Rule of Experts

Rule of Experts

Egypt, Techno-Politics, Modernity

TIMOTHY MITCHELL

University of California Press

BERKELEY LOS ANGELES LONDON

University of California Press
Berkeley and Los Angeles, California

University of California Press, Ltd.
London, England

Library of Congress Cataloging-in-Publication Data

Mitchell, Timothy, 1955–.
Rule of Experts : Egypt, Techno-Politics, and Modernity / Timothy Peter Mitchell.
p. cm.
Includes bibliographical references and index.
ISBN 0–520-23261-5 (alk. paper).—ISBN 0–520-23262-3 (pbk. : alk. paper)
Cataloging-in-Publication data is on file with the Library of Congress.

Manufactured in the United States of America

10 09 08 07 06 05 04 03 02 01

10 9 8 7 6 5 4 3 2 1

The paper used in this publication is both acid-free and totally chlorine-free (TCF). It meets the minimum requirements of ANSI/NISO Z39.48–1992 (R 1997) (*Permanence of Paper*). ♾

To Lila

Contents

Illustrations

Acknowledgments

Several of the chapters gathered here I first drafted while staying in a village in southern Egypt. All of them I rewrote and completed in the same place. Occasionally the histories told by neighbors and friends in the village have made it into parts of the book. In two of the chapters I lay out in more detail some of the things I learned there.

During more than a dozen stays over the past decade, for periods ranging from a few days to a few months, I incurred many unrepayable debts. Among the numerous people owed thanks, I want to mention Khairy Muhammad Ibrahim, his parents Muhammad and Fatna, and their family; Hamida bint al-Kumiya and her family; the households of the late Salim ʿAbd al-Warith, in particular Ahmad, Muhammad, Jamal, and their families, as well as the absent Sayyid for the use of his house; Hajj Lamʿi Ahmad Muhammad and his family; Shahhat Shihittu; the family of Mahmud ʿAbdullahi; and Hasan Murad. I am grateful to all of them for their help and generosity.

Two chapters of the book were published in full elsewhere and have been revised here only slightly. They speak the slightly different language of the time and place they first appeared. Read again in the surroundings of this book, I hope they can be interpreted in new ways. Chapter 5 was published as "The Representation of Rural Violence in Writings on Political Development," in *Peasants and Politics in the Modern History of the Middle East*, edited by John Waterbury and Farhad Kazemi (University Presses of Florida, 1991), and chapter 7 appeared as "The Object of Development: America's Egypt," in *Power of Development*, edited by Jonathan Crush (Routledge, 1995). In addition, the first two-thirds of chapter 4 consist of a slightly revised version of "The Invention and Reinvention of the Egyptian Peasant," *International Journal of Middle East Studies* 22: 129–50.

The final third of the chapter, however, presents new material that alters the significance of the part I previously published.

Three other chapters draw on material published in partial or preliminary form elsewhere. Parts of chapter 6 are from a paper presented at the Sixth Biennial Conference of the International Association for the Study of Traditional Environments, "Manufacturing Heritage / Consuming Tradition," Cairo, December 15, 1998, published in the proceedings of the conference, *Consuming Tradition, Manufacturing Heritage: Global Norms and Urban Forms in the Age of Tourism,* edited by Nezar AlSayyad (E. F. Spon, 2001). A preliminary version of chapter 8 was presented at a conference in Aswan in April 1997 and published in Cairo in *Directions of Change in Rural Egypt,* edited by Nicholas Hopkins and Kirsten Westergaard (American University in Cairo Press, 1998). The first half of chapter 9 was published in an earlier form as "No Factories, No Problems: The Logic of Neo-Liberalism in Egypt," *Review of African Political Economy,* no. 82 (1999), 455–68. I am grateful to the editors of the publications just mentioned for their invitations to contribute my work, and for their many helpful suggestions for its improvement. I am also grateful to Cambridge University Press, Routledge, and E. F. Spon for permission to republish the earlier material.

My research in Cairo in 1996–97 was supported by a fellowship from the American Research Center in Egypt, funded by the National Endowment for the Humanities. The directors and staff of the center, especially Amir and Amira Khattab, helped in numerous ways. A fellowship from the International Center for Advanced Study at New York University in 1999 gave me the opportunity to make progress on the writing.

In Egypt, a number of friends and colleagues offered intellectual support, hospitality, criticism, and opportunities to present my work in seminars and publish it in Arabic. I want to thank Mahmud Abdel-Fadil, Elwi Captan, Rania Fahmy, Ferial Ghazoul, Muhammad Hakim, Nawal Hassan, Ali Eddin Hilal, Siona Jenkins, Dalila al-Kirdani, Reem Saad, Mustafa Kamal al-Sayyid, Olivier Sednaoui, Hilmi Sha'rawi, David Sims, and Soraya al-Torki. I owe special thanks to Bashir al-Siba'i, poet, historian, and extraordinary translator.

It would be impossible to list all those from whose advice and criticism I benefited at meetings where I have presented my work over the last few years, or at N.Y.U. Among the many who have helped are Muhammed Hamdouni Alami, Nezar AlSayyad, Sophia Anninos, Arjun Appadurai, Talal Asad,

Joel Beinin, Jennifer Bell, Tom Bender, Ethel Brooks, Nathan Brown, Terry Burke, Ray Bush, Koray Çaliskan, Dipesh Chakrabarty, Partha Chatterjee, Ken Cuno, Veena Das, Nick Dirks, Samera Esmair, Khaled Fahmy, Munir Fakhr al-Din, Jim Ferguson, Leela Fernandez, Robert Fernea, Michael Gilsenan, Peter Gran, Christine Harrington, Nicholas Hopkins, Huri Islamoglu, Wilson Jacob, Deniz Kandiyoti, Zachary Lockman, David Ludden, Kristine McNeil, Uday Mehta, Leila Mustafa, Fred Myers, Roger Owen, Stefania Pandolfo, Karen Pfeifer, James Piscatori, Panayiota Pyla, Gyan Prakash, Marsha Pripstein-Posusney, Anupama Rao, Vyjayanthi Rao, Yahya Sadowski, Omnia el-Shakry, Caroline Simpson, Susan Slyomovics, Kees van der Spek, Nancy Leys Stepan, Joe Stork, Sandra Sufian, James Toth, Robert Vitalis, and Jessica Winegar.

None of those mentioned here is responsible for the views the book expresses or for whatever errors or oversights it contains.

Lynne Withey, associate director of the University of California Press, waited patiently for this manuscript and then steered it expertly through review and publication. I also want to thank Mary Francis, Cindy Fulton, Marielle León, and Sharron Wood.

Dr. Boutros Wadieh holds a special place among these expressions of gratitude. No one I know combines his breadth of knowledge of Egyptian and Arab history with such sympathy for the demands of ordinary lives. Several chapters of this book have benefited from his insights on almost every page. Janet Lippman Abu-Lughod and the late Ibrahim Abu-Lughod have given not only intellectual and moral support over the years but the example of their own political and intellectual commitment. The members of my own wider family in England have been an unfailing support. Adrian and Justine have lived their whole lives with this book, becoming ʿIdris and Yasmin in the village and enduring many other abrupt changes in their circumstances with great spirit and understanding. Lila Abu-Lughod knows herself how much I have relied on her.

Najʿ al-Hajir, Egypt
April 2001

Note on Transliteration

I have tried to ensure that the reader with little or no knowledge of the modern politics of Egypt will be able to follow the arguments of the book and enjoy discovering aspects of an unfamiliar history. In transliterating the Arabic names of persons and places I have used common English forms where they are available, and otherwise used a simplified form of a standard transliteration system. (Two Arabic letters have no easy equivalent in the Latin alphabet. In the name ʻA'isha, the ʻ represents the Arabic letter *ayn,* and the ' represents the letter *hamza.*) For simplicity, I have omitted diacritics, long vowels, and initial hamzas. Occasionally the transliteration reflects the Arabic spoken in Upper Egypt rather than the standard written language. The term "acre" refers here to the Egyptian acre or *feddan,* whose area was fixed in the nineteenth century at 0.420 hectares, equivalent to 1.038 British or U.S. acres. To indicate the Egyptian pound I use the symbol E£ rather than the older French form, LE (*livre égyptienne*).

Introduction

We have entered the twenty-first century still divided by a way of thinking inherited from the nineteenth. Nineteenth-century Europe learned to understand the modern world as the outcome of history. People came to believe that the pattern of human affairs manifested neither the working of a divine will nor the self-regulating balance of a natural system, but the unfolding of an inner secular force. There were several ways of accounting for this inner dynamic, all of them referring to the increasing power of human reason to order social affairs. The movement of history could be ascribed to the growing technical control that reason acquired over the natural and social world, to the power of reason to expand the scope of human freedom, or to the economic forms that were said to flow from the spread of rational calculation and freedom—the exchange relations of modern capitalism. Whichever aspect of modern, secular rationality one emphasized, everything could be understood as the development of this universal principle of reason, or a reaction against it, or its failure, delay, or absence.

In the twentieth century, as the study of society became a university profession and was divided into the separate disciplines of social science, each field inherited the assumption that a singular logic provided the unseen dynamic of social life. Different disciplines took different approaches to deciphering this logic. Some, like economics, depicted the rationality of social life in ideal form, proposing to understand particular cases in terms of their degree of deviation from this unreal abstraction. Others revealed the logic of modernity in large patterns of social and political change. In some fields, especially in the later decades of the twentieth century, there were also attempts to show the limits of this logic. Social historians, cultural anthropologists, and scholars in new fields like area studies, gender studies, and cultural studies looked at the weight of resistance to the spread of rationalization, the market, and what came to be called globalization. They showed the complexity of local variation in the patterns of modernity, the mixtures of the modern with the nonmodern, even the survival or revival of alternatives. Yet in attempting to uncover the complexities and limits of modernity's singular logic, these critiques for the most part continued to assume such a logic was at work. Despite the richness of the new work, this common assumption left us heading into the twenty-first century as captives of nineteenth-century thought.

The critiques that were made of the more systematic and nomothetic kinds of social science took two common forms. The first was to reveal how things that orthodox inquiries took for granted were inventions. Categories that nineteenth-century social science had grounded in the material, racial, biological, or psychological nature of human societies—class, race, nation, gender, modernity, the West, and many more—were shown to be "socially constructed." The second was to show how the categories' artificial nature and the subterfuges involved in their invention made these constructs less universal, stable, pure, singular, and transparent than was usually assumed. In some cases even the underlying idea of historical time, as the homogeneous chronometric within which human social action is contained, was placed in question. These achievements defined the fields variously called interpretive social science, cultural studies, or, in a loose sense, poststructuralism. Such fields, with all their differences, seemed to be marked by their common distance from the systematizing social sciences, both those operating at the individualist level of hypothetico-deductive methods, and those at the structural level of historical systems and processes.

Yet this distance itself became a problem. It left the older kinds of social science untroubled. It did so by failing to contest the territory on which they were established. Focusing on the process by which social objects are imagined or discursively constructed made the work of imagination into its own sphere. Demonstrating that everything social is cultural left aside the existence of other spheres, the remainder or excess that the work of social construction works upon—the real, the natural, the nonhuman. Insisting on the centrality of the cultural tacitly recognized those other dimensions—the material, the economic—in relation to which the cultural gains its distinctiveness. Attending to the significance of the local acknowledged the weight of the global, in reference to which the local is experienced and defined. Recovering the importance of particular alternatives, mixtures, and variations acknowledged the force of the universal, to which such variation always refers.

Although the more cultural or critical approaches to social understanding might object to the methods, assumptions, generalizations, or limits of those social sciences that claimed the rigor of a hypothetico-deductive logic or the inclusiveness of a systemic analysis, they had already granted the existence of the terrain that those methods defined as their own. By admitting the existence of a universal process (modernity, capitalism, globalization) and of forces that, when all is said and done, underlie it (the forces of nature, the material, the technological, the economic), these ways of thinking again and again handed over to the systematizing forms of social science a territory and a logic they would never so easily have been able to establish. It is that territory and that logic that this book contests.

It is a curious fact that while critical theory has interrogated almost every leading category of modern social science, it has left perhaps the most central one untouched. It has critiqued the concepts of class, nation, culture, society, state, gender, race, personhood, and many others, but not the idea of the economy. It is as though the varieties of cultural theory had to leave in place a residual sphere of the economic, as a reserve whose existence in the distance made cultural analysis secure. Everything else could be understood as cultural, including particular forms of economic practice or local ways of thinking about the economy. Anthropological studies of communities that do not know the modern concept of the economy could show that nonmarket societies had other ways of understanding value and organizing exchange. But even these emerged as an alternative kind of economy, rather than as ways of questioning the foundation of the concept. Indeed, the classic work of Malinowski helped, if anything, to universalize the idea of the economy when taken up by later scholars. The economy always remained, tacitly, as a material ground out of which the cultural is shaped, or in relation to which it acquires its significance.

Even when the modern concept of the economy has been studied, its surprising history has been missed. From the work of Karl Polanyi in 1944 to some of the last writings of Michel Foucault, published in English in 1991, there have been several accounts of the emergence of the economy as a sphere of government or self-regulation in Europe during the eighteenth and nineteenth centuries. Polanyi understood its emergence as the separation of market relations from the wider social networks in which they were previously embedded and constrained. During the modern period, he argued, the economy was disembedded from society. Foucault relates the formation of the economy to the birth of "government" in the eighteenth century, a term that in those days referred not to the institutions of the modern state but to the methods of enumerating, regulating, and managing a population, out of which the modern state and modern social sciences were gradually formed. The practices of government, in this view, formed the economy as a field of political regulation.

These and other studies overlook an unexpected fact. No political economist of the eighteenth or nineteenth century wrote about an object called "the economy." The term "economy" in that period carried the older meaning of "thrift," and in a larger sense referred to the proper husbanding of resources and the intelligent management of their circulation. The classical political economists expanded its meaning to refer to this proper management at the level of the political order. They used it in ways similar to the term "government," in the sense that Foucault explores. "Political economy" was concerned not with the politics of an economy, but with the proper economy, or governing, of a polity.

The idea of the economy in its contemporary sense did not emerge until the middle decades of the twentieth century. Between the 1930s and 1950s, economists, sociologists, national statistical agencies, international and corporate organizations, and government programs formulated the concept of the economy, meaning the totality of monetarized exchanges within a defined space. The economy came into being as a self-contained, internally dynamic, and statistically measurable sphere of social action, scientific analysis, and political regulation.

Was the economy, then, one more "social construction," a recent product of the collective imagination to place alongside the ideas of culture, society, class, or the nation? Or was it, as most would probably argue, just a new and more coherent name for economic processes that already existed? After all, since the formation of professional economics fifty years earlier, in the final decades of the nineteenth century, a body of scholars had been constructing models and descriptions of the mechanism of market exchange, treating the mechanism as a self-contained and self-regulating process. Moreover, they traced their ideas back to the work of François Quesnay or Adam Smith, a century or more before, if not to earlier studies of "political arithmetick" or the writings of Aristotle.

The answer I propose here is that it was neither. It is not adequate to describe the economy as a social construction, or an invention of the social imagination, for such an approach always implies that the object in question is a representation, a set of meanings, a particular way of seeing the world. This kind of analysis leaves the world itself intact. Intentionally or not, it depends upon maintaining the absolute difference between representations and the world they represent, social constructions and the reality they construct. It is an analysis that leaves the economists to carry on undisturbed, pointing out that they are not concerned with the history of representations, but with the underlying reality their models represent.

Should we agree, then, that at some level the "economy" was just a new word—or even a new way of imagining—something that always existed? That will not do either. The birth of the economy did not occur only at what is called the level of language or the social imagination. Its arrival can indeed be traced in the writings of economists such as John Maynard Keynes; in the organization of a new branch of the discipline, macroeconomics, in relation to which most earlier economic theory was repositioned as "micro"; in the development of the field known as econometrics, which attempted the mathematical modeling of the entirety of a nation's economic system, and of the techniques known as national income accounting, which presented a statistical enumeration of this totality; and in numerous other intellectual developments of the 1930s and 1940s. Equally important to the birth of the economy, however, was a series of events outside the professional fields of economics and statistics, which those fields had little or no ability to comprehend. These included the collapse of the international financial system in the interwar period; the domestic crises of the Great Depression; the development of Soviet, New Deal, fascist, and other forms of state control of production, trade, employment, and investment; the wartime management of technology, information, supply, and consumption; and, of particular significance, the collapse in the years during and on either side of World War II of the global structure of political and economic affairs formed by the European and Japanese empires. Out of this series of political implosions, social disintegrations, financial failures, and worldwide conflicts emerged this new object, the economy.

The economy did not come about as a new name for the processes of exchange that economists had always studied. It occurred as the reorganization and transformation of those and other processes, into an object that had not previously existed. The crises and forces that brought about this transformation lay partly in actions economists had always studied, but for the most part were far wider and more diverse. These "extraeconomic" origins of the economy made possible new forms of value, new kinds of equivalence, new practices of calculation, new relations between human agency and the nonhuman, and new distinctions between what was real and the forms of its representation.

So is the conclusion one should draw that the birth of the economy occurred as a transformation at the material level as much as the level of representations? Not at all. If we begin from the assumption that these separate levels are something fixed and occur in a given relation to one another, such a transformation cannot be understood. The distinction between the material world and its representation is not something we can take as a starting point. It is an opposition that is made in social practice, and the forms of this opposition that we take for granted are both comparatively recent and relatively unstable. In an earlier book, *Colonising Egypt,* I explored the making of the modern practices of representation in the colonial politics of the nineteenth century. In the twentieth century, the time span on which this book is focused, the economy became arguably the most important set of practices for organizing what appears as the separation of the real world from its representations, of things from their values, of actions from intentions, of an object world from the realm of ideas. We take these kinds of distinctions as something foundational, as the basis on which our ordinary understandings of social life are built, and as the framework of the modern social sciences. However, since the mechanisms that set up the separations precede, as we will see, the separation itself, the foundation is not as stable as it seems. This problem occurs with special force in the case of the economy, because its organization and understanding are so dependent on the distinctions in question.

I suggested just now that one important contribution to the making of the economy was the collapse of a global network of European and other empires. Before the 1930s it would have been difficult to describe something called the "British economy," for example, in part because the forms of trade, investment, currency, power, and knowledge that might be constituted as an economy were organized on an imperial rather than a national scale. There was no easy way, therefore, to enclose them within a single space, to envisage them or organize them as the kind of bounded territorial entity that the making of an economy required. In fact it may have been at the level of the colony, rather than the metropolitan power, that this territorial framing of an economy was first possible. Keynes, who was a key figure in the making of the economy within economics and government, wrote his first book while employed at the India Office in London, the successor to the East India Company, the corporate colonizing power in which James Mill, Robert Malthus, and John Stuart Mill, three of the leading figures in nineteenth-century political economy, had all held senior positions. The book Keynes wrote, *Indian Economy and Finance,* addressed issues that were critical to his later formulation of the concept of a national economy—the state's control of the circulation of money within a defined geographical space. There are excellent studies of the role that ruling India played in the formation of modern British political theory. However, the question of how far twentieth-century economics also has a colonial genealogy has been overlooked.

This book examines the making of the economy, and broader questions about politics and expertise, in a postcolonial context. In common with other uses of the term, the word "postcolonial" in my title does not refer to the period after the end of colonialism (an end it might be difficult to locate). It refers to forms of critical practice that address the significance of colonialism in the formation and practice of social theory. Colonialism, from this perspective, was not incidental to the development of the modern West, nor to the emergence there of new forms of technical expertise, including the modern social sciences.

The possibility of social science is based upon taking certain historical experiences of the West as the template for a universal knowledge. Economics offers a particularly clear illustration of this. Certain forms of social exchange, contract law, disposition of property, corporate powers, methods of calculation, dispossession of labor, relationship between public and private, organization of information, and government regulation that were formalized in western Europe in the nineteenth century as "market exchange" were abstracted by economics into the framework of a social science. The new science ignored the importance of a larger structure of empire in making possible these domestic arrangements. At the same time, it presented these categories and arrangements as a general standard, for both scientific knowledge and social practice. Every country in the world was now to be measured and understood in relation to this universal model.

I draw attention to this history not, it should be emphasized, to make the facile argument of cultural relativism: that economics works in the West, but since other cultures are different they need their own social sciences. The concepts of the social sciences can always be translated from one context to another, as Dipesh Chakrabarty reminds us. They can operate just as well outside the West as within, and just as badly. The formation of the so-called market practices of the nineteenth century and earlier was, as I said, a global phenomenon. And a worldwide project involving colonial government, the colleges of the East India Company, American academic visitor programs, metropolitan universities, intergovernmental organizations, the Ford Foundation, and other agencies transformed economics into a global form of knowledge—the term global referring to a widespread but very thin network of ties and exchanges.

Unlike an argument about cultural relativism, a postcolonial perspective locates these problems of colonialism, global expansion, and translation within the history and practice of the science, rather than outside it as secondary issues that might be addressed after the science is already formed. And it examines the reasons for and significance of the silence on these issues in the scientific field, or their location as something secondary. Although the offices of the East India Company in London have now given way to the headquarters of the International Monetary Fund in Washington, D.C. or the World Trade Organization in Geneva, and the production and export of technocratic expertise is organized from American university campuses rather than the company's Haileybury College in Hertfordshire where Malthus taught, the issues raised by postcolonialism are no less relevant today—and perhaps more so—than in the days of Malthus and Mill.

The chapters of this book span both ends of this history, from the apex of British colonial power in the later decades of the nineteenth century, to the structural adjustment and financial stabilization programs of the IMF at the close of the twentieth. All the chapters deal with events in one particular place, the country of Egypt. This gives an element of continuity, I hope, to discussions that in other ways are quite diverse. Not all of them are concerned directly with the question of the economy. The issues I have just raised emerge in the first two chapters and are addressed directly in the third, and I look at them again from a variety of contemporary perspectives in the final three chapters.

The book as a whole examines a wider set of issues concerned, to express them too abstractly, with problems of social calculation, agency, abstraction, violence, law, capitalism, and expertise. By writing about these abstract issues in a particular place, I also locate them in particular episodes, projects, conflicts, and transformations. This is a book of political theory, but it sets forth a kind of theory that, for reasons that will become clearer, avoids the method of abstraction from the particular that usually characterizes a work of theory. The theory lies in the complexity of the cases. This introduction abstracts from these particulars in ways that are misleading, and perhaps at times opaque. It therefore offers no substitute for what lies in the chapters themselves.

The first theme to which I want to draw attention is the question of "the character of calculability." Borrowed from the German sociologist Georg Simmel, the phrase provides the title of chapter 3, but the theme is taken up in several other parts of the book. The economy, I have already suggested, can be understood as a set of practices that puts in place a new politics of calculation. The practices that form the economy operate, in part, to establish equivalences, contain circulations, identify social actors or agents, make quantities and performances measurable, and designate relations of control and command. The economy must also, as Michel Callon has argued, operate as a series of boundaries, distinctions, exceptions, and exclusions. For example, the economy depends upon, and helps establish, boundaries between the monetary and the nonmonetary, national and foreign, consumption and investment, public and private, nature and technology, tangible and intangible, owner and nonowner, and many more. How are these boundaries and exceptions made? What calculations do they make possible? What problems arise and what costs are incurred? These kinds of questions are explored at several points, from a variety of angles, especially in the book's final three chapters dealing with the contemporary period. Chapter 3 looks back to the first half of the twentieth century, however, to ask how certain forms of calculability were first formatted.

Great Britain invaded and occupied Egypt in 1882, to put down a popular revolt against government misrule and European financial control. After putting an end to the uprising and reestablishing Cairo's authority over the countryside, one of Britain's first preoccupations was a vast project of calculation. To reorganize the tax revenues and pay the country's debts to European banking houses (emergency measures to pay the debts had precipitated the revolt), the colonial power set out to determine, for every square meter of the country's agricultural land, the owner, the cultivator, the quality of the soil, and the proper rate of tax. To collect, organize, and represent this information, the authorities decided to produce something never achieved before, a "great land map of Egypt." The map was intended not just as an instrument of administrative control or geographical knowledge, but as a means of recording complex statistical information in a centralized, miniaturized, and visual form. It was to provide not just a diagram of reality, but a mechanism for collecting, storing, and manipulating multiple levels of information.

In recent years the production of maps has often been taken to epitomize the character of colonial power, and by extension the power of the modern state. The map signifies the massive production of knowledge, the accuracy of calculation, and the entire politics based upon a knowledge of population and territory that Foucault characterizes as governmentality, the characteristic power of the modern state. The map can also be said to prefigure the work of twentieth-century economics, defining a contained geographical space to be organized later as a national economy, and addressing issues of statistical information that were to play a central role.

Although the great land map of Egypt was celebrated for its accuracy and for solving several technical problems in the conduct of large-scale surveys, its successful completion in 1907 obscured something important.

The map did not produce a more accurate or detailed knowledge of its object than earlier forms of governmental practice. In fact, the calculations that it was supposed to enable were never quite made possible. What exactly, then, was new about this novel politics of calculation, and from where did it derive its power and appeal? Chapter 3 opens with these questions, then relates them to the larger project that emerged in Egypt, as elsewhere, over the following decades: the making of the national economy.

The question of calculation is related to a second theme I want to identify, that of human agency. In the social sciences, the ability to calculate often defines the existence and power of human beings as social agents. In economics and in parts of other disciplines, social explanation is organized around the question of the calculations made among individuals, presenting particular arrangements or events as the outcome of a sequence of interacting computations. (Conversely, the supposed inability of certain social actors—peasants, for example—to calculate their situation, as we will see, provided the justification for an entire politics of social improvement, and for later programs of technical development.) In chapter 1, I present a complex story from the mid-twentieth century in which the forms of agency involved appear to be not only those of humans. A variety of other forces come in to play. These might be called the forces of technology, disease, hydraulics, war, nature, chemistry, and several others—except that, because of the way they interact, it would be difficult to contain them within any of these categories. One of the things with which they interact, in different ways, is what we call human intention. The results of the interactions are complex, and in several cases disastrous. As one unravels these interwoven forces, human agency appears less as a calculating intelligence directing social outcomes and more as the product of a series of alliances in which the human element is never wholly in control. Is human agency a disembodied form of reason, observing, calculating, and reorganizing the world before it? Or is it rather more of a technical body, manufactured out of processes that precede the difference between ideas and things, between human and nonhuman? If so, what consequences follow for thinking about social explanation, or the logic of history, or for analyzing processes, such as the economic, that are formatted as the outcome of human calculation?

The issues of agency and calculation raise common questions about the way the modern world is divided—into objects and ideas, nature and culture, reality and its representation, the nonhuman and the human. Several other parts of the book explore these divisions in further ways. In each case, I am interested in the local methods of organization, the particular political techniques, and the novel social practices, that seem to secure this bifurcation of the world. In each case, the scale and thoroughness with which the distinction is set up is quite remarkable. Yet at the same time, on closer examination, and focusing on the process rather than what is presented as the end result, the status of the binarism is less certain.

Another variety of this separation, one that plays a critical role in the making of the economy, is the phenomenon of the rule or the institution. Economic theory, as I discuss later in the book, depends upon maintaining a continuous but difficult distinction between the act of exchange and the formal and informal rules or institutions that structure the exchange. At the wider scale of the economy as a whole, the same problem arises of distinguishing between the totality of economic exchanges, whose aggregation is measured as the economy, and the powers of government, law, statistical production, and economic knowledge that structure the economic whole.

In a market economy, a central example of such an institution is the law of property. Property depends upon a set of rules and sanctions that determine an individual's power to dispose of an object in the act of exchange. The rules also establish his or her power to exclude or limit the claims that others may make upon that object. In the closing decades of the twentieth century, there was a significant global movement to reinforce, redefine, and universalize the rules of property. Egypt was one of many countries in the world where the privatization of state-owned enterprises, the reform of corporate and contract law, the reorganization of trade barriers, and expanded claims about the corporate ownership of what is called intellectual property attempted in different ways to recast and extend the rules of property. In the final part of the book, I examine some of the difficulties and questions this project encountered.

The law of property gains its power by appearing as an abstraction. It seems to stand as a conceptual structure, based not on particular claims or histories but on "principles true in every country," in the words of a British colonial administrator. Chapter 2 explores this issue in the context of a question about the origin and status of such rules, examining the genealogy of the law of landed property in Egypt and its relation to the formation of the larger institutional structure of the modern state. The government officials and European advisors who helped establish the law considered it the opposite of the older forms of rule that the modern state replaced, which appeared to them to rest upon arbitrary decision, the making of exceptions, and the prerogatives of unrestrained power. (The same distinctions were made at the end of the twentieth century, when the universal rules of property and the price mechanism were advocated as a replacement for forms of central command, arbitrary state power, and the irrational allocation of resources that characterized nonmarket political economies.) The genealogy presented in chapter 2, as well as my later discussions of the contemporary period, suggest we should be suspicious of this distinction. Did the establishing of a law of property replace the forms of arbitrariness, particularism, and force said to characterize the old order? Or was it rather a process that redistributed, concentrated, and concealed within itself these negative elements? What role do the negatives that colonialism or contemporary reform programs claim to banish play in making possible the rule of law or the market, or the institutionalized forms of power that accompany that rule?

The discussion of the rule of property and the institutionalization of the law-state connect with a number of other themes that recur in the book, to which I will refer briefly. The first is the question of territory. If the modern state is characterized by what appears as a structure of rules or institutions whose regularity and abstractness separates it from the social order it governs, it is also distinguished by its territorial character. It seems to acquire a new clarity and absoluteness in its control over a particular geographical region. The containing of individual political and economic exchanges within a framework of rules appears to be matched by the containment of collective exchanges, movements, values, and identities within a territorial frame. Frontiers are demarcated as fixed lines, the movement of population and goods across those lines is controlled in unprecedented ways, and marginal forms of political life, where allegiance to the central authority was graduated or variable, increasingly give way to more uniform and rigorous methods of control. These are issues raised in chapter 2, but their discussion continues at several further points, including chapters 6 and 7. These discussions relate the production or materialization of territoriality both to the possibility of making the economy and to the power to make rules, technics, or institutions appear separate from the supposedly material world they govern.

The production of this new territorial power also makes possible the making of the nation. It is often forgotten that the modern state that emerged in the Lower Nile valley in the eighteenth and nineteenth centuries was not yet a national state. Cairo and its hinterland were ruled as part of the Ottoman Empire, and although Ottoman sovereignty was increasingly tenuous, especially after the British occupation, the link with Istanbul was not formally ended until the eve of the Empire's collapse, in 1914. Even beyond that moment, until the Ottoman defeat in World War

I, Ottomanism remained the larger context of local political identity, especially after 1913, when military modernizers led by Jamal Pasha and Enver Pasha took power in Istanbul. After the war the British reorganized the local Ottoman dynasty in Cairo as a national monarchy, and saw their own control reduced by the measures of partial independence they were forced to negotiate with a new constitutional government in 1922 and 1936. In the course of these events a national politics emerged, but the tensions between nationalism, monarchism, and colonialism—and broader popular pressures that none of these could represent—ended in a military coup in 1952 that brought an end to both the British and the monarchy, and enabled a fuller measure of national independence.

It is a minor but indicative fact that the first two leaders of postindependence Egypt, men born in the final months of the Ottoman Empire in 1918, had been named by their fathers after the two Ottoman generals, Jamal and Enver. The governments of Jamal Abdul Nasser and Anwar Sadat helped complete the recasting of local history as the history of an Egyptian nation, so the wider Ottoman past, and the alternative futures it had contained, were forgotten or overwritten by the newer identities of pan-Arabism. The idea of Egypt as a nation was projected back into the nineteenth century, and the nineteenth-century rulers of Cairo were transformed into protonationalists. History, once again, could be understood as the unfolding of a singular logic—the awakening of a nation into the universal consciousness of modernity.

Making the nation was not a project completed in the earlier part of the century, for the nation is an identity that must be continually remade. National history is something taught in schools and inculcated in the forms of public culture, but it is also performed in the lives of ordinary citizens. In Egypt, the performance of the past involved questions of the relationship of Cairo's political elites to the West, and at the same time their relationship to their own wider society, especially the mass of people known as "the peasantry." Chapter 6 considers the struggle over defining the nation's past, examined through two interconnected episodes involving a village in southern Egypt. What happens when the politics of making contemporary Egypt works through the making of its national past? Through what forms of politics, expertise, violence, and resistance does the identity of a nation get made?

Nationalism and violence lead back to the question I raised at the start about the logic of history. Throughout the book I am concerned with the question of how one can relate what happens in a particular place to what we call the global forces of modernity, of science and technology, and of the expansion of capitalism. Chapter 1, for example, examines a series of seemingly global forces—technology, science, imperial power, and capitalism—and asks how one might understand the working of these different forces in a way that avoids lending to any one of them a logic, energy, and coherence it did not have. In particular, I consider how one might write about capitalism or the economic without attributing to them an internal rationality, an element of sameness, or an inherent power that is then given the credit for what happened.

I also explore in different parts of the book how the logic or rationality attributed to modernity, the market, law, science, technology, or capitalism tends to produce a certain restricted understanding of violence. Violence is thought of as the opposite of these forms of reason or logic. It usually appears to belong to nature, or to the forms of reaction against the more universal logics of history. Such reactive violence is a perennial theme in discussions of the countryside: the violence of the peasantry, its resistance to change, and its reluctance to accept authority, whether expressed in great rebellions or in everyday forms of refusal. Chapter 5, for example, deals with a brief period in the mid-1960s when battles for political control at the center of state power were also fought in the villages. Events in the Egyptian countryside coincided with the arrival of a new generation of American social science, focused for the first time on the non-Western world. New fields such as peasant studies, a form of expertise whose genealogy is examined in chapter 4, had been built up by the 1960s, and the questions of violence, disorder, and change in the countryside were a major concern. Chapter 5 examines how these new forms of expertise addressed the issue of rural violence. It explores how the logics of social science translated the question of violence into a reactive, backward, irrational, and often invisible force.

Similar issues are raised in a different way in the last three chapters of the book, where I examine the contemporary politics of national development, foreign expertise, and economic reform. I show how the outcome of the reform programs was not the forms of market relations or capitalist development promised by the reformers, but a complex rearrangement of social practices driven by a series of different and intersecting logics. I ask about the dangers of talking about this kind of transformation in terms of the rationality and power of capital, the market, or, in the language of the 1990s, globalization. Rather than contributing further to the impression that these forces have the coherence, energy, and logic they claim for themselves, I argue the need for a more careful consideration of what can be learned from the rather more violent and unpredictable interactions these terms are used to describe.

A final theme is the one from which the book takes its title. In each of the chapters that follow, we encounter modern forms of expertise. We meet the engineers who built the Aswan Dam, the administrators who defined the law of property, the scientists and public hygienists who attacked epidemic disease, the surveyors who made the Great Map, the political scientists who diagnosed rural politics, the experts who confirmed the irrationality and violence of the peasant, and a series of development practitioners and economists who devised programs of financial aid and economic restructuring. From the opening of the twentieth century to its close, the politics of national development and economic growth was a politics of techno-science, which claimed to bring the expertise of modern engineering, technology, and social science to improve the defects of nature, to transform peasant agriculture, to repair the ills of society, and to fix the economy.

Three questions run through my examination of modern techno-politics. First, how do the binarisms fixed in place in modern politics open up the distance that requires and enables this expertise: in a particular way of writing about the peasant, for example, in a form of development practice that treats Egypt as an object laid out like a map, or in hydraulic engineering projects that reorganize the river Nile and transform the distribution of power, technology, and information across countryside? In each case, the place and the claims of expertise are constituted in the separation that seems to open up, opposing nature to technology, reality to its representation, objects to their value, and the economy to the science of economics. Second, if those separations, as the book argues, are not what they seem, if they occur not as fundamental oppositions but as uncertain forms of difference constituted, and at the same time undermined, in the political process, how is the expertise actually formed? What can we learn from its difficult and divided genealogy? Third, if these separations allow reason to rule, and allow history to be organized as the unfolding of a locationless logic, how does expertise attach itself to this logic? What strategies, structures, and silences transform the expert into a spokesperson for what appear as the forces of development, the rules of law, the progress of modernity, or the rationality of capitalism?

I

PARA-SITES OF CAPITALISM

1 Can the Mosquito Speak?

In the summer of 1942 two forces invaded Egypt, and each provoked a decisive battle. Only one of the two was human, so only that one is remembered, although the casualties in the other battle were greater. On the northwest coast, Erwin Rommel's Afrika Corps crossed the border from Libya and was halted on its march toward Cairo by the British Eighth Army at al-Alamein. Four months later the British counterattacked. After a two-week tank battle they routed the German and Italian forces, whom they outnumbered in men and tanks by more than two to one. Al-Alamein was the Allies' first decisive land victory in World War II and, along with the Soviet victory a month later at Stalingrad, appeared to turn the tide of the war. No count of the casualties was possible given the scale of violence and the disarray among the defeated forces, but somewhere between fifty and seventy thousand soldiers may have been killed, wounded, or missing.[1] Long after the armies moved on, moreover, the battle continued to claim its victims. Al-Alamein marked the first use of land mines as a major weapon of war. It was responsible for three-quarters of the twenty-three million uncleared mines Egypt accumulated in the twentieth century, the largest number of any country in the world.[2]

Meanwhile, at the other end of the country another invader arrived, descending down the Nile valley from Sudan: the *Anopheles gambiae,* a mosquito native to sub-Saharan Africa but previously unknown in Egypt. The gambiae mosquito carried in its stomach the malignant form of the malaria parasite, *Plasmodium falciparum.*[3] Other species of malarial mosquitoes existed in Egypt, but these carried a more benign form of malaria and were confined to small pockets in the north, where the local population had developed a degree of immunity. There were no local defenses against *Plasmodium falciparum.* The first reports of an outbreak of gambiae malaria came in March 1942 from the villages of Nubia, the country lying across Egypt's southern border with Sudan. The epidemic reached Aswan by July and Luxor by August, then continued north to Asyut, the largest city in the south. As at al-Alamein, the number of victims was unknown and unknowable. It was estimated that three-quarters of a million people may have contracted the disease in the three years of the epidemic, and between one and two hundred thousand died.[4]

I first heard about the 1942 malaria invasion in 1989 from a man named ʿAmm Ibrahim, who lived in a village near Luxor where I was spending time.[5] Then in his eighties, he was the most informed narrator of the history of the village, and the story of the malaria epidemic was always the most vivid part of his narrative. It killed one-third of the village, he used to say, and there were not enough healthy men left alive even to carry the dead. People were hauled to their graves on the back of a camel.

The war and the epidemic interacted with a third threat to the country, a severe wartime shortage of food. The shortage had complex causes of its own. In 1933 the dam across the river Nile at Aswan, built at the turn of the century, had been increased in height, completing a network of dams, barrages, and canals begun in the mid-nineteenth century that converted most of the country's agricultural land to year-round irrigation.[6] Only one-fifth of the Nile valley was now irrigated by the river's annual flood, which in the past had fertilized the soil by depositing a layer of silt and nutrients. The other four-fifths required chemical fertilizers.[7] By the end of the 1930s Egyptian farmers were using 600,000 tons of fertilizer a year—mostly the new artificial nitrates—at the highest rate per cultivated area in the world.[8] An international cartel among chemical manufacturers had assigned 80 percent of the Egyptian market to a consortium led by the German business group I. G. Farben, one of whose companies had invented the process for synthesizing ammonium nitrate.[9] These supplies were cut off by the outbreak of war.

The lack of fertilizer caused the yield of wheat and other crops to drop by as much as a quarter. The government introduced food rationing to supply the cities and the British troops, and introduced fertilizer rationing and acreage controls to force landowners to switch half the country's cotton fields to the cultivation of food.[10] In the far south, however, the main commercial crop was sugarcane rather than cotton, for which no controls were introduced. The owners of the cane plantations extended the crop's acreage by as much as 30 percent during the war, exacerbating the shortage of staple foods in the region hit by gambiae malaria (and increasing the breeding grounds for mosquitoes).[11] In the second year of the malaria epidemic casualties were much higher, since many households had been too sick to harvest the previous year's food crop and were weakened by famine and malnutrition. The highest casualty rates were recorded among the workers on the sugar estates.[12] At one of the largest cane plantations, a few miles south of Luxor, the manager estimated that malaria affected 80 to 90 percent of the people, and the doctor in the nearby town of Armant reported eighty to ninety deaths a day.[13]

The elements combining to cause the disaster of 1942–44 represented some of the most powerful transformations of the twentieth century. First, there was the damming of the river. The building of the original barrage at Aswan in 1898–1902 helped inaugurate around the world an era of engineering on a new scale. Schemes to block the flow of large rivers were to become the century's largest construction projects. Dams were unique in the scope and manner in which they altered the distribution of resources across space and time, among entire communities and ecosystems. They offered more than just a promise of agricultural development or technical progress. For many postcolonial governments, this ability to rearrange the natural and social environment became a means to demonstrate the strength of the modern state as a techno-economic power.[14] Second, there were the synthetic chemicals. The manufacture of artificial nitrates introduced a transformation even greater than the building of dams. From the largely synthetic-free world of 1925, the production of new chemicals, led by nitrates, grew at a phenomenal rate. In the United States output increased tenfold in each decade. By the 1980s there were four million synthetic chemicals in production, sixty thousand of which were in common use. This transformation had an impact at the level of the cell and the organism to rival that of dams at the national level.[15] Third, there was malaria, which took advantage of irrigation schemes, population movements, and changes in agriculture to become the world's most deadly infectious disease. *Plasmodium falciparum* represented only 30 percent of clinical malaria cases but was responsible for up to 90 percent of the deaths. It was so widespread that no one could agree even to the nearest million how many lives it was taking each year.[16] Finally, there was the war. Al-Alamein was remembered as the first great mechanized conflict, in which the German panzers, used in new kinds of tactical combination with antitank guns and aircraft, engaged the larger Grant and Sherman tanks. Yet the battle front was so narrow, and the German and Italian machinery so short of fuel and ammunition, that the two-week battle was fought at close quarters, like a battle of World War I. It epitomized a new and lethal interaction of man and machine.

Dams, blood-borne parasites, synthetic chemicals, mechanized war, and man-made famine coincided and interacted. It is not surprising to find disease brought by environmental transformation, industrial chemistry shaped by military needs, or war accompanied by famine. Nevertheless, their interaction presents a challenge. How exactly did tanks and parasites and synthetic nitrates affect one another? What kind of explanation can bring them together?

The war and the epidemic interacted on several levels. At the outbreak of hostilities Britain had reimposed martial law on Egypt, after the country had enjoyed almost two decades of partial independence from the colonial occupation established in 1882. The authorities censored reporting of the malaria epidemic, hoping to contain it in the south. Already preparing to evacuate Cairo in case Rommel broke through at al-Alamein, the British were unwilling to divert men and resources from the north to meet the invader from the south. This helped the gambiae mosquito advance. The British also faced a shortage of quinine, the only treatment against the infection, for in the same month that gambiae malaria was reported in Nubia the Japanese had occupied Java, cutting off the Dutch cinchona plantations whose trees supplied the drug to Europe.[17] So the Egyptian Ministry of Health was left to launch its own antimalaria campaign. Its eradication teams attacked the disease vector—the mosquito—rather than the parasite itself, spreading Malariol, diesel oil mixed with a spreading agent, on pools of standing water. The oil formed a film on the water surface, which prevented the mosquito larvae from hatching. Malariol tended to go missing, however, since irrigation pumps could use the diesel oil as fuel, which the war had made it difficult to obtain. The eradication teams later replaced it with Paris green, a mixture of arsenic powder and copper acetate used originally as a painters' pigment, which proved a more reliable larvicide, or at least one less liable to be taken over for other purposes.

The war may even have brought the epidemic. The anopheles mosquito has a range of only two miles, so to reach Egypt it needed vectors of its own. One view was that it must have arrived by airplane, a mode of travel not unusual for mosquitoes. German air and submarine attacks had made the Mediterranean unsafe, so the British were flying a new supply route to Cairo via West Africa and Sudan. But the hostilities may also have enabled the mosquito to reach Egypt by boat. The war had increased river traffic with Sudan, and the building and raising of the Aswan Dam had created new breeding places for the insect along the route. Once in Egypt, the mosquito continued to travel north, moving by boat, train, and motorcar. To prevent its movement, these vehicles were treated by a new technique, the pyrethrum spray, developed over the previous decade to combat a major outbreak of malaria in Natal Province on the east coast of South Africa—like Upper Egypt, a region producing sugarcane. Pyrethrum powder, made of the dried flowers of the pyrethrum variety of chrysanthemum and sometimes burned to fumigate houses against insects, was mixed with green soap and glycerine and then forced through the spray nozzle of a stirrup pump, making a fine poisonous mist that killed the adult mosquitoes.[18]

Disease often moves with the changing movements of people, and modern war causes large numbers to find routes outside existing networks of trade and migration. But having taken advantage of new kinds of transport and traffic routes, the insect also needed ways to establish itself by colonizing new territory and populations. The patterns of war and transportation had to intersect with other developments, in particular changing hydraulics. In the same years that the gambiae mosquito began to move north from equatorial Africa along the Upper Nile valley, it also crossed the Atlantic to the coast of Brazil. In both Brazil and the Upper Nile the mosquito took advantage of recent irrigation works and changed patterns of water use. In the case of the Nile, the British had extended the control of the river at Aswan by constructing further storage reservoirs in the Anglo-Egyptian-occupied Sudan. Dams were completed across the Blue Nile at Sennar, two hundred miles south of Khartoum, the Sudanese capital, in 1925, and across the White Nile at Jabal Aulia, thirty miles above Khartoum, in 1937. These projects were followed by reports of new levels of endemic disease, including schistosomiasis (a parasitic worm infection carried by an aquatic snail that would eventually affect all of Egypt, and whose treatment later introduced another endemic infection, hepatitis C, in possibly the world's largest transmission of blood-borne pathogens from medical intervention) as well as malaria.[19] The linking together of the river control projects enabled the mosquito to jump barriers from one region to the next. The accompanying cultivation based on perennial irrigation created many breeding places among a thicker population of human hosts that often lived much closer to the water now that flooding no longer occurred in many areas. The engineers who built the irrigation works had not considered the possibility that snails or mosquitoes would make use of their work to move, or that certain parasites would travel with these hosts, or that devastating consequences would ensue. In a private report in 1942, however, the British acknowledged that the surest way to restore the health of the Egyptian population would be to destroy the dams and return to basin irrigation.[20]

The irrigation works led to other unexpected effects. The damming of the river altered the distribution and timing of its flow, as well as the temperature and chemistry of the water. This affected the riverbed and banks, altering the character of the riverine environment. Microorganisms and plants dependent on the balance of the river's ebb and flood disappeared, while other, more aggressive species took advantage of the change. Curly pondweed, or *Potamogeton crispus,* one of the most invasive aquatic plants, began to form large islands of weed, which the river's current carried in clumps downstream. An Egyptian malaria expert established that the *Anopheles gambiae* in turn made use of the pondweed, which transported the larvae of the mosquito from one breeding area to the next.[21]

If the gambiae mosquito benefited from the changes in the flow and chemistry of the Nile, its parasite, needing human bodies for reproduction, was also able to take advantage. As a spore-forming parasite, the plasmodium did not set out to kill its human victims, but entered their bodies merely to complete its unusual life cycle. Transferred by the bite of the female mosquito, the young spores take up residence for about a week in the cells of the victim's liver. Each spore then bursts apart and releases into the bloodstream up to forty thousand offspring, which feed off the blood's cell hemoglobin and multiply into further offspring, some of which assume separate male and female forms. The explosive reproduction is not intended to kill the victim, but to ensure that with the bite of another mosquito a number of spores are ingested back into the stomach of the insect, where they fertilize and complete the reproductive cycle. However, the malignant form of the parasite brought by the new invader to southern Egypt makes the red blood cells of its victims particularly sticky, clogging the arteries and depriving the body of oxygen. Most victims survive after a severe fever, which ensures that the parasite still has hosts in which to live. But if the brain or another vital organ is deprived of oxygen, the unwilling host can die.

In Upper Egypt the plasmodium found a population with no immune response to interrupt its infection cycle, for it was a new arrival. It also found a population whose bodies had been transformed by the sugar industry. From the 1920s Egypt's newly independent government was for the first time able to protect local manufacturing, in particular sugar production, the country's oldest and largest modern industry. Price protection against the global market in the 1930s and 1940s combined with the irrigation work supported the extension of cultivation. Perennial irrigation and cane cultivation reduced the fertility of the soil and the land available for food production. When the war interrupted the supply of artificial fertilizer, these factors combined to make the people of southern Egypt far more vulnerable to the plasmodium parasite. In contrast to the badly nourished residents of southern Egypt, none of the government officials, medical workers, or eradication teams, nor the wealthy women from Cairo who launched a charity relief operation in the south, lost their lives in the epidemic.[22] Furthermore, reports from Brazil indicate that sugarcane juice, which those working on sugar plantations consumed on site by breaking and chewing the cane, can worsen the effects of malaria.[23] Thus on several levels the parasite found that sugar had left the bodies it encountered less able to resist infection. The chemistry of the epidemic operated at the level of the nation and of the cell.

The fertilizer shortage that contributed to malnutrition also represented the interaction of forces on several levels. After German nitrate supplies were cut off by the war, there was a larger reason why alternative sources of chemical fertilizer could not be found. Natural supplies of ammonium nitrate were available in only one place in the world, the Atacama Desert in Chile, and the U.S. processing companies operating there could supply Egypt with only small amounts. Along with the manufacturers of artificial nitrates, they were using their fertilizer factories for a more urgent purpose. Ammonium nitrate provided the main ingredient for two chemically similar but socially different processes, each concerned with life and death: the fertilizing of crops and the making of high explosives. Europe and America had converted their fertilizer plants to the manufacture of wartime ammunition. The lack of nitrates for Egyptian agriculture, and the consequent food crisis that left much of the population undernourished, was due not only to the loss of a particular source of supplies. The chemical powers of the nitrates contributed to the course of events.

Finally, war provided the method used to defeat the epidemic, for pyrethrum sprays and Paris green were not enough. After the first winter of the epidemic the government declared the gambiae mosquito eradicated, but in 1943–44 there was a second and much more severe outbreak. Part of the problem was that the eradication campaign, influenced by current public health concerns about the unhealthiness of stagnant water, had concentrated on the large standing pools often found on the edges of villages, whereas this particular mosquito was willing to breed in the smallest ditches and irrigation channels and in the borrow pits left by the construction of railway embankments, which were not associated with disease and were often overlooked.[24]

The Egyptian government was able to turn for help to a new form of transnational secular body, the nonprofit corporation. Early in the century,

U.S. military expansion in the Caribbean, in particular the building of the Panama Canal, had encouraged extensive efforts to control mosquitoes, which carried both malaria and yellow fever. (Ferdinand de Lesseps, the man who organized the construction of the Suez Canal, had been the first to attempt to dig a canal across the Isthmus of Panama, but in 1889 was forced to abandon the ten-year effort, in part because of deaths from these two diseases.) In 1915, the year after the canal's completion, the newly established Rockefeller Foundation took over the mosquito campaign from the U.S. army and launched a worldwide program to study and control the two mosquito-borne diseases. Thus the global movements of the mosquito gave shape to a transnational corporate philanthropy.

Yellow fever was a more immediate concern than malaria, for it threatened to use the Panama Canal to cross into the Pacific. Rockefeller set up a program in Brazil to eliminate the disease from the coastal areas of South America.[25] The leader of the campaign, Dr. Fred Soper, developed eradication methods based on modern warfare, in which "brigades" of uniformed men armed with spray guns went on search and destroy missions. Disease was to be defeated not by improved social conditions or medical intervention but by the physical elimination of the enemy species. Detailed maps and index cards recorded the location of houses to be searched, the discovery of each mosquito, and the routes and timing of missions to spray or dump the chemicals. With its focus on yellow fever, the Rockefeller Foundation headquarters in New York was not interested in reports that the gambiae mosquito had reached Brazil. However, Soper saw in the arrival of the new and relatively well contained *Anopheles gambiae* an ideal opportunity to demonstrate his technical methods. He organized a campaign in 1938 that eradicated gambiae malaria by the early 1940s. The success made Soper the world's most influential malaria expert, able to reshape tactics and lay down the new methods of total species eradication, methods that were not seriously challenged for another fifty years.[26]

In November 1942, in coordination with the British offensive at al-Alamein, the United States entered the Mediterranean war, landing troops in French North Africa. Disease was again a concern, but in this case it was typhus, which had killed tens of thousands of soldiers in World War I. To develop ways to protect its forces, Washington set up a Typhus Commission with its headquarters in Cairo. Fred Soper of the Rockefeller Foundation was seconded to the commission and sent to Egypt. As in Brazil, his arrival on an unrelated mission coincided with an outbreak of gambiae malaria.[27] The intersecting networks of U.S. philanthropic and military power had once again brought Soper and the gambiae mosquito together. He drew up a plan for a military-style eradication campaign, but the British authorities, objecting to this introduction of an American influence into Egyptian politics, forced the government to shelve the plan. When the epidemic reemerged in 1943–44, the British began to fear that it threatened the population centers and troop concentrations of the north. They agreed that the Egyptians should appoint "a sort of malaria dictator" to organize a campaign against the disease (the word "dictator" was in vogue in those days).[28] They were forced to drop their earlier objections and allow the Egyptian government to follow the Brazilian model of eradication, advised by Soper.[29] The Egyptian teams finally identified and destroyed the last gambiae larvae in February 1945, a few kilometers to the south of ʿAmm Ibrahim's village near Luxor.

The chain of events in Egypt seems to create a triangle, formed by the interconnection of war, disease, and agriculture. War in the Mediterranean diverted attention and resources from an epidemic arriving from the south, brought by mosquitoes that took advantage of wartime traffic. The insect also moved with the aid of the prewar irrigation projects and the ecological transformations those brought about. The irrigation works made water available for industrial crops but left agriculture dependent upon artificial fertilizers. The ammonium nitrate used on the soil was the main ingredient in the manufacture of explosives and was diverted for the needs of war. Deprived of fertilizer the fields produced less food, so the parasite carried by the mosquito found its human hosts malnourished and killed them at the rate of hundreds a day.

The chain is in fact more than a triangle. The connections between a war, an epidemic, and a famine depended upon connections between rivers, dams, fertilizers, food webs, and, as we will see, several additional links and interactions. What seems remarkable is the way the properties of these various elements interacted. They were not just separate historical events affecting one another at the social level. The linkages among them were hydraulic, chemical, military, political, etiological, and mechanical. No one writing about Egypt in this period describes this interaction. There are studies of military tactics, irrigation methods, Anglo-Egyptian relations, hydraulic engineering, parasites, the sugar industry, and peasants. But there are no accounts that take seriously how these elements interact. It is as if the elements are somehow incommensurable. They seem to involve very different forces, agents, elements, spatial scales, and temporalities.[30] They shape one another, yet their heterogeneity offers a resistance to explanation.

The resistance may have something to do with the mixing of natural and social worlds. Chemical and biological processes are surely of a different order than military and political forces. Each of these processes and forces has its own science, which identifies the agents, time lines, geo-spatial scales, and modes of interaction appropriate to its analysis. This tends to leave each of them isolated in their separate sciences. The isolation may be appropriate for the task of a particular science or technical expertise, but its limitations are striking as soon as one begins to ask about the kinds of interactions I have described. Since those interactions belong, as I suggested, to some of the most profound transformations of the modern era, this presents a problem for social science. Instead of developing the kinds of analysis that might address these interactions, responding to the techno-scientific transformations of the twentieth century, social theory is still largely trapped in the methods and divisions of labor of the nineteenth century.

There are two characteristics of social explanation relevant to this problem. First, social theory typically operates by relating particular cases to a larger pattern or process. Events in a place like Egypt are explained as the local occurrence of something more general, or an exception to what generally occurs, or a particular variation in the general range of possibilities. In some of the social sciences this aim is quite explicit, expressed in rules of method and styles of writing. In others it is implicit but still at work, for example in historical scholarship, in which the narrative may focus on a specific context but draws its structure and relevance from an implied comparison with other, more general cases. Inevitably the generic case in such accounts is the history of Europe or the West, and the particulars of what happened outside Europe are explained as replicas of Europe's history, or variations from that historical pattern, or alternatives to it.[31] In studies of Egypt, for example, events like those I have been describing fit into a variety of larger narratives: the story of the nation and its development, the growth of new social classes and other national actors, and the rise of the modern state, often placed in the context of the development of capitalism, the expansion of Europe, or the global history of modernity. The story takes it shape from the way it fits into a sovereign narrative told about every place, the story of rationalization, technological and social progress, the growth and transformation of production, and the universalization of the culture and power of the West. This assumption of a universal armature is the foundation that makes social theory possible. The development of forms of explanation placing particular events into a universal framework coincided, of course, with a quite palpable expansion of Western power, wealth, and technical knowledge. The issue is not whether such expansion occurred, but its relationship to the grounds on which social theory is built. The universal to which social theory aspires is a category founded within and expressed by the particular history of the West.

The second feature of social explanation follows from the first: all the actors are human. The protagonists of the history of the nation, of modernity, of capitalism, are people. Human beings are the agents around whose actions and intentions the story is written. This is necessarily the case, for it is the intentionality or rationality of human agents that gives the explanation its logic and enables particular cases to fit as instances of something general. The general or universal aspect of events that social theory attempts to identify occurs precisely as the spread of this human reason, technical knowledge, or collective consciousness. By contrast, although the river Nile is transnational, and anopheles mosquitoes are quite global, their generality is not the same as that of capitalism, the idea of the nation, or modern science. The Nile is not considered an abstraction, nor is the mosquito experienced as an expression of the universal.

The result of these two features of social theory is that in the explanation of events one always knows in advance who the protagonists are. Emile Durkheim once described the resistance that nature offers to understanding compared to the ease with which society is explained. "While the scientist who studies physical nature is very keenly aware of the resistance it offers him, and which he has so much difficulty in overcoming, the sociologist seems to move in a sphere perfectly transparent to his view, so great is the ease with which the most obscure questions are resolved."[32] What is this ease, this transparency? It arises in part from having already decided who counts as an agent. It is not that social analysis necessarily ignores disease, agriculture, chemicals, or technology, but that these are externals—nature, tools, obstacles, resources—whose role is essentially passive. Even on the occasions when they are given a more independent force, there is still a fundamental divide between human agency and the nonhuman elements.

Social science is always founded upon a categorical distinction between the ideality of human intentions and purposes and the object world upon which these work, and which in turn may affect them. There is little room to examine the ways they emerge together in a variety of combinations, or how so-called human agency draws its force by attempting to divert or attach itself to other kinds of energy or logic. No explanation grounded in the universalizing force of human projects and intentions can explore whether the very possibility of the human, of intentionality, of abstraction depends on, at the same time as it overlooks, nonhuman elements. These appear merely physical, secondary, and external.

If the web of events in wartime Egypt offers a certain resistance to explanation, part of the reason may be that it includes a variety of agencies that are not exclusively human: the anopheles mosquito, the falciparum parasite, the chemical properties of ammonium nitrate, the 75mm guns of the Sherman tank, the hydraulic force of the river, and one or two more to be introduced shortly. These do not just interact with the activities of human agents. They make possible a world that somehow seems the outcome of human rationality and programming. They shape a variety of social processes, sometimes according to human plans, but just as often not, or at least not quite. How is it, we need to ask, that forms of rationality, planning, expertise, and profit arise from this effect?

In social theory there is an important exception to the rule that human action is put at the center and the external world is treated as an arena for such action rather than the source of forms of agency and power. It is found in the work of Marx. For Marx, individual capitalists are to be understood not as agents in their own right, but as those who personify the power of capital. The "main-spring" that powers the movement of capitalist history is not human intention but the expansion of value through the exchange of commodities, in particular the exchange of labor power. An individual possessor of money becomes a capitalist, Marx writes, when this expansion of capital through exchange becomes his subjective aim. He then "functions as a capitalist, that is, as capital personified and endowed with consciousness and a will."[33] Thus Marx understands capital as something twofold. It arises from the circulation of money, the development of technical processes, and particular patterns of commodity exchange and power relation. Yet these material processes acquire a quasi-human form. Through exchange, the powers of objects take on a consciousness and a will. Most analyses that draw on Marx move quite quickly over this idea. The ability of certain historical actors to personify the force of capital is easily taken for granted. There might be disagreement over which particular actors achieve this role, and how successfully they accomplish it. But what does it mean for capital to become personified? How exactly do nonhuman things or processes form this hybrid with the consciousness of humans? What does it mean to think of capital as something whose power depends on being simultaneously human and nonhuman? Marx, as Derrida says, was "one of the first thinkers of technics," the first to grapple with the hybrids of man-machine, capital-consciousness, automatism-will.[34] His writing grasped that human consciousness is an artifactual body, even if in the end he always wanted to ground his critique of consciousness in absolute distinctions between real and abstract, presence and representation, object and value, labor and ideas. These are distinctions whose apparent stability we must explore. How is the ambivalent relation between the nonhuman and the human, or the real and the abstract, constituted? How are the irreducible exchanges or tensions between the two resolved in modern politics into so simple an opposition?

To begin this task, we need to find a capitalist, someone who can function in our story as capital personified. Fortunately there is such a capitalist available, and a big one. As it happens he had a large house on the same plantation at Armant mentioned above, where eighty or ninety workers a day were dying of malaria. He was, it will be no surprise to learn, the plantation's owner. Ahmad ʿAbbud also controlled the processing mill five hundred yards down the river, together with the eighteen other large sugar factories in Egypt that made up the country's sugar industry, and he was one of the most powerful figures in Egyptian business and politics.[35] Trained as an engineer at the University of Glasgow, he had worked on irrigation schemes in Ottoman Iraq before World War I and on the railway system in Syria and Palestine during the war. He started business in Egypt in 1924 by obtaining a contract to dredge and maintain the new government-financed irrigation canals, his wealth expanding with the expansion of the public irrigation system.[36] His construction company worked on increasing the height of the Aswan Dam in 1929–33 and other large state projects. Like a handful of other successful entrepreneurs, he used these lucrative government contracts and concessions to move into other business sectors, including shipping, public transport, real estate, trade, and banking. He joined Egypt's new class of big landowners by acquiring the six-thousand-acre sugar plantation at Armant, and in 1939 took control of the Egyptian Sugar Company, the country's oldest and largest industrial venture, which enjoyed a state-protected monopoly over the processing of raw cane and the sale and export of sugar.[37] By the outbreak of World War II, as his business empire moved its headquarters into Cairo's first high-rise structure, the eighteen-story Immobilia Building, ʿAbbud controlled one of just two or three family-based entrepreneurial groups competing to monopolize large sectors of the country's finance, trade, transportation, and industry. Following the war, the international press was to rank him as one of the ten richest men in the world.[38]

The growth of ʿAbbud's empire depended upon his making and remaking circuits of political and social power. In February 1942 the British forced the appointment of an Egyptian government led by the Wafd party, which had earlier negotiated the country's partial independence from Britain and seemed its most reliable wartime ally. Through a business association with the Wakil family, cotton merchants and landowners whose daughter Zaynab was married to the Wafdist prime minister, ʿAbbud reestablished earlier ties with the Wafd, began to finance its activities, and helped put his allies and business associates in control. Three months after the party took power, ʿAbd al-Wahid al-Wakil, a brother of ʿAbbud's business partner, was made minister of health, just as the ministry received the first news of the arrival of gambiae malaria.[39] At the same time ʿAbbud secured the dismissal of the Wafd's new minister of finance, who had tried to introduce sugar rationing (and to prosecute the Wakils for the wartime smuggling of cotton textiles).[40] The minister's removal gave ʿAbbud's sugar monopoly a free hand to negotiate a lucrative deal with the British. As the negotiations neared completion in February 1943, the British ambassador spent six weeks visiting ʿAbbud and his Scottish-born wife Jemima at their spacious red-tiled villa on the sugar estate (a long anticipated trip that became a "nightmare" after the ambassador suffered a dangerous fever and ʿAbbud was twice almost killed, first in a plane crash and then in a driving accident when his horse bolted and threw him against a brick wall).[41] Following the stay ʿAbbud concluded his "thief's bargain," as the disgruntled British called it in private, agreeing to sell the British military authorities his company's "surplus" stock of sugar (at a moment of famine on the sugar estates) for a considerable profit. The deal also gave ʿAbbud scarce supplies of fertilizer, officially earmarked for other crops, to use on the sugar plantations.[42]

Over the following months, as the malaria epidemic took hold again, ʿAbbud embarked on an audacious scheme to use his profits from the sugar deal and the expansion of cane cultivation to make himself into what a British official, invoking once again the nomenclature of the day, called "a kind of commercial dictator."[43] ʿAbbud maneuvered to take over the bank and the affiliated enterprises of the country's other major business conglomerate, the Misr group, which had a dominant position in textile manufacture, the cotton trade, air transport, cinema, insurance, and other fields.[44] At the same time he revived a plan from the 1930s for Egypt's largest industrial scheme, to install hydroelectric turbines in the dam at Aswan that had recently been made higher. He proposed to use the electricity to manufacture and supply the country's entire demand for fertilizer.

The interwar years had seen a growing struggle among the rival business groups for the dominant position in what Robert Vitalis calls the "rent circuits" of Egyptian politics, meaning the profits to be made from privileged control of the economic resources circulating through the country. Controlling the circulation of rents, however, was dependent upon the control of resources that had other, interconnected forms of circulation. These included the complex networks of family power and colonial affiliation whose significance I have already suggested. But at the center of these struggles from the 1920s to the 1950s was an effort to command, or at least turn to profit, one particular kind of circuit, the flow of the waters of the Nile.[45] The Aswan Dam offered the opportunity to reorganize and concentrate into fewer hands a series of further circulations—hydraulic, electrical, political, chemical, and agricultural. ʿAbbud and his rivals competed for the lucrative rights to build a hydroelectric power station at Aswan and convert the force of the river's flow into the power to drive industry, which in turn would fuel agriculture. Large quantities of electric power would be used to convert nitrogen into artificial fertilizer. Just as alluvial silt had once been carried and deposited by the floodwaters of the Nile, synthetic chemicals would in future be transported in sacks from the nitrate plant at Aswan and deposited across the country's fields to restore a little of the lost fertility of the soil. The complex flows of the Nile flood, channeled into storage basins, held for several weeks to allow silt and nutrients to settle, and released again into the river, were to be reorganized and transformed into the narrower flows of waters through turbine wheels, high voltages along transmission cables, electrical energy into nitrates, fertilizer sacks across the countryside, and ammonia from the soil into the proteins of cane and cotton plants. The political struggle to control rent circuits was a battle to build and control these interconnected circuits. And it was through these same circuits—dams, irrigation, sugar cultivation—that the mosquito had entered Egypt.

Should we explain ʿAbbud's power and wealth in terms of his ability to "personify" capital and become the conscious representative of its power to reproduce and expand? This seems preferable to the alternative of saying that ʿAbbud's success resulted simply from his skill as a calculating agent who was able to out-calculate his rivals and make an ever larger profit. The latter explanation attributes all the success to ʿAbbud himself. It does not even ask what arrangements (of law, property, political economy, engineering, irrigation, and much more) made such calculation possible, or what agencies kept those arrangements in place. The former at least gives some credit to another power, the circulating force of capital. Capital can circulate and, by combining with further forces, go through metamorphoses into other forms—from money into property and labor, property and labor into sugarcane, sugarcane into processed sugar or alcohol, and back again into money—using resources and arrangements that do not come from ʻAbbud alone.[46] Clearly, however, the movements and metamorphoses of capital were not the only circulations at work in ʻAbbud's success. His struggle to divert rent circuits to his own advantage was at the same time an effort to develop and direct a whole series of interconnected circuits: water, electricity, nitrates, military requisitions, cane, processed sugar, cotton, and several others.

Clearly, too, the idea that these circulations and forces are "personified," or represented by the actions of particular individuals, is too simple. Individuals may at times secure control of certain elements, and they may even claim to represent those elements in the social world. But no individual masters them, or submits the world to their intentions. More often there occurs a series of claims, affinities, and interactions, all of which exceed the grasp or intention of the human agents involved. Human agency and intention are partial and incomplete products of these interactions. This incompleteness, as we will see, means that no single line divides the human from the nonhuman, or intentions and plans from the object-world to which they refer.

But why insist on all these additional agencies, circulations, and forces? Surely the task of social science, like all science, is to simplify, to identify a limited number of more decisive agents. Why not accept a simpler but more powerful story, one that can depict the big picture and even identify certain patterns or predictions? There is an old answer to this question: that if the world is a complicated and indeterminate place, with many agencies and forces at work, then an accurate picture of that world will be a complex and indeterminate one.[47] But the answer I want to propose here has to do with the role of expertise and reason, explanation and simplification, in the politics of the twentieth century. Politics itself was working to simplify the world, attempting to gain for itself the powers of expertise by resolving it into simple forces and oppositions.

This is not, therefore, a question of introducing a natural or hydraulic determinism to replace the determinism of modern technological innovation or capitalist expansion. If social and economic networks were connected with the changing ecology of one of the world's longest rivers, this does not mean attributing social outcomes to changes in nature. Long before the Aswan Dam, before all the irrigation work of the nineteenth century, the river was already as much a technical and social phenomenon as a natural one. Its waters were channeled, stored, raised, distributed, and drained by the interaction of mechanical, human, animal, and hydraulic power. William Willcocks, the director of reservoirs for the Egyptian government, whose studies of Nile hydraulics were used to determine the engineering of the Aswan Dam, considered the old system of channeling floodwaters in sequence into hundreds of interconnected field basins, holding them for a certain period, and releasing them in sequence again into the river a more complex irrigation mechanism than the enormous but singular barrage and reservoir that replaced it.[48] The old methods had manufactured a geography that was no more natural than it was human, and no less. Rather, it was always both.

Nature was not the cause of the changes taking place. It was the outcome. The very scale of the technical and engineering works of the twentieth century produced a new experience of the river Nile as exclusively a force of nature. A visit to the Aswan Dam inspired a European writer to publish the first popular account of the river, which he called a "biography" of its life. "When, at the end of 1924, I first saw the Great Dam at Aswân," wrote Emil Ludwig, "its symbolic significance burst upon me with such force that I seemed to comprehend the River Nile forwards and backwards from this crucial point in its course. A mighty element had been tamed by human ingenuity so that the desert should bring forth fruit, an achievement which the centenarian Faust had attempted as the highest attainable to man in the service of his fellow-men."[49] The reference to Faust is quite appropriate. Goethe's great novel of the colonizing transformation of nature was inspired by conversations with Saint-Simonians, secular priests of engineering who had traveled to Egypt in the nineteenth century and initiated the irrigation projects completed, and transformed, with the Aswan Dam. The new scale of twentieth-century engineering, of which the Aswan Dam was among the first and most dramatic examples anywhere in the world, turned the bizarre religion of the Saint-Simonians into an everyday belief: that "human ingenuity" could now dominate the "mighty elements" of nature. In manufacturing the dam, the engineers also manufactured nature.

Several features of the new construction helped produce the effect of a world divided into human expertise on one side and nature on the other. First, there was the concentration of the river control mechanisms at one site. The old irrigation mechanisms were distributed along the length of the valley, formed out of hundreds of canals, drains, dikes, basins, sluices, pumps, and water wheels, as well as the channel of the river itself, and drew upon steam, animal, hydraulic, and human power. It would have been difficult in describing these arrangements to say where natural forces ended and technology began, or to draw a line between ingenuity and nature. In contrast, the dam at Aswan gathered all the engineering into one location, providing an observation point where writers like Ludwig could stand and suddenly "comprehend" the river as a force of nature tamed by man. Second, the concentration of engineering required a parallel concentration of capital. Building the original dam cost £2,440,000 sterling, and a further £280,000 was spent to strengthen the base immediately after the reservoir was filled.[50] To organize, and later justify, this expenditure required a series of proposals, plans, financial statements, political memoranda, annual reports, and newspaper accounts, all of which in different ways described, enumerated, calculated, and argued about the building of the dam. The arguments and calculations accompanying the old hydraulic system had been distributed over a much wider territory. Thus a significant reorganization and concentration of accounting, calculation, description, and knowledge accompanied the concentration of hydraulic power in the dam. These and other reorganizations were the kinds of processes through which the world came to be simplified into what seemed nature on one side, and human calculation and expertise on the other.

Life was now to be increasingly resolved into this binary arrangement, rendering up a simple, dualistic world of nature versus science, material reality versus human ingenuity, stonework versus blueprints, objects versus ideas. This dualism, however, as the Aswan example indicates, was an artifact of particular projects and politics. Like all dualisms, and all artifacts, it was neither original nor completely stable. The artifactual is the effect of a process.[51] If one turns back from the effect created by the engineering at Aswan, from the force of the "symbolic" that Ludwig was able to experience when standing before the completed dam, to recover the process itself, then the distinction between nature and science, between masonry and symbol, between the river to be tamed and the expertise that later claimed to have tamed it, one can locate any number of episodes, elements, and forces that disrupt the effect created by the final artifact. Engineering the dam was a messy, uncertain, conflict-ridden, and haphazard project. Public finances were controlled by an International Debt Commission, which forced changes in the alignment of the dam. The original plan had allowed "more play and choice of alignment" to take advantage of the soundest rock for the foundations. Instead, the granite under the foundation was rotten, causing delays to the construction and uncertainty about its future stability. The delays forced the contractors to abandon plans to build the masonry work using mortar manufactured from local lime and to import ready-made, faster-drying Portland cement instead. The cement mortar was less flexible and watertight than lime, leading to problems with leakage through the structure. The water spilling through the dam's sluices began to erode its base. The engineers had neglected to consider thermal stresses. The dam cost twice the original budget.[52] Subsequent problems of silt accumulation, seepage, and evaporation from the reservoir were so great that instead of increasing the water available, the mean annual discharge of water below the dam was almost one-fourth less in the fifty years following the dam's construction than in the thirty years before it was built.[53] None of these problems was foreseen by the experts at work on the dam. So complex were the forms of calculation required by dam construction, it later gave rise to the new field called cost-benefit analysis. But as hundreds and eventually thousands of large dams were built around the world in the course of the century, the accuracy of calculation cannot be said to have improved.[54]

Still, it might be argued, science one by one solved the problems it encountered. Many of them were overcome, it is true, but then one would have to acknowledge that science did not direct the engineer's work as a preformed intelligence. The projects themselves formed the science.[55] Solutions were worked out on the ground. Engineering was an expertise given shape in these and similar undertakings. The British engineers returned to London after each season of construction in Aswan to present papers at meetings of the Institution of Civil Engineers. These were published in the *Proceedings* of the institution, or in professional journals such as *The Engineer.* On a site, engineers could refer to R. B. Buckley's *Irrigation Pocket-Book,* which quoted figures for the adhesion of mortar joints or the expansion of different materials due to the penetration of moisture, based on observations drawn from earlier projects.[56] The expertise was hybrid, not an exterior intelligence applied to the world, but another artifactual body. If one adds to this Willcock's view that the older system of basin irrigation was more sophisticated than the barrage and reservoir that replaced it, the conclusion that follows is that in some ways, rather than applying knowledge to the world, the engineering work took it away. British engineers were taught things by the dam and carried this knowledge into scientific journals and irrigation manuals, but the farmers and local irrigation experts who had managed and maintained the earlier hydraulic system had much of their knowledge taken from them.[57]

The questions and disputes posed by the building of the dam were not restricted to debates within professional journals and discussions among engineers at the site. The problems spilled over and drew in government officials and employees, archaeologists, the national and European press, entrepreneurs and investors, and an increasing number of Egyptian intellectuals and political figures. The reservoir behind the dam inundated the great

Temple of Philae and other ancient sites. Archaeologists campaigned against the building of the dam in the European press and at scientific congresses.[58] Cost overruns led to conflicts among financiers, government engineers, contractors, and outsiders, which continued for years and were taken up in national politics. In 1919 Willcocks criticized the postwar plans of the Ministry of Public Works to build two further dams in Sudan, claiming the plans were based on faulty calculations of the Nile flow and pointing out that one of the dams, at Jabal Aulia, would submerge valuable agricultural land and displace and cause suffering to a large population.[59] Science was formed in these wars, and so was the country's new national politics. Willcocks's proposal to increase the height of the Aswan Dam a second time as an alternative to controlling the Nile from Sudan was taken up by the nationalist movement during the 1919 uprising against the British. Willcocks found himself put on trial for sedition and criminal libel.[60] The disputes continued, especially after commissions of inquiry discovered that the ministry's program included further, more serious miscalculations.

The aim of those involved in the disputes, one might say, was to "personify" the forces of nature in politics, that is, to translate their potential into human projects. As with ʿAbbud's later attempt to personify certain circulations of capital, chemical fertilizer, and electricity, the forces put to work, although portrayed as nature or material resources and therefore subject to human expertise and planning, never quite accepted this secondary role. There were always certain effects that went beyond the calculations, certain forces that exceeded human intention. Scientific expertise and national politics were produced out of this tension.

The gambiae mosquito, as we know, figured nowhere in these rival plans and calculations for the dam, or in the technical and political battles that followed. When it took advantage of the new reservoirs and river movements and arrived unexpectedly in Aswan, however, a similar struggle developed to draw the insect into a variety of political alliances. In interwar Cairo the political problems of the countryside, associated with the spread of perennial irrigation, the development of commercial agriculture, the growth of large estates, and increasing poverty, indebtedness, landlessness, hunger, and parasitic infection among the fellahs, or peasants, were translated by those in power into problems of what was called "public health." They were to be solved by government programs of rural social improvement and hygiene. The Wafd government of 1936 created a Ministry of Health, and when the party returned to power with British help in 1942, one of its first acts was to pass the Law for the Improvement of Village Health. "The growth of the democratic and national spirit in Egypt after the war," wrote an Egyptian political economist in 1940, referring to the period since World War I, "has made the nation aware that helping the fellah is not only a duty but also an insurance against social unrest. . . . The creation of a Ministry of Health in 1936 and of an independent Section of the Ministry of the Interior devoted to the planning and execution of rural reforms, is a welcome sign of increased public interest in the fellah."[61] The arrival of gambiae malaria was interpreted by those in power as evidence confirming the need for this program of social and hydraulic engineering. The problems of Egypt were those of limited natural resources and a deficient public health, and were to be overcome by the methods of techno-science. In December 1942 the new minister of health, ʿAbd al-Wahid al-Wakil, blamed the malaria epidemic on the failure of previous governments to carry through with the hydroelectric scheme promoted by his friend ʿAbbud and with further irrigation projects, arguing that these would have raised the standard of living in the south and made its population healthy enough to resist the epidemic.[62]

Before the war, the program of public health and public works allowed no place for more radical discussions of the question of private property in the countryside. Warning that the rural population, in the language of public health, was "dead as regards healthy nationalistic life," a number of political figures had called for limited measures to alleviate the increasing hardship caused by commercial agriculture and large-scale landownership, and even the government tried to introduce agricultural rent controls. But the issue of property rights was not raised.[63] It was symptomatic of prevailing attitudes toward entitlement that when the wartime fertilizer crisis led to food rationing, supplies were assigned to different groups according to income, with higher income groups getting bigger rations.[64]

But the impact of the mosquito's arrival was not so easily controlled. If ʿAbbud's associates translated the malaria epidemic into renewed arguments for projects of public health and public works, the mosquito could be taken up by rival groups in other directions. A group of women from wealthy families closely associated with the Egyptian royal family, which opposed the Wafd government and the British, organized soup kitchens and other relief projects in the south to aid the malaria victims. By drawing attention to the crisis they provided the royal palace with an opportunity to embarrass the government.[65] But they in turn could be embarrassed by the mosquito. The wealthy women invited a young journalist to visit and describe their relief efforts. The journalist, later to become a leading writer, reported instead that the women themselves were like mosquitoes. They belonged to the class of Egyptians who "suck the people's blood and turn it into cakes, caviar and champagne." The rich were the real epidemic, he wrote, and their opulent palaces were no better than the stagnant pools in which the mosquitoes bred.[66]

The mosquito was put to work by critics of the ruling order to alter the terms of national debate. As the malaria epidemic in the south became public knowledge in Cairo, a number of individual reformers turned the crisis into an argument for more radical change. Rejecting the government view that the high death toll reflected poor sanitary conditions in the countryside and the need for further public works, they linked the crisis to the unequal distribution of land. One deputy in parliament claimed that the standard of living in the Soviet Union, where land was held in common, was much higher, and others drew attention to the successful land reform programs of Eastern Europe. From 1944 to 1947 and again in 1951, bills were introduced into parliament modeled on these reforms, proposing to bar owners of more than fifty acres from acquiring additional land.[67] The measures were blocked in parliament and no party made land reform an issue.[68] Instead, in March 1948 the government launched a program to distribute land reclaimed from the desert in five-acre plots to small farmers, who also received "hygienic houses" grouped in four villages, each equipped with a school, mosque, health unit, and public bath.[69] With such measures, made possible by the raising of the dam at Aswan, there seemed no immediate threat to the power of men like Ahmad ʿAbbud, who were able to consolidate their political and economic position. Yet thanks to the malaria epidemic and to the food shortages and poverty it had made visible, the question of land reform was now in circulation.

ʿAbbud's electricity and fertilizer schemes were interrupted in October 1944, when his political rivals managed to bring down the Wafd government. Five years later, however, he formed an alliance with the rival Misr group, and together in 1950 they helped put the Wafd back in power and secure their monopolistic economic positions. ʿAbbud's empire expanded with acquisitions in tourism and textile manufacturing, and new ventures to manufacture paper and perfumes, both using byproducts of the sugar industry.[70] He abandoned the proposal to build a nitrate plant at Aswan powered by hydroelectricity, which was to become a government project. In its place he took advantage of capital loans and a new nitrogen-fixing technology available from the United States to build a fertilizer factory at Suez, powered not with Nile waters but waste gases from the nearby Shell oil field.

The fertilizer factory was funded by the United States as an emblem of its postwar role in the country, "the most substantial, tangible example of American economic assistance to Egypt," as the U.S. Embassy reminded Washington.[71] The Americans planned to build political influence and at the same time subsidize their own industrial technology through a program of "technical assistance," which would organize postwar international relations around a politics of techno-economic development. Besides the fertilizer factory, in its first years the assistance program also funded a pilot scheme for the introduction of hybrid corn, the supply of six helicopters from United Helicopters of Palo Alto, California, for spraying crops with new chemical pesticides (more on that in a moment), a demonstration project for well drainage to restore land that, thanks to the dam, was "deteriorating from excess irrigation and salinity," and a new technology for building houses of mud brick.[72] People in the Nile valley had been building their houses with mud brick for several millennia, of course, so this last item needs explanation. Arthur D. Little, the Boston-based consulting firm advising the U.S. mission, had determined that an improvement to mud bricks was "an essential part" of Egypt's techno-economic development. The peasant's house "is never clean," the embassy reported to Washington. "The very nature of the mud brick promotes dust rather than cleanliness. Its surface is porous and will not readily take whitewash or paint."[73] The consultants received a contract to build twenty mud brick houses by a new process, using "a special mud brick making machine" instead of the traditional wooden mold, and improving the normal mixture of mud and straw by the addition of oil. From the twenty demonstration houses, it was hoped, "the knowledge of how to build such a house will be spread throughout Egypt."[74]

There were three significant features of this new politics based on technical expertise. First, as with the dam at Aswan, it represented a concentration and reorganization of knowledge rather than an introduction of expertise where none had been in use before. Technical knowledge was to be focused into pilot projects and demonstration sites, from where it would spread throughout the land. Villages in Egypt already had a straightforward method of plastering over mud brick, using particular local clays mixed with straw, employed whenever a house needed smoother or more impressive walls. But existing practice, like the old knowledge of irrigation, involved an expertise that was too widely dispersed to provide a means for building imperial power—or the profits of a Boston consulting firm.

Second, as with the engineering at Aswan, the projects encountered continuous practical difficulties. In fact, every one of them failed. The seedlings of hybrid corn "withered," the oil-stabilized mud brick was a failure, the use of helicopters had "run into various complications" (they broke down), and the new nitrogen-fixing technology for the manufacture of fertilizer did not work as planned. "It will be a long time before the fertilizer plant will produce satisfactorily," the embassy reported to Washington in November 1951. "The basic process is faulty from the design standpoint. Some of the engineering was done in New York and parts in London and it turns out to have been a weak job."[75] As at Aswan, the technical experts tried to learn from these failures. Repairs were improvised, opportunistic alternatives were introduced, and goals were reformulated. But what this means is that technical expertise did not work by bringing science and technology to develop natural resources. It happened just as much the other way around, and in ways that tended to be incomplete or unrealizable. So-called nature formed the expertise, which never completely escaped its compromising origins.

Third, however, it was an important aspect of the politics of technical expertise that these failures and adjustments were overlooked, in fact actively covered up. Techno-science had to conceal its extrascientific origins. Nowhere, first of all, was it mentioned that every one of these technologies—crop spraying, high-yield corn, drainage mechanisms, fertilizer plants, or a mud brick more resistant to disease—were themselves responses (and unsuccessful responses) to problems caused by earlier techno-scientific projects, in particular the Aswan Dam. Beyond this, the fundamental difficulties were presented as minor issues of the improper implementation of the plans, unexpected complications, bureaucratic delays, or the need to follow up. The hybrid corn, it was decided, needed to be recultivated with greater quantities of pesticide. The helicopters needed a larger and more continuous supply of spare parts from California. The new mud brick technology had to overcome political objections from the Ministry of Social Affairs, which believed that modern housing should be built of concrete. The pattern was set from the very start with ʿAbbud's nitrate factory at Suez. Since the factory was built to manufacture not just fertilizer but the political effectiveness of an imperial power, the mistakes in design and engineering could not be made public. No one was to be told that the engineering was a weak job, or that the entire plant was wrong, as the jargon put it, "from the design standpoint." The embassy promised ʿAbbud and his U.S. partners that "we would cooperate fully in keeping the situation quiet. In response to inquiries we would continue to say that operating difficulties in the early phases are to be expected from any new chemical process factory."[76]

Techno-politics is always a technical body, an alloy that must emerge from a process of manufacture whose ingredients are both human and nonhuman, both intentional and not, and in which the intentional or the human is always somewhat overrun by the unintended. But it is a particular form of manufacturing, a certain way of organizing the amalgam of human and nonhuman, things and ideas, so that the human, the intellectual, the realm of intentions and ideas seems to come first and to control and organize the nonhuman.[77]

ʿAbbud's new fortunes were short-lived. Postwar protests against conditions in the countryside intensified, and a popular campaign against the British role in Egypt culminated in the Cairo fire of January 26, 1952, when Shepeard's Hotel, symbol of the British presence, was burned down. A newly appointed government began to move against ʿAbbud's business monopoly. After failing to get him to pay E£5 million in tax arrears, the Ministry of Finance decided to nationalize his sugar company. ʿAbbud in response was reported to have bribed the king, who dismissed the government after four months in office.[78] As the political crisis developed, on July 23, 1952, junior officers in the Egyptian army led by Jamal Abdul Nasser carried out a coup d'état. Within six weeks they passed a land reform law and announced that postwar proposals to build a second and far larger dam at Aswan would go ahead, as the centerpiece of postindependence state building.

These actions, followed by the 1956 nationalization of the Suez Canal and the Suez crisis, brought on by the abrupt U.S. withdrawal of support for the Aswan High Dam, are now remembered as a turning point in Egypt's politics. But Nasser and his fellow officers had not seized power with the aim of carrying out land reform or building a postcolonial state around the Aswan project. Concerned principally with the incompetence and corruption of the army high command, they took control when they suddenly feared their own arrest.[79] They forced the king to abdicate in favor of his infant son and appointed a reformist prime minister with the aim of restoring a less corrupt and oligarchic parliamentary order. Since proposals for land reform were circulating, however, and were even advocated by the U.S. Embassy (as a defense against an imagined communist threat), they offered the means for an insecure new regime to win popular approval and weaken the few dozen oligarchs like ʿAbbud obstructing political reform. The army regime went on to expropriate all the estates of the royal family, but for others set the maximum holding relatively high, at three hundred acres.[80] The high limit and the ease with which it was evaded ensured that relatively little land was redistributed, but the reform did establish rent controls and tenant rights that improved conditions in every village, until their abrogation in October 1997. ʿAbbud lost most of his six-thousand-acre sugar plantation, and subsequently, as the military government moved against "the monopolies" and other rival sources of power, his business empire as well.[81] Hydropolitics had made ʿAbbud rich, but had also set in motion other forces, not least the mosquito, that combined to bring him down.

Similar combinations formed the genealogy of the High Dam, involving exchanges among hydropower, fertilizers, economic collapse, and war. During World War I American fear of Germany's new nitrate technology, and its own dependence on the single natural source of nitrates in Chile, persuaded Congress to include in the National Defense Act of 1916 the funds to build a mammoth nitrogen-fixing plant at Muscle Shoals in northern Alabama. The project included the construction of a large dam nearby, with a hydroelectric power station to supply the great quantities of electricity consumed in nitrogen fixing. At the war's end, after a $100 million federal investment, both the factory and the partially completed dam and power station were uneconomic and useless.[82] This technical failure, however, enabled something much larger to result. In July 1921, Henry Ford proposed a scheme not just for this corner of northern Alabama, but for the entire river basin to which it belonged, linking together industry, hydroelectric power, transmission grids, river navigation, soil improvement through artificial fertilizer, and scientific agriculture. The proposal envisioned an expansion of the industrial coordination schemes that Ford had pioneered, from the scale of car factories and suburban lifestyles, to the transformation of the entire ecology of a geographic region, organized around the technicized space of the damming of a river system and the transforming of its energy into unlimited hydropower. The scale of federal support that Ford demanded for the project ensured the opposition of his business rivals, and the proposal was rejected. But with the economic collapse of the Great Depression the project was revived by the federal government. In 1933 an act of congress put Ford's scheme into effect as the country's largest public works project, the Tennessee Valley Authority.[83]

The TVA, the child of earlier technical and political failures, came to epitomize the new possibilities of development and planning, especially in arid regions such as the Middle East. Large dams offered a way to build not just irrigation and power systems, but nation-states themselves. In 1949 the United Nations sent an economic survey mission to the Middle East. Its head was Gordon Clapp, the chairman of the TVA board. The following year, two World Bank experts writing on development in the Middle East explained how since 1930, "the popular imagination has been captured by the idea of the development of entire river systems."[84] In the following years the old schemes of ʿAbbud and his rivals for a hydroelectric plant and fertilizer factory at Aswan were taken up by the new military government in Egypt. But they now formed part of a TVA-inspired scheme to build the second dam, on a mammoth scale, just above the existing dam at Aswan. Work began in 1964 and was completed in 1971. Ignoring the costs of salinization, waterlogging, declining soil fertility, the displacement of the people of Nubia, the loss of an archaeological heritage, increased disease, coastal erosion, the destruction of a large fishing industry, the loss of water due to evaporation and seepage, and other problems already evident from the first dam, and without even attempting studies of costs and benefits, the Aswan High Dam became the centerpiece of postwar nation making in Egypt.[85]

Marx published some famous lines about an insect—not the mosquito, but the bee. Although it builds itself an elaborate hive, he wrote, the bee is no architect, for the architect "raises his structure in imagination before he erects it in reality."[86] Since Marx wrote those words we have come to believe more and more that this Cartesian notion of the mind-as-architect's-office is what captures the difference between ourselves and nature. The work of imagination puts together plans, images, ideal structures—in fact entire systems of culture and meaning—before they are taken outside and erected in reality. We have made do for too long with this misleadingly simple view of the world that Marx himself placed in question. I have already suggested by describing the work of the engineers at Aswan why this is misleading, and have offered other examples elsewhere.[87] I could make the point again simply by recalling the work an architect actually does: the visits to the site and consultations with the client that precede any attempt at drawing; the long, eye-straining hours with the CAD program; the printing and distribution of drawings; the meetings around a table with the plans spread out to negotiate the rules of building codes and planning regulations; the day-to-day supervision of the building contractor; the arbitrating among electrical, plumbing, and ventilation contractors installing rival networks of cables, pipes, and ducts; the measurements that do not fit; the overlooked details; and the changes of mind as things are taken apart and redone. There is no disputing that all this involves a constant work of imagination, but none of it precedes or stands apart from doing things in reality. There is no other, more real world. Nowhere does one suddenly step from imagination to reality, from plan to real thing, any more than did the engineers at Aswan.

Yet if we return to the case of the anti-malaria campaign in Egypt, it might be said, surely the difference between the mosquito and the human expert is clear. *Anopheles gambiae* may have been clever to make its way across the African continent, but it was no match in the end for the powers of chemical science, human ingenuity, and planning. Perhaps not. Yet here, too, the story of expertise versus nature is too simple. After all, the eradication teams did not kill the mosquitoes barehanded. They needed a lot of nonhuman assistants. Since the end of World War I, the J. R. Geigy company in Switzerland, a manufacturer of dyestuffs for the textile industry (and member of the I. G. Farben chemicals cartel), had been trying to find a safe, effective, and long-lasting substance to use as a mothproofing agent for textiles.[88] In 1941, with Rommel advancing in North Africa and the gambiae mosquito making its way northwards from Sudan, a company chemist named Paul Müller discovered the toxicity of dichloro-diphenyl-trichloroethane. Mixed 5 percent in an inert powder, the chemical was found to kill clothes moths and many other insects yet seemed to have no effect on warm-blooded animals. Since it was a contact rather than an oral poison, it proved to be a potent killer even of bloodsucking insects, which do not ingest poisons, including human lice, the parasite responsible for transmitting typhus.[89] The disease that brought Fred Soper of the Rockefeller Foundation to Cairo the following year, typhus was a major threat to soldiers at war and civilians in war-torn cities. The British Ministry of Supply named the new Swiss chemical after its initials and began manufacturing DDT in April 1943, giving its production the highest wartime priority alongside radar and penicillin.[90] The following year, Soper persuaded the Egyptian government to replace pyrethrum—the powder of chrysanthemum flowers—with DDT in the gambiae eradication campaign in southern Egypt. Houses were treated with the chemical, and the ceilings of trains were spray-painted with a mixture of DDT and kerosene, an innovation later copied around the world.[91]

Neither the companies manufacturing DDT nor the eradication teams using it in Egypt had any idea how the chemical worked. They just admired its potency. In fact, no one knew how it worked, not even the man who introduced its powers. When Müller received the Nobel Prize in Medicine or Physiology in 1948, he won the award for having demonstrated that DDT killed arthropods, not for knowing why.[92] Bringing its powers into action had required several years of methodical work, testing hundreds of synthesized organic substances on flies trapped inside a Peet-Grady chamber. This was an enclosure or room that simulated an insect's environment, such as a desert, a rainforest, or the kitchen of an apartment. The insects and the chemical agent were introduced into the chamber while an observer watched through one-way glass.[93] The discovery that DDT killed the flies was made in the Peet-Grady chamber, not in Müller's head. Techno-science involved not so much planning in advance or raising structures in the imagination; it involved erecting a room inside the research lab, which rearranged so-called nature, much like the dam at Aswan, concentrating its elements in one place, transporting the rainforest onto the premises of a chemical company, and providing a place where it could be continuously observed. The chain of events that took DDT from the Peet-Grady chamber to the field was a process of borrowing, translations, and things invented for one purpose taken over by other forces, all modulated by the politics of U.S.-British rivalry over Egypt, the needs of war, the accidents and ambitions of a Rockefeller career, and the impact of sugarcane production and irrigation works.[94]

What is more important, as we now know, while the malaria campaign used the new power of DDT, the pesticide had purposes of its own, well beyond the intentions of the research chemists and the eradication teams. In 1944 the U.S. Army Public Health Service and the American Entomological Society had already begun to issue warnings: that DDT would kill beneficial as well as harmful insects, was poisonous to fish, and was potentially harmful to all forms of plant and animal life. The warnings were ignored. After the "success" of the new chemical in Egypt, and a more famous success in eliminating head lice under Soper's supervision in Naples (in fact both campaigns mostly employed pyrethrum, with DDT used only at the end, after the epidemics had largely passed), Soper agreed with the advocates of DDT that it was "an almost perfect insecticide."[95]

DDT was not in fact a more lethal insecticide than pyrethrum or other chemicals it replaced. Like pyrethrum, it did not attack the malaria parasite directly. The plasmodium spores were too small and too numerous to reach with poison. The new chemical simply interrupted their breeding cycle by intervening at its most vulnerable point, when millions of spores were concentrated in the bodies of a relatively small number of much larger hosts, the female mosquitoes. DDT's greater effectiveness against mosquitoes was due to its very stable chemical structure. It was practically insoluble in water and resisted degradation by sunlight or soils. So it remained in the environment not for days or weeks, but years and decades. (When it does break down, it was later discovered, the resulting products include DDD, which is also toxic and resists decomposition for up to 190 years.) When sprayed in a house DDT lingered, so it "vaccinated" the place long enough to interrupt the mosquito's breeding cycle, and without the impractical need to seal up the house, as the pyrethrum spray required.

In Egypt, however, DDT (and pyrethrum) also gained their effectiveness from special features of the gambiae mosquito—or rather, of the social relations between the mosquito and its human hosts. As in Brazil, the insect was a new immigrant, so it was not well established in the local community and was comparatively easy to isolate. At the same time, the *Anopheles gambiae* is the most social form of malarial mosquito. It is especially dependent on its human hosts, preferring human blood to animal.[96] Thus it is generally found only around human habitation. This makes it unable to travel long distances, hence the importance of boats, trains, and floating weeds for its travel. But the dependence on humans also made it easier to eradicate, because the spraying of houses and vehicles only was relatively effective. For all these reasons, a methodical and relentless vector eradication campaign, taking on the mosquito pool by pool, house by house, and village by village, was successful.

As a result, the malaria experts drew the wrong lessons from Egypt. Success there suggested, mistakenly, the possibility of a worldwide species eradication using hunt-and-destroy campaigns and the killing power of the pesticide. In 1946 Soper and the Rockefeller Foundation embarked on a malaria campaign in Sardinia, designed to show that DDT could be used not just to control malaria, but to eliminate it. They sprayed the chemical from airplanes and helicopters and employed a total of twenty-four thousand men in ground teams, whose equipment included flame-throwers. Yet despite extending the campaign for five years, they failed to eradicate the mosquito. It was too well entrenched. Hundreds of thousands of pounds of DDT were spread over the Sardinian landscape, but tests showed that the mosquito larvae survived concentrations of the chemical twenty-five times greater than those used in the eradication campaign—for reasons no one could quite explain.[97]

Undeterred by this failure, four years later, in 1955, the World Health Organization (WHO), which had taken over responsibility for the worldwide administration of antimalarial campaigns from the Rockefeller Foundation, adopted a plan for the global eradication of malaria using DDT. Countries where the anopheles mosquito was relatively thinly established reduced or even eliminated the vector, especially in Europe, but in many more places eradication was not effective. Although described as "global," the eradication program ignored Africa, the world's major malarial region, aside from one or two pilot schemes. Elsewhere the parasite gradually developed resistance to quinine and other drugs and returned in large numbers.[98] Meanwhile, DDT produced other, more destructive effects. Only in 1969 did the WHO agree to move toward programs of vector management rather than eradication and begin to warn of the risks of DDT, leading to its banning (but not elimination), at least in agriculture. At the end of the

1990s the United Nations Environment Program sponsored negotiations to end the use of DDT altogether by 2007.[99]

By this time there was a better understanding of DDT's long-term effects. While almost insoluble in water, it dissolves easily in fat, so it accumulates in the fatty tissue of animals, an accumulation that is magnified through the food web. Although no one still quite knew how it worked, it was believed that it acts like a hormone, mimicking or disrupting chemical messengers in the body, affecting the development and functioning of the organism. It weakens the immune system, decreases lactation, causes male animals to develop female reproductive organs, and leads to other disruptions of sexual development.[100]

Since these powers were not limited to killing the lice, clothes moths, and mosquitoes for which DDT had been developed, its use quickly spread to other areas, especially agriculture. Far more of the pesticide was used worldwide in farming, to support the increased use of synthetic fertilizers, than in public health programs. One of the most popular worldwide applications was in the protection of cotton crops.

In Egypt, by 1950 the use of chemical fertilizers had returned to their prewar levels, the highest in the world. The fertilizers were producing "lush vegetation and flowering," it was reported, which encouraged insect pests, in particular the cotton leaf worm.[101] Two local companies began importing DDT to combat the cotton pest. With U.S. help the government acquired the six helicopters from United Helicopters to use for spraying the chemical from the air.[102]

Meanwhile, the country's two dominant business monopolies, the ʿAbbud and Misr groups, whose increasing power I mentioned earlier, consolidated their control by forming a political and economic alliance, which in 1950 helped bring the Wafd party back to power. The two groups prepared the way for this collaboration a year earlier by agreeing to coinvest in a new joint venture with the U.S. chemical company Monsanto—to build a local plant to manufacture DDT.[103] A major ingredient of DDT is ethyl alcohol, which was to be made by Egypt's only commercial distillery, the Société Egyptienne de Distillerie, owned by the sugar baron Ahmad ʿAbbud, using molasses supplied by his sugar monopoly.[104] ʿAbbud had got rich helping to build the Aswan Dam, which enabled the spread of sugar plantations but also required the introduction of fertilizer. The use of fertilizers brought insect pests, which needed treatment with DDT. Now the DDT would be made from ʿAbbud's sugar.

By the time of Nasser's military coup two years later, the government had decided to build the pesticide factory itself using the assistance of international healthcare agencies. One week after the coup, on August 2, 1952, in perhaps its first international act, the new government signed an agreement with WHO and UNICEF to build a factory at Kafr Zayat that would produce two hundred tons a year of finished DDT.[105] With healthcare agencies financing this mass production of the new pesticide, the U.S. Embassy was able to report with optimism that while "Egypt consumes at present less pesticides than would be the case if the average farmer were better educated," as his education progressed, "increased demand for such products should develop."[106] Demand did indeed develop. Standard doses of pesticide were soon found to be ineffective. The DDT had been killing off natural predators, so the pests that survived the chemical were able to reproduce explosively. The quantities used had to be doubled and then trebled. Without the government having to spend a penny on further education for farmers, but through the working of the chemical's own poorly understood powers, the use of pesticides progressed.

Today the *Anopheles gambiae* has disappeared from the story of Egyptian politics. Even the one good account we have of the malaria epidemic, by Nancy Gallagher, does not give the mosquito or its parasite much credit. As in every other explanation of this kind of politics, history has a limited number of actors, and the insect arriving from the south is not one of them. There are the British, manipulating Egyptian politics while resisting the incipient postwar usurpation of their role by Americans; there are the national elites—the monarchy and the small landed aristocracy—losing their power to a more dynamic class of commercial landowners, entrepreneurs, and military officers; and, now and again, there are the subaltern communities—the rural population, the urban working classes, women—making up the rest of the social order. The mosquito, on the other hand, is said to belong to nature. It cannot speak.

As part of nature, the gambiae mosquito became a problem of public health. With the mosquito's help, questions of hygiene, disease, housing, and ignorance emerged as the principal way of addressing the situation of rural Egypt. National politics was organized around programs of health improvement, rural reconstruction, technical development, and above all the engineering of the river Nile and the transformation of its power into electricity, fertilizers, irrigation, and the growth of agriculture and manufacturing. The resources and limits of nature and, by extension, of rural society were to be transformed by the dynamic activity of technical development, which required the application of scientific and social scientific expertise.

These projects began to arrange the world as one in which science was opposed to nature and technical expertise claimed to overcome the obstacles to social improvement. The malaria eradication campaign presented an opportunity to bring the intelligence of medical science, with its resources of chemistry, hygiene, past experience, and worldwide information, to work upon the insect vectors, protozoan parasites, fevers, poverty, and malnutrition that made up the defects of the material world and had to be defeated. In irrigation projects, the power of technical assistance and engineering was to overcome the limits of natural resources. At al-Alamein, the first great battle of technicized warfare, two opposing generals, it is said, combined the mobile powers of mechanized weapons and the new, large-scale deployment of mines to determine the course of history. Such programs and campaigns manufactured a world that appeared as natural resources versus technology, bodies versus hygiene, men versus machines, the river versus human ingenuity.

Yet the projects that produced this binary world could emerge only by engaging a series of other logics, forces, and chemistries: the hydraulic energy of the Nile River, the chemical properties of ammonia, the feeding patterns of the anopheles mosquito, the career making of a Rockefeller epidemiologist, the supply lines sustaining an army at war, the reproductive cycle of the plasmodium parasite, the anticolonial struggle of Egyptian nationalism, the world's increasing chemical addiction to sugar, and DDT's preference for fatty tissue, to name a few. Although technical development portrayed the world as passive, as nature to be overcome or material resources to be developed, the relations of science and development came into being only by working with such forces.

The same was true of what was called the development of capitalism. The circuits that 'Abbud tried to control and transform into sources of profit involved family networks, the properties of sugar and nitrates, the labor of those harvesting cane, imperial connections, and the shortages brought by war. The production of profit, or surplus value, came about only by working within and transforming such other forces and reserves. Thus a term like "capitalist development" covers a series of agencies, logics, chain reactions, and contingent interactions, among which the specific circuits and relations of capital formed only a part.

Introducing these other forces is not a question of describing the resistance of nature or material conditions. It is not a matter of acknowledging nonhuman forces that worked against human expertise or created obstacles to technical progress and capitalist development. The reports describing the problems of the Aswan Dam, the setbacks in malaria eradication, or the failure of technical assistance programs often used such formulations to express the difficult relationship between human intention and the world of experience. Expertise, however, did not confront such resistance externally, after it was already complete, nor did the power of capital. Plans, intentions, scientific expertise, techno-power, and surplus value were created in combination with these other forces or elements. The technology of dam construction was formed at the construction site in Aswan, and in earlier and subsequent projects. The methods of mosquito eradication developed in Brazil and Egypt were the outcome of working with *Anopheles gambiae* in particular locations, among a new population of human hosts. What is called nature or the material world moves, like the plasmodium, in and out of human forms, or occurs as arrangements, like the river Nile, that are social as well as natural, technical as well as material. The world out of which techno-politics emerged was an unresolved and prior combination of reason, force, imagination, and resources. Ideas and technology did not precede this mixture as pure forms of thought brought to bear upon the messy world of reality. They emerged from the mixture and were manufactured in the processes themselves.

Resolving these processes into reason versus force, intelligence versus nature, or the imagined versus the real misapprehends the complexity. But this misapprehension was necessary, for it was exactly how the production of techno-power proceeded. Overlooking the mixed way things happen, indeed producing the effect of neatly separate realms of reason and the real world, ideas and their objects, the human and the nonhuman, was how power was coming to work in Egypt, and in the twentieth century in general.

Social science, by relating particular events to a universal reason and by treating human agency as given, mimics this form of power. The normal methods of analysis end up reproducing this kind of power, taken in by the effects it generates. In fact, social science helps to format a world resolved into this binary order, and thus to constitute and solidify the experience of agency and expertise. In much of social science this is quite deliberate. It tries to acquire the kind of intellectual mastery of social processes that dams seem to offer over rivers, artificial nitrates over sugarcane production, or DDT over arthropods. It is less important whether one understands how things work, more important how effective are the immediate results. But more careful forms of historical or cultural analysis can do the same thing in less obvious ways, by leaving technics unexamined, or talking about the "social construction" of things that are clearly more than social.

To put in question these distinctions, and the assumptions about agency and history that they make possible, does not mean introducing a limitless number of actors and networks, all of which are somehow of equal significance and power. Rather, it means making this issue of power and agency a question, instead of an answer known in advance. It means acknowledging something of the unresolvable tension, the inseparable mixture, the impossible multiplicity, out of which intention and expertise must emerge. It requires acknowledging that human agency, like capital, is a technical body, is something made. Instead of invoking the force and logic of reason, self-interest, science, or capital and attributing what happens in the world to the working of these enchanted powers and processes, we can open up the question, as I have attempted here, of what kinds of hybrid agencies, connections, interactions, and forms of violence are able to portray their actions as history, as human expertise overcoming nature, as the progress of reason and modernity, or as the expansion and development of capitalism.

2 Principles True in Every Country

In 1863 Isma'il Pasha, the Ottoman ruler in Cairo, gave one hundred acres of land to his coffee maker. He gave another hundred to his head barber. He had succeeded his uncle Sa'id as viceroy in January of that year, and within eighteen months he allocated to those around him more than sixty thousand acres of the Nile valley. The recipients were military officers and high officials, family members and household staff. In the same short period he also added more than fifty thousand acres to his own estates.[1]

To Europeans, actions like these expressed everything that was wrong with the East. They exemplified the shortcoming for which colonial officials liked to criticize "native" systems of rule: their arbitrariness. Compared to the universal rules of a modern system of law, native government proceeded by personal decision and the caprice of power. "With respect to general propositions," wrote an English administrator in India, "I have yet seen no reason to admit that principles, unquestionably true in every other country, should not be applicable in Bengal. It is in the nature of justice and good government to deduce its arrangements from undisputed points of original right. It is in the nature of arbitrary power to make exceptions."[2] In non-European government the exceptional was the rule; power gained its strength from its arbitrariness. Modern government, like modern science, the European believed, was based upon principles true in every country. Its strength lay in its universalism.

This language belongs to an earlier century. But the views it expresses remain current. At the end of the twentieth century, the law of property reappeared at the center of Egypt's political and economic life. As chapters 8 and 9 of this book describe, a program of political and economic restructuring reasserted the primacy of property rights as the institutional framework for the introduction of market relations. The universal rules of property were to replace the system of arbitrary political controls, special claims, and institutional exceptions that had restricted their operation. The political economy of Egypt was to be reestablished on the basis of principles true in every country.

THE RULE OF PROPERTY

How is the general character of law produced? How do the rules of property achieve the quality of being universal? There is no straightforward answer to this question. Modern jurisprudence sees law as self-establishing, existing as a system of rules whose validity is established only by other rules.[3] Modern economics sees the existence of property as self-evident, representing an axiomatic set of rules without which the act of exchange could not occur. In the positive accounts of law and economics, the genealogy of what is taken to be a universal system of rules is not open to investigation. This is inevitable, for if the axiomatic had its origins in particular histories and political acts, its claim to universalism would be lost.

In Cairo, the answer to this question about the origin of modern property rights was first formulated in 1882. The British occupied the country that year, following a political crisis caused by Isma'il's debts to European banks. They set up the Commission of Enquiry into the Land Tax, whose purpose was to examine property rights and taxes and propose measures for their reform.[4] These would remove irregularities from the tax system and increase the revenue, to pay off what was owed to Rothschilds and the other banks. The reforms required a cadastral survey to establish the owner and tax rate of each plot of land. This was not completed until after the turn of the century, so the revenue reforms had to wait. But right away the Ministry of Finance published a study of property relations, *La Propriété foncière en Egypte.* Written by the secretary to the Commission of Enquiry, the study explained property claims in the country in terms of the history of a concept: the evolution of the right of private ownership.[5]

The author drew on the work of contemporary French writers to argue that under the laws of the Ottoman Empire, which had ruled Cairo since 1517, all land was considered the property of the state.[6] French scholars had popularized this interpretation of Ottoman practice to justify the seizure of village land by French settlers in Algeria. Private property, they believed, was the foundation of civilization. Its absence in the territories of the Ottoman Empire demonstrated the uncivilized state of Muslim peoples and the progress that colonization would bring them.[7] This progress would come in the form of ideas. European legal principles, it was said, were based upon universal principles that can be applied uniformly to particular cases, by the process of abstracting from a particular circumstance to the general principle that governs it. Drawing on elements of this colonial view to portray a similar transition toward modernity in the Nile valley, the Ministry of Finance study became the text on which subsequent histories of the Egyptian law of property depended.[8]

Before the development of twentieth-century economics and jurisprudence, which offered ways to be silent about the genealogy of what claims to be universal, this kind of account was the only way, outside theology, to explain the general character of law. Law could claim to be universal, and thus nonarbitrary, only be appearing as the expression of civilization. The growth of civilization represented the spread of the principle of human reason, which overcame the limits of habit, prejudice, caprice, and ignorance. The faculty of reason gave men the power to step outside these local constraints, it was thought, and thus acquire a universal vision and understanding. European colonialism, understood as the contemporary expression of the spread of civilization and reason, established the abstract forms of law, in relation to which particular histories of the right of property could be written. Such histories occurred as the local expression or realization of this universal abstraction.

A certain contradiction is apparent. The virtues of a universal right of private property were articulated to support seizing land by force in North Africa. The land could be taken because those who farmed it had not heard of this universal right. The principle of property was presented as the opposite of arbitrary power or coercion, represented by the state ownership of land; but it justified a violent exercise of power, and in fact was established by this violence. The British were now articulating the same principle in Cairo, a city they had seized by force after first bombarding and destroying a large section of the country's second city, Alexandria. Private property was seen as the reversal of the old order of state ownership. Law based on private rights represented a rupture with the previous world of arbitrary and despotic power. Yet many of the property claims that were to be consolidated as private rights, especially the largest ones, came into being through the "arbitrary" grants that Isma'il had made, and those of his uncles and grandfather before him. The author of the Ministry of Finance study, Yacoub Artin, was himself a product of this history of large estates. His grandfather, Sukias Tcherakian, an Armenian from Istanbul, moved to Cairo in 1812 soon after Isma'il's grandfather, Mehmed Ali, came to power to manage the estates of one of Mehmed Ali's sons.[9] Rather than there being a rupture, the old had helped form the new.

The history of private property is rather silent on the conditions that produced it and the precedents incorporated into it. In fact it is silent on a lot more, as we will see. Presented as a history of legislation, of an abstraction, it has little to say about how private property was actually constituted in a particular place. The abstract arrives from elsewhere, and its particular histories are incidental rather than part of its nature. If its emergence had something to do with individual appropriations, exceptional decisions, or acts of violence, these belonged to the past, from which the present was now ruptured. The break in history caused by the colonial occupation, by the arrival of modernity and civilization, helped to establish the universal character of law. The ad hoc, violent, and exceptional character of the law of property was entirely hidden by the presentation of law as something abstract, as a universal rule, with its origins elsewhere, applied to particular circumstances.[10]

Compared to Artin's study of 1882, we have a better understanding today of landholding in the Ottoman Empire before the colonial occupations. We know that the view that all property was "owned" by the state is too simple and that for several centuries land in the Nile Delta had been treated as something that individuals could buy and sell.[11] We also know that landholding did not refer to land as an object, to which single individuals claimed an absolute right. It referred to a system of multiple claims, and not to the land itself but its revenue. The claimants included the Ottoman ruler, the ruler's local representative, the legal-religious authorities, the cultivators themselves, and other customary claimants within the countryside, such as the indigent. The doctrine of state ownership of land did not correspond to the modern notion of property but registered the ruler's political claim to a share of the revenue, while also acknowledging both the revenue claims of local political forces and the subsistence claims of the cultivator and other members of the village.[12] The network of claims, moreover, involved not just the land but a variety of processes and relations: grain as distinct from other crops, trees and their fruits, grazing rights, the supply of water, the maintenance of irrigation works, and so on. The claims were related to a wider discourse of justice and reciprocity reproduced in social practice. They were not fixed in an abstract code of law, but were guided by legal precedent and by prescriptions developed in response to actual circumstances and events.

This understanding opens up further questions. How was it possible to reduce the productive processes of the countryside to the single issue of who controlled the land? How was the question of its control moved away from the competing claims and obligations of those who lived on the land

and those who ruled them, and turned into a "right" that could be exercised absolutely, even by a person who had no relation to the place? How were these issues abstracted from forms of justice and reciprocity recognized (sometimes only in their violation) at the level of agricultural life, and located elsewhere—in the city, in its courts and police forces, and at some still more distant and abstract level, in propositions "true in every country"? How, in short, did modern law acquire its power and authority?

Let us return for a moment to Isma'il's method of establishing claims to the land. In September 1863, to take a representative example, he issued the following instructions to his secretary of the treasury:

> We have decided that three hundred acres are to be granted as an estate to His Lordship Nuri Bey, Governor of Sharqiyya. We have given an order to His Excellency the Inspector of the Lower Nile to have the said lands surveyed, their boundaries marked, and the list of the boundaries sent to the treasury. As soon as the list of boundaries reaches you, you are to record them and issue from the tax registry the required title deed in the name of the aforementioned and send it to him. This is the reason we have written this to you.[13]

Power seems to operate through a chain of personal orders and interconnected prerogatives rather than a generalized regime of government. It is not exactly arbitrary. The document refers to a legal process of recording, boundary marking, and bookkeeping. But the written record that results does not invoke any universal rule. In fact, it insists on its own specificity: "This is the reason we have written this to you." Compared to the universal rules of a modern system of law, the document, and the actions and claims it performs, appears not so much ad hoc, but as a form of power whose specificity is not disguised. The law announces its specificity, tracing its own steps. The act of granting land, the inspector's survey of the boundaries, the placing of boundary stones, the recording of measurements and sending them to Cairo, listing them in the taxation register, and issuing the title deed: all these acts are prescribed in the decree. The performance of the law will gain its authority from following this particular sequence of acts.

The order of private property that replaced this was just as particularistic. It, too, was based on individual acts, orders, seizures, descriptions, and inscriptions. But these processes were reorganized so that some seemed particular and others general: some appeared fixed, singular, anchored to a specific place and moment, like objects, while others appeared mobile, general, present everywhere at once, universal, unquestionably true in every place, and therefore abstract. One set of actions, people, and sites was fixed in position as "land" and "peasants," made into objects to supervise and control. At the same time a series of removals, rearrangements, delaying maneuvers, simplifications, and silences established other sites and other actions as what seems the opposite of this: nonlocal, outside actuality, and therefore universal. This was to create the effect of a fundamental difference: land versus law, the particular versus the general, the physical versus the abstract, thing versus idea, force versus order. To understand how this difference was made we have to reopen the connections between what was separated, follow the links from one action to another, and see how one set of elements in this relationship was subordinated, removed, reserved, or silenced. This will bring to light what is buried when we write theories of "property," "law," and "the state," when we begin with metaphysical abstractions rather than asking what methods of politics and expertise divide the world into metaphysics on the one hand and mere physics on the other.

PUTTING VILLAGERS IN THEIR PLACE

Cotton and sugarcane, the modern world's two main industrial crops, did not grow in the temperate climates of Europe. They needed the warmth of semitropical zones, where northern Europeans found it difficult to work or settle. Over several hundred years the English and French had developed what many considered a sophisticated institution to solve this difficulty—the slave plantation. Developed in the Caribbean, it had been expanded by the Americans across the southern United States. The government in early nineteenth-century Cairo was keen to import modern European and American ways of doing things. In fact it sent its European-officered army to invade the Sudan in July 1820 to establish control over the sultanates that ruled the Upper Nile and import slaves to the north. However, the efforts at mass enslavement failed. A system of industrial agriculture based on the importation and private ownership of humans could not be introduced into the Nile valley. Instead, the government tried a number of different methods to create an industrial discipline among the existing agrarian communities. The result was a further series of failures.

Before the nineteenth century methods of government in the parts of the Nile valley controlled from Cairo were based on dividing the revenue of the land. Farmers paid a part of their main crop—a food grain—to the authorities in exchange, they were told, for the security and justice that authority guaranteed. This method would not work with the modern industrial and export crops in demand in Europe, such as cotton and sugar, or opium. Farmers had no interest in growing a crop they could not eat, or process to serve local needs. The authorities, on the other hand, needed a way to take the whole crop. For the first time they needed a method of making farmers grow something they did not want and hand it over entirely. Or perhaps they had often thought of doing this but only now believed, thanks to the power of the new, disciplined army, that they had the means to achieve it. As John Bowring, friend of Jeremy Bentham and advisor to Mehmed Ali, later reported to the British parliament, "nothing but despotic authority would have forced the cultivation of many of those important articles such as cotton, opium, sugar, indigo, etc., of which Egypt furnishes so large a supply."[14] Thus a "monopoly" system was introduced, backed by military discipline, that compelled villagers to grow certain crops and deliver them to government warehouses.

The response of the rural population was a straightforward one. Large numbers refused to farm and in many cases abandoned their villages. Tens of thousands deserted their homes and moved to agricultural regions outside government control, or escaped to Cairo and other towns, or moved further abroad to Palestine and Syria. The Ottoman governor, Mehmed Ali, responded by instituting a more elaborate system of overseers and penalties and ordering the confinement of peasants to their villages, with permits required for those who wished to travel outside their locality.[15] These measures failed to stop the exodus. In 1842 the authorities began to compile a register with the names of all those reported to have deserted their villages.[16] At the same time they introduced a new system, allocating officials of the ruling household, or in some cases local notables or merchants, the responsibility for the tax arrears of particular villages.[17] Yet desertion remained a serious problem, continuing under Mehmed Ali's successors.[18]

The next response to the problem of keeping the rural population in place was a series of measures between 1847 and 1862 to restrict or eliminate the customary claims of those who abandoned their land. These are the regulations later assembled by the Ministry of Finance into the account of the emergence of private landownership discussed above. Cuno shows the regulations were concerned less with individual rights and more with stabilizing the existing land regime after the disruptive agrarian programs of the first half of the century.[19] While Cuno's arguments are persuasive, we can state more specifically that the new laws were a response to the continuing crisis of desertion, legalizing the expropriation of the land of those who fled and seeking to deter others from fleeing. Four of the six provisions of the first land law in 1847 were concerned with limiting the claims of those who had deserted their land. Deserters who returned to claim land that had been allocated as a tax responsibility to someone else were entitled to recover only half the land and required to reimburse the taxes paid. The 1855 land law was an amendment to this regulation, setting further limits on the ability to recover land. After fifteen years returnees lost all rights to their land and would receive instead only a subsistence plot of between half an acre and three acres. An 1858 law reduced the period after which deserters lost all rights to their land to five years.[20] Despite these measures the problem of desertion continued. A further decree of December 7, 1862, not mentioned in the histories of landownership but confirming the preoccupation with desertion, was still more severe: any native who deserted his village would have his land seized and sold off after two months, unless he deserted during the cultivation season, in which case it would be seized and sold immediately.[21] Far from representing a gradual accumulation of rights by the individual, the land laws of the mid-nineteenth century represented a series of attempts to compel individuals to remain at work on the land and to confirm the seizure of land from those who fled.

These measures were related to another process, also usually omitted from histories of private property: the incorporation or erasure of political communities that occupied the margin, neither outside nor completely within the jurisdiction of Cairo. Before the middle of the nineteenth century, most people inhabiting parts of the Nile valley beyond the immediate reach of Cairo lived in autonomous political communities referred to as tribes or emirates, and were relatively independent of the Cairene authorities.[22] Historical sources refer to these populations as *ʿarab,* a term usually translated as "Bedouin" and used in contrast to the fellahs, the settled villagers. Although the word *ʿarab* historically refers to the pastoral nomads of the desert, in the Nile valley large numbers of them farmed the land and lived in villages. What distinguished them from other villagers was not necessarily nomadism but their relative autonomy from Cairo and often their domination over the fellahs themselves. They lived on the geographical margin, partly within and partly beyond government control. Their lands were seldom registered or taxed, but they often payed some collective form of tribute. They were involved in agriculture but did not belong to the "peasantry." They formed a complex economic and political borderland.

The new control over the countryside involved eliminating these border forms of political life. Modern accounts of this process, assuming that the *ʿarab* were nomads, describe it as "the settlement of the Bedouin."[23] In fact it involved, once again, the attempt to construct a new kind of control over their lands and livelihoods, and much of their so-called nomadism was simply the dislocation caused by this attempt. The government of Mehmed Ali initially recognized the Arab claims to land used for pasture or seasonal cultivation.[24] But from the 1840s, members of the ruling household began to take such land to create large estates for themselves.[25] Violent struggles broke out, and by the end of the 1850s the "Arab troubles," as official sources refer to the conflict, had become so severe that large numbers had abandoned agriculture and moved with their herds to areas beyond the reach of government troops, or fled abroad.[26]

When Isma'il came to power in January 1863 and began granting estates to his officials and relatives, he was responding to a series of failures and increasingly violent reactions in the search for new methods of controlling the way crops were grown. He had spent the preceding years organizing new estates of his own in the south, developing the production of cotton and sugarcane and running a sugar refinery that was described as the country's most impressive industrial project.[27] He brought the expertise acquired in the managing of sugar mills and plantations back to Cairo, and began reorganizing the whole country as a system of agricultural estates.

In his first week in office he abrogated the 1862 law penalizing rural desertion. He ordered the governors of every province to draw up lists of those who had lost their land, together with the value of the land and the names of those who had taken it over. From now on natives who abandoned their land were to be treated according to established principles, which presumably meant restoring the five-year limit of the 1858 law.[28] He also encouraged the Arabs to return to their lands. To those without property he offered parcels of abandoned land, giving two acres to every household of five persons.[29] In exchange, the Arabs were required to submit to the authority of a military officer appointed in each district to oversee their affairs. They were to give the officer a list of the heads of the sections of each tribe, with the number of persons and a description of each individual enumerated "tribe by tribe, section by section, name by name." The officer would then issue a permit with the name, physical description, and tribe of every individual under his authority. A person who wished to move from one tribal section to another, or one part of the country to another, required this permit to travel.[30]

A MAD FANATIC AND A COMMUNIST

We know very little about the impact of these events on people's lives. Most of what we can learn about those lives is from the traces they left elsewhere. We know about the flight of villagers from the land largely through such sources as the further acts of dispossession with which government tried to punish them. On occasion, however, the violence of property making, which was also the violence of nation making, provoked a more concerted reaction. These events left larger traces, although still only partial.[31]

The uprising against British rule in India in 1857–58 provided a warning of what could develop, and the British were soon to bring the lessons they learned in India to Egypt. But the popular message from India arrived sooner, reaching the Upper Nile provinces of Jirja and Asyut, where Isma'il was building his sugar plantations. To convert flood basin agriculture to the year-round cultivation of cane, workers were digging the Ibrahimiyya Canal, the largest construction project ever undertaken in the Nile valley and reported to be the largest canal in the world, extending more than four hundred kilometers from Asyut to Cairo.[32] Both the cane plantations and the canal required large amounts of forced labor.[33]

A sign of the impending troubles was a murder that took place in June 1863 in Tanagha, a village about thirty kilometers south of the town of Asyut, in an area where Isma'il had acquired several sugar estates. The victim was someone of significance, at least to Isma'il, for the viceroy personally ordered that all firearms be confiscated from the inhabitants of the village and that the same be done in any village in Asyut province where a killing occurred. If any villager was subsequently found with a weapon, the village head was to be dismissed and his sons and relatives forbidden to assume the headship.[34]

In the winter of 1864–65 the crisis came. In October Isma'il took over a large estate, which included a sugar mill and steam pumps, at the village of Naj' Hamadi, claiming the land had belonged to his elder brother Ahmad (who had been drowned in a railway accident six years earlier).[35] The difficulties created by the spread of plantations were aggravated by serious flooding in the autumn, which devastated the nearby town of Jirja and destroyed homes and crops throughout the region.[36] By February there were severe food shortages and most of the cattle were dead. Yet the government continued to impose burdens. Orders reached local officials to make a levy of camels to support the continued occupation of the Sudan; to begin work immediately on improved flood defenses at Jirja, requiring 1,085,000 hundredweight of stone; and to provide another fifty thousand men as forced laborers on the Ibrahimiyya Canal.[37] "The system of wholesale extortion and spoilation has reached a point beyond which it would be difficult to go," wrote a European resident. "Egypt is one vast 'plantation' where the master works his slaves without even feeding them."[38]

A month later an armed uprising broke out, beginning in the village of Qaw, near Jirja, and four neighboring villages, but reaching as far as Asyut forty kilometers to the north.[39] The revolt was led by Ahmad al-Shaqi, known as al-Tayyib, the Good, native of the village of Salamiyya, near Luxor, and said to be the disciple of an anticolonial religious militant from India who had escaped abroad after the defeat of the 1857–58 revolt and spent several years near Asyut. The seriousness of the uprising is indicated by the seniority of those sent to suppress it. Mehmed Fadil Pasha, inspector of the Upper Nile region, came by steamer from Cairo with an armed force, and Isma'il himself followed. The secretary of war, Isma'il Pasha Abu Jabal, commanded the troops. They burned Qaw and its four neighboring villages to the ground and sent the surviving male inhabitants as prisoners to the Sudan. The women and children were distributed among other villages. Ahmad al-Tayyib was rumored to have escaped, but his relatives from Salamiyya, men, women, and children, were taken in chains to Qina. Reports of the number of villagers who were killed ranged from several dozen to sixteen hundred. One eyewitness described how Fadil Pasha "had the men laid down by ten at a time and chopped with pioneer axes." Fadil was rewarded after his return to Cairo with promotion to the Council of Justice.[40]

British consular reports attributed the revolt to the labor that villagers were forced to supply on Isma'il's estates. The food shortage had caused prices to jump, and local wages had also risen. Measures introduced in January to control prices from Cairo by setting up a Prices Committee and provincial Commerce Committees had failed to halt the increases.[41] The fixed wage of two and a half piastres a day that Isma'il had introduced on his estates two years earlier represented only one-quarter of prevailing wages by 1865.[42] Local reports agreed that although religious appeals provided al-Tayyib's legitimation, his object was the new land regime. "He is a mad fanatic and a communist," a European resident in the area was told. "He wants to divide all property equally and to kill all the Ulema."[43] Isma'il blamed the events on the negligence of the governor of Jirja, whom he removed and put to trial. He also appointed a separate administrator for his estates in the south, divorcing their management from those in the Delta.[44] The effort to turn much of the region into his plantation was proving difficult.

Despite the violence with which the government demonstrated its resolve, the problems of villagers abandoning the farming of overtaxed land and rejecting the authority of Cairo continued. In 1865 the viceroy issued a decree forbidding officials to grant anyone permission to abandon their land.[45] Later that year he ordered the sale of rights to all abandoned land, and of any cultivated land that was not registered in the tax registers, while the period after which those who deserted their villages lost their rights was reduced again, from five years to three.[46] Another order of the same year noted that despite the efforts at conciliation the Bedouin were still refusing to submit to the viceroy's authority. Instructions were given that any Arab found in a town, at a market, on a road, or in any other place carrying a firearm was to be arrested.[47] Several orders were also issued in the same period to inspect and reorganize the country's numerous prisons.[48] In June 1865, the inspector of the Lower Nile region reported a large increase in theft, including attacks at night on villages and isolated estates, in which property and animals were looted. Ismaʿil declared this to be the work of evil and malicious individuals, many of them former convicts, who had to be eliminated—by further incarceration. He ordered the head of every village and Arab tribe to round up within thirty days all "depraved and malicious persons and suspicious characters" in their localities. Those arrested were to be sent to the army or navy if fit, otherwise to labor in the stone quarries at the Nile Cataracts. If any such persons were found in their districts after thirty days, the headmen themselves would be punished.[49]

Desertion of the land and armed rebellion were not the only problems the new agriculture faced. The extensive irrigation works required by industrial crops brought two additional forces into play: disease and debt. In May 1865, as the rebellion in the south subsided, cholera appeared. The cholera vibrio followed the same route an anticolonial militant from India would have taken, coming from South Asia to Mecca with the annual pilgrimage, then continuing on by boat across the Red Sea and overland to the Nile valley.[50] The main routes reached the Nile in the south, where the disease struck hardest. It claimed some sixty thousand lives, with the highest death rates in the provinces of Jirja and Asyut.[51] As with the gambiae malaria epidemic of the 1940s, the irrigation work in these two provinces exacerbated the disease. Villages that drew their water from the Nile escaped infection, while adjacent villages that used the standing water in the new canals suffered badly. In the town of Qina, near Jirja, 250 people were reported dead in a single day. "Shaikh Yussuf laid the mortality at Kenah to the canal water," wrote a European resident, "which the poor people drink there."[52] When the disease reached Alexandria in the north, it panicked the European business class and sent them fleeing. Thirty thousand left by ship within a fortnight, bringing all major commerce in the country to a standstill.[53] Their flight carried the cholera to all the main ports of the eastern and northern Mediterranean, helping turn the disease into a pandemic that circled the globe for a decade.

Meanwhile, the cotton boom the country had enjoyed during the blockade of the Confederate ports in the American civil war had come to an end.

Isma'il had taken large loans from European financiers during the boom years. One of the largest of these was in response to an earlier epidemic, the cattle murrain of the summer and autumn of 1863, which had killed anywhere from 250,000 to 900,000 head of cattle, wiping out most of the country's draft animals used for ploughing and irrigation. Loans from European finance houses enabled Isma'il to import hundreds of thousands of animals from Europe and Asia, along with steam pumps and ploughs and emergency supplies of food.[54] But the food and the loans came too late to enable people to feed themselves that winter, and tens of thousands lost their lives.[55] The slump of 1865 was followed by the collapse of European speculative finance in the stock market crash of May 1866. Isma'il managed to obtain further loans to keep up interest payments to the banks. These loans only compounded the debt, however, postponing the crisis but making the eventual collapse more severe. The debt, as we shall see, was to provide a mechanism that would lever into place the new law of property, and with it the colonial occupation.

THE PRIVATE VILLAGE

The obstacles to the consolidation of a new kind of control over the countryside included the occurrence of theft and armed attack, the continuing problem of desertion, the difficulty of establishing authority over the Arab population, the waves of modern epidemic disease, and what must have seemed the ever-present risk, demonstrated by the events in Jirja in 1865, of an armed revolt. These events, and the violence to which they were responding, constitute the local context that was omitted from the history of private property. Private property emerged in the form of large agricultural estates. Beginning by the 1840s, and expanding rapidly from the 1860s, the estates represented a further effort to find ways of establishing a detailed and continuous control over the rural population. This time it was more successful.

By granting an estate to one of his functionaries, family members, or servants, the viceroy effectively subcontracted to the recipient, whether high-ranking officer or household coffee maker, the problem of policing and extracting revenue from that district. In fact the estate first emerged in the 1840s not as a form of private property, but as a means of making an individual official liable for paying the revenue arrears of a particular village. Any villager who owed taxes was thereby placed in debt bondage to the official and compelled to work the land to the benefit of the official until the debt had been paid.[56] (I will return in a moment to this issue of debt, a mechanism of coercion working within the right of property.) The estates Isma'il created in the 1860s and 1870s continued the practice of making villages or parts of villages the responsibility of individual officials. At the same time, the much lower tax rates on estates made them a potentially lucrative reward for the loyalty of those who received them. The reward provided a means of binding the recipient in allegiance to the ruler and thus strengthening his authority.[57]

In the 1870s the estates were transformed from tax responsibilities into landholdings over which the recipient enjoyed what came to be called private ownership. This change did not occur because the holders sought the development of private rights. It was forced upon them by the government's and the foreign bankers' further demands for revenue. In 1871, sinking deeper into debt, the viceroy offered full ownership rights and the halving of future tax liability to anyone who would pay a sum equivalent to six years' tax. The revenue from this arrangement was pledged to European bankers as security for another loan. The offer was unattractive to most landholders, so three years later the payment was made obligatory, in twelve annual installments. The "equivalent" *(muqabala)*, as the payment was called, in effect a 50 percent increase in taxation, became the principal cause of indebtedness among landholders.[58] Private ownership emerged not as a right won by individuals against the state but as part of a penalty imposed upon them as a means of paying government debts, a penalty that in fact caused many smaller landholders to fall into debt themselves and lose their land.

The advantage of the estate did not lie in higher productivity. The argument that large holdings were more productive than small farms was made after the British occupation and would be made again at the end of the twentieth century, as we will see, when the restrictions placed on the formation of estates in subsequent decades were once again removed. Small village farms were considered four times as productive as the large estates of the ruling family.[59] The estate's advantage was that it enabled the most powerful households to achieve a direct and continuous control over the process of farming and claim complete possession of its product. The estate represented a system of supervision and coercion that succeeded for the first time in fixing cultivators permanently in place on the land and preventing them from abandoning cultivation or moving to another region. They could now be forced in large numbers to grow crops under the orders and for the benefit of an outsider.

This power was achieved in several ways. First, the cultivators lost control not just of the land but of their households and living arrangements.

They were made to live under close supervision in a "private village," owned by the new owner of the land. Private landownership was in many cases the private ownership of a village.

With the creation of large estates, especially those that brought former flood basins or wetlands under year-round cultivation, the owners required housing for the labor they used. At first they left the workers to construct their own huts, but they later discovered that greater power could be acquired over a workforce by taking control of their living arrangements. There were several recent precedents for the building of supervised accommodation for large groups of men, including the construction of barracks for a modern mass army and similar housing for the labor forces employed on major construction projects such as the Suez and Ibrahimiyya canals and the new railway lines.[60] There was even an attempt to control the accommodation of ordinary villagers, in the form of a program announced in 1846 to rebuild every village in the country according to a precise and regular plan. A number of model villages were built on the estates of the ruling family, "in order to show the fellahs how to construct their villages" (as the consultants Arthur D. Little were to try again a century later).[61] The sketch of the village of Gezzaye (see fig. 1), drawn by an Armenian engineer named Hekekyan, "shows the general style of these villages," several of which were built in Lower and Upper Egypt. As the drawing indicates, the village consisted of three classes of houses: those for sheikhs and the well-to-do, those for "the middling class of fellahs," and "lines of huts for the last class of fellahs." A separate row of houses accommodated government officers and travelers, with a house of prostitution located conveniently behind. In the northwest corner, adjacent to the house of prostitution, was the manor house for the lord of the estate. The irregular size and shape of this compound, Hekekyan notes, represented a characteristic "derogation from the rule imposed on the rest of the place." He added, however, that by the time of his visit about five years after the building of the village, "we found the streets already traversed in several directions by huts and stables in the manner of epaulements to secure privacy."[62]

In the later part of the century, beginning once again on the viceregal estates, landowners began to construct large numbers of "organized" villages, in which "the owner imposed on his tenants a plan where everything had its logical place." The typical layout consisted of several rows of mud huts to house the workers and their overseers, and at the center of these was the group of buildings known as the *duwwar,* consisting of a courtyard lined on three sides by storerooms and workshops and on the fourth by the offices, which had accommodation for the manager of the estate on an

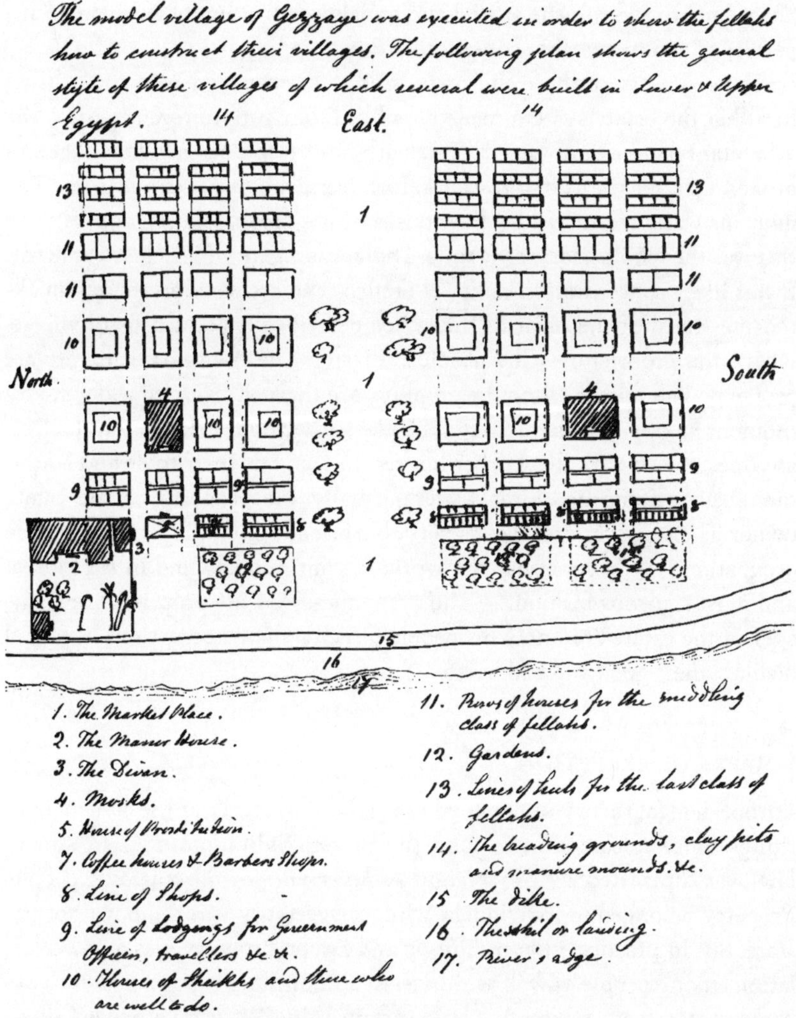

The model village of Gezzaye was executed in order to shew the fellahs how to construct their villages. The following plan shows the general style of these villages of which several were built in Lower & Upper Egypt.
14
East.
14
North
South
1. The Market Place.
2. The Manor House.
3. The Divan.
4. Mosks.
5. House of Prostitution.
7. Coffee houses & Barbers Shops.
8. Line of Shops.
9. Line of lodgings for Government Officers, travellers &c &c.
10. Houses of Sheikhs and those who are well to do.
11. Rows of houses for the middling class of fellahs.
12. Gardens.
13. Lines of huts for the last class of fellahs.
14. The treading grounds, clay pits and manure mounds. &c.
15. The dike.
16. The sahil or landing.
17. River's edge.

Figure 1. The model village of Gezzaye, 1852. Source: Hekekyan, "Journals 1851–54," folio 355. Reproduced by permission of the British Library.

upper floor. On the largest estates the administration, housing the management offices and lodgings for the agricultural engineers, would be located at the center of the property or in the nearest village, while the workers would be housed in a series of compounds around the estate, each built as a walled enclosure with double doors set in a high gateway, like "a sort of fortress." The housing formed a permanent "agricultural colony," isolated from the main village and known as the *ʿizba.* By extension, the term

ʿ*izba* came to refer to the spatial and social organization of cultivators, supervisors, and owner that constituted the estate.[63]

The geometry of these sites expressed the new power over the cultivators that the estate system made possible. From a more recent period, the inhabitant of a medium-sized estate with ninety-five acres of land that was broken up after the 1952 agrarian reform remembered it as a prison. "The *duwwar* was surrounded by the houses of the *zurra*ʿ (sharecroppers), and this was the whole ʿ*izba* at the time. There was a gate which closed at night. It was like a concentration camp."[64] French scholars who carried out an extensive study of the ʿ*izba* in the 1930s described it as "a private village, where the proprietor is the absolute master. The houses are his private property. The fellahs whom he employs are there at his invitation; at any moment he can send them away if he pleases, without being accountable to anyone."[65] Not only the worker houses, in fact, but their tools and equipment, even domestic animals, were usually the property of the estate owner. The larger estates had "a veritable brigade of employees whose sole occupation was to supervise the workers, continuously and in the closest and most rigorous fashion."[66] The system enabled the proprietor or manager of the estate "to know his people directly, their needs, their likes and dislikes, their good and bad habits."[67]

POWERS OF EXCEPTION

European legal theory understood the right of property as the control over things. Since at least Montesquieu, this private right (*dominium* in Roman law) was contrasted with sovereignty *(imperium)*, or the rule over people. Property belonged to individuals, while sovereignty was the power of the state. But in practice, in both Europe and Egypt, property was a power relation among people as well as things. At a minimum, it was a power to exclude others from taking or using certain things. If people needed those things to survive, then property rights conferred much wider powers, including the ability to make people do as the owner wished.[68] The proprietor of the estates that spread across the Nile valley was a sovereign, an "absolute master." He was accountable to no one. He could imprison, expel, starve, exploit, and exercise many other forms of arbitrary, exceptional, and, if necessary, violent powers. The law of property claimed to be a universal right, based upon undisputed principles true in every country. But this general truth enclosed within it a zone of arbitrariness. The walls of the ʿ*izba* encircled a realm of exception, within which power operated without rights. The architecture that formed the enclosed agricultural colony, a microcolonialism within a larger colonial domain, went hand in hand with a legal architecture that constructed territories of arbitrary power within the larger space of legal reason and abstraction.

The power of this sovereignty was constituted not only within the estate, but from the relations between the enclosed domain of the estate and the wider countryside in which it stood. The estate could operate as a sort of prison, in part because to escape from the estate meant to become both landless and homeless. Reinforcing the discipline created by the walls and gates of the *ʿizba* was the power generated by the wider arrangements of which it was a part. This was the other side of the successful control of labor: the expansion of the estate system to eliminate the opportunity of escape to a less coercive alternative. One estimate indicates that by 1863 estates already covered more than one-seventh of the cultivated area.[69] Over the next twelve years their area almost doubled. A local writer noted the exploitation now suffered by landless agricultural laborers, who were "compelled to work for whatever wages it is possible to get from the owners, depending upon their pleasure, even though this amount be extremely small and incommensurate with the labor. This is particularly so in areas where there are a great many workers, who then accept diminished wages and compete with one another in this, to the benefit of the landowners."[70] The landless were as much a part of the arrangement as the workers tied to the estate. Their role lay not just in the discipline they helped enforce among estate workers by their availability to replace them, but in the provision of extra labor at harvest and other periods of peak demand for which the proprietor did not have to provide year-round support. There developed mobile brigades of workers, controlled by labor contractors and overseers, resulting in a dual labor force.[71] The estate represented a method of fixing workers in place and at the same time making other workers mobile. Both the fixing and the mobility depended upon the rapid removal of land from village control and its transformation into estates.

A census carried out on the eve of the occupation in 1882 indicated that there were then five thousand estates in the Delta alone, housing 12 percent of the population. Three years later regulations were introduced to govern the creation of estates, restricting them to properties of more than fifty acres. Yet by 1901, half the country's agricultural land was held in estates of this size. In 1912, in a further attempt to slow down the rate at which villagers were losing their land and their homes, the British introduced the Five Feddan Law. Modeled on a similar measure in the Punjab, the law prevented creditors seizing from small farmers their last five acres (feddans) of land, their essential farm tools, two draft animals, and their house. Nevertheless, by the 1920s it was estimated that more than one-third of the agricultural population in the Delta had become landless, while the number of estates in the country as a whole had reached about seventeen thousand.[72] In an official list of place names published in 1932, more than half the localities listed were private estates.[73]

These islands of sovereignty were in the majority of cases seized from villages. It is impossible to determine exactly what proportion of the land taken as estates was previously uncultivated and what proportion was cultivated land or pasture belonging to villages. Some of the so-called uncultivated land had been made that way by the failed coercions of earlier decades, and other areas had formed part of the transhumant agriculture of the Bedouins forcibly ended by the government. These issues aside, the decline in the taxable area of village lands between 1863 and 1875 suggests that about two-thirds of the land taken as estates was cultivated village land. The villages may have lost even more, for many of the lands taken as estates continued to be registered as village land.[74] Barakat has shown how large proportions of the estate land seized by Isma'il and his predecessors was taken directly from the villages.[75] Even when estates were formed from land officially categorized as uncultivated, untaxed, or abandoned, it was sometimes at the expense of the villages. The recipient of the uncultivated lands of a village would in some cases forcibly exchange them for an area of more fertile village land already under cultivation, claiming the need for a consolidated acreage for the estate in place of the dispersed fragments of less fertile, uncultivated soil.[76] Villagers themselves later made it clear that they considered the big estates to have been created largely by the appropriation of cultivated village land.[77]

A further means of control was provided by the mechanism of debt. With the village itself under private sovereignty, cultivators could now be required to work for less than a living wage. The typical arrangement was to employ the workers without payment or below subsistence wages on the labor-intensive cotton crop, which was grown on a three-year (sometimes two-year) rotation. On the land rotated out of cotton the workers grew food and fodder crops, each worker receiving a small plot to provide for the subsistence of his household and surrendering the rest of the crop to the owner. In some cases the workers rented rather than sharecropped their subsistence plots, but in either case the owner tended to retain control of irrigation and the choice of crops. Only the owners had a surplus to sell, so they alone had access to capital. The owners therefore provided the working capital for the subsistence plots. When workers were unable to repay this or other loans they were placed in debt bondage to the owner.

The wages for working on the cotton crop were then absorbed in debt and interest payments, and the workers became an unpaid, bonded workforce.[78]

The mechanism of debt was not only a power available within the sovereign space of the estate. In 1876 the government agreed with thirteen European powers and the United States to establish the Mixed Courts, a parallel judicial system based on French law governing legal relations between foreigners and local subjects.[79] Administered mostly by foreign lawyers and judges, the new courts for the first time enabled creditors to seize ownership of a cultivator's land for nonpayment of debt. In five years fifty thousand acres in a single province were lost by distraint to moneylenders, who ranged from large mortgage banks to the small Greek and Levantine traders that had opened shops in almost every village.[80] A British parliamentary inquiry later reported that the local population regarded the courts simply as "a machine for transferring the land" from the native cultivators to their creditors.[81] Once again the law of private property created a power that was much more than a control over things. It manufactured this "machine" that concentrated into certain hands enormous powers of violence. An individual creditor could now use its force to evict a farmer from the land, seize possession of draft animals and ploughs, and demolish houses. Since the Mixed Courts did not govern relations among local subjects, but only those between locals and foreigners, this power was another enclave of privilege reserved for Europeans, another exceptional power made possible by a supposedly universal law.

The powers of debt were soon concentrated into a much larger force, providing the leverage for colonial occupation. "By the irony of fate," as Britain's colonial governor of Egypt later put it, the machine was used to take over the estates of the country's largest landowner, Isma'il himself, and turn the country into a European colony.[82] In 1874 a global economic depression began, brought on by the crisis of speculative European banking, including the large loans to Isma'il and his government. As the depression caused the price of cotton to fall and made further credit unavailable, Isma'il was unable to postpone any longer the financial collapse. In 1876 the banking houses established a Debt Commission in Cairo, which took control of the country's finances and used the new Mixed Courts to take possession of Isma'il's estates. When Isma'il resisted the takeover the British and French governments had him deposed in favor of his son Tawfiq. The latter began to lose power to a popular constitutionalist movement, led by junior army officers and disaffected notables.[83] In 1882 the British invaded the country, established a military occupation to eradicate the populist movement, and reasserted European control over finances, including all of the viceregal estates.[84] This course of events was ironic, perhaps, but the powers at work were not particularly those of fate.

MAKING A DIFFERENCE

The development of the agricultural estate transformed the Nile valley in the nineteenth century. I have argued that we should describe this development not as "the emergence of private property," but as the development of new ways to manage those who farmed the land, achieved after earlier failures, through new methods of devolution, incarceration, surveillance, and exclusion. This is not simply a matter of reversing the image, as has sometimes been proposed. Instead of portraying the estate as the culmination of the development of private rights against the excessive powers of the state, an alternative view portrays it as an arrangement created by the state to bring order to the system of landholding and increase its own powers over rural society.[85] This image makes better sense of what occurred. Yet the argument that large-scale *private* property emerged as a more efficient form of *state* control begins to exceed the terms in which it is expressed. The argument assumes a distinction between rural society or economy and the state. The former is constructed out of private persons and their rights, and the latter consists of public powers. One has to take the distinction between state and society not as the starting point of the analysis, but as an uncertain outcome of the historical process. It is a difference whose genealogy parallels the one we are tracing between the abstraction of law and the materiality of land. The new methods of management cannot be understood in terms of an entity called the state imposing its power upon rural society. What is clear from the details of how the estate emerged is that it was neither exactly an arm of the state nor a private arrangement standing in opposition to the state. This is not because the estate was a dual entity, but because until this period neither state nor society was imagined to exist. As the new methods developed, some took forms that began to be categorized as aspects of the state, and others took forms that would be labeled as part of society. Some of the new powers for the control of land and labor would later appear as public powers, others as private. A vocabulary readily existed for labeling certain practices or bodies as viceregal *(miri)* and for distinguishing what was public or general *(ʿamm)* from what was exclusive *(khass),* but such terms did not correspond to our contemporary vocabulary of state and society or name such distinct entities. Rather, it was out of the new practices that these categories began to emerge.[86]

The estates granted to officials and servants of the viceroy illustrate this point. The grant was a means of forcing these functionaries to become responsible for extracting tax payments. As new canals and steam pumps made it possible to convert flood basins to year-round cultivation, the grant was also a means to make the recipients responsible for organizing the labor, machinery, and other resources required for converting the land. The estate holders had the local power to command the collection of taxes, but also to command forced labor for irrigation and conversion projects and to police the converted land.

Yet the estates were never mere agencies of the central power. Some estates were formed not by functionaries of the ruling household but by rural lords, tribal heads, or provincial merchants, who enjoyed local networks of power independent of the system of central authority. Even functionaries of the viceroy could use their position to build larger estates, amass personal revenues, and exercise local powers well beyond what the regime in Cairo intended. They made unrecorded acquisitions of land, confiscated land from those unable to pay taxes, or simply seized village land for their own use.[87] The viceroy's repeated efforts to prevent government servants from independently enlarging their landholdings suggests the scale of this problem. On October 25, 1864, Isma'il instructed the Council of Justice to enforce a ruling issued under his predecessor that prohibited provincial employees—clerks, engineers, surveyors, military officers, medical officers, and others—from purchasing or renting village land in the province in which they were employed.[88] A year later the viceroy ordered the inspectors of the Upper and Lower Nile to inform all provincial governors that those who held a village district as an official estate were forbidden to purchase privately held land within the district, whether belonging to natives of the district or outsiders.[89] Isma'il also frequently transferred provincial officeholders to new districts, made several unsuccessful efforts to ban the use of unpaid forced labor on estates, and tried more than once to undertake a new land survey and offer rewards for revealing unregistered land.[90] None of these measures succeeded in keeping provincial officials and other estate holders under control. The local powers generated by the estate system served the purposes of the central authority but always exceeded its control. This excess of power cannot be grasped in terms of any simple distinction between state and society.

Even more difficult to analyze in these terms are the estates of the ruling family. Like his predecessors, Isma'il made his largest seizures of land to create estates for himself and members of his family. In a single week in October 1863 he took more than thirty thousand acres belonging to twenty-six villages in the province of Sharqiyya and all the land registered as untaxed or uncultivated on the borders of the neighboring province of Daqhaliyya.[91] By the end of his reign Isma'il and his family controlled 916,000 acres, or almost one-fifth of the taxable agricultural area of the country, including much of the most productive land.[92] The governing power was the largest "private" landowner.

The revenue collected on the viceregal estates was not paid into the government treasury but held by the estate itself.[93] A separate administration was set up to manage the "domain" *(da'ira)* of each family member, each with its own treasury, staff, and equipment and paying its own salaries and pensions. The domain of Ilhami Pasha, son of Isma'il's uncle and predecessor 'Abbas, for example, "owned six steamboats, six palaces, 3,855 animals, an unspecified number of factories and carriages, and a primary school for the owner's male slaves. It paid monthly salaries and pensions of 129,531 piastres to 666 employees and former employees, including translators, accountants, and clerks."[94] The domains functioned as separate sovereignties, with far more power and autonomy than ordinary estates. Yet they cannot, as Hunter concludes, "be regarded as extensions of state power."[95] Their status became still more ambiguous as they were pledged as security for loans and fell, like the country as a whole, under the control of European financiers. In May 1865 Isma'il separated the administration of his own estates from the rest of the family holdings, and pledged them as security for a loan.[96] In 1878 he signed over the remaining family domains to Rothschilds. The family domains were transferred to the government after the Europeans took control and renamed state domain, to distinguish them from those mortgaged earlier. Yet state domain referred to lands controlled and managed not by the state but by the House of Rothschild. These distinctions were elaborated as a part of the functioning of political control. They do not define two original and neatly separable objects. The domains represented another zone of exception, minisovereignties established by the powers of property, debt, and mortgage, and used as levers of occupation.

What is the genealogy of the law of property? How do general principles become true in every country? The old answer, set forth in Cairo in 1883 by Artin's study for the Ministry of Finance, described a series of nineteenth-century laws, and read them as the steps gradually instituting the principle of private ownership. It presented this process as the history of a conceptual structure, the framework of individual rights. The origin of the structure lay outside the Nile valley, in the rational scheme of European legal theory. Artin's account reinforces the impression of a nonlocal origin, and thus of law as something ideal, for it abstracts the laws from the actual circumstances and political struggles out of which they came.

We cannot read such history as an accurate representation of the genealogy of the law. We can, however, read it as a text that, in its silences about actual circumstances and struggles, *performs* the origins of law. The ideal structure of law is produced by its difference from the particular history and materiality of local events. The absence of the local and the actual in the Ministry of Finance study enacts, and reproduces, the difference. Presenting the law of property as a conceptual structure whose origins lie outside actuality is part of a process that establishes the law in terms of this dualism.

The local origins of the law are necessarily hidden, for they lie in questions of power, discipline, coercion, and dispossession. They are tied up in specific histories, now largely forgotten, of the failed coercions of an earlier system and the depopulation of hundreds of villages, of laborers forced to dig canals and embankments on an unprecedented scale and farmers made to grow crops they could not eat, of permits and travel restrictions and the spread of new epidemic diseases, of rebellions crushed with overwhelming force and prisons and labor camps filled and refilled. Scarcely a word about these events is found in the standard histories of how the universal right of property arrived, and today they can be only partially retold.

The colonial presentation of law as a conceptual structure brought from abroad performs the silencing of the actuality out of which property is made. But it is not just the colonial legal texts that produce this difference. The very act of colonial occupation produces it. By the time the law of property was in place, the British could claim that the days of the old abuses were over. The colonial occupation marked a rupture with the past, and the arbitrary rule of despots had given way to the rule of law.

The rupture of colonial occupation was not a complete break with the past, however. The rule of property consolidated by the British confirmed a distribution and control of land put in place over the preceding decades. The exceptions, privileges, injustices, and coercions that produced this distribution of power and resources were to become a permanent part of the new order. The new legal order, rather than ending exceptional forms of control, created a thousand arbitrary powers. Every one of the new private estates, with their high walls and fortresslike gates, was its own sovereignty, a private realm of arbitrariness. Law was presented as the opposite of violence, exception, arbitrariness, and injustice, yet somehow these features were all incorporated within it. How could law be both order and violence, justice and injustice, universal and exceptional?

Rather than creating a rupture with arbitrary forms of power, the rule of law rearranged the arbitrariness. It redistributed its operations and its effects. The mechanism of this rearrangement was the estate. Law ruled on the outside, arbitrary power was hidden on the inside, just as it was hidden in the histories of the law. This happened at many levels, from the village strongman whose power was now that of local landowner to the larger estates of the absentee landlords, from the great domains of the ruling household to the state domain of the European banks, and beyond all these, the country as a whole, reorganized by the same methods as the domain of colonial power. Thus universal law was founded upon exceptions. Each of these domains was a zone of exceptionality, a sovereign territory within which the principles that established it did not apply.

Since law must establish itself as the opposite of violence, and since principles become universal by fixing their difference from what is exceptional and local, the rearranging was also a process of denial, differentiation, and exclusion. The system of private property achieved this not only at what is called the level of language or representation, in writings like Artin's that presented law as a conceptual system. It built the difference between the actual and the ideal, the material and conceptual, into the architecture of the countryside. The estate divided the world into law on one side and land on the other, abstraction versus material reality. The *'izba* was much more than a prison. It was a principle of order. It presented the new structure of difference, enacting it in the regularity of its lines and the repetition of its forms. These inscribed the effect of an absolute opposition: on one side an agricultural colony consisting of labor, animals, resources, implements, and land, all of them now objects to be owned; on the other, administration, bookkeeping, order, property, the right of ownership.

The production of private property created the object quality of modern space. The forces, powers, processes, and claims whose tension and interaction gave rise to rural life were to be replaced by a world resolved into two dimensions, the inert materiality of land on one side, legal codes and property rights on the other. Thing versus idea, reality versus abstraction, space versus its meaning. With the rapid expansion of the estate system, these methods became a central feature of the production of "Egypt" itself as a closely managed geographical and political object. Alongside the system of estates, several other processes employed similar methods in a new politics of the production of space. In the later nineteenth and early twentieth centuries, practices such as the demarcation and policing of frontiers, the transformation of the country's agriculture from a system based on capturing floodwaters to one based on permanent canals, and the overcoming of distances through the construction of railways, roads, shipping canals, and telegraphs all involved the creation of surfaces and enclosures that could be opened, closed, extended, mastered, and improved. Producing Egypt as an object of state power was the outcome of these novel techniques.[97]

Most of the time we take for granted the notion that land and even labor are objects, commodities that can be bought and sold. Following Marx, it is possible to say that turning labor into a commodity marked a violent act of alienation in which human life, a living force, was reduced to the status of a thing. Following Lefebvre, it is possible to make a parallel argument about land. The "production of space," as Lefebvre termed the transformation of landscape into object, leveled the "natural and sacred contours" of the landscape under the exchange values and sign systems of capital.[98] Both are arguments of alienation that trace how a living reality is reified, turned into a mere thing. They are arguments of misrecognition: capitalist relations of exchange disguise the real social relations and natural values embodied in living forces. They are powerful arguments, but they are arguments that work within a binary or dialectical logic. They oppose nature, a living actuality, to a nonpresent, regulating ideality. We have located the power of law in a further series of binarisms—those that appear to establish the universality of law by securing its difference from the actuality of colonial history, the ideality of property in terms of its difference from the materiality of land and labor, and the order of colonial rule in terms of its difference from the arbitrary violence of the past. If our goal is to destabilize these dualisms, then a critique that rests on a dialectical logic, however powerful, cannot serve. The law of property does not take nature or life and turn them into objects. Law is produced as the difference between the ideality of rights and the physicality of nature, between the abstraction of the code and the actuality of life. The concepts of nature or life in which a dialectical critique is grounded are produced in the political process we are examining.

The principle of abstraction on which the order of law depends can be generated only as the difference between order and violence, the ideal and the actual, the universal and the exceptional. But the violent, the actual, and the exceptional—all of which the law denounces and excludes, ruptures itself from and supersedes—are never gone. They make possible the rupture, the denunciation, and the order. They are the condition of its possibility.

3 The Character of Calculability

In 1903 the German sociologist Georg Simmel published an essay describing modern life as a world of unrelenting calculation. People had developed, he wrote, "a purely matter-of-fact attitude in the treatment of persons and things." He attributed the new mentality to the growth of large cities, which encouraged the development of an impersonal, individualized rationality at the expense of the more deeply felt emotional ties of life in the countryside and small towns. A calculating mentality was connected with the concentration of commercial transactions in the large city, or what he called "money economy": "The metropolis has always been the seat of money economy," Simmel argued, "because the many-sidedness and concentration of commercial activity have given the medium of exchange an importance which it could not have acquired in the commercial aspects of rural life."[1] If money economy had made the modern mind "more and more a calculating one," this could be connected with the way modern science was transforming the world into questions of mathematics:

> The calculating exactness of practical life which has resulted from a money economy corresponds to the ideal of natural science, namely that of transforming the world into an arithmetical problem and of fixing every one of its parts in a mathematical formula. It has been money economy which has thus filled the daily life of so many people with weighing, calculating, enumerating, and the reduction of qualitative values to quantitative terms.[2]

The new "character of calculability" had introduced a precision and unambiguousness in social relationships, Simmel concluded, "just as externally this precision has been brought about through the general diffusion of pocket watches."[3]

"The Metropolis and Mental Life," as the essay was called in English, became one of the most widely read works of twentieth-century social theory. At the University of Chicago, built with John D. Rockefeller's money into a powerhouse of the new professional fields of social science, the essay was translated into English by Edward Shils and incorporated in 1936 into the syllabus of a new, unified social science curriculum, to be read by every undergraduate. Yet just fourteen years later, in 1950, another translation appeared, which changed the terms of Simmel's argument about money economy and the growth calculability.[4] The alteration followed a change in the meaning of the English word "economy" that had occurred in the same fourteen years.

In the 1930s the word "economy" (and *Wirtschaft* in German) meant something like "the principle of seeking to attain, or the method of attaining, a desired end, with the least possible expenditure of means," to quote the 1925 edition of *Palgrave's Dictionary of Political Economy.*[5] By extension, "money economy" referred to the attitudes and transactions of commercial exchange, a way of "dealing with men and things," in Simmel's phrase.[6] By 1950 the word had acquired a new meaning. It no longer referred to a set of attitudes and relations but denoted a distinct social sphere, "the economy" (now always with a definite article), the realm of a social science, statistical enumeration, and government policy.[7]

This change was reflected in the changed wording of the 1950 translation of Simmel's essay. The definite article was inserted into both passages quoted above: "The metropolis has always been the seat of *the* money economy," wrote Gerth and Mills, the authors of the second translation, adding the innocent word I have italicized. "The calculative exactness of practical life which *the* money economy has brought about corresponds to the ideal of natural science."[8] The modification made it seem as though Simmel were referring to this newly realized object, the economy. Simmel was not the only German social theorist to suffer this revision in American hands. Talcott Parsons did the same thing in the same period to Simmel's more famous contemporary, Max Weber.[9]

The definite article that slipped gently into the world between the 1930s and the 1950s was a marker of one of the most profound intellectual and political changes of the twentieth century. Its importance is only confirmed by the fact that no one has noticed it took place. Polanyi, Tribe, Dumont, Foucault, Buck-Morss, and others have argued that the economy became a distinct sphere of social practice and intellectual knowledge in the eighteenth or early nineteenth century.[10] Yet the political economists of that period do not describe a distinct structure called "the economy" or use the term in its mid-twentieth-century sense. They use the word only with the meaning defined by Palgrave, above, or in an older sense referring to the "proper governing" of the community's affairs. The term "political economy" refers to this economy, or governing, of the polity, not to the politics of an economy. Even Friedrich List, the nineteenth-century German–American political economist and entrepreneur who is sometimes singled out and said to be writing precociously about "national economy," was writing in this sense.[11]

Only toward the end of the 1930s was the new idea of "the economy" realized, and as late as the 1950s writers still sometimes felt the need to explain what the word now meant.[12] It came to refer to a self-contained structure or mechanism whose internal parts are imagined to move in a dynamic and regular interaction, separate from the irregular interaction of the mechanism as a whole with what could now be called its exterior. A variety of other spaces could now be conceived in terms of their relationship to this hermetic field: the sphere of politics or the state; the sphere of law (previously at the center of questions of political economy); the sphere of science and technology; and the sphere of culture.[13] Among these objects, the economy was distinguished by the fact that it stood for the *material* sphere of life. At the same time, as the sphere of rational and numerical calculation, it was the one most easily represented in statistical and algebraic forms. For this reason, the most abstract and mathematical of the social sciences, economics, claimed the task of representing what seemed the most real aspect of the social world.

In the Introduction I criticized culturalist or constructivist approaches to social understanding for leaving ultimately undisturbed the distinction routinely made between the constructed and the real, the cultural and the material, the social and the economic. So my argument here is not going to be that the economy was a "cultural construction" of the twentieth century, that it was something imagined or invented. Rather, I would like to suggest that in the twentieth century the economy was *made*. The economy was an artifact and, like all things artifactual, was made out of processes that were as much "material" as they were "cultural," and that were as "real" as they were "abstract." Indeed, these distinctions cannot provide a basis for making sense of how the economy appeared, for the apparent bifurcation of the world into the real and the abstract, the material and the cultural, does not precede the making of the economy. On the contrary, the economy was a set of practices for producing this bifurcation. It was both a method of staging the world as though it were divided in this way into two, and a means of overlooking the staging, and taking the division for granted.

To uncover the genealogy of the economy, this chapter looks at the earlier decades of the twentieth century, and puts aside the fact that we know (or think we know) what an economy is. How did those attempting to manage the political and economic problems of their times make sense of things? This approach differs from the normal procedure, in which one assumes that those dealing with finance, trade, agriculture, landownership, manufacturing, population, urban growth, and related topics were dealing with "the economy"— even if they did not give it this name and often dealt with things that today might not be considered part of the economy. Such an approach attributes to earlier periods a way of dealing with the world that they did not have, in terms of an object—the economy—that had not yet been made. It gives us no way of telling what difference was made by one of the most powerful new objects of the twentieth century. The realization of the economy made possible new practices (of development, management, and government, to name a few), new claims to expertise, new equivalences, and new silences, not one of which is easy to uncover when we project the economy onto periods whose politics were not organized around this object. On the other hand, by examining what it means to be living in a period when no one knows what will constitute the economy, or even that such an object might materialize, perhaps we can get a better sense of what its materialization involved.

The chapter explores these questions in early twentieth-century Egypt. Examining what happened in Egypt will enable us to introduce the issue of colonialism into the history of economics. It is important to appreciate to what extent the realization of the economy belongs to the history of colonialism. The economy appeared in the context of the collapse of an imperial order. World-encircling arrangements of investment, management, production, information, and trade based on the political control of colonial resources gave way to arrangements based on ostensibly national economies. The economy was constructed by definition and default as a national rather than imperial space.[14] The nation, and the national economy in particular, provided the format of what could appear as a postimperial political topography. John Maynard Keynes, a critical figure in the making of the economy, published his first book, *Indian Currency and Finance* (1913), while employed at the India Office in London.[15] The book addressed a set of questions whose larger answer was later to be formulated as the national economy: how to conceptualize, measure, and manage the circulation of money within a defined geographical space. Indeed, it was in relation to the problems of colonial rule that several of the problems of managing the enclosed spaces of the economy were originally worked through. Moreover, as an apparatus to be managed and made more efficient, the economy was the object upon which the new politics of development was built after the 1930s. The development of economies provided the forms and formulas through which European colonial powers could attempt to restructure the relationship with their colonies in the mid-twentieth century, and through which imperial powers whose reach was still expanding, in particular the United States, could find a new mode of operation.

THE GREAT MAP

In 1909 a group of bankers, businessmen, government officials, and scholars established in Cairo the Société Khédiviale d'Economie Politique de Statistique et de Legislation. The society met in a mansion near the Nile that housed the new national university, founded a few months earlier.[16] It drew its members from Cairo's cosmopolitan elite, both native Cairenes and members of the large community of expatriate Europeans. In January 1910 the society launched what became an influential journal of political economy, *L'Egypte Contemporaine,* publishing articles in English, French, and Arabic. The aim of the society was to organize and support research, congresses, and journeys of study, exploring "the problems of national life." Its rules forbade any discussion of a purely political or religious nature.[17]

Rather than leaving this intellectual activity to the initiative of individual members, most of who were involved in business or government, the founders of the association launched a collective research project to which all members might contribute. Searching for the broadest possible topic, they proposed an investigation of landed property *(propriété foncière)* in Egypt, describing this as the country's "great problem."[18] They published an outline of the research program in the journal. The outline makes clear that with this topic they intended to encompass something far broader than the question of landownership: Part I, *La Nature et L'Homme,* would cover geography and climate, population (the 1907 census, immigration and emigration, the legal status of natives and Europeans), and the distribution of property. Part II, *La Mise en Valeur du Sol,* would examine different owner-producer relations, agricultural methods, capital, and forms of production. Part III would deal with the marketing of agricultural products, including the relation between the market, prices, and the land's value. And Part IV would examine the social and economic condition of the producers. For the founders of the society, the existence of landed property provided a way of organizing and picturing a great diversity of social phenomena and economic relations. It portrayed these diverse relations as established within a common physical space, the space defined by the agrarian property relations examined in the previous chapter.

The idea that a country's social and economic relations can be pictured in terms of agrarian property draws on the nineteenth-century tradition of Anglo-Scottish and French political economy, the tradition of Quesnay, Smith, and Say, but especially of David Ricardo. For Ricardo, the dynamic of creating wealth began not with the act of exchange, but with the process of settling and cultivating an empty land, a space of colonization. The power to colonize the land gave rise to private property, and thus to rent, or the income that flows from exclusive control of the land. As colonization spread and inferior land was brought under ownership and cultivation, the difference in rent between land of different quality opened up the possibility of an increasing profit, and thus the general expansion of wealth.[19] The entire question of wealth was framed by the space of colonization and the possibility of landed property.

Ricardo's work was transformed by John Stuart Mill, and again by Marx, to take account of the production of wealth in manufacturing, and the novel forms of spatial organization, discipline, and power out of which the modern factory was built. Then, from the 1870s, a new, academic economics abandoned this entire tradition, putting in its place a locationless notion of "exchange." The space of the act of exchange was formulated geometrically, by the axes of a chart, as the two-dimensional plane in which the desires, or utilities, of a buyer and a seller intersected. This planar space carried no reference to the countryside, the city, the factory, or any other conception of place.

The older tradition of political economy was not abandoned, however, but was developed in Europe outside the field of economics, especially in faculties of law. It was French and Italian professors of law who helped develop the field of political economy in Cairo. The salience of the older tradition in Cairo reflected the situation there at the turn of the twentieth century. The system of private estates, examined in the previous chapter, was now established. The new space of landed property—a protonational space, but not the space of a national economy—provided the means to address and seek to solve "the problems of national life."

In 1907, on the eve of the founding of the Société d'Economie Politique, the Ministry of Finance completed a project that helped format and make knowable this new spatial order: a countrywide survey of the cultivation and ownership of land.[20] Apart from the reporting of deaths and contagious disease, the survey was the first large statistical operation the British undertook in Egypt. An older Bureau Central de Statistique, set up in 1870 and revived after a period of inactivity in 1878, had been closed down by the British. The bureau had carried out a census in May 1882 on the eve of the colonial occupation, and its closing as part of a reduction in government expenses in March 1883 impeded the processing and publication of the census returns.[21] Although another census was taken in 1897, and statistics on foreign trade were compiled at the port of Alexandria, there was no continuous and systematic government production of statistical knowledge until the launching of the land survey. The survey therefore played a central part in making a space of national calculation available.

Begun in 1898, the survey was based upon a novel technique of figuring the relationship between people and land embodied in the law of property: the large-scale map. In the surveyors' decade of work they produced twenty thousand separate maps depicting the country's entire agricultural area, field by field and plot by plot, at a scale of 1:2,500 (one centimeter representing twenty-five meters, or about twenty-five inches to one mile). For every plot, the smallest of which were just a few millimeters square on the map, the name of the owner was listed, and these names were compiled into registers of landowners and their tax liabilities.[22] By 1908, a year after the completion of the survey, the government had distributed some 100,000 of these map sheets, issuing 82,008 to government departments and selling 17,685 to the public.[23] In less than a decade the countryside had been transformed from a place in which maps played no role in administrative practice, legal argument, or financial calculation, to one of the most closely mapped terrains in the world.[24]

The making of these maps introduced new forms of measurement, representation, and calculation. They seemed to be part of the new character of calculability, in Simmel's phrase, that would define the politics of the twentieth century. But what precisely was new? There had been modern maps of different parts of the country for several decades, and the calculation of land areas and tax liabilities in the Nile valley was probably the oldest continuous example of administrative practice in the world. A closer look at what was novel in the making of the cadastral map offers us a way to understand the new practices of calculation that contributed to the twentieth-century making of the economy.

The cadastre, or official register of landholders, their lands, and their tax liabilities, was a long-standing institution, renewed with each foreign conquest of the country. When the Ottomans seized Cairo and the Nile Delta in 1517 they ordered a survey of landholdings that took sixty years to complete in the Delta and another thirty to extend toward the south. No new survey was carried out prior to the French occupation three centuries later.[25] Mehmed Ali ordered a cadastral survey and compiled a new tax register in 1813. All these surveys involved measuring the size of each plot in each village under Cairo's authority, and recording the total land and tax liability of every household and village. The information was recorded in village registers and in a government register in Cairo. It was never depicted on maps.

Mapping the countryside was probably attempted for the first time in 1853–59, when Mehmed Ali's successors carried out a comprehensive new cadastral survey. But the mapmaking was soon abandoned in favor of the old method of recording landholdings in registers, and any maps produced were lost. In 1858 a team of astronomers and surveyors began a detailed topographic study of the country. This provided information for a forty-five-square-meter relief map of the Delta and Middle Egypt that was the centerpiece in the palace representing modern Egypt at the famous 1867 World Exhibition in Paris.[26] Maps of the Delta were eventually published in 1871, although on a scale too small to show landholdings. The mapping of the south was never completed.[27]

The failure to produce a cadastral map continued after the Europeans took direct control. The Anglo-French Debt Commission and the International Inquiry that took over the country's revenues in 1878 ordered a land survey based on maps. The mapping was interrupted the following year when Isma'il, the Ottoman viceroy in Cairo, dismissed the Europeans and briefly put in charge an American (whose survey work the British later declared unreliable). It was slowed after Isma'il's deposition and Britain's military occupation, by the budget cuts of 1883, and by a cholera epidemic the same year that took more than fifty thousand lives. It was finally abandoned in 1888 with less than one-sixth of the country's agricultural area mapped.[28]

A decade later, with the collaboration of the Debt Commission, the new British survey began. Unlike earlier attempts at map making, the survey was based upon triangulation.[29] Instead of starting at the level of each village and building the map, plot by plot, by taking measurements with wooden rods or iron chains, the surveyors first laid a grid that would extend over the entire Nile valley. Using theodolites and signaling mirrors set up on the desert plateau on either side of the cultivated riverbanks, they established a network of lines each up to twenty-five kilometers long, crisscrossing the valley and connected into triangles from whose angles the length of each line could be determined. These they subdivided into smaller triangles with sides of about 3.5 kilometers. Individual villages, fields, and plots were then fixed within this triangulate web, the surveyors measuring each plot with chains and checking position and accuracy by further triangulation, establishing triangles within triangles within triangles. The "great land map of Egypt," as the *Geographical Journal* in London called it, would be based for the first time on a "rigorous framework" and "planned upon [a] connected system."[30]

The accuracy of the framework depended on the precise measurement of the baseline of its first triangle. The base was laid out along a railway track at Giza, near Cairo, in 1898, using five-meter laminated fir rods fitted with steel points at each end. The rods were checked against a standard bar that had been obtained forty years earlier from the firm of Brünner in Paris for the 1858 mapping project, and was itself sent back to Europe to be checked at different air temperatures against standards in Paris and Madrid. After measuring the Giza base, the survey office was dissatisfied with the accuracy of the rods and decided to replace them with a pair of 100-meter brass and steel Jäderin wires ordered from Stockholm, but these did not arrive until 1906. So for their second baseline, established at Seila in Fayyum Province in 1900, they used a 100-meter steel tape. The director of the survey, Captain Henry Lyons, gives the following account of how the base was measured. Along the baseline, approximately three kilometers (two miles) in length,

> stout wooden pickets were driven into the ground at intervals of a tape-length apart. On the head of each picket was nailed a plate of zinc, with fine cross lines ruled on it the intersection of which marked the point at which the measurement was to be made. The base was levelled on August 10, 1900, and the measurements occupied the following two days, one being made at dawn before the sun rose, and the other after sunset, since the sandy desert became so intensely heated by the sun's rays during the daytime as to render it inadvisable to measure between sunrise and sunset. The air temperature was determined for each tape-length by sling thermometers used at each end of the tape.[31]

With his British assistants and team of locally recruited chainmen, Lyons stretched and supported the tape by having it

> laid on blocks of wood of triangular section, in order to reduce friction as much as possible, so that it rested on the wooden edges of the blocks, and only for about two-thirds of its length on the surface of the desert;

> it was strained to uniformity of tension by means of a spring balance during the first two measurements, and to 15 kilograms during the last two. Uniformity of tension was secured by having the tape raised clear of the ground just before the measurement by three chainmen at equal intervals, who then lowered it gently into position.[32]

Repeating this procedure between each of the thirty pickets, the surveyors read off the difference between the end of the tape and the crosshairs marked on each picket head, "with the aid of finely-divided ivory scales." The results were adjusted for the inaccuracy of the tape, the tape's tension, the air temperature, the difference in level along the line, and the height above sea level. After taking the average of the dawn and evening measurements, writes Lyons, "we obtain for the length of the Seila base: 2,902.474 metres ± 0.0043 metre."[33] At the end of three days work, they had measured a line almost two miles long to within an accuracy of one-eighth of an inch.

This kind of precision was repeated in the theodolite traverses and chain measurements, and in the offices of the survey in Cairo, where the figures from notebooks compiled in the field were transcribed, computed, and checked. Great accuracy and speed were achieved, it was said, "by instituting an almost mechanical system of work, and by carrying the principle of the division of labour to its extreme possible development." The mechanical organization of labor made this human calculating machine self-checking, so that "any part not up to the requisite standard was automatically rejected."[34] The measurements and computations were then translated into the twenty thousand separate map sheets, which together for the first time made the country available in the form of a continuous "paper landscape."[35] The information on property owners and tax liabilities was compiled as an index to the maps. It was organized into two different kinds of register. The main register, for each village in the country, listed the land of the village, by field *(hod)* and plot, and for each plot listed up to twenty-five items of information, including area, class of land, tax, owner, and occupier. The second register listed the same information organized by landowner.[36]

As a method of producing official knowledge of the country, the cadastral map was considered to have four advantages. The first lay in its spatial presentation of landownership. The old tax registers could record the dimensions of every plot of land and relate each plot to an owner, but could not indicate the relationship between one plot and another. The new map showed not only the size of a particular landholding, but also its relation to all the others. The simultaneous presentation of adjoining plots produced a new kind of knowledge, the knowledge of irregularity. Since tax rates were based on the quality of the land, and plots in the same field tended to be of similar quality, "any anomalies in the rate of tax are at once visible."[37] In this way the map revealed facts that were previously invisible. The spatial display could show other distinctive or anomalous features, such as areas of land under reclamation that might need reassessment in future years. And as Lyons pointed out, it would now be impossible to record the same plot of land twice under different owners.[38] More importantly, although Lyons did not mention this, the map made immediately visible any plot of cultivated land that had not been registered under an owner, and was thus evading taxation. This was information the old cadastral register could never produce.

Political power now had a new form: the knowledge and command of space. The old cadastre was assembled from a knowledge of households and villages. Land claims and tax liabilities were the claims and liabilities of communities of persons, and expressed the relations of those communities both to the land and to those in power. Movements of information, revenue, and control flowed through these relations. Under the new system, the list of persons was merely "complementary" to the map, supplying additional information "that could not conveniently be inserted on the plan of a piece of land."[39] Power over persons was to be reorganized as a power over space, and persons were merely the units arrayed and enumerated within that space. The spatial order of knowledge was reflected in the method of mapmaking. The survey began by establishing coordinates not within the village but across the entire country, built upon a "rigorous framework." It recorded every community in terms of its graticulation within this nationwide context. The nation was emerging as this space, this material/structural extension, within which villages, persons, liabilities, and exchanges could be organized and contained. The connections, linkages, commands, and flows of information that made up this political order no longer seemed to pass through particular persons and communities. They appeared to arise in the space of separation between the land and the map, the social community and the state, the revenue and its statistical representation.

A second advantage the surveyors claimed was that the map made visible and recorded the tremendous changes that had occurred over the previous generation. The thousands of hamlets created to house workers on the new estates (the *ʿizbas* discussed in chapter 2), which had developed outside and largely at the expense of the existing system of village communities, and thus outside the system of village surveying, were named and attached to villages. New boundaries of each village were established topographically and their land area was mapped and measured. The irrigation works that accompanied the creation of private estates had reorganized the old system of flood basins into which landholdings had previously been grouped. In many cases the basins no longer provided a coherent division of the land, so holdings were reorganized into standardized parcels of fifty to one hundred acres. For each of these parcels the names of the landowners were inscribed and then listed in corresponding registers, fixing the land as a system of objects to be possessed and exchanged.

What the surveyors saw as recent changes, however, as I discussed in chapter 2, were at the same time a series of exceptions. The estates had come into being through the exercise of arbitrary and often violent forms of power, whether through grants from the ruler or the prerogatives of the European-controlled Mixed Courts. The mapping erased the signs of this arbitrariness, removing the scars, the abnormalities, through which the violence could still be traced. By giving each estate an official name and set of boundaries, and intercalating each one among the old system of village names and land claims, the arbitrariness of large landownership was merged into a uniform national space and made invisible. If the map made some kinds of abnormality newly visible, it made other forms disappear. Later on, when the economy comes into being, it will not be just a new and more detailed set of representations. Like the map, it will occur as practices that redistribute forms of knowledge and ignorance, and rearrange the normal and the abnormal.

A third advantage of the map was claimed not directly in the official account, but by implication. The map moved the site where all this knowledge was held. The old cadastre rested on the knowledge of the village surveyors. These men possessed a vital skill, especially in the south, where the Nile flood still inundated most of the fields each year. After the floodwaters had drained away, the surveyors marked out the plots along the dikes. The same expertise produced the old cadastral registers, and was still relied upon for local assistance in producing the new cadastral maps. The maps were made in the same years as the building of the first Aswan dam. As we know, the dam was to reorganize the distribution of expertise, taking away most of the local knowledge of flood basin irrigation, distributed along the length of the river, and concentrating technical control at one site.[40] After its raising in 1912 and 1933, the dam left only one-fifth of the land under flood basin irrigation, so the annual work of local surveyors was also taken away. The map contributed in its own way to a similar redistribution of knowledge. The cadastral knowledge of the village surveyors was now to be transferred into the map. The reason for the "mechanical" level of accuracy in the survey work was that the map had to be precise enough to allow the area of a plot, and thus the tax liability of its owner, for the first time to be calculated from the map itself. Instead of measuring the land, tax officials would measure the map.

A final advantage the map seemed to have, it follows, was its unprecedented degree of accuracy. The first chapters of Lyons's account of the project were devoted to a history of surveying in Egypt, beginning with the Pharaonic system and moving on to the Coptic methods of measuring and calculating area. These methods were still in use as Lyons began his survey, including the survival of Coptic notation in arithmetic, despite efforts since Mehmed Ali in the early part of the century to eliminate the use of Coptic numerals in surveying (the Coptic fractions had survived). Lyons described what he considered the inaccuracies of the Coptic method of calculating area before going on to chronicle the failures of nineteenth-century attempts to introduce more modern methods, leading to his own survey, presented as the culmination of this history of increasing precision, and thus representing the most complete and accurate measurement of the land.

Yet the historical presentation of the cadastre in terms of the evolution of precision—as another history of abstraction, that is, another account of the growing power of human reason to order and take the measure of the world—hid something. Lyons could not claim, in fact, that the survey he directed resulted in a more accurate measure of the land. Accuracy is always a question of where one stands. As we shall see, the new maps were in significant ways less accurate and more cumbersome than the old methods of recording landholdings. However, thanks to the gap opened up between field and map, the question of accuracy could now be recast. It was now an issue of one, simple relationship: the correspondence between the map and "the real world."

The twentieth century's new regime of calculation did not produce, necessarily, a more accurate knowledge of the world, despite its claims, nor even any overall increase in the quantity of knowledge. Its achievement was to redistribute forms of knowledge, increasing it in some places and decreasing it in others. At the same time, it transferred this knowledge to new sites. By a series of removals, it opened up a certain distance, the distance between the field and the computing office, between the farmer and the colonial survey officer, between the iron triangulation marker and the paper map.[41] The distance of such removals, repeated countless times in the cadastral survey and in increasing numbers of other projects, was to have a strange effect. The act of removal began to appear not as an action but as something more profound. The distance from the field to the map and back again, from the village to the computing office, would come to mark what seemed an absolute gap: the divide between reality and its representation, between an image-world and its object. The question of accuracy or truth could now be cast as the degree of correspondence between the object-world on one side of this divide and the maps, images, and numbers on the other. This strange effect gave rise to new objects and forms of calculation—among the most important of them, the economy.

AN ORGANIZATION OF THINGS AND POWERS

Surely, it may be said, even if an object called the economy was not named before the middle decades of the twentieth century, and the statistical practices that measured it had not yet been developed, nevertheless there was plenty of activity of an economic nature in earlier periods, and governments tried to regulate and even direct this activity. In that sense the economy was always there, one could argue, and the transformation I am describing occurred more at the level of ideas and representations than in material and political relations themselves.

It is certainly true that many of the activities that contributed to the making of the economy had long histories. But it would be a mistake to minimize in this way the importance of the change that occurred. There was no economy before the twentieth century because the economy belonged to a world that was being reorganized around a new axis, the axis that appears to divide the world into image and object, representation and reality. This could not be a transformation only at the level of representations, for the modern belief in a disembodied yet secular realm of representation was one of the outcomes of this kind of transformation. Many quite real things had to be reorganized to make the world appear to separate cleanly along its new divide.

The great land map of Egypt was not just a new way of representing an existing object, private property. The map helped to constitute and consolidate the new institution of private property and the forms of debt, title, dispossession, and violence on which it depended. Ordered by the Debt Commission, the maps in particular enabled the commissioners to reestablish boundaries for the hundreds of thousands of acres of state domain, many parts of which had been encroached upon, or reclaimed, by local farmers, and to begin auctioning these former khedival estates to private investors.[42] Thus mapping played a role in producing the distinction between land as "mere object" and the abstractions of law, taxation, and title. Likewise the making of the economy was not just a new way of representing certain forms of production and exchange, but part of a general reorganization of forms of calculation, appropriation, and government.

In the case of Egypt, I have stressed the importance of landed property in forming a new space of economic processes, to be imagined and organized as the economy.[43] However, private landownership was connected with a series of further transformations that were to form, and be formatted, as the national economy.

First, there was the increasingly widespread cultivation of cotton, which by the second decade of the century accounted for 92 percent of the country's recorded exports of goods.[44] A century earlier in England, when Ricardo first outlined a simplified idea of the making of wealth as the expanding control of agricultural land and the consequent increase in agricultural income, his model of the circulation of wealth was based on the cultivation and consumption of a single product, wheat.[45] With the expansion of large landownership in England, the wheat crop had replaced a more diversified grain agriculture and played a dominant role in farming, trade, and consumption. So perhaps it seemed reasonable, especially to an immigrant banker turned estate owner like Ricardo, to simplify the circulation of wealth to the movements of a single commodity.

This situation had changed dramatically in the 1870s. In a single decade, from 1868 to 1878, Britain went from producing four-fifths of its basic food and fiber to producing scarcely one-half.[46] In the same decade, the tradition of political economy built on the work of Ricardo was put aside (except by Marx) as a new professional economics began to emerge. Stanley Jevons, Karl Menger, and Leon Walras laid the foundation of the new profession by abandoning the image of wealth making based on land acquisition and the grain cycle and proposing in its place, as I mentioned, a mathematical model of the act of exchange, simplified into an action involving a single buyer, a single seller, and a single, unnamed commodity.[47] It was no longer possible to consider material relations to be expressed by one dominant commodity, such as wheat, so economists narrowed the study of wealth to this contentless act of exchange.

In Egypt, however, the transformations of the 1870s had worked differently, and brought the country closer than perhaps any other place in the world to the old Ricardian idea of wealth as the expansion of private property and the circulation of a single commodity. The creation of private property transferred most of the power to choose what crops to grow from those who cultivated them to a new person, the landowner. The transfer and concentration of power, together with the irrigation works allowing year-round cultivation, led to the replacement of food crops with cotton production across large areas of the countryside. As agricultural production, at least that part that served the market, tended toward monoculture, cotton began to provide a single commodity that could be taken to represent economic processes as a whole. In March 1910, an article in the second issue of the journal of the Society for Political Economy, *L'Egypte Contemporaine,* noted, "To study the economic situation in Egypt comes down to studying the agricultural situation, for the development of every branch of commerce and industry, the situation of the banks and property companies, in one word, the wealth of the country and its general prosperity, depends almost exclusively on the cotton crop and the price at which it is sold."[48] The importance acquired by cotton made possible a new kind of calculation. It made it possible to simplify and homogenize economic relations by representing their complexity in the form of a single commodity. Once again, the forms of calculation whose genealogy we are tracing did not emerge as a new representation of existing realities, but in new arrangements that would help simplify the world into reality and its calculation.

There were several other new arrangements that developed in this period related to the regime of private property and the monoculture of cotton, all mentioned in the passage just quoted: the new world of property companies, local and foreign banks, and commercial houses. These multiplied around the turn of the century and produced in turn a new kind of demand for statistical information. At the same time, their own activities provided a set of processes for such statistics to represent.

The joint stock company was a critical development. The Cairo bourse was founded in the 1890s to enable these companies to trade their shares and raise capital. By the early twentieth century it was one of the three or four most active stock exchanges in the world. The capital of joint stock companies established in Egypt or conducting their primary activities there doubled in two decades, it was reported, from £19,357,358 sterling in 1882 to £40,372,347 in 1902, and more than doubled again in just five years, to £92,617,219 in 1907.[49] Most of this capital was held by property development companies, involved in both rural land development and building and speculation in new urban neighborhoods of Cairo, and by mortgage companies (the latter accounted for £30 million sterling of the £52 million increase in capital from 1902 to 1905). So the proliferation of joint stock companies was connected with the new regime of private landed property and the growth of the metropolis.

Joint stock companies were a new kind of semipublic institution. Historically, it should be noted, the limited liability company was not a private institution that began to open its ownership to the public. It was a form of public institution taken over by private interests. Before the later nineteenth century, the legal privileges of corporate existence and limited liability were granted only for purposes that could be portrayed as a benefit to the public. In England limited liability corporations could be established only by an act of Parliament and were created for public works such as canal, railway, harbor, and bridge building, and above all for colonization.[50] The oldest and largest of the British colonizing corporations, the East India Company, had played an important role in producing the modern science of economics. Three leading nineteenth-century political economists, James Mill, Robert Malthus, and John Stuart Mill, spent their working lives as employees of the company, and after its nationalization and renaming as the India Office, as we know, it gave the most famous economist of the twentieth century his first employment. In Egypt from the 1890s, this form of public/private body also played a role in the generation of economic knowledge. It generated a new public of shareholders, and the managers and directors answerable to them, whose financial decisions required the publication of share prices, financial results, and other kinds of statistical information, as well as general information about the financial and political condition of the country.

The financial and commercial activities related to the economics of cotton production in the countryside, including investment and speculation in land, were imagined to have their location in the country's expanding cities of Cairo and Alexandria. Whatever the actual location of the cotton, the processing industries, the speculation, and the money, if these diverse materials and activities were imagined to have a single location, it was the city. In fact the idea of the city offered both a parallel and an alternative to landed property as a space that gave concrete and visual form to the new relations of wealth creation. Simmel's essay with which we began this chapter proposed a special relationship between "money economy" and the mental or cultural life of those who inhabit the large city. Prior to the making of the economy in its mid-twentieth-century meaning, the idea of the metropolis could be used in this way to imagine the density and tangibility of economic relations. In the formative decades of the professional social sciences, sociologists were preoccupied with the question of the city. It held a place later to be filled by the idea of the economy.

How was this density of the economic imagined? How were certain everyday transactions among people and things to become something as solid and tangible as "the economy"? How was the economy to be made into an object, something people would take to be real? Simmel's essay on the city suggests part of the answer. In the metropolis, Simmel wrote, ideas and values took on the appearance of objects. A dense built environment generated what he called "objective culture." Objective culture, or objective spirit, referred to the way in which ideas and values no longer seemed to reside within the individual, but to have migrated into the bodies of things. The institutions, buildings, and technologies of the city seemed to be more than just physical structures. They were themselves a form of "spirit" or "life." In the metropolis, "the development of modern culture is characterized by the preponderance of what one may call the 'objective spirit' over the 'subjective spirit,' " Simmel wrote.

> The individual has become a mere cog in an enormous organization of things and powers which tear from his hands all progress, spirituality, and value in order to transform them from their subjective form into the form of a purely objective life. It needs merely to be pointed out that the metropolis is the genuine arena of this culture which outgrows all personal life. Here in buildings and educational institutions, in the wonders and comforts of space-conquering technology, in the formations of community life, and in the visible institutions of the state, is offered such an overwhelming fullness of crystallized and impersonalized spirit that the personality, so to speak, cannot maintain itself under its impact.[51]

The terms of Simmel's argument sound strange today. We no longer talk of a world full of crystallized spirit (or rather, when we do we no longer use those words). The phrasing reflects Simmel's effort to describe "an enormous organization of things and powers," which had not yet been named "the economy." Yet this world already appeared to be dividing along the axis that would make it possible to fabricate the economy. It was a world of things and powers, a world in which the quality of being objectified belonged to ideas as well as things. Ideas and values no longer belonged to individuals, just as the measurements of the fields were no longer the property of village surveyors. New forms of architecture, engineering, science, schooling, statistical knowledge, finance, commerce, and government were ordering up a world in which buildings, educational establishments, technologies, commercial houses, and the "visible institutions of the state," in Simmel's phrase, presented to the individual what now looked like an "objective culture." The metropolis appeared divided into these two dimensions: on the one hand, its material fabric of buildings, institutions, and technologies, on the other the "crystallized spirit" that these new spaces and structures seemed to embody.[52]

For Simmel, this separation can be understood only as the result of an act of alienation. Ideas and values—the forms of "spirit" taking on an objective existence—must previously have resided within the individual, from whose hands, or mind, they have now been torn. There is no reason for us to subscribe to this thesis of alienation. No doubt this is how the new world was experienced, for it was a place increasingly organized to isolate and create a sense of lack or absence within the individual. It would be more reasonable to assume, however, that forms of ideality and value, the occurrence of the metaphysical and the meaningful, were always distributed much more widely in the world, never simply locked inside people's heads. The new "organization of things and powers"—the new institutions of government, architecture of the metropolis, and forms of money economy—like the new methods of the cadastral survey, were redistributing ideas and values in a simplified way, to manufacture the apparent separation of objects and values, things and powers. Only a world reorganized to generate this simple two-dimensional effect could give birth to the economy.

Another turn-of-the century development in Cairo, also connected with the property regime, the growth of the city, and land speculation, both enabled and demanded a new range of statistical information: the introduction of a single national currency and of paper money. The circulation of a national currency was to provide the critical means to imagine, and to format, the twentieth-century economy.

Mehmed Ali Pasha had introduced his own money system in 1834, based on a gold coin of one pound. But this coexisted with other Ottoman and European coins, many of which were no longer legal tender in Europe or traded at different values from their European value. An 1885 law refixed the value of the Egyptian pound and determined which other kinds of coin would be accepted in public accounts and at what value. Despite these reforms Egyptian pounds did not circulate in large quantities. The British preferred to deal in the gold coins (chiefly British sovereigns) that flowed into the country each year with the export of the cotton crop.[53] The situation began to change from 1898, however, when the statutes of the privately controlled National Bank of Egypt were approved, with the right to issue banknotes. The bank was required to cover half the value of the notes in circulation with reserves of gold. By 1914 there were only E£2.4 million in banknotes in circulation, but thereafter the volume rose rapidly, reaching E£12.65 million by the end of January 1916 and E£67 million by 1919.[54]

If the system of landed property brings into being a topographical space that defines the extension of economic processes, the cadastral survey translates this into a paper landscape, cotton production generates a simplified measure of the production and circulation of commodities, and the building of the metropolis provides a material expression of the intensity and expansion of exchange relations, paper currency plays another part in the formatting of social processes as an economy. The new money forms a system of circulation, one that somehow occurs both as the movement of wealth and its representation. It seems to work on two levels of representation. First, the notes themselves are a representation. They circulate as a system of financial signs that carry value because of the reserves of gold to which they refer. Second, since these signs are more mobile than the old forms of gold coinage, the volume of the notes moved and the velocity of their movement become themselves a system of signs. From 1914, the Ministry of Finance in Cairo began to publish statistical tables of credit and circulation. These showed figures for the annual circulation of banknotes since 1900, as well as the gold reserves and other deposits of the bank, together with data for the current year indicating the circulation of banknotes month by month. This picture of the circulation of money, the government suggested, could be used to measure the general activity of "the Egyptian market."[55] The following year it proposed that the same statistics be used as "a barometer of the financial situation of the country."[56]

When John Maynard Keynes began to write of an object called "the economy" in the 1930s, he introduced the term when searching for ways to account for the special nature of money, whose significance Walrasian theory had been unable to grasp. As we saw, these were issues that had preoccupied him since before World War I, when he tried to understand the peculiar problems of finance in colonial India. The statistical figures with whose help the economy was gradually constructed—national income (later called the gross national product), investment, savings, and money supply—were all measures of the movement of money from hand to hand within the nation. In its basic form, the economy was conceived as the sum of every occasion on which money changed hands. Since money works, as I just mentioned, on two levels of representation, once again we should not understand the emergence of the economy in terms of the distinction between new economic practices and their representation. The representational forms of money bring into being the new kinds of movement that will be figured as the economy. The separation of the economic from its representations is not a single line dividing the material world from a world of ideas, or the economy from economics. It is an uncertain difference established in multiple places within those practices that form the economy.

One more factor played a role in the production of the new object of knowledge, and indeed was an aspect of all of those already discussed: Egypt's colonial condition. Colonialism had helped institute the regime of private property and the monoculture of cotton; European-owned property companies and banks had driven the speculative growth of Cairo; large European financial houses owned the country's debt and had demanded the cadastral survey and the production of many other forms of statistical information; and European speculators were largely responsible for the growth of the stock market and the increasing circulation of paper money. Whether organized from Cairo or the European capitals, this colonial activity was the activity of outsiders, those for whom Egypt itself existed as an object of speculation, investment, government—and curiosity. Foreign investors and colonial administrators shared with visiting archaeologists and tourists an outsider's fascination with Egypt as a strange and unusual "case." *L'Egypte Contemporaine* welcomed the publication of the *Annuaire Statistique* in 1910, with its wealth of social facts, saying

> there are few countries where some of these facts present themselves with a relief as striking, sometimes also as strange, as in Egypt. Her situation and geographical particularities, the character of her present activity, the diversity of races that live there, make Egypt interesting not only to the archaeologist and tourist. It is also, for the economists and sociologists of all countries, one of the most fascinating crossroads of the modern world.[57]

I suggested earlier that Keynes's experience in the problems of colonial financial administration may have been significant in the later development of his work. Colonialism opened up a distance, a space of separation, a relationship of curiosity, that made it possible to see something as "a case," a self-contained object whose "problems" could be measured, analyzed, and addressed by a form of knowledge that appears to stand outside the object and grasp it in its entirety.

This colonial relationship with India or Egypt as a peculiar social and economic case was gradually supplemented by an increasing demand from the major powers and the international organizations they established for statistical information making every country in the world comparable. Some of this demand goes back to the late nineteenth century. The establishing of the country's first Bureau de Statistique in 1870 directly followed the khedive's visit to the Exposition Universelle in Paris, where the presentation of statistical data on each country in the world was one of the organizing principles of the exhibition.[58] The *Statistique de l'Egypte* published for three years (1870–72) by E. de Regny, the Frenchman appointed to head the bureau, presented material modeled on that of the world exhibitions. It was collected not for internal administrative purposes but to present at future exhibitions, beginning with the Vienna World Exhibition.[59]

In the twentieth century the international demand for countries to produce statistical representations of themselves became more frequent and systematic. In 1922 the new International Labour Office in Geneva asked member states to compile national figures on population movement. The International Institute of Agriculture in Rome, forerunner of the FAO, organized world agricultural censuses in 1929 and 1939, which were the reason for the only surveys of this sort that Egypt carried out in the interwar period. The Middle East Financial Conference, convened in Cairo by Britain and the United States in 1944, called on governments in the region to collect and publish accurate banking statistics, showing all debits to current accounts, so that "changes in the velocity of circulation of bank deposits can be kept fully under review as an indicator of the volume of business activity."[60] It called for bank balance sheets to be published in the standard form drawn up by the League of Nations in 1934, and for improved statistics on balance of payments. The conference also called for the compilation of statistics on national income and output, and proposed that countries send staff to be trained in this new statistical practice in London or Washington, so that the accounts would be produced in a uniform (and Anglo-American) way.[61] In response to this proposal, following the war the Egyptian Ministry of Finance sent an employee to complete a doctorate at the University of London, where he produced as his thesis the first systematic study of Egypt's national income.[62]

Landed property, cotton production, joint stock companies, the speculative growth of Cairo's built environment, and the increasingly rapid circulation of money provided a series of processes that constituted new fields of social and economic calculation. Colonialism provided an effect of separation, like that between the village and the survey office, that helped establish this space of calculability as an object. The fields of calculation contributed to their own "objectivation" by collecting and putting into circulation the statistical information on which they depended. In 1905, the government set up a Statistics Office, which published its first *Annuaire Statistique* (Statistical Yearbook) in 1909.[63] The statistics service was initially an office within the Survey Department, which was part of the Ministry of Finance. The location was partly a practical matter. As the cadastral survey reached completion in 1907, some of its personnel became available for other kinds of statistical work.[64] But it also reflected the continuity between the statistical work of the survey and the emergence of a new kind of economic calculation within the country. In 1911 the Statistics Office became a department of its own within the Ministry of Finance. The statistics that the government produced, moreover, were made available by a new method of circulation. The statistics published in the early years of the *Annuaire Statistique* represented information that ministries and other public bodies had already been collecting on activities such as the railways, the cotton trade, and import duties, much of it assembled on the orders of foreign creditors who had been allotted the income from these sources. The Department of Statistics lacked the resources to conduct large-scale studies of its own, and no legislation was provided to compel public or private bodies to supply it with information. Nor did it benefit from any system of local government, or local business or agricultural syndicates, as found in many parts of Europe, engaged in their own collection of data on which the central statistics office could draw. In its early years, therefore, the Statistics Office was largely restricted to the role of obtaining information collected internally by other government departments, by the customs and excise authority, by public bodies such as the railways, telegraphs, and telephone, and by shipping and other joint-stock companies. This information was gathered together and published as the *Annuaire Statistique.*

What characterized this new statistical process, therefore, was not the collecting of such information so much as the act of making it public. On the eve of his retirement as director of the Statistics Department in 1924, I. G. Lévi noted that the department

> each year puts into print at least 7,800 manuscript pages of figures, amounting to more than three million numbers per year or 10,000 numbers per day, which it must calculate, register, verify, and transcribe! It prints in its offices some 11,000 reports and has 32,000 books or pamphlets distributed by the press each year. It receives, reads, and files a little under one million documents per year, sends more than 6,000 letters, and receives 10,000.[65]

Statistics were no longer just to serve the administrative needs of the individual departments or organizations that collected them. They were to be put together and circulated, partly for the benefit of other departments of the state and partly for making arguments to the political powers in the metropole, but also for a new kind of user—the public. In the same way, the new Société d'Economie Politique declared that its role was to study questions of political economy, statistics, and legislation, "for the instruction not only of its members but also of the public."[66] The *Annuaire Statistique* was published partly to meet this same demand. *L'Egypte Contemporaine* welcomed the *Annuaire* as "the essential foundation for all economic and social study relating to Egypt." It added that such studies were important not only for residents of the country but "for so many others who have sent their capital there or conduct commercial relations with it, and follow anxiously from outside the fluctuations of its wealth and of its economic progress."[67] The statistical information, as this suggests, did not simply represent a preexisting sphere of economic activity. It helped to bring this sphere, with its anxious participants, into being.

This new concern, not just to collect statistical data but to have it in regular circulation among "the public," seems to distinguish the use of statistics in the twentieth century from earlier practices, at least in the case of Egypt. Colonial powers had long made use of statistics, whether for administrative needs or to produce a larger "illusion of bureaucratic control."[68] Toward the end of World War I, as Britain and other colonial powers faced a harder task in justifying the continuation of colonial occupation, new statistical work could clarify the purpose and authority of imperial government.[69] But the circulation of statistics among a "public," like the newly visible circulation of currency, enabled them to take on the form of an "objective culture," something with a solidity or substance of its own. One could begin to conceive of the gap that seems to set this circulating body of information apart from the processes and activities it refers to. The gap appears as a divide between two worlds, a sphere of figures, numbers, facts, and trends on the one side, and the world to which these refer on the other. The latter must stand as its opposite, the realm of the material, the real.

At this point, in the early decades of the twentieth century, there was no single term for this realm. Writings I have already quoted indicate the variety of phrases used to invoke the object to which this emerging sphere of representation referred. The phrase "the Egyptian market" was used occasionally, although the term "market" did not have the abstract force it would take on at the end of the twentieth century. "The wealth of the country and its general prosperity," the "social condition and general economics of the country," its "wealth and economic progress," and its "economic situation" were among the other expressions writers used. Just as often they invoked phrases like the one that launched *L'Egypte Contemporaine*, "the problems of national life."[70] The *Annuaire Statistique* of 1914, which was twice the length of earlier volumes and introduced the use of graphs and introductory essays summarizing the statistical picture, suggested that these "taken together form a summary of the general situation of the country and show the progress of each of the branches of its activity."[71] The word economy itself was not used in any of these senses: in English, French, and Arabic it still carried the older meaning of management or the conserving and rational use of resources, and it did not necessarily refer to what were now sometimes called "economic" issues. The Société d'Economie Politique divided its activities into three sections, which it termed the Section de Legislation, the Section d'Economie Politique (later adding "et Statistique"), and the Section d'Economie Sociale.[72] Social economy and political economy were terms referring to the sound government or arrangement of affairs, not to "the economy" as an object or sphere.

Even a generation later, toward the end of World War II, the use of the word "economy" to indicate something that could be managed and made to grow was an Anglo-American neologism that did not always survive translation into French and Arabic. In 1944 the Middle East Financial Conference published policy recommendations to enable Middle Eastern countries after the war "to expand their economies." The French translation rendered this phrase as *"de renforcer leur economie"* and the Arabic as *"tanmiyat quwaha al-iqtisadiyya"* (to develop their economic forces).[73] Within a few years, however, the term economy was widely used in Arabic, but almost always in phrases such as "the national economy" (*al-iqtisad al-qawmi*) rather than standing alone. In 1950 the Statistical Department, along with the State Domains Administration, the Fisheries Service, and the Department of Tourism, were joined together to form the Ministry of National Economy (still without a definite article in the English translation).[74] In December of the same year, the country's leading newspaper, *al-Ahram,* began to publish its business supplement as a separate monthly magazine. Initially it kept the old name, *al-Ahram fi khidmat al-tijara wa-ʾl-sinaʿa* (al-Ahram in the Service of Commerce and Industry). A year later, expanded in size, it added beneath this title the motto "A monthly magazine dealing with affairs of the national economy." Two years later, following the July 1952 military coup, it changed its name to *al-Ahram al-iqtisadi.* The lead story of its first issue following the coup was headlined "The national economy in the new era."[75]

READING DIFFICULTIES

Producing this new object of calculation was not an easy process. The difficulty lay in a particular feature of the way the new statistical practices emerged. I have described some of the processes that defined the space of economic and social relations and gave them a movement and circulation that could be measured. But these same processes giving rise to a character of calculability created other effects that undermined the fixed and measurable nature of such relations. Private property, monoculture, the stock exchange, paper currency, and colonial power all began to contribute to forms of movement, instability, and crisis that destabilized the process of making a world of calculation.

The difficulties can be seen with particular clarity in the cadastral survey. Lyons noted that "the country is ever becoming more densely populated and every portion of the cultivable land is being reclaimed as fast as circumstances admit." The maps could not keep pace with the changes, and they themselves became overcrowded and "confusing to read." The difficulty was compounded, Lyons felt, by the fact that maps were annotated in Arabic, which, he believed, "does not possess the numerous different types of letters that are available in European writing."[76] Further difficulties arose from the tiny size of the plots: in 1907 40 percent of holdings were under half an acre and 90 percent under five acres, a fragmentation increasing as more land was concentrated into larger estates, leaving the majority of the rural population less and less to share.[77]

Difficulties also arose from the fact that the surveyors were attempting to map not just what was changing, but something contested. The incorporation of land into large estates had exacerbated the problem of boundary disputes. Lyons admitted that where title to the land was unclear, or where encroachment may have occurred, big landowners tended to win out. In the last four years of the survey, the government received 42,962 complaints about inaccuracies in the recording of property boundaries. Some three thousand of these were acknowledged to result from incorrect measurement, but 39,073 were declared unfounded.[78] Through such declarations, inscribed onto the map, the arbitrariness of the large estates was to be erased. The villagers had no means of appeal, but evidently they developed their own response. At the completion of the survey the government acknowledged the problems of inaccuracy and noted that the third- and fourth-order triangulation, which relied on triangulation points placed within the cultivated area, would have to be redone. It had been impossible to establish permanent points. This was due in part to the character of agriculture in the Nile valley, in which every meter of available land was cultivated and the borders of plots were marked only by irrigation ditches, redug after each flooding or ploughing. There were no hedges or other permanent features marking plot boundaries, which might be used to establish survey points. But it was also due to the fact that the large stones and lengths of angle iron used as survey points were frequently lost, sometimes by accident but "more often by wilful interference."[79] In some cases villagers assumed they were boundary markers, and quite sensibly moved them to the edges of their plots. They also found them useful to employ as building materials, or as levers and weights for the irrigation machines they now required to lift canal water into their fields.[80]

A related source of difficulty was that reorganizing the control of agriculture according to a system of permanent property rights did not stabilize the countryside, despite the new system that identified each plot of land and tied it to a named owner. On the contrary, as we saw in the previous chapter, private property rights led directly to a process of eviction and dispossession of small owners and tenants through debt foreclosure and other mechanisms. By the turn of the century the evictions reached a point of crisis. In 1912 the government was forced to introduce rules to limit the disruption, preventing the eviction of holders of less than five acres or the seizure of their houses, essential farm implements, and working animals. Despite the law, the problem of landlessness continued to grow, producing an ever-larger population of mobile workers and temporary or permanent migrants. This unfixing of the population from the land through the system of private property made subsequent efforts at census taking or the measurement of agricultural income increasingly difficult. By 1950 there was still not even an approximate statistical measure of the size of the landless agricultural labor force. The agricultural censuses of 1929 and 1939 made no attempt to include a survey of the seasonal and migrant work force.[81] A study published in 1950 tried two different methods of estimating the size (and the income) of the agricultural labor force. One method produced a total about 40 percent higher than the other, and there was no way of deciding between the two figures.[82]

Another set of problems resulted from the ever-wider cultivation of cotton, as excessive cropping and perennial irrigation caused a series of difficulties. In the first decade of the twentieth century the crop suffered from increasing infestation by the cotton worm, forcing emergency legislation in 1905 to draft every boy between the age of ten and eighteen from agricultural households into compulsory labor in the fields, to remove and burn the infested leaves (boys who refused to be drafted could be imprisoned for up to a week). With no annual flood to fertilize and drain the fields, the soil became poorer and more saline. Crop yields began to decline rapidly, dropping by almost 50 percent from 5.8 *qantars* (hundredweight) of cotton per acre in 1897 to 3.25 in 1909. To compound the problem there were rapid swings in the price of cotton, from year to year and month to month, producing serious difficulties and sometimes crisis.[83] The Cotton Commission was set up in 1908 to establish causes for the declining yields but found its work hampered by the lack of accurate statistics on areas planted and yields. This prompted the Survey Department to publish the *Collection of Statistics of the Area Planted in Cotton in 1909,* which analyzed the accuracy of the data on cultivated areas provided by the village *sarraf* or tax official. Ernest Dowson, who had succeeded Henry Lyons as director-general of the Survey Department, proposed to improve the reporting by the *sarrafs* and the interpretation of their reports, in particular by identifying the fields planted with cotton on the Survey Department's new maps. It was hoped in this way to turn taxation statistics into a source of more general agricultural information, which could be used to address the problems of cotton production.[84] In 1910, on the recommendation of the Cotton Commission, the British administration agreed to a long-standing demand to establish a Department of Agriculture, to coordinate efforts to stem the decline in cotton yields.[85]

Similar problems affected the stock market and the new national currency. It used to be thought that the standardization of national currencies made money into a more homogenous, controllable, and therefore countable measure of collective wealth. Simmel's fear that "money economy" was "transforming the world into an arithmetical problem" became the common view of the homogenizing effects of the new money.[86] Yet as Zelizer shows in the case of the United States, the standardization of legal forms of money was typically accompanied by a proliferation of other kinds of monies—multiple forms of credit, coupons, tokens, shares, checks, savings schemes, and other varieties of currency, both official and unofficial—which made the circulation and measure of wealth no less heterogenous than before.[87] The possibility of calculating the "velocity of money" arrived and disappeared at the same time.

In addition, the speed and volume of circulation even of official forms of currency and wealth produced its own crises. In 1911 the new stock market crashed, forcing dozens of companies into bankruptcy. The *Annuaire Statistique,* which had prided itself on its increasingly detailed reporting of the activities of joint stock companies, was unable that year to publish any statistics relating to the stock market. Due to "the crisis," it reported, too many companies had disappeared, merged with others, or been re-formed. The printing of paper money also led to crisis. First there was the surge in prices, especially in the first decade of the century, which resulted in several attempts to develop explanations of the phenomenon. The most popular was to blame it on the abolition of the *octroi* (the tax on commodities brought into the town from the countryside for sale), which was eliminated from the last two towns, Cairo and Alexandria, at the start of 1903. Yacoub Artin's "Essai sur les causes du renchérissement de la vie matérielle au Caire" (1908) dismissed this explanation, and produced copious data relating the price inflation to the general increase in population, production, trade, and the size of cities over the preceding decades.[88] This was very much an explanation in terms of nineteenth-century political economy: the problems caused by paper currency itself, although affecting everyone, were not yet visible to economic analysis. The situation worsened during World War I, when the government quietly ignored its own rule that the printing of money had to be backed by reserves of gold covering 50 percent of its value. The supply of banknotes increased rapidly during the war, as I mentioned, and the increase was backed by British treasury bonds instead of gold. By 1919, when E£67 million in banknotes were in circulation, gold reserves were down to E£3.33 million, or less than 5 percent. Britain had taken the rest of Egypt's gold to finance the wartime Arab Revolt against the Ottomans. As a result, the Egyptian pound was forced off the gold standard onto a "sterling exchange standard," exposing the country to all the crises that sterling faced in the interwar period.

This range of crises and inexplicable developments made the continuing work of the Statistics Department both more necessary and more difficult. The volatility of economic events made the collection of data more arduous and unreliable. At the same time, the economic crises often deprived the department of the resources or personnel required to collect the information that such crises seemed to demand. There were several attempts to introduce the surveying of prices and to measure the new concept of "cost of living." The first effort, in 1914, had to be abandoned because the outbreak of war made prices so unstable that they could not be reliably measured. After the war, in 1921, T. L. Bennett, controller of the Statistics Department, managed to compile a survey of consumer prices. But the effort to make this an annual exercise failed when the following year Bennett suffered a "deplorable accident."[89] Subsequently the office lacked the resources to continue his work.

Efforts to measure the movement of commerce and population faced similar difficulties. There were good statistics on the export and import of commodities. Giuseppe Randone, a protégé of the famous Italian statistician Luigi Bodio, had been brought to Egypt to help organize the 1882 census and then set up and ran a statistics office for foreign trade within the Alexandria customs office, before becoming the first director of the Central Statistics Office in 1905.[90] The system of reporting and classifying imports and exports that he set up in Alexandria became a model for other countries. But it did not work elsewhere in Egypt. In 1913 an attempt was made to reproduce a similar system for internal commerce, by carrying out what was intended to be an annual survey of river navigation on the Nile. The attempt was abandoned when the ports and ship owners refused to supply adequate information. Another effort was made to survey this information in 1928, but it was only partially successful.

Much more difficult was the attempt to measure the invisible part of foreign trade, the import and export of capital. A 1910 report listed the following obstacles: the "fictitious circulation" created by banks and commercial houses, which was completely unmeasurable; the impossibility of establishing the value of the credit notes created for the import and export of commodities; tourist expenses paid by checks, letters of credit, and foreign banknotes; letters of credit or checks issued to Egyptians who summered in Europe; payments for the army of occupation; profits or losses of Egyptian speculators in foreign stock exchanges; fees paid by ships in port or transiting the Suez Canal, or for the loading of coal; rent and investment income of foreigners resident in Egypt; and rents, interest, and profit on foreign capital invested in Egypt, especially in banks and joint stock companies.[91] Note that every one of these obstacles relates to the colonial situation of Egypt.

Similar difficulties existed in establishing the movement of the population into and out of Egypt. Passports were introduced after World War I, but were used to record only arrivals, not departures. In 1922, as I mentioned, the International Labour Office in Geneva asked member states to compile national figures on population movement in order to establish currents of international migration. The Statistics Department eventually persuaded the passport office to introduce a system of passport cards that would match arrivals and departures, but the effort was derailed by the slump of 1929. The measurement of population movements was not resumed until during or after World War II.

The measurement of personal and company income was also very slow to be established, and once again the colonial situation was part of the reason. Prior to 1936, foreigners resident in Egypt were under the jurisdiction of their own governments rather than the government of Egypt. The foreign governments refused to agree to the imposition of an income tax, so income tax was not introduced until 1939. This meant that there was no requirement for individuals or companies to report annual income, or to organize their financial affairs as a yearly system of income and expenses. Even joint stock companies, which did publish annual figures, followed no uniform method of accounting, so incomes of different companies were not comparable. In the countryside, there was no systematic attempt to measure agricultural income until 1942. This effort was undertaken in response to the wartime crisis of food supply, discussed in chapter 1. But the crisis led to the introduction of crop controls and rationing and dramatic shifts in the crops grown and in prices. There was no reliable way to measure income in the midst of such disruption, so the attempt had to be abandoned.

These problems made it impossible to calculate in any convincing manner the country's total "national income," despite recent attempts to narrow the meaning of this term and transform it into a concept that could be represented statistically. In 1922 A. L. Bowley published an article in the *Economic Journal* in London entitled "The Definition of National Income." He proposed that the term be defined to include only monetary income, thus excluding, for example, "the value of women's domestic services," or the annual value of using one's clothes, furniture, or motorcar. Even so, he acknowledged, it would be many years before methods of calculating national income were feasible, especially given the financial distortions caused by the war.[92] Later that year, however, I. G. Lévi, the director of the Statistics Department, published the first attempt to estimate a national income for Egypt.[93] The attempt coincided with Egypt's formal independence from Britain and had a directly political purpose: to argue that the country's national income was much higher than the British had believed, and that it therefore possessed the resources to embark on a program of industrialization, to which Britain was opposed. (Lévi went on to become the head of the Egyptian Federation of Industries.) Yet there was no agreement on how to calculate the total. British statisticians accused Lévi of overestimating national income by 50 percent, in particular because his accounting method failed to deduct many of the expenses incurred in the production of income, especially in agriculture.[94]

The political rivalry in the production of economic statistics was not an isolated incident. Indeed the entire history of statistics in the early decades of the twentieth century was caught up in the struggle between Egypt and Britain, with France and other European powers often intervening against the British. The founding of the Société d'Economie Politique in 1909 was directly supported by the French government, which paid for a French political economist, Germain Martin, to spend six months in Egypt helping to organize the association and establish its journal.[95] The initiative was connected with the founding of the first Egyptian national university the year before, which the British attempted to block and refused to give financial support.

Such political rivalry was an aspect of a more general set of factors affecting the growth of statistical knowledge. The European colonization of Egypt made the very economic facts that statistics wished to fix far more elusive and difficult to define. The fluid movement of capital and population, the multiplicity of languages and jurisdictions, and the legal privileges and prerogatives enjoyed by foreign communities in Egypt made it enormously difficult to represent the country as a singular, national economy. Consider the problems faced by what might seem the relatively straightforward process of counting the inhabitants of the country. The 1917 census, said to be the first reliable enumeration of the population, was carefully scheduled for the month of May, the only period when the population was thought to be in its "normal state." It was the only month in which there were no foreign tourists, movements of agricultural laborers, summer exodus to Europe, or major popular feasts. The census still had to deal with the displacements of labor and restrictions on movement imposed by the war and the large army of occupation.[96] And although the census was planned to capture the entire population on a single day, in fact it took two weeks to conduct. In addition, those responsible described the following difficulties that they faced:

> 1. Illiteracy rates of 86.3 percent for men and 97.9 percent for women, making it necessary for the census agents to fill in the forms themselves—but among the Muslim population (91.4 percent), the agents were forbidden access to the home.
> 2. The population's "inveterate suspicion of all demands for information coming from the government" (despite a public campaign to convince them of its innocent purpose).
> 3. The population's opposition to putting on paper any information relating to their economic situation, or the ages or even names of boys.
> 4. The political situation in which "one part of the population, the natives, detests the government and the other part, the foreign colonies, consider themselves to form little states within the state and do not readily acknowledge the right of the local Administration to interfere in their affairs without the permission of their diplomatic representatives."
> 5. The absence of a definition of Egyptian nationality, with Greek, Ottoman, and Persian subjects rarely declaring their true nationality, "in order to hold open the door of declaring another nationality in case of need."

6. The considerable number of homeless people living on the streets of the cities.

7. Minor officials in the provinces who have the habit of not discussing orders from the central government, even to ask for an explanation to ensure a better execution, "leading to illogical actions and dangerously liberal interpretations."

8. The "absence or frequent changing of street names, formation of new villages, division of these or transfer from one administrative district to another, the absence of numbers on buildings and maps of towns."

9. The presence of a large nomadic population on the outskirts of certain provinces, "so unapproachable and fiercely jealous of their independence that ordinary census methods could not be applied."

10. The multiplicity of languages spoken and the confusion of different nationalities and races, often in the same buildings and residential quarters, "so that census agents must be accomplished polyglots and full of tact to accomplish their task."

11. The circumstances in paragraphs (4) and (10) required the use of numerous languages in both the questions and replies, demanding educated, professional decipherers.

12. The Europeans who directed the census, lacking close contact with the natives, were liable to "overlook in the Arabic versions improper expressions that may influence the results."[97]

These were the disruptions and displacements that resulted from the colonial situation: the confusion of jurisdictions, languages, and races, the absence or illegibility of street names and numbers, the formation of new villages and shifting of their boundaries, and the persistent threat of improper decipherment and translation. Native officials in the provinces, operating at a distance from the European authorities in Cairo, made "dangerously liberal interpretations." Europeans at the center, distanced from the natives, were unable to keep out the improper expressions that contaminated the Arabic texts and distorted the results.

Attempts to calculate the country's national income faced a similar range of difficulties. Following I. G. Lévi's much criticized attempt in 1922–23, the first comprehensive calculation was *A Study of the National Income of Egypt*, the doctoral thesis published by Mahmoud Amin Anise in 1950. The author depended for his calculations on whatever existing statistical information was available, including the population census (with all its problems) and a variety of partial surveys of various aspects of production, prices, and incomes, each relating to different years and different parts of the country. He also faced the difficulties of Egypt's particular position in relation not to the colonial powers but what were now called other "national economies," from which, despite the new terminology, it was not exactly separate. "One of the peculiarities of the Egyptian economy," the author explained, "is its cosmopolitan [sic] and to a certain extent its dependence on foreign capital and technical knowledge. In answering the question whose income we are attempting to measure I was not completely satisfied."[98] Industry and commerce, he pointed out, had been developed mostly by foreign capital or by foreigners resident in Egypt. He decided to define national income as income accruing to any resident of the country, whether a national or foreigner. But his income totals for the country also included profits and dividends going abroad.

The problems of measuring the size of the agricultural workforce have already been mentioned, one method of estimating producing a figure between 30 and 40 percent higher than another method, with the result that measures of agricultural income were a complete guess. Industrial income was similarly difficult to estimate, in part because most establishments did not keep annual accounts. Most businesses classified as manufacturing were in fact engaged in repair work, another reflection of the colonial situation, making it impossible to calculate the proper value of raw materials and output.

A further problem was that international organizations now demanded that statistics be measured and presented in standardized forms, so that comparison was possible from one country to the next. In practice the standard form was usually based on the social and economic arrangements found in the West.[99] For example, the agricultural census was to be organized as a study of "farms." These were the units to be counted and measured and by which the animals, crops, workers, and machinery were to be enumerated. Most agricultural households in Egypt worked dispersed fragments of land that were not organized as farms, and many held machinery or animals in partnership. Large estates, on the other hand, were more than farms, as we have seen, and were operated as "private villages." For this reason many aspects of the census were impossible to apply. Such standardization reproduced on the international level a process of homogenization and averaging that is a characteristic of statistical work in general.

Although colonialism provided an impetus and field for the development of statistical and economic knowledge, the stabilization of this knowledge as the "national economy" would not be possible until the era of the nation-state—and indeed would be part of the constitution of that transient era.

By mid-century, in Egypt as in many other places, politics had acquired a new object. The economy had come into being as a sphere that could be measured, managed, developed, analyzed, restructured, and compared. I have traced some of the practices that helped form the economy, involving a range of processes from mapping and statistics to property, law, agricultural transformation, and colonial power. The mixture and form of these processes would vary, of course, in other places, but the details of what happened in Egypt can enable us to look more closely at what occurred. I have also traced the "reading difficulties" that arose. There are four things we can learn from these events about the making of the economy.

First, although economic and statistical practice will claim, like Lyons, to map this sphere with great precision, we should notice what those involved actually do. They are often very careful and precise, and they always stress the accuracy of their work. But we should not be misled by their claims into thinking that the novelty and usefulness of this knowledge lay in its accuracy. Once more the cadastral survey can illuminate the point. As we saw, the attraction of the use of mapping was that from now on information about landholding would be contained on the map. To calculate the area of a holding it was no longer necessary to measure with rods or chains on the ground. Thanks to the accuracy of the map, one could read the measurement from the surface of the map. The site of control and calculation had been transplanted from the field to the office.

Yet this calculation from the map was very difficult. There was a problem of shrinkage, as the moisture in the map paper dried out. Even after drying the paper for three weeks prior to drawing the map, the surveyors had to include a calculation for shrinkage of the paper when calculating the area of an individual plot from the map.[100] But the larger problem was how to calculate this area in the first place. No plot was perfectly regular, so measuring the sides alone from the map would not work. To solve the difficulty, the surveyors introduced a device developed by the Revenue Survey of India, which they called the feddan comb. This consisted of a small frame made of stiff cardboard, 21 × 17 centimeters (about the size of this page), with dots printed through the card at 5 millimeter intervals along the long sides through which fine black threads ran in parallel lines from side to side, dividing the area within the frame into strips 5 millimeters in width. When placed over the map, the threads divided a plot into strips whose breadth corresponded to 12.5 meters on the ground. The surveyor used a pair of dividers to measure the length of each strip, stepping out the dividers to read off each measurement against a translation scale printed on the border of the card. The sum of these measurements gave the area of a plot.[101] The method was ingenious but far from accurate. "The weak point about the feddan comb," Lyons acknowledged, "is that it is almost impossible to keep the threads tight and parallel. Further, to thread them through the exact positions is difficult and the dots are not always placed at the correct distance apart, which may be due to shrinkage of the cardboard after printing."[102] The shrinkage of the cardboard, the shrinkage of the map paper, the inaccurate placing of the dots, and the difficulty in holding the threads tight and parallel meant that it would not, after all, be possible to measure landholdings and determine tax liabilities directly from the map.

The cardboard frame illuminates an important aspect of the making of expertise in the twentieth century. The new statistical methods did not generate a more accurate knowledge, or even a greater amount of knowledge. Captain Lyons was forced to admit that after ten years of work, the survey had produced a knowledge of the area of each landholding that was less precise than before. Although he criticized the old Coptic rules of arithmetic—while admitting the rules were accurate enough when plots were not too far out of square, and in fact most plots were relatively square—his own methods resulted in a less reliable calculation. What the survey accomplished was a series of removals, of transferences, that tried to shift the site where calculation would occur. In place of the village surveyor walking with his rod along the boundaries of each plot, the employee in the survey office would walk his dividers across the feddan comb, stepping them backwards and forwards from the threads to the scale.

The problem of accuracy was not specific to the survey or the difficulties of drawing maps. Similar difficulties arose with other forms of knowledge. The new statistics on the price of cotton, for example, represented an approximation. The farmer may well have had a more accurate knowledge of the cotton price. He knew it from day to day, in his locality, for the variety of seed he grew, among the particular merchants with whom he had to deal. The figures collected in the statistical yearbook, or even the weekly prices published by the Ministry of Agriculture, were not the price of any particular cotton, or of all the different cottons at all the different places cotton was sold. Likewise, as we just saw, the agricultural census organized information in terms of "farms," a simplification that could never accommodate the forms of knowledge and relationship that constituted the world of the countryside. Here, too, one might say, there were shrinkage problems. Once again, the statistical knowledge cannot be said to be a more accurate knowledge, or even a greater amount of knowledge. Instead, it represents a reformatted knowledge, information that has been translated, moved, shrunk, simplified, redrawn. What is new is the site, and the forms of calculation and decision that can take place at this new site.

The second point follows from this act of removal: the new forms of economic and statistical knowledge did not stand in relation to the economy in the simple relation of a representation to reality, the way a map is thought to represent the real world. And yet this is how it would appear. The removal and concentration of knowledge into new sites opened up a distance, a gap that came to seem an absolute divide. The movement from the field to the survey office was not to be experienced as a chain of social practices, but as the distance between reality and its representation, between the material and the abstract, between the real world and the map.

This is a point we have encountered in different ways already, in discussions of the making of the Aswan Dam, for example, of the concentration of property claims into the rules of law, or Simmel's experience of the metropolis as a world of objectified culture. Both the old system of surveying and the new involved a variety of social practices, every one of which might be thought of as a mixture of action and thought, measurement and calculation, object and idea, thing and value, reality and representation. The village surveyor might read off distances with his rod and chain, clean off a boundary mark with his foot, write down measurements in his register, argue with the owner of the next plot, and report alterations to the tax office. All these processes involved mixtures of what are called real and representation, thing and value, or object and idea. In fact it would be impossible to hold them apart according to such a distinction. In the same way the mapmaker, holding the feddan comb in one hand, trying to keep the cardboard flat and its threads taut, walking the pair of dividers with the other hand, making sure its point does not slip as he reads the measurement off the scale, cursing the heat that has shrunk his paper, and trying to prevent the whole sheet lifting into the air under the ceiling fans whirling above his head, is involved in as much a practical activity as a mental one, dealing with an object as much as a representation. Saussure, the famous theorist of linguistic representation, describes the difference between an idea or representation and the material that represents it as no more than the difference between two sides of the same sheet of paper. For the mapmaker the difference is even less, and that is exactly the source of his difficulty. The dimensions of the paper are a representation, the signifier of a certain distance on the ground. But the size of the paper, the distance from one pen mark to another, is also a distance "on the ground," or at least on the table, a real distance, and one that will not stay still. He cannot keep reality out of his representation.

Our world is made up of technical bodies, hybrids that are neither wholly objects nor ideas, more than just things but not disembodied spirits (hence appearing as crystallized spirit), not properly divisible into nature and culture, or reality and representation. The clerks in the survey office converted theodolite and chain readings from the field into distances to be drawn on the map. Their computational labor was divided up and correlated to form "an almost mechanical system," something close to a piece of machinery. A calculating apparatus, made out of men, had the mechanical powers of a computer. Like all computers, it was a mixture of hardware and software. But at the same time, the new world of modern politics is organized to manufacture the effect that this difficult, unstable, temporary distinction between hard and soft, physical and mental, real and representational, is a permanent, fundamental, and ontological divide. The map presents itself as a mere representation, an idea or abstraction, set apart from the real, fixed, physical reality it depicts. It erases and hides the contested, political, representational nature of the world it portrays, in the same action with which it denies its own (shrinking) physicality. The mechanical organization of labor, the movement from the field to the office, the repeated accounts of the precision and accuracy of the work, all operate together to produce the effect of a bifurcated world. It is as such an effect that the economy is brought into being.

Third, it is these processes of organization, movement, reformulation, and exclusion that set up the economy as a new sphere of calculability. The making of the economy, it follows, does not lie outside the forms of knowledge that enable statistics and economics to know it.[103] Another example—the introduction of price barometers—can illustrate this. In July 1910, I. G. Lévi and Germain Martin pointed out that "while for the theoreticians of economic equilibrium a market consists of the fixity of prices, at a given moment, for a quantity of products of the same type and of the same quality, in Egypt prices vary in relation to certain commodities from place to place, beyond the costs of movement and transportation, especially in the villages." The price variation can be found, they pointed out, even between villages only a few kilometers apart. To remedy the anomaly, they proposed the publication of price barometers in all the villages of Egypt, listing the current prices of commodities in nearby towns.[104] This simple proposal illustrates the method of constituting the economy. It is repeated in the work of the surveyors. They found rural property relations contested, the subject of multiple claims, agrarian transformations, and violent histories. Their response was not to record these multiple claims and histories of violence on the map, but to help format the world they surveyed, dividing it into fields and plots, determining ownership, naming estates as villages, marking boundaries, and rejecting appeals for adjustment. Lévi and Martin found forms of social practice that did not correspond to the abstract theories of the market. Their answer was not to alter the theory, to take more accurate account of what happens, but to propose an alteration to what happens, to bring it closer to the simpler practice of theory. Expert knowledge works to format social relations, never simply to report or picture them.

The economic historian Karl Polanyi is remembered for his argument that the modern world was formed in the "Great Transformation" of the nineteenth century, in which market relations became disembedded from the wider social ties in which they were previously contained.[105] The separation of economic ties from other forms of social practice that had previously governed and limited them, he argued, gave rise to the self-regulating market economy (which quickly proved itself incapable of its own regulation). *The Great Transformation*, published in 1944, was one of the most influential works to depict the construction of "the economy" as a separate sphere in the nineteenth century. It can be reread today, however, not just as an account of nineteenth-century European history, but on another level as one more contribution to the twentieth-century production of the economy. The event that Polanyi projects back onto the nineteenth century, the emergence of the economy as a separate sphere, was in fact realized only in the mid-twentieth century. And theoretical essays such as Polanyi's wartime writing were part of this work of production. The economy came into being not by disembedding market relations from a larger social ground that previously contained them, but by embedding certain twentieth-century practices of calculation, description, and enumeration in new forms of intellectual, calculating, regulatory, and governmental practice. The economy, in Callon's phrase, is embedded in economics, and in social theory, in colonial administration, in national income accounting, and in all the other practical activities of mid-twentieth-century social life that formatted, shaped, and made the new field of national politics.

Finally, it should be recalled, this attempt at formatting, at relocating the site where calculations occur in the uniform space of a national economy, was not successful. As we have seen, the forms of social practice that gave rise to the new kinds of calculability, and that calculation attempted to format, also continually rendered the world more mobile, uncertain, and incalculable. The surveyors' map presented itself as a picture of a reality on the ground. But that reality "on the ground" did not stay out there, it entered into the making of the map—not only in the problems of shrinkage, but in everything from the moving of survey marks and the disputing of boundaries to the entire politics of rural property claims that were involved in the act of survey. The experts themselves tried to limit this disruption, to frame and define the world that they hoped to measure and survey. But in the very act of framing, they were continually exposed to the difficulties of drawing limits, of successfully transferring political conflicts to the narrow sites of calculation they had mastered.[106]

Following the completion of the cadastral survey of Egypt in 1907, Henry Lyons returned to England and to a career as director of the Science Museum in London (previously obscure and ill arranged, it is said, but transformed by Lyons into one of the great technical museums of the world).[107] His successor as director-general of the Survey Department, Ernest Dowson, remained a professional surveyor in the colonial service. He accompanied the British army as it occupied Palestine and Iraq in World War I. In this capacity he helped to spread the new survey expertise developed in Egypt across the Near East, and later to sub-Saharan Africa. In 1945 he published an article criticizing the "divorce" that had developed between the practical and technical aspects of surveying on the one hand and the legal and political on the other. Surveyors needed not just technical expertise but "knowledge of the social structure, agricultural practices and land tenures, customary as well as statutory, of the community concerned," the article claimed. "For it is only in the light of these conditions and of the juridical, fiscal, economic or other objectives sought, that they can adjust the technical to the other interlocking requirements effectively."[108] These "interlocking requirements" illuminate the impossible character of calculation. Any attempt to set the limits of the technical operations of calculation must first establish and understand those limits. This opens the problem of calculation to an interminable difficulty, the need to know all those other social, agricultural, and legal practices out of which the object to be mapped is constituted.

II

PEASANT STUDIES

4 The Invention and Reinvention of the Peasant

Among the figures in the scholarly imagining of the postcolonial world, "the peasant" is a strange kind of presence. With this abstraction a category of human being became a field of expertise, the subject of his own scholarly journals and the object of a distinct body of theory and description. "What are villagers in India, in Egypt, in Mexico *really like?*" the anthropologist George Foster asks, as he begins a brief history of the field. "For nearly fifty years anthropologists (by no means to the exclusion of others) have searched for answers [to this question] . . . living with villagers in order to question them and to observe their behavior, describing their findings in books and articles." At first they called their research the study of "folk" societies, Foster says, but after World War II scholars "came to realize that 'peasant' is a more appropriate term, and thus was born the new subfield of 'peasant studies.' "[1]

Foster makes these remarks in his foreword to the book *Shahhat: An Egyptian,* by Richard Critchfield, which he recommends for its accurate portrayal of what peasants everywhere are really like, and which became a favorite of both hotel bookstores in Cairo and college-level introductions to the Third World in the United States. The book belongs to a genre of peasant studies for which scholarship on the Middle East, more than other parts of the Third World, has provided an important home, a genre I would call descriptive realism. Critchfield sets before us the peasant's life "like a series of wonderfully composed photographs," wrote one of the book's reviewers; "when taken together, they make us see and feel the contours and the substance of fellah culture."[2] Despite the claims of photographic realism, however, a careful reading of Critchfield's book reveals his "real peasant" to be something constructed out of earlier representations, as a collage of familiar Orientalist images juxtaposed with clippings taken—in fact plagiarized—

from earlier writings, in particular from the previous popular study in a similar genre, *The Egyptian Peasant* by Henry Ayrout.

This chapter examines the genealogy of Critchfield's Egyptian peasant, not just to bring to light these forms of repetition and borrowing, but to ask some larger questions. What is the nature of this realist genre in peasant studies? Why is the Middle East, with its dearth of more critical examinations of rural society, so well represented? Why are the results so widely accepted, acquiring so easily the status of classics? Why does the realism of the peasant's portrayal seem to require not only the borrowings from earlier writings but also the exclusion from the picture of history, of the West, and of the presence of the Western author? Overall, what political processes are at work in the producing and reproducing of all this realism?

The emergence of peasant studies as a new field of expertise more than half a century ago can be located quite precisely in the widespread rebellions that rural populations were able to organize against occupying European powers during the interwar years. In the Arab world, for example, rural uprisings in Egypt, Morocco, Syria, and Iraq in the years after World War I were followed by the Palestinian uprising of 1936–39, the first sustained anticolonial revolt, which required one-third of Britain's armed forces to suppress it and a commission of colonial experts to examine rural life in Palestine and explain the rebellion's causes. In Indochina, peasant uprisings during the early 1930s that succeeded in establishing self-governing soviets were the background to studies such as Pierre Gourou's classic *Les Paysans du delta tonkinois* (1936), a work advising the colonial authorities of the "delicate" task they faced in preserving the existing Vietnamese "moral and social" system that it so meticulously described, along with the peasants' "strikingly wretched material conditions." The book warned that if the author's words were ignored and this "traditional" world were allowed to collapse, the peasantry would then "have a clear picture of its poverty and would center its thoughts on it."[3] As the rebellions spread, the experts kept up. The uprising in Palestine affected provincial Egypt, where political organizing and economic protest intensified in 1938 and 1939.[4] Several diagnoses of the peasant condition were put into print, including Ayrout's famous study of the Egyptian peasant, first published in 1938 under the title *Moeurs et coutumes des fellahs,* which claimed to "photograph" for the first time "the realities of peasant life" among Egyptians—and which compared itself, in turn, to the work on Vietnam by Gourou.[5]

The picture of what peasants are "really like" has a curious history, as the subsequent reissuing of these kinds of texts reflects. Gourou's study was translated into English in 1955 by the Human Relations Area Files, and between the late 1960s and mid-1970s it became one of the most important sources for studies on peasant revolt in Vietnam.[6] Ayrout's work, written in France where its Egyptian author was training to become a Jesuit priest, was translated into Arabic (1943) and English (1945), and then, following the shifting focus of foreign interest in Egypt, into Russian in 1954, and finally into English again in the United States in 1963.[7] By the early 1960s American scholarship was becoming increasingly interested in the question of peasant politics, urged on by events in Indochina and elsewhere and by figures such as undersecretary of state Chester Bowles, who as chairman of the Democratic Platform Committee in the 1960 elections had secured American commitment to a new economic policy toward the Third World.[8] Ayrout's *Egyptian Peasant* was published with an introduction by the sociologist Morroe Berger of Princeton, at that time considered the senior American scholar of the contemporary Middle East. Berger noted, twenty-five years after the book's first edition, that although political feelings in rural Egypt had still "hardly begun to develop," the government of President Nasser was now seeking "to awaken ambition and expectation among the peasants."[9] These observations were preceded by a foreword from Chester Bowles himself, warning that everywhere in Asia, Africa, and Latin America, "peasants are rousing themselves from apathy and despair to ask hard economic and political questions," and that with the spread of "communist agitators" they now "constitute fertile ground for subversion and unrest."[10]

American interest in helping Nasser deal with rural agitation and unrest subsided in the mid-1960s, after the Egyptians failed to fit their domestic and foreign policy to America's expanding regional interests. The need to expand American power reflected problems elsewhere in the world, in particular the intensification of the war against Vietnam. It is no coincidence that Vietnam was where Richard Critchfield first acquired his anthropological interest in peasant villages, while serving there from 1964 to 1967 as a reporter for the *Washington Star.* "What began as the reporting of events (conventional journalism)," he explained autobiographically, "ended in the study of the culture of ordinary people (amateur anthropology). It was that kind of war," he added, echoing a generation later the sentiments of the French ethnographer Pierre Gourou: "by 1967 the restoration of traditional Vietnamese values was the only chance left of saving the country."[11] Critchfield's first book, *The Long Charade: Political Subversion in the Vietnam War* (1968), presented to American readers the views of

British military advisors in South Vietnam, who represented a colonial expertise in dealing with rural "terrorism" accumulated earlier in Malaya and Palestine. The war in Vietnam, he explained with their help, was not a struggle for national liberation but a problem of "law and order." The government's police force had been weakened by terrorism in the countryside, and only by reestablishing "permanent security in the towns and villages" could "traditional" leaders and values be reestablished.[12] "The villagers were the key. But how to *get to know them* well enough to help them against the terrorism which was destroying their confidence and their culture," Critchfield wrote.[13] After leaving Vietnam Critchfield went on to visit and write about villages in Indonesia, India, Mauritius, Iran, and finally Egypt, where he spent several months during the years 1974–75 getting to know the Upper Egyptian village that was to be the subject of *Shahhat: An Egyptian,* his first full-length village study.

The years 1974–75 marked the beginning of a new American interest in rural Egypt, as President Sadat abandoned his predecessor's policies, aligned his foreign policy with the United States, and reopened the country to private capital investment. *Shahhat* was published in 1978, two months after Sadat's journey to Jerusalem and at the height of his popularity in the United States. The chairman of the Democratic National Committee this time around had been Robert Strauss, who was now a Middle East advisor to the White House and the coordinator of Sadat's visits to the United States, including the Camp David negotiations later that year with Israel. Although *Shahhat* failed to get a foreword from Strauss to match Ayrout's foreword from Chester Bowles, the author's introduction inadvertently locates the study of peasants in the context of U.S. interests in Egypt, including the interests of men like Robert Strauss. The introduction summarizes an interview the author obtained with Sadat, who is described as "Egypt's first ruler of truly *fellaheen* origins" (in fact he was the son of a minor functionary employed by the British army in Egypt, and moved from the provinces to Cairo as a young child).[14] The president, we are told, "was deeply concerned about the disruptive effect of rapid change as raised in this story, especially in the villages," and his plans for rural Egypt included switching to "high-value cash crops" and "investing heavily in agri-industry." Transferring farmland out of village control into large commercial hands coincided with the interests of American agribusiness corporations, including Coca-Cola and Pepsico, for whom Camp David confirmed the ending of the Egyptian boycott of American soft drink companies and the opening up of an important new market. Both companies embarked on investment projects in Egypt in the late 1970s, including a twenty-thousand-acre citrus-growing project to produce soft-drink concentrates negotiated jointly by Taha Zaki (an advisor to the Egyptian government on "food security") and a director of Pepsico—the White House advisor Robert Strauss.[15]

It was in this new period of renewed American interest in the economy and society of Egypt that Critchfield published his account of what rural Egyptians are really like. As with "any story set in the Third World today, particularly the Arab world," we are warned, the book deals with the difficult ground of "cultural and psychological turbulence." Shahhat, the rather petulant adolescent who is the story's central character, is said to be in many ways "typical of the great mass of poor Egyptians," and since his fellow villagers "all represent people found in the Third World today," the author tells us that he "found Shahhat and his problems exemplary." The problems involved are those that face a violence-prone adolescent as he adjusts to the recent death of his weak and alcoholic father amid the demands of an adoring and overbearing mother (as Robert Fernea remarks in his review of the book, "Freudian constructs haunt the scene").[16] Presented as "the story of how a deeply traditional Egyptian, when faced with sudden changes in his way of life . . . comes of age," Shahhat's life is to be read as an individual enactment of the larger drama of "modernization," in which villagers who have "never changed their way of life" in more than six thousand years are forced to adjust to modernity in less than a decade.[17]

The notion of a village life unchanged in sixty centuries is, of course, a complete fiction. To take just the nineteenth century, this region of Upper Egypt had seen the decline and virtual elimination of long-distance trade with India, Arabia, and the Sudan, the collapse of the local textile industry, and the introduction and spread of private landowning, export crops, steam-driven irrigation pumps, and epidemic diseases such as cholera. Large commercial estates were established, including the "feudal" estate to which Shahhat's village belonged up until the 1952 revolution, which became a sugarcane plantation supplying the Egyptian Sugar Company. European armies arrived—the village of Qurna, adjacent to Shahhat's village, was long remembered locally for its inhabitants' armed resistance to the French soldiers of Napoleon[18]—and villagers themselves were conscripted for the first time into a modern Egyptian army and forced to pay the taxes to support it. In 1822–23, artisans and peasants in the region rebelled against conscription, taxation, and the destruction of local textile manufacturing, gathered a force of several hundred armed men, and established their headquarters in Shahhat's village of Buʿairat. They marched on the local garrison and sacked it, causing the rebellion to spread throughout the surrounding countryside. The government dispatched European-officered reinforcements who burnt Buʿairat to the ground and rounded up and massacred the insurgents.[19] Police stations and telegraph lines were later built, and steamships and railways came, carrying government inspectors, European engineers, and great quantities of tourists and archaeologists, many of whom encamped in or near Shahhat's village, which lies at the foot of the Theban necropolis, burial place of King Tut, perhaps the most famous archaeological and tourist site in the world. It is this place that Critchfield introduces to us as an untouched and therefore typical corner of the Third World, a hamlet "so obscure it barely has a name" (xxv).

This blindness to historical transformation is carefully achieved. The essence of Critchfield's method is to assure us at frequent intervals that everything we encounter in rural Egypt we have somehow seen before, in some exotic image from the past. Egyptian peasants are familiar in advance to those who have visited museum exhibits of ancient Egypt. Shahhat's mother, for example, is immediately recognizable, for she has "the peculiarly straight nose, oval face, fair complexion, and large lustrous eyes familiar from ancient Egyptian statues and paintings" (4). In fact throughout Upper Egypt, we are told, "the facial and physical appearance of the villagers" resembles that of "the hundreds of statues and busts in the Cairo Museum" (xv). Then there are the inevitable echoes of the Bible. When Shahhat rescues a blonde female tourist from the cliff above the village, angrily chasing off some village boys who were following her, we are told that Shahhat, "in his black robes against the blindingly white rocks with the open blue sky all about, seemed very much a wrathful Old Testament figure" (111). We also get a quotation from the *Rubayyat* of Omar Khayyam (195), and several reminders of the *Thousand and One Nights.* A villager named Mitri, we are told, "resembled an old gnome out of Arabian Nights" (101) and even the infamous Habu Hotel, built in the village about a decade before as a hangout for the younger kind of European tourist, has "a medieval Arabian Nights air" (138).[20] Everything is encountered, it seems, as the original of something ancient and exotic that one has already seen in a museum, or read about in the literature of Orientalism, or imagined from the distant past.[21]

But Critchfield's most important means of making peasant life seem something exotic and thus unchangingly familiar is his reliance on more recent writings, in particular the 1938 work of Henry Ayrout. He paraphrases *The Egyptian Peasant* from the opening pages. "Foreign conquerors have come and gone—the Persians, Greeks, Romans, Byzantines, Arabs, Turks, French and English. As Henry Habib Ayrout once observed, while the Upper Egyptian villagers changed their masters and their religion, their language and their crops, they never changed their way of life" (xiii).[22] Even

Shahhat's village of Buʿairat, where Critchfield stayed, is seen through Ayrout's eyes.[23] The Egyptian village, wrote Ayrout, "forms a closed system . . . [of] habits, customs and taboos handed down from the distant past" (106). Forty years later Critchfield discovers that Shahhat's village "was in fact a closed system," which "preserved habits, customs, and taboos handed down from pharaonic times" (89). The peasant, Ayrout explained in his most famous line, "preserves and repeats, but does not originate anything" (132). Egyptian peasants, Critchfield unselfconsciously reiterates, "preserved and repeated, but did not originate, create, or change" (xvi).

Thus Critchfield's village turns out to be the exotic kind of place we have somehow always visited before, in museums, Arabian nights, and guidebooks, but above all in studies of the Egyptian peasant. As we will see, the extent of this familiarity is quite astonishing in Critchfield's case. Yet he is not the first to present rural Egypt as a living museum, familiar to us in advance through countless earlier texts and images. If one turns back to Ayrout, one encounters a similar problem. Rural Egyptians, Ayrout tells us in his first chapter (entitled "Changelessness"), are "as impervious and enduring as the granite of their temples, and as slow to develop." The images one has of their daily life, whether from "Pharaonic tombs or from Coptic legend, from Arab historians or the *Description of Egypt,* from early English researchers or the travellers of our own day, seem to form a single sequence. . . . These scenes, though separated by so many centuries, only repeat and confirm one another" (20). The American edition of Ayrout adds that urban Egyptians who know nothing of the countryside and find it inaccessible by private car can now visit instead an agricultural museum in Cairo, which has been built "to introduce them to village life."[24] Like Critchfield, however, Ayrout also reads rural Egypt through the pages of a more popular text, in this case the work of the turn-of-the-century French social psychologist Gustave Le Bon. Before continuing with my reading of Critchfield and showing the extent of his dependence on Ayrout, I will examine Ayrout's own dependence on the work of Le Bon and explore how this dependence helped establish Ayrout's book as the classic study of the Egyptian peasant.

Le Bon's writings, including *Les lois psychologiques de l'évolution des peuples* and his famous work *Psychologie des foules* (The Crowd), both of which were translated into Arabic and widely read in Cairo, were addressed to two pressing political questions of his day: how to explain scientifically the difference between advanced and backward societies, and how to explain scientifically the difference within a society between the mass of its people and the elite.[25] To account for these differences Le Bon introduced the concept of a people's psyche or soul, a "collective mind" that consists of ideas, feelings, and beliefs and is created by a process of slow, hereditary accumulation. This accumulation, claimed Le Bon, which is the measure of a people's evolution, occurs not among the mass of a nation but largely among its elite. Between the masses in a country such as Egypt, therefore, and those in parts of Europe, the difference in level of development might be small. "What most differentiates Europeans from Orientals is that only the former possess an *élite* of superior men." It is this elite that "constitutes the true incarnation of the forces of a race."[26] In his work on the crowd, described by Gordon Allport as "possibly the most influential book ever written in social psychology," Le Bon employed the same principle to explain social differences within a society.[27] The crowd or mass *(la foule)*, he explained, is composed of cells so merged together that they constitute a "provisional being," with an unconscious collective mind. In this merger individual mental differences, the source—as he had shown—of all excellence, are lost. The loss of individuality, Le Bon concluded, makes the crowd into a less intelligent being, like a child, or like a backward nation or race. The backward nation and the crowd represent parallel states of mental inferiority, both caused by the absence of individuality.[28]

Henry Ayrout adopted the vocabulary and thinking of Le Bon to explain the nature of the Egyptian peasant. "The fellah should always be spoken of in the plural," he wrote, "because he lives always as a member of a group, if not of a crowd" (94). The peasant "is like a primitive man or child" (134), he explained, for like the primitive or the child he has "little individuality." This is reflected in the "formlessness" of his village (116), where "all is dust and disorder. There is no plan or system, and not a single straight line" (100).[29] The lack of form and structure indicates the absence of individuality because without straight lines one cannot have individual houses. Like their occupants, the buildings are not separate units but are merged together and indistinguishable from one another, like cells "in the agricultural hive" (116). The absence of individual houses reflects, in turn, the absence of distinct families. The family, too, has no individual identity but simply "shades off into a wider community more or less closely interrelated by blood and marriage . . . . Just as the house is not a complete unit by itself, neither is the family which lives in it. As there is no real 'home' . . . so there is no real 'family' " (125). Individuality and structure are also missing at the level of the village: "nothing is more like one Egyptian village than another Egyptian village. Here is another example of the monotonous uniformity"

(95). The village itself, it follows, "is not a community in the social sense, not an organism, but a mass *[une foule]*." And, finally, at the level of the peasantry as a whole and of the nation: "One might well talk of Egypt in the plural. There is no single Egyptian people . . . but only a seething assemblage of the most varied types. . . . Neither is there a true peasant community, but only a homogeneous mass *[une foule homogène]*" (33).

All these absences in turn reflect a more fundamental absence, the lack of individual mental life, or what Ayrout, following Le Bon, calls "personality." The peasant is "as little of a personality as he is of an individual," Ayrout explains (110). The development of his intelligence, it seems, has "atrophied," and what there is of it "is collective rather than personal." He does not engage in "individual thinking." Several "essential features" of the Egyptian mentality follow from this situation. The peasant is habitually distrustful and therefore selfish, "cunning to the point of duplicity," fond of a "semi-conscious" state of torpor, and yet violent in the extreme when roused. His sense of justice is corrupt, and he lacks frankness, curiosity, ambition, sensibility, and initiative (132–38). How to account for these monstrous mental absences? "Some sociologists put it down to masturbation, which is fairly common in the Islamic East." But according to Father Ayrout, that particular vice seems to be more common in urban areas, whereas these personality problems are more pronounced in the countryside (132). He explains them instead in terms of the miserable condition of rural life, though the "real evils" are not the poverty and hardship itself but the peasant's "lack of education and culture," as a result of which "he does not feel the depth of his suffering" (154), as well as the indifference of those who might help him, who have failed to notice "the distress which he himself could not put into words, and perhaps only half felt" (15).

The solution Ayrout suggests for this problem of an *assemblage sans architecture, matériellement et intellectuellement,* as the French original puts it, is a material and mental "reconstruction of the Egyptian village."[30] He supports the various proposals being put forward in the 1930s and 1940s to replace the villages of Egypt with geometrical "model villages" of the sort already built on many of the country's large commercial estates (his father was a well-known Cairo architect),[31] combined with a program of rural education (to which he devoted his own later life) that would provide villagers with the mental architecture needed to cope with straight lines and separate houses.[32] Such a program, Ayrout argues, is the responsibility of the Egyptian elite, or more specifically of a group he names the "rural middle class," men like the nationalist leaders Saʿd Zaghlul and Mustafa Nahhas, "conservative, gain-loving, unpretentious" types who "live in the country and keep a close eye on the yield of their feddans." This class is to be distinguished from the very largest landowners, who live only in the city and, like their allies the British and the European-owned credit companies and agricultural processing industries, are opposed to rural reform.[33]

As these proposals make clear, Ayrout's work forms a part of the political debate emerging in the late 1930s and 1940s, mentioned above in chapter 1, in which an educated Cairene elite began to see the rural population as a social problem. In 1938 alone, for example, the year Ayrout's book was published, there appeared Mirrit Butrus Ghali's *Siyasat al-ghad* (Policy of Tomorrow) and Hafiz Afifi's *ʿAla hamish al-siyasa* (Notes on Politics), each of which includes an analysis, in different terms, of the situation of the rural population.[34] Ayrout's contribution to this debate, in the familiar vocabulary of Le Bon, is to demonstrate how the peasantry lacks the ability even to feel their own suffering, and therefore requires the political intervention, as Le Bon had always stressed, of the nationalist elite, whose role is to "revive" the rural population, and yet, indicating the political dangers involved, to "awaken without exciting" (158–59). The duty of the elite, explains Ayrout, is "to liberate the fellah's spirit from its stifling envelope of mud. . . . The initiative can never come from his own community, which is completely numbed and powerless, but only from the classes which overshadow him, from the *élite,* who with their riches of mind and money can vitalize him. In this dough must work the leaven of intelligence and sympathy" (23).

This is the complex genealogy of the work that was to reappear in the United States in 1963, described on its cover by the dean of British and American Orientalists, Hamilton A. R. Gibb, as "a classic in its field."[35] By what process had *The Egyptian Peasant* become a classic? First, there was what the *American Sociological Review* called "its continued relevance and its virtual monopoly of the subject"—twenty-five years after the first edition. The book was not the only study of the Egyptian peasant, as we have just seen—indeed if there were any classics they were Ibrahim ʿAmir's *al-Ard wa-ʾl-fallah* (The Land and the Peasant, 1958), which influenced a generation of Egyptian scholars, and the writings of the French scholar Jacques Berque, but none of this work was translated into English.[36] Ayrout's book had acquired its continued relevance and hence monopoly in the minds of Western scholars by its ahistorical method of explanation, in which the condition of rural Egypt is attributed not to political and economic forces of the day but to a timeless peasant mentality.[37] Morroe Berger, the senior American social scientist who wrote the introduction to the U.S. edition, had used this account of the peasant mind as a source for his own study, *The Arab World Today* (1962), generalizing Ayrout's views to help answer the question, "what kind of person is the Arab?" Berger was able to report that "The Arab seems to harbor two major contradictory impulses," combining "extreme self-assertion" with "an inability to assert independence as an individual," not to mention his "virtual obsession with oral functions." Prejudices of this sort, to which Ayrout's milder stereotyping could lend authority, were not considered abnormal. To the contrary, Berger was at that time the chair of the Near and Middle East Committee of the Social Science Research Council and three years later became the founding president of the Middle East Studies Association of North America.[38]

Then there was Ayrout's realism. H. A. R. Gibb claimed that the book "holds up a mirror to the peasantry as they are." A mirror was the correct metaphor, but, as we saw, it was a mirror reflecting not some original peasant reality but a series of other mirrors, ranging from the French *Description d'Egypte* and the writings of nineteenth-century European travelers to the exhibits in the Egyptian museum and, above all, the work of Gustave Le Bon. Such a system of mirrors produced an image of the peasantry appropriate to the writer's political concerns and pastoral sympathies. But their overall effect was to make the book appear to confirm everything Orientalism had always suspected concerning the mentality and way of life of the Arab, thus guaranteeing its reception as a classic. It was no accident, furthermore, that Father Ayrout had been educated in France and wrote his study in French as a dissertation for a French university. Unlike works in Arabic, it was readily available for translation into British, Russian, and American editions. The final mechanisms for rendering the book a classic were the requirements of postwar American politics, in particular the complex of development programs and university Middle East courses. The English edition of 1945 was made available in the United States through the Human Relations Area Files, and apparently an initial American translation was produced by the U.S. Point Four program, presumably as an introduction to rural Egypt for American development experts.[39] "There is no better book," the *Economist* remarked confidently when the Beacon Press edition finally appeared in 1963, "on the magnitude of President Nasser's domestic task in rural Egypt."

Despite its status as a classic, the book required updating for the American edition, and also some minor yet significant rewriting by the author. Several references to the political violence commonly used by Egyptian peasants against the authorities were deleted or amended in the U.S. edition, replacing them with an image of "passive and obedient" villagers. For example, the original text describes the reaction of a group of peasants to an attempt to take possession of their *'izba* (the workers' housing complex on a large commercial estate, discussed in chapter 2, which often evolved into a self-contained village while the houses, fields, agricultural equipment, and even domestic animals remained the estate owner's property) by a financial institution that had foreclosed on its owner:

> When the bank's bailiff arrived to carry out the seizure, the villagers resisted him, and the police had to interfere. The assistant chief constable of the *markaz* [district] arrived on the scene at the head of an armed force, but was attacked by the people. Seeing that the situation promised to grow more serious, he felt himself obliged to order shots to be fired in the air to frighten the fellaheen. The effect was to exasperate them. They proceeded to cut the telephone wires and to burn the bailiff's car. A new body of police soon came to the rescue, but proved as useless as the first. Finally the Mudeer [provincial governor] appeared on the scene at the head of yet a third force and order was re-established only when further shots had been fired into the air. Seven of the policemen were wounded by stones thrown at them by the villagers. Several villagers were arrested, and a judicial enquiry was opened. This incident, which took place in 1936, is by no means abnormal. (41–42)

In the American edition this paragraph has been removed and replaced by a single sentence: "Occasionally it was necessary to put the ordinarily passive and obedient peasants down with police force."[40] With such amendments some of the few references in Ayrout to particular historical and political episodes were eliminated, and the book's portrayal of a hapless peasantry inhabiting a changeless countryside was ready for the American reader.

We can now return to Critchfield. We have seen how he invokes Ayrout to support the image of an Egyptian village unchanged in six thousand years, and we have seen the sources of these images in Ayrout, especially the borrowings from Le Bon, and their acceptance in the United States as a relevant and realistic portrayal of rural Egypt in the second half of the twentieth century. Critchfield's role is to take up these fading images in the last quarter of the century and reprint them in new colors.

It is not just that Critchfield has read Ayrout before he arrives in the village and sees the place through the earlier text. Matters are much worse—he is unable to put Ayrout down. For example, when Critchfield goes with Shahhat to the local market *(suq),* he cannot help turning again to *The Egyptian Peasant*. The market, Ayrout had explained,

> lasts from dawn to midday. The sellers . . . make their way to it at daybreak in long files, choose a spot to lay out their wares, and squat down behind them to wait for customers . . . . All is a noisy, confused mêlée of men, cattle and goods. (104)

"The *suk*," Critchfield tells us,

> lasted from dawn to mid-morning, and if Shahhat wanted to sell something, he came at daybreak, chose a spot along the road to display his vegetables or tether his sheep, and squatted down to wait for customers. By eight o'clock the *suk* was a noisy, confused hubbub of men, women, children, cattle, and goods. (86)

Further on Ayrout continued:

> Here again can be seen the love of the fellaheen for crowding together and moving only in congested groups. If they have to cross the Nile . . . the fellaheen throng so densely into the ferry-boat . . . that accidents are frequent. When they set out on foot or on donkey-back, laden with astonishing bundles, it looks like an evacuation. . . . When they have to travel by train, they arrive several hours beforehand, cluster on a corner of the platform, and scramble all together into one carriage, even if there is plenty of room elsewhere. (106)

And Critchfield:

> Though there was plenty of space along the road, they all crowded together in one small area for the *fellaheen* loved congested groups. When they crossed the Nile everyone would throng into the same small ferry so that it was a wonder accidents were rare. When they took the train, they would arrive two or three hours early, cluster on one end of the platform and then scramble all together into a single carriage, even if there was plenty of room in the next one. The road through the *suk*, with so many people hurrying by on donkey or on foot—most of them laden with enormous bundles . . . —resembled an evacuation. (86–87)

But not as much as it resembled Ayrout's book.

How do the characters in Critchfield's drama cope with the strangely constructed world in which they find themselves? There is no problem, for they are constructed the same way. They are as preserved and repeated as the countryside they inhabit. In the chapter of his book "The Peasant's Body," Ayrout describes under the heading "Race and Type" the racial features of the Egyptian—drawing, incidentally, on the scientific racism of writers like Gustave Le Bon. Ayrout notes that the peasant of Upper Egypt, being a mixture of Egyptian and "negro," is

> heavily built [with] rather prominent cheekbones, a thick nose . . . and a heavy jaw. His features on the whole are rugged . . . neither very sensitive nor very expressive. [The Arab nomads] differ markedly from the fellaheen by their finer features . . . their more excitable temperament [and] their cruelty in vengeance. (79–80)

Critchfield tells us that, "except for his curly black hair, with its hint of African negro blood," Shahhat "looked more Arabian than Egyptian." Most of the other young men in the village were

> more heavily built, and had strong cheekbones, thick noses, and heavy jaws. Among their rugged faces, Shahhat's stood out as singularly sensitive and expressive. His finer, more Semitic features and more excitable temperament, his sense of vengeance that was not without its cruel side . . . (5)

made Shahhat resemble the nomads of the desert—or at least the nomads of Ayrout's racial classification.

This racial vocabulary, once borrowed from Ayrout, recurs throughout Critchfield's story. The "vengeful Bedouin streak in Shahhat's blood" is continually invoked to explain his habitual violence (63). His friends and associates are contrastingly "negro." In the "dark brown skin, curly hair, thick lips, and strong cheekbones" of his friend Snake, "there was something plainly African" (59); Faruk, Shahhat's sharecropper, has "wet, open lips" (15), later described as "full, wet lips" (51); and Abdullahi, owner of the local bar, has a head and chest covered in "frizzy hair like a negro's" (35). The racist effect is enhanced by most of the other descriptions of people's facial features. Hagg Ali, for example, has "cunning, calculating eyes, a hawk nose, wrinkled face, and an ingratiating, obsequious manner" (20). When he gets annoyed this "cunning face" is "twisted into an angry, purple fury . . . the veins swelling on his forehead" (55). (Veins and muscles are continually swelling: when Shahhat gets angry his face and neck turn "crimson with all the muscles strained" [12], we meet another whose "neck muscles stood out like ropes" [74], and so on.) The face of Abdullahi, the bar owner, is "hideously pock-marked," and those of his customers always have "a demoniac look" (35). Bahiya's eyes are "dull and squinty," whereas Su'ad has "sly, viperish eyes" (41–42). Sheikh al-Hufni is "a bent, emaciated, toothless old man" (44), as opposed to Yusef, who is "bent, toothless, and garrulous" (50). El Got is "a slight, weaselly, pale little man"

(60); Mitri is "frail and wrinkled" like "an old gnome" with "rheumy blue eyes" (101); the father of Faruk, the sharecropper, is a "shrunken little man"; Hasan, a "drunken scoundrel," has "such a short, thick neck he looked hunch-backed"; Ali, Hasan's son, is a "dull, slack-jawed youth" (147–48); and so on.

To complete the racist effect, these characters are all made to speak, as it were, like foreigners. None of them knows how to say "a lot," for example, so they are always saying things like "there is much grain left" (155), "he must love money much" (120), and "in the past there was much wheat. . . . Now we cultivate sugar cane and oh, so many crops and get much money . . . [and] eat and drink much" (95). When a sharecropper gets dismissed he says, "All right. Finish. I wanted that" (150), and when Zacharias criticizes the government a woman announces "The speaking of Zacharias is good" (121). Someone leaving home says "Tell your mother goodbye. We go to Cairo" (205), and when he returns they say "Best arrival to you" (212), unless the arrival is unexpected, when they say "What a strange coming" (169).

Within this racial framework, Shahhat's whole character seems to have been determined in advance by Ayrout. "Rural, gregarious, stay-at-home; such is the Egyptian people in its dominant characteristics" (30), wrote Ayrout, noting later "their love of the soil, their sense of rhythm, and their taste for songs, stories and colours." The peasant's intellect, he said, "is controlled by his senses, and remains close to things felt and done. . . . Life to him is a succession but of todays" (133–34). Sure enough, Shahhat turns out to be "rural, gregarious, stay-at-home. . . . With his love for the soil, his feel for physical labor and nature's rhythms, his taste for songs, stories and gossip, his mind was governed by the senses and stayed close to things done and felt; life to him was a succession of todays" (38). Not to mention a succession of plagiarisms.

Explaining the views on sexuality among his village hosts, Critchfield also borrows from Ayrout. "The temperament of the fellaheen," Ayrout tells us,

> is very ardent and sensual . . . [but] the heat of passion is short-lived. At thirty a fellah woman is no longer attractive, but the children she has borne her husband bind him to her. . . . The men . . . are kept faithful less by virtue than by village law. (119)

According to Critchfield,

> Ommohamed [Shahhat's mother] knew that young men like Shahhat were ardent, sensual, and romantic, but that the heat of such passion

> cooled all too soon; after thirty or so it was the children . . . that bound a husband and wife together. In her eyes men were kept in place less by their own virtue than by Islamic law and village social pressure. (29–30)

Perhaps even Ommohamed had been reading Ayrout.

Taking his cue from Ayrout, Critchfield turns the sexuality and violence of villagers into a major theme of the book. His Author's Note at the beginning suggests that in Upper Egyptian villages "the occurrence of adultery, fornication, and sodomy, despite severe Moslem penalties, seems an assertion of pagan sensuality absent elsewhere in Egypt" (xv). The opening pages set the scene by invoking ancient Egypt as the source of this obscene and violent paganism. Shahhat's mother is described, twenty years earlier, stealthily entering the ruins of a temple at night and observing the local Pharaonic art. There are wall paintings portraying "a procession led by the god of the penis," and reliefs depicting the pharaoh's military victories that show "mass decapitations and castrations, with heaps of genitals carved in stone." The very sight of these genital heaps, we are told, causes local villagers to become "filled with lust" (9). Soon after we are informed of the young Shahhat's "growing sexual hunger" and told how "the size of his penis" became the object of village comment. Pride in their masculinity, it seems, creates in local men "a drive to reduce competing males to lesser status through domination, sadism, and even sodomy; dominance was everything." It comes as no surprise that the villagers, described in this way as animals, commonly practice sodomy not just with other males but with animals, too. Shahhat himself, Critchfield informs us, used to do it with a female donkey (17).

The rest of the book follows in much the same tone, telling us, page after page, of fights and stabbings and robberies and murders, of men who rape, men who bite off people's noses, and men who kill people and cut them into little pieces. Most of these events occurred before Critchfield came to the village, or while he was away in Cairo, and are related to him second- or third-hand by Shahhat, through an interpreter. Their secondhand quality is obvious. One story, for example, involves Shahhat's sharecropper, Faruk, a "drunkard and voluptuary" according to the caption under his photograph, who is involved in "every sort of debauchery, drinking heavily, smoking hashish, chasing women, and spending long hours gambling" (16). One night, we are told, he met in the fields with a woman from a nearby village who used to sell herself occasionally for money. The couple were discovered, however, by two other villagers—"coarse, filthy, dishonest and drunken men"—who hit the woman, beat Faruk and tied him up, stripped the woman naked, and took turns raping her, pausing when they were finished to untie Faruk and beat him again, "pounding and kicking him until he lost his senses." Almost every line of the story is clichéd, from "Faruk could not tear his eyes away as he listened to the woman's moans," to the description of the woman's breasts as, inevitably, "full" and "firm." We are also told by the author that she enjoyed being raped (78–79). The book's tone is persistently misogynist; another rape victim is shown in a photograph, smiling at the camera, with a caption that describes her as a "willful, flirtatious fourteen-year-old" (103).

Critchfield retells this tale not as an example of how a vexatious village youth offers colorful stories to a visiting American, but as a detail for his picture of what villagers, as Professor Foster's foreword puts it, are really like (indeed, Foster particularly praises Critchfield for bringing into view the "darker side" of peasant behavior—which, he assures us, given the peasants' poverty and lack of opportunity, "is highly adaptive" [x]). Critchfield's factual presentation of such episodes is especially surprising given that he admits elsewhere in the book that local stories could become "exaggerated and dramatized" as they "spread through the village" (139), and that Shahhat in particular "had ceased to be able to distinguish" between tales he had heard from others and those he had invented himself. "The most fantastic unreality easily paled and mingled with the real." An "educated outsider," Critchfield adds, "might be expected to grow bored and skeptical" (100).

He or she might indeed—especially as Critchfield seems to share Shahhat's problem of being unable to distinguish the unreal from the real, and with the help of Ayrout has put some additional tales of violence into the mouths of his informants. Describing the military conscription of the peasant, Ayrout had explained that

> to ensure his rejection he may put out one of his eyes, or cut off a couple of fingers. . . . If he can, he will hide or escape. . . . When there is no way out, and he cannot avoid leaving home to join the army, the family receives condolences and abandons itself to mourning as if for a bereavement. To leave the village is like going abroad. *Partir, c'est mourir.* (107)

Critchfield relates that

> Shahhat had heard how in past times young men in the village had been known to cut off their fingers or put out an eye to be rejected, or try to hide in the desert to escape. If there was no way out and they

> could not avoid going into the army, their families received condolences and abandoned themselves to formal mourning as if their sons were already dead. In the old days, to leave the village was to die. (162)

Describing the working of vendettas in rural Egypt, Ayrout had said that sometimes

> the feud is kept up in every family from generation to generation. . . . The antagonism, though usually latent, will show itself suddenly over some trivial matter, such as the shifting of a boundary mark, a theft of manure, or a *gamoossa* trespassing. Then human life counts for nothing. (109)[41]

Critchfield tells us that even in Buʿairat

> a feud, once started over a diesel pump or some other trivial affair, could go on a long time. Antagonism might show itself over something so trifling as a trespassing sheep, missing fodder, or the shifting of a boundary marker, and before long it could seem as if human life counted for nothing. (89)

Ayrout's account had continued:

> Thus life is lived in constant insecurity. To feel this one must spend a night in a village. As soon as night falls . . . the dogs begin to bark . . .

He goes on to describe an incident in the village of Qalandol in 1936 (another of the historical episodes eliminated from the U.S. edition of the book), where to avenge an earlier killing in a struggle over the selection of the village headman, a man was stabbed in the marketplace. The victim's friends then

> bore down on the spot with rifles and staves, crying "Allah, Allah!" . . . By midnight the two parties [were] determined to fight to the death. . . . The police had the greatest difficulty in restoring order. (109–10)

Critchfield's passage continues with a description of the village adjacent to Buʿairat:

> But in Qurna life was lived in constant insecurity. As night fell, the dogs would start to roam and bark. . . . Sometimes a fight could start for no good reason and before long men would come running to reinforce both sides, armed with rifles and staves and shouting "Allah, Allah!" In no time both parties would vow to fight to the death and the police faced great difficulty in restoring order. (89)

Note that in Ayrout's story the violence arose out of a serious political dispute, whereas the only point of originality in Critchfield's version is that violence now occurs "for no good reason."[42]

In this construction of what the Egyptian—and Third World—peasant is "really like," there is more than just a persistent plagiarism and the addition of invented incidents. There is also something missing. The account is written entirely in the third person, rendering the author, who was partly present in the village, completely absent from the scene. Critchfield only presents himself at the end, in an afterword, in which there is a photograph of him standing in the village and a careful explanation of his method. He always begins the study of a "traditional village" by laboring in the fields, working alongside the person he refers to, using the possessive, as "my peasant subject." He then works with interpreters, using two of them a day ("interpreters tend to tire after five or six hours of steady translation"), to compile a voluminous ledger of his subject's recollections of past adventures and dialogues. "These became seven hundred pages of single-spaced typewritten notes," we are told. "Shahhat and I," the author adds, "were together, virtually every waking hour, for almost a year" (227–31). Moreover, we have been assured in the preface that the names of the characters in the story, as well as the photographs that illustrate it, are all "real" (xiv). The result is "as true a portrait" as he can write, Critchfield concludes, ending the book with a circular, almost desperate, assertion about Shahhat's story: "A real person, his identity and existence are its verification" (233). The claims, the details of how the account was constructed, and the confidential and possessive tone in which they are imparted to us—all placed outside the telling of the story itself—are intended to establish the author's authority.

While in the village, Critchfield adds in the afterword, he and his interpreter "tried, as much as we were able, to remain observers and not participants, and I think, in the main, we succeeded." But this required the "restraining influence" of the interpreter, for on several occasions, Critchfield informs us in the same paragraph, he and his peasant subject "had violent, usually drunken fights, Arab-fashion, coming to blows, once throwing chairs at each other, and sometimes actually knocking each other down." Although these bouts of "Arab" violence left the villagers "always upset," the American "rather enjoyed them," as did his subject. "With the possible exception of one or two other peasant subjects, I doubt if I have ever gotten to know anyone, including members of my own family, as intimately as I grew to know Shahhat." This intimacy, secretly confided to us, is intended to increase rather than undermine the author's authority, for apparently it has nothing to do with what Critchfield calls "the story": "when it came to events that represented progress in the story, [the interpreter] and I kept carefully aside" (231–32). Thus the device of the confessional afterword assures us of the author's intimate understanding, while the removal of all traces of the author's presence from the story itself creates an effect of objectivity.[43]

In my own copy of *Shahhat,* however, some of the book's pages are bound out of place, with the result that a part of the afterword comes in the middle of the "story." In the heat of a violent quarrel Shahhat is having with his mother and uncle, which causes him to leave the village for Cairo, Critchfield himself accidentally appears, speaking to us in the first person: "Advised of the quarrel by Shahhat in Cairo, I returned once more to the village. Hence I was physically present during the more dramatic episodes of the closing section." In one of these episodes, he mentions, "I had to throw a violently hysterical scene" (230–32). After one more misplaced page we return to these very episodes, which are now haunted by this invisible, inadvertently announced presence. The separation of the author from his story is subverted, and the effect of objectivity slips away.

Yet even if your own copy of the book is correctly bound, you will sense another subversive presence haunting its pages. The storytelling elides the presence not only of the American author, but of the Westerner in general. The Western tourists and archaeologists who frequent the village and its surroundings are mentioned, but only obliquely and at a distance. Like the author, they are never allowed a presence of their own. The only straightforward account of them is the humorous description of a fleeting visit by a busload of tourists to the local Pharaonic temple. The sudden intrusion is shown strictly from the villagers' point of view: the village square is shaken into life, chairs are put out in front of the café, Coca Cola and fake antiques are brought out to peddle, children demand *baksheesh,* and guides shout their instructions to the harried visitors. Then suddenly the bus is gone again, and the village regains its peace and quiet (107). Nevertheless, despite this deliberate distancing of the American and European presence, several other signs slip in to indicate a more pervasive relationship.

First there is the Habu Hotel, built in the early 1960s, where Critchfield himself stayed. He describes it disingenuously as a "country inn" (227). As far as I know, however, it catered not to local travelers but largely to northern Europeans, attracted across the river from Luxor by the cheap rates for rooms and the even cheaper rates for local hashish. The village café, where Critchfield often spent his evenings, seems to have catered to a similar clientele; it was where villagers learned their English. Several of the key characters in the story earn their livelihoods and have even made fortunes from tourism or archaeology. Shahhat's uncle, Ahmed, who we are told represents in the story the kind of Egyptian that "accepts modernization and its values" (xiv), works as a night watchman at the largest tourist hotel in Luxor (30). His father's cousin, the notorious Hagg Ali, "had grown mysteriously rich in a short time," allegedly from illicit dealing in archaeological treasures (19). He also organizes the supply of laborers for American archaeological digs all over Egypt, and is well known to organizations like the American Research Center in Egypt. Archaeology and tourism, in fact, appear to be a significant source of income for the village and certainly an integral part of its life. One or two more successful villagers have themselves become Egyptologists, including a man from the village who went on to study for a French doctorate at Montpellier and became a professor of Egyptology in Cairo.[44]

The book ignores the village's dependence on archaeology and tourism, just as it ignores Shahhat's dependence on the author. Critchfield arrived in Buʿairat just after the death of Shahhat's father, when the boy's family suddenly found itself seriously in debt. The opportune arrival of an American writer, willing to pay a village youth for his stories, can hardly have been irrelevant to the relationship that developed between them. Yet these forms of dependency upon Westerners and the Western economy are not discussed ("spending patterns remain traditional," we are told [xviii]), and there is no attempt to analyze the larger causes of local poverty and debt essential to such dependence. The story is one of "cultural and psychological turbulence," and the closest it comes to discussing economic dependence is a passing reference to the male prostitution that is often part of these contemporary forms of the colonial relationship. Shahhat's friend Snake had often told Shahhat, who in turn had told Critchfield, "that if the foreign tourists who came to visit the tombs of Qurna were more interested in himself than the fake antiques he peddled, he took them out into the desert, where he would provide any service, as long as he was paid handsomely. It was not an uncommon way of earning money among the young men of Qurna." But Shahhat himself, we are reassured immediately, "had little to do with tourists" (107).

Since the 1970s tourism has become the largest industry in the Nile valley in terms of foreign earnings. Shahhat's village might actually be somewhat "typical," therefore, although not in any of the ways Critchfield suggests. In its inhabitants' employment as peddlers, guides, café owners, hotel staff, part-time prostitutes, archaeological laborers, and native informants, the village perhaps typifies some of the novel ways in which the world of the West reorganized areas such as rural Egypt in the late twentieth century, and put the villager once more to work. Thus by eliding the presence of the tourist and archaeological industries, as well as his own presence as a writer, Critchfield helps conceal the multiple ways in which villagers continue to be organized as producers for nonvillage consumption.

Concealment, however, is the wrong word, for *Shahhat* itself forms a part of this system of production. Its role is to produce the peasant voice. Although we are assured in the afterword that Shahhat "knew no English" when Critchfield first met him, we have been told in the story itself that he had picked up some English "listening to foreigners in the café." But, it is quickly added, "he never talked with them. If his friends asked why, he would say, 'God gives me my work. I have land. Why should I speak with these foreigners . . . ? My work is to cultivate the land' " (228, 108). Until, of course, Critchfield arrived at the Habu Hotel and finally persuaded the peasant boy to speak. Thanks to Critchfield, as Foster puts it in his foreword, "Shahhat the man speaks for and to us" (xii). Just as Ayrout put into words for us the misery of peasants who were unable to feel their own suffering, Critchfield translates for us the words of a peasant who knows no English, enabling him finally to find a voice and communicate with us.

In this way, removing from the village both the presence of the American author and the playing of the world economy creates not just an effect of objectivity but also of a peasant subjectivity. Like many infinitely more respectable studies of the Third World peasant, Critchfield's writing produces a peasant voice that appears self-formed. The voice is presented not as the product of an American writer, or even of the peasant's encounter with the writer or with other local forms of Western hegemony, but as the speaking of an autonomous subject. Thanks to the invisible writer, the figure of the peasant is given a place in the monologue of the West, reaffirming with his presence our myth of partaking in a universal human dialogue. In this manner the peasant subject is produced for nonpeasant consumption, packaged by a university press and sold in the tourist hotels of Luxor and Cairo and the campus bookstores of American universities.

Should Critchfield's book be dismissed as merely an unfortunate and isolated case of plagiarism by an author who is more a popularizer than a scholar? After all, it might be said, he is clearly an enthusiastic writer whose sense of adventure and evident enjoyment of the company of some of those he writes about gave him a far greater exposure to villages around the world than any of his former colleagues among American foreign correspondents.

I do not think so; not just because inserting the missing quotation marks around the passages plagiarized from Ayrout would do little to improve things, but because, in the years since its publication, the book itself and the realism it claims to present have never been dismissed. The problem posed by *Shahhat* is not primarily a question of plagiarism, but the question of why a book that reproduces yet again the racist stereotype of the Third World peasant, with all colonial history removed and all the effects of neocolonialism made invisible, can still be so easily and widely accepted.

Shahhat was described in the *American Anthropologist* as "an excellent dramatization of peasant life," in the *Journal of American Folklore* as "enjoyable and readable," and in the *American Ethnologist* as capturing, despite its "undisciplined subjectivity," "the vividness and passionate intensity of Upper Egyptian life."[45] George Foster's foreword calls the book "one of the most absorbing accounts of peasant life I have ever read," and stresses "the extent to which it illuminates and confirms the points anthropologists have made about peasant society" (xii). A note at the beginning of the book informs us that Richard Critchfield writes about the Third World for the *Economist*, the *New York Times*, the *Los Angeles Times*, the *Christian Science Monitor*, the *Washington Post*, *Foreign Affairs*, and the *New Republic* and is the author of numerous other books and articles about peasant life. These include a subsequent work, *Villages* (1981), in which he updates the story of Shahhat and gives what he admits are brief, "rambling" accounts of about a dozen other villages he has visited, including those from his days in Vietnam. "Somewhat unexpectedly," we are told in the paperback edition, *Villages* "drew serious attention from agricultural scientists, students of development, and Washington policymakers."[46] In 1988 Critchfield's first book on peasants, *The Golden Bowl Be Broken: Peasant Life in Four Cultures*, was republished by a university press as a text "recommended for course use."[47] Critchfield's research in Egypt was financed with a grant from the Ford Foundation (and he subsequently received grants from the Rockefeller and other foundations and was employed as a consultant on Third World villages by the U.S. Agency for International Development. His "realism" in the portrayal of the peasant was supported, in other words, by a mass of reviewers, editors, publishers, development experts, policy makers, grant committee members, and university teachers.

In December 1981, not long after the publication of *Shahhat* and immediately following the appearance of *Villages*, Critchfield was named as one of the first half dozen recipients of the new MacArthur Foundation fellowships, a $250,000 award nominated secretly by unnamed scholars and given annually to individuals whose work is of outstanding intelligence and originality. Besides "the peasant," and the Middle Eastern peasant in particular, is there any stereotype in the Orientalist portrayal of the non-West whose racism and ahistoricism could remain so acceptable that the author of its latest incarnation might find his work so well received and rewarded?

POSTSCRIPT

This chapter was first published as an article in the *International Journal of Middle East Studies.* Following its publication I was contacted by the sisters of Henry Habib Ayrout and indirectly by Richard Critchfield. These contacts led to further discoveries and opened additional questions.

The reader may be little surprised to learn that Father Ayrout wrote his classic study of the Egyptian peasant without any firsthand knowledge of rural Egypt. He had grown up in Cairo and left Egypt secretly in 1926 at the age of eighteen, against the wishes of his father, who intended him to follow his two other sons into the father's profession of architecture. Dressed in a cassock and carrying a passport supplied by the French Jesuits, at whose school he had studied in Cairo, Ayrout left for twelve years of training at a Jesuit college in Lyon. He completed his study of the Egyptian peasant as a dissertation ten years later, relying on books such as Winifred Blackman's *The Fellahin of Upper Egypt* and on correspondence with former school friends in Cairo whose fathers owned large agricultural estates. He himself never visited rural Egypt while writing the book, and had probably seen no more of the countryside than the view from the train on his way to Alexandria.[48]

Ayrout returned to Egypt in 1941. The German army had occupied Lyon, leaving the Jesuit schools in Egypt and the Levant deprived of funds from France and forced to reduce their operations or close down. With no conventional Jesuit employment available, Ayrout began his educational and missionary work in Upper Egypt, eventually founding more than a hundred schools among the Coptic community and becoming the resident authority on rural Egypt for foreign scholars and journalists.[49] "Anyone coming to Egypt to study the fellaheen, the peasants," wrote Jay Walz, the *New York Times* correspondent in Cairo from 1959 to 1964, "sooner or later called on the dynamic, bristly-haired Jesuit priest."[50] In 1968 the Ford Foundation decided to tap Ayrout's expertise, commissioning him to spend seven months touring villages in East Africa and then flying him to New York to give eight lectures at Columbia University on rural development. On reaching New York in April 1969, he suffered a heart attack and died.[51]

Ayrout's sister, Janette De Bono-Ayrout, who graciously invited me to her apartment in Cairo, did not believe the work of Gustave Le Bon was ever read by her brother or his circle, as she had never heard the name mentioned. After tea, she invited me to see the personal library of her late husband, the Egyptian historian Jacques Tagher. She was gently surprised when we found on the shelves a two-volume edition of Le Bon's *L'Homme et la Société.*

Richard Critchfield acknowledged in a published response to my essay that he had "paraphrased" Ayrout. Busy with further studies of peasants in Mindanao and Java, however, he had forgotten to add the references when copy-editing *Shahhat*. He promised to add them to a future edition.[52] I pointed out in reply that he would need not just references but quotation marks, since many of his borrowings from Ayrout were verbatim; that he would also have to do the same with passages copied from other authors not mentioned in my essay, such as the nineteenth-century Orientalist Edward William Lane, which may have been more numerous than those copied from Ayrout (even the description of Shahhat's house, for example, including its architectural details, comes almost word-for-word from the account of "dwellings of the lower orders" in Lane's famous 1835 study, *The Manners and Customs of the Modern Egyptians*); and finally, that he would have to explain to the reader why his description of Shahhat's house comes from a book written a hundred years before it was built and the portrait of Shahhat's visit to the market, his work in the fields, his character, and his facial appearance were taken from an account written almost a generation before he was born.

I wrote the original essay without visiting the village of Buʿairat, for the improbability of Critchfield's account was clear enough from its ignorance of recent history and its stereotypical image of an unchanging village life. I subsequently visited the village several times, however, and found the book's portrait even more bizarre than I had suspected. Critchfield suggested that the location of Shahhat's hamlet within Buʿairat, adjacent to Medinet Habu, the ruined temple of Ramases III, indicated that this was a particularly ancient community and had preserved more Pharaonic practices than most. In fact, while the main village a mile to the south was probably the result of an Arab settlement (on an ancient site) within the previous three hundred years, Shahhat's hamlet was built within the preceding fifty years.[53] Most of the families that settled there came to serve the needs of modern archaeology and tourism. Shahhat's great-grandfather Khalifa is said to have moved to the area from Karnak across the Nile, possibly when the French-run government antiquities service for which he worked began excavations nearby. In the 1880s he served as a guide and assistant for an American archaeologist and antiquities collector, Charles Wilbour.[54] Together with another family, who also worked for the antiquities service, Khalifa's descendants built most of the hamlet. Many of Shahhat's uncles and cousins continued to work for French archaeologists, others for Americans from the University of Chicago, who had begun excavations at Medinet Habu in the 1920s. Three of the uncles invested their income in the building of small hotels. Shahhat's father was less successful. He became the local supplier of alcohol to the foreign archaeological missions, and died of his alcoholism. Shahhat himself, although happy to hoe a field when a tourist turned up to videotape the character from Critchfield's book, had to spend most winters elsewhere in Egypt as a foreman and labor contractor on French archaeological digs—and struggled himself against his father's illness.

This long history of relations between local families, foreign archaeology, and a small-scale tourist industry, mixed in with the agrarian economy of sugarcane and household farming, has formed the complex reality of Shahhat's village. We cannot read Critchfield's work as a portrait of this reality, for the book deliberately ignores the relations between locals and outsiders that have formed it. We should see the book, at best, as one more aspect of those relations.

Richard Critchfield died on December 10, 1994, in Washington, D.C. He had gone there to attend a publication party for his tenth book, *The Villagers,* in which he retold stories from the dozen or more villages he had described in his earlier works.[55] His obituary in the *New York Times* mentioned that he was survived by an elder brother, James Critchfield, of Delaplane, Virginia. James Critchfield, I subsequently discovered, worked for the United States Central Intelligence Agency. The discovery led to further questions about the production of Critchfield's portraits of the Third World peasant.

James Critchfield belonged to the founding generation of the CIA. After working closely with former Nazi intelligence officers in postwar Germany, he was appointed the first director of CIA clandestine operations in the Near East in 1959, and went on to become a senior architect of U.S. policy in the Middle East for three decades.[56] One of his first actions, in February 1960, according to a later Congressional investigation, was an attempt to murder the president of Iraq, General ʻAbd al-Karim Qasim. Critchfield's idea was to have the president killed with a poisoned handkerchief prepared by the CIA's Technical Services Division. (The attempt failed, but Qasim was killed three years later in a coup welcomed and possibly aided by the CIA, which brought to power the Baʿth, the party of Saddam Hussein.)[57] The attempted murder of Qasim was one of the actions for which James Critchfield's supervisor, Richard Helms, the director of Central Intelligence from 1966 to 1973, was mildly sanctioned by the U.S. Senate in 1977, for allowing the CIA to function as though it had "a licence to operate freely outside the dictates of the law."[58]

One cannot assume without further evidence that Richard Critchfield worked in the same profession as his brother. However, he certainly moved in the same circles. *The Villagers,* his last book, acknowledged the "advice, suggestions, help and hospitality" he received from Cynthia Helms, the wife of his brother's former supervisor; from Robert S. McNamara, the former U.S. secretary of defense; and from a number of other figures associated with the CIA and the politico-military establishment. These were unusually well placed associates for a man who insisted in each of his books that he was just a journalist who wrote about peasants in obscure parts of the world.

One might also notice the way his choice of villages, always portrayed as out-of-the-way places, followed the changing focus of U.S. imperial concerns, some of them at the time quite secretive. He was in India and Nepal in 1959–62, the years coinciding with probably the largest CIA operation of the time: a secret program based in Nepal to train and arm Tibetan refugees to fight the Chinese occupation in Tibet.[59] Critchfield's visits to Nepal were spaced between spells teaching journalism at the university in Nagpur, the birthplace and headquarters of the rising Hindu fascist movement. By the mid-1960s, an account of the CIA program in Nepal reports, "CIA officer James Critchfield described the guerrillas' achievements inside Tibet as 'minimal.' . . . In any case, the CIA's attention was shifting to Indochina."[60] Richard Critchfield followed suit, arriving in Vietnam in 1964 as a reporter for the *Washington Star* and writing the book that promoted the views of British military intelligence, which the CIA was then urging Washington to adopt. From Vietnam he took trips to Java, then spent a year there in 1966–67, just after the CIA had helped the Suharto regime seize power and carry out the killing of as many as a million political opponents. He also spent a year in Washington as a White House correspondent for the *Star,* which had its own connections with the CIA.[61]

In 1969 Critchfield abandoned the *Star* to become a full-time "reporter from villages," with a grant from the Alicia Patterson Fund.[62] For his first long stay in a single village he chose the seemingly out-of-the-way island of Mauritius, in the southern Indian Ocean. The Indian Ocean, however, was then at the center of another U.S. military expansion. Mauritius had just acquired its independence from Britain and was offering naval facilities to the Soviet Union. The United States was building its own Indian Ocean naval and intelligence base on the island of Diego Garcia, previously attached to Mauritius but retained by Britain and leased to the United States. To ensure the secrecy of the new base, Critchfield's friend McNamara demanded that the entire population of the archipelago to which Diego Garcia belonged, the Chagos Islands, be removed. Britain agreed to secretly round up the inhabitants, against their will and in violation of international law, and ship them to Mauritius. As Critchfield arrived on the island, Britain and the United States were paying the Mauritian government £650,000 to help settle the Chagos Islanders, in the hope that news of their illegal deportation would not reach the West.[63]

Building the base on Diego Garcia was part of an expansion of U.S. power in the Gulf and the eastern Mediterranean, an expansion that involved new relations with the two leading non-Western military powers in the region, Iran and Egypt. Critchfield's village studies over the ensuing years followed these shifting concerns. He lived in a village on the border between Iran and Iraq in 1971, just as his brother had helped persuade President Nixon to start building Iran into a heavily armed ally of the United States and begin secretly destabilizing the Baʿthist government in Iraq. In 1974 he arrived in Egypt, within weeks of Washington reestablishing diplomatic ties with Cairo. Although most of rural Egypt was still off-limits to visiting Westerners, by choosing a village on the edge of the tourist area near Luxor Critchfield was able to spend time in the Egyptian countryside during this critical period of renewed U.S. involvement in the country.[64]

So was Critchfield an American spy? I do not know and do not think this is the interesting question. A few years after Critchfield's book appeared a leading Egyptian journal published a series of articles warning about the "penetration" of Egypt by American scholars and development experts, whose research posed a threat to the country's "national security."[65] One article reported the views of the sociologist Saʿd Eddin Ibrahim, who gave the example of an American study that had collected data on local leadership in four hundred Egyptian villages, warning that such information could be used in ways detrimental to Egypt.[66] This seems unlikely. Given the evidence of Critchfield's writings, it is hard to imagine him gathering anything in the way of useful information, just as there is very little one could learn from a survey of "leadership" in four hundred, or even forty, Egyptian villages. As I explain in later chapters, it would be difficult to point to any American research on Egyptian rural development that gathered information reliable enough to threaten the country's security. If there was any threat it lay in the danger of invoking the shibboleth of "national security," an invocation aiding those forces of repression for whom this is always a useful term. Saʿd Eddin Ibrahim himself became a victim of this repression when he was sentenced a decade later to seven years in prison for alleged activities threatening national security.[67]

The importance of Critchfield's connections with America's "national security" regime, whether direct or indirect, lies elsewhere, in unraveling the political genealogy of such expertise on the Middle East, and on the question of "the peasant" in particular. Only recently has it been understood how pervasively the CIA influenced the production of academic and intellectual culture around the world in the second half of the twentieth century. The story of the Congress for Cultural Freedom, established by the CIA in Paris, is now well known, including its funding of the British magazine *Encounter.* The CIA's efforts extended well beyond this, to include the funding of art exhibits, in particular those promoting abstract expressionism; concerts featuring the work of avant-garde American composers; academic and cultural congresses; and books, translations, and a wide variety of journals willing to criticize Marxism or the Soviet Union and to support, or at least remain silent on, American violence in Vietnam and other parts of the world.[68] Among the journals the agency funded overseas was an Arab counterpart to *Encounter* magazine, *al-Hiwar,* established in Beirut in 1962 under the editorship of a distinguished Palestinian writer, Tawfiq Sayyigh.[69] *Al-Hiwar* ceased publication in 1967 after the CIA funding of the Congress for Cultural Freedom was revealed.

These connections with the clandestine U.S. production of cultural and academic expertise may have extended not only to work like Critchfield's, but also to the U.S. publication of Ayrout's *Egyptian Peasant.* The book was published in the United States, as I noted, a quarter of a century after it was first written, but coinciding with a renewed American interest in domestic Egyptian affairs. Its publication was arranged by Morroe Berger, who had played a role in the creation of the National Defense Education Act in 1958 and, as I mentioned earlier, was the first chair of the Near and Middle East Committee of the Social Science Research Council and the founding president of the Middle East Studies Association of North America. As a student in New York in the late 1930s, Berger had been a member of the New York Trotskyist movement, with others like Irving Howe, Seymour Martin Lipset, and Gertrude Himmelfarb, many of whom became active anticommunists after the war and in several cases moved far to the right.[70] Some of them, including the journalist Irving Kristol, the N.Y.U. philosopher Sidney Hook, and the editor of *Encounter,* Melvin Lasky, were later funded and promoted by the CIA. Like many other scholars who came to area studies after World War II, Berger had worked in intelligence during the war, and he, too, had connections with the CIA. He was a member of the Congress for Cultural Freedom and was the scholar who recruited the editor for the Arab counterpart to *Encounter* magazine, *al-Hiwar.* The generous amount of CIA money that he offered the prospective editor carried with it one stipulation: that the journal publish articles dealing with the unfavorable position of Muslim communities in the Soviet Union.[71]

The most serious questions raised by this story are neither Critchfield's plagiarisms of Ayrout, nor the possible connections with the activities of U.S. intelligence work and the clandestine political funding of American journalism and scholarship. The most important issue is the structure of academic expertise that enabled these forms of prejudice, ignorance, and misrepresentation to flourish and gave such dubious books their circulation and acceptance.

5 Nobody Listens to a Poor Man

The discussion of rural politics and violence has always been strangely one-sided. Resistance and rebellion in the countryside have been the object of a long series of studies. But it seems to be a convention of the literature that rural violence refers to the violence of the poor and the powerless. The phrase is not usually taken to mean violence used against these groups. Although the latter may be discussed in explaining the context of rebellions or the reactions they provoke, it is seldom itself the focus of analysis.[1]

Part of the reason for this one-sidedness is that any attempt to write about the everyday use of violence against the powerless faces the problem of evidence. Violence directed against people within a small community often relies on the power to impose silence. Victims can disappear, survivors may fear to speak, investigations, if they occur, produce only accusations and hearsay, or are organized to serve larger political purposes. The original act of violence is therefore easily lost, and writing about it becomes an almost impossible effort to reconstruct events out of fragments and recover the voices of the missing.

Yet the silence imposed by local forms of violence is seldom total. A violence that erased every sign of itself would be remarkably inefficient. The death, the disappearance, the physical abuse or the act of torture must remain present in people's memory. To acquire its usefulness in the play of domination, violence must be whispered about, recalled by its victims, and hinted at in future threats. The disappearance or the hidden act of terror gains its force as an absence that is continually made present.

The missing evidence, it follows, is not simply a methodological problem that limits the feasibility of writing about everyday violence, making it impossible to reconstruct a meaningful analysis. Rather, in a very basic way, in a culture of fear, meaning itself is made possible by what is missing.

To elaborate a cultural economy that can manufacture terror, obedience, and submission depends upon the ever-present reference to what has disappeared, upon deaths remembered and violations recalled. Paradoxically, then, the void that seems to undermine the foundations of a scholarly account of political violence turns out to be a crucial empty space—"the space of death" as Michael Taussig calls it, invoking a phrase of Walter Benjamin—by reference to which the construction of an economy of fear can proceed.[2] It also follows that the recollections, reports, and rumors that refer us to what is missing are not just secondary evidence, to be employed as tools offering a partial and unreliable access to the original event. Without the patterns of recollection there would be no significance to the original event, and in that sense no event. It is the combination of violence and its recollection, of the absent and its representation, that constitutes the event.

By realizing the hybrid nature of its occurrence, we can perhaps be more attentive to the problem of political violence against the poor, and question the ways rural politics is described. This chapter takes the case of Egypt in the 1960s, a critical period of political struggle in the countryside, and reexamines the accounts of peasant politics. It considers the kinds of writing through which this period was represented, particularly in the United States, looking for the signs of violence that were missed and asking how far the narratives that were written were capable of addressing the question of violence. I will begin by presenting some fragmentary evidence of political violence against the poor, gathered in rural Egypt in the 1960s.

The evidence consists of accusations made by the inhabitants of Ghazalat ʿAbdun, a village in Sharqiyya Governorate in the Nile delta, as recorded in a secret report drawn up in October 1966 by the Criminal Investigation Department of the Egyptian army and reproduced, twenty years later, in an appendix to an American study of the politics of rural Egypt.[3] The document is one of about three hundred such reports that were submitted to the Higher Committee for the Liquidation of Feudalism, a government body set up in 1966 by President Gamal ʿAbd al-Nasser in response to popular demands that the government investigate and curb the provincial power of large landowners.[4] The report accuses Ahmad Hasan ʿAbdun, a former member of parliament and the largest landowner in the village, of eleven "criminal and terrorist" offenses.

"Approximately ten years ago," according to the report, Ahmad Hasan "was accused of killing Muhammad al-Qalshani Ibrahim from the village." The victim "vanished from sight and no traces of him were ever found. No one came forward to testify against him out of fear. The investigations were suspended for lack of evidence." Ahmad Hasan then "took possession of the land belonging to the slain peasant, which amounts to more than four feddans [acres] of the village *zimam* [cultivated area]." Five years later, the report claims, Ahmad Hasan "beat and tortured the farmer Hasan Ahmad ʿAli, known as Hasan Naqah, who was his private guard." The torture "led to bleeding and death," but "no one in the village dared to lodge a complaint against him." He dealt with another farmer, according to the report, "by tying him to his car and dragging him along the village roads until he reached the front of his store. The victim was naked and he was beaten and maimed in front of his mother. This took place because the victim demanded the conversion into *hiyaza* [registered tenancy] of a plot of land he was cultivating," of which Ahmad Hasan was the owner.[5]

Three years ago, the report further claims, Ahmad Hasan "beat and tortured the lawyer ʿAbdel ʿAzim ʿIdrawis by burying him up to the shoulders in a cemetery at night. He was rescued by his relatives. But as a result of this incident the aforementioned lawyer lost his mind. He now lives as an insane person in the village." On another occasion Ahmad Hasan "beat the citizen Ahmad Yusif in the mosque while he was praying. He also assaulted his wife." When the local schoolteacher, a nephew of the wife, intervened, Ahmad Hasan assaulted him as well, "hitting him with a liquor bottle which he held in his hand." In some cases the accusations refer to sexual harassment, including a murder alleged to have taken place "because the victim refused to comply with the wishes of the feudalist's wife, who was known for her bad behavior," and the claim that Ahmad Hasan himself enticed "the wife of the fruit seller ʿAbdel Latif ʿAli to run away from her marital abode and coaxed her to stay with him for a long time until her husband was forced to divorce her." Ahmad Hasan then married the woman, "and she continues to be his wife until now."[6]

What can we learn from this kind of fragmentary evidence? In the first place, the report seems to indicate that a typical cause of violence in the village was conflict over the control of its land. More than half the crimes it mentions occurred in response to the victims' demands for cultivation rights. On one occasion, it is claimed, Ahmad Hasan "beat and tortured the farmer ʿAbdel Wahid al-ʿArushi, who died as a result of his injury. The reason was a dispute over a demand made by the victim for the conversion into *hiyaza* of a plot of land he was cultivating, but owned by the feudalist. This incident took place some four years ago and no one in the village dared to complain." In another case the farmer made his demand during the holy month of Ramadan, and in response Ahmad Hasan mistreated the man's wife "by forcing her to break her fast. He then beat her children, while her husband was lying sick. They were expelled from the village and went to settle in ʿIzbat al-Manshiyya." Another dispute involved land in a neighboring village. According to the report, Ahmad Hasan "led a group of regular and private guards as well as members of his gang in an attack on the estate of Hajj Ibrahim Najm, close to the village of Ghazalat ʿAbdun. They fired several rounds of ammunition to terrorize the peasants. The attack was caused by an old dispute between him and the owner of the estate over a piece of land."[7] The prevalence of disputes over access to land suggests it would be possible to explain many of these incidents of violence in fairly straightforward terms: they represent a struggle over local economic resources between parties of vastly unequal strength.

Such struggles over access to the land appear again and again in the reports on other powerful families that were submitted to President Nasser's committee, not included in the American study. The Salih family, for example, who owned extensive property in the village of Beni Salih and nineteen neighboring villages and hamlets in the district of Fayyum, south of Cairo, were accused by the local villagers of dozens of acts of violence and exploitation—including at least six killings and the shooting of the village carpenter.[8] A summary of some of the other complaints against members of the family seems to reveal the same conflict over cultivation rights behind their use of violence. Complaints were made against Salih ʿAli Salih by Mursi ʿAbd al-Al Qandil ("appropriated the produce of the land"), by Mujawir ʿAbd al-Ghani Mujawir and his mother ("illegal seizure of half an acre"), and by the heirs of Muhammad Radwan ("arrested and evicted from the land"); against Anwar ʿAli Salih ("eviction of ʿAbd al-Qawi Sanhabi after he demanded a rental contract in writing"); against Anwar Mahmud ʿAli Salih by ʿAbd al-Tawwab ʿAli Muhammad ʿAbd al-ʿAziz ("illegal seizure of land he owned, which the former then sold"); and against ʿAbd al-Zahir ʿAli Salih by Muhammad Muhammad ʿAbd al-Rahman Hasanain ("land illegally seized"), by Mizar Makkawi ("appropriated the produce of the land"), by Naish Tusun ʿAwad ("land illegally seized"), by Sufi Muhammad Muhammad Musʿad and his father Muhammad Muhammad Musʿad ("blocking a canal from which they used to obtain free irrigation, after which they had to pay for water") and many others.[9]

The logic of these disputes seems clear. The demands for secure access to the land come from those who, like most villagers in Egypt, own virtually no land or none at all. Government figures suggest that in 1965, after the agrarian reforms of the 1950s and early 1960s, 45 percent of agricultural families were still landless.[10] Among those owning or renting land, 95 percent held less than five acres, at an average of just over one acre per holding, while the top 5 percent of owners continued to control 43 percent of the cultivated area.[11] These official figures, moreover, are an unreliable measure of the inequality of ownership. As we have seen, the villagers' complaint is that large landowners had the power to misrepresent the extent of their control.[12] Studies of individual villages almost invariably indicated a far greater inequality. A study in 1980–81 of a village in Upper Egypt showed that the village's 4,500 officially registered landholdings were consolidated into about 1,250 farms, including two of more than three hundred acres.[13] A study of three Delta villages in 1984 found that the official landholding records in one village "only began to hint at the degree of concentration of economic and political power." Although the largest dozen owners officially farmed an average of less than fifteen acres each and none controlled more than fifty acres, in fact one individual farmed an estate of 150 acres and his extended family controlled three times that amount, or about one quarter of the village's cultivated area.[14] Another village study, conducted in 1979, found that the largest landowner in the village owned about two hundred acres but was registered as owning only thirty acres. The study concluded that in those days a widespread fear of a future lowering of the land ceiling led "most rich farmers to register their land under more than one name."[15] The family of Ahmad Hasan ʿAbdun owned 290 acres, according to the report from which I have been quoting, although the village registers showed him owning only 100 acres. He, too, had violated the agrarian reform laws by registering the land under different names.

This kind of control of the land provided a means, in turn, for constructing a broader economic and political power. In the case of Ahmad Hasan it enabled him to monopolize both the village's labor and its agricultural produce. "Tenancy contracts do not exist between him and the peasants," the report notes, "and he exploits them in the worst manner because he appropriates all the crops, while leaving to them only meager amounts of rice and wheat." Also, "he imposes forced labor on peasants to work in his orchards without payment of wages or against very low wages. Whoever opposes him is punished by beating and torture to be followed by expulsion from the land and the village."[16] Ahmad Hasan's power was further extended through his control of an irrigation pump and the supply of water to the fields, and through an attempt to monopolize the supply of fertilizer from the government cooperative in the village. When the clerk of the cooperative, a relative of his, tried to resist his demands for more fertilizer than his quota, Ahmad Hasan "put the warehouse of the cooperative on fire causing damage amounting to £180, which was paid by the aforementioned clerk.

This incident took place in 1963. He also incited some of his assistants to let the water flow into the warehouse, which damaged the fertilizers stored there, in order to mete out vengeance on the cooperative's clerk."[17]

The significance of these forms of violence, however, is not simply a question of their economic utility. In fact, as Taussig remarks, it would be a mistake to make do with a neatly utilitarian explanation of such events.[18] Although most of the violent incidents in the report on Ahmad Hasan can be related to a particular dispute over land, labor, or crops, the violence seems to exceed this kind of utility: a man is buried alive, another is tied to a car and pulled naked along the village streets, and other forms of torture are even worse. The excess appears inexplicable and leads one to question the reliability of the reports. The Egyptian army's Criminal Investigation Department, after all, was notorious for its own use of terror in collecting information. Yet despite the problems of reliability in such circumstances, the accusations against Ahmad Hasan include a kind of detail that suggests the reports come from the villagers themselves. A certain beating takes place in front of the victim's mother, another occurs during the month of Ramadan, the weapon used in a third case is a liquor bottle. The dates, the locations, the financial sums, and the relationships between the parties involved are all precisely recalled. The details suggest, if not the absolute reliability of the events, their status as stories that have been placed carefully in memory and told and retold among the victims. The accounts, by what seems to us their excess (something we have no way of measuring), reveal a culture of fear.

It is in this context that we should consider the question of reliability. Our impulse is to get to the bottom of such stories, to establish their truth. But as I suggested at the start and as the accusations against Ahmad Hasan seem to confirm, the truth of a culture of fear is built upon absences, upon tortures "no one dared to report," victims who "vanished from sight" and investigations "suspended for lack of evidence." "Despite all these criminal incidents," the report on Ahmad Hasan concludes, " . . . no one dared to accuse him, out of fear."[19] To take these accusations seriously as the signs of a culture of fear is not to imply that such fear and violence was typical of all Egyptian villages in this period. But it does raise the question of what exactly, in that case, such reports can be taken to represent.

Some writers on rural Egypt have taken these reports, in a sense, as highly representative. They are taken to represent not the typical landowner, but the very limited extent of this kind of exploitation and its essentially feudal nature. In a country of about five thousand villages, it is pointed out, the

Higher Committee for the Liquidation of Feudalism produced reports on only some 330 families. From this the conclusion is drawn that there were only "pockets" of illegality and resistance to land reform during Nasser's rule and that exploitation in the countryside was "successfully ended by the reforms of the Nasserist period." Any further reference to "exploitation," therefore, "cannot be other than political propaganda."[20] The problem with this use of the Higher Committee's reports is that conflicts over control of the land were not confined to those villages the committee investigated. On the contrary, its investigations were deliberately limited to families subject to the first agrarian reform law of 1952 (those owning more than three hundred acres) in order to divert a far broader popular discontent with the exploitative power of large landholders in the countryside, a power that in many cases the land reforms had strengthened, by misrepresenting the problem as the survival of the remnants of a pre-1952 "feudalism."[21]

We should not be misled into making the reports represent, in this way, the near absence of rural violence. Although the violence was no doubt less severe in many other cases, conflicts over the land may have been endemic. In a study of local conflict in three villages in Middle Egypt between 1967 and 1970, ʿAbd al-Muʿti found constant disputes in each village that focused on the same three issues: tenant farmers falling behind in the payment of rent, the consequent attempts by the owners of the land to evict them, and the demand of the tenants to have their rental agreements put in writing.[22] It is true that these disputes were handled by village committees, whose records were the only available evidence for such a study, rather than by the more invisible methods of violence favored by Ahmad Hasan. Like other local institutions, however, the committees were dominated by the landowners and generally ruled in their favor. They thus served the useful function of diverting and dissipating the grievances of tenant farmers (they did nothing for the landless), while legitimizing the underlying relations that are the source of coercive power.

Given the nature of the subject, we cannot resolve the question of how representative are the reports of violence like that of Ahmad Hasan ʿAbdun. To ask how many other large landowners were like Ahmad Hasan or how many other Egyptian villages endured a similar culture of fear would be fruitless. What we can do is to employ what this case tells us about the elusive nature of rural violence against the poor to interrogate and perhaps unsettle other accounts. Rather than passing over the details found in the reports of the Higher Committee for the Liquidation of Feudalism, I want to use them to examine the representation of violence against the poor in American academic accounts of rural Egypt. I will argue that these accounts developed ways of writing that, given the nature of rural violence, tended systematically to exclude it from the picture.

A symptom of this exclusion is that in the American study, published in 1986, the report on Ahmad Hasan was consigned to an appendix. Nowhere in the text itself does the author refer to its details or consider their significance. The book opens with another case of rural violence, a detailed recounting of the story of a murder in the village of Kamshish, to which I will come back. However, even this account is strangely disconnected from the rest of the text. Despite an avowed concern with "local community relations," the author, Hamied Ansari, follows Leonard Binder in examining the national influence of the rural bourgeoisie rather than the local construction of its power.[23] Other studies of rural politics in Nasserist Egypt show a similar neglect.[24] The only passage of which I am aware describing the role of violence in creating a culture of fear is the following paragraph from Iliya Harik's 1974 study of a village in the Nile Delta summarizing the conduct of Mustafa Samad and his brother, who until the end of the 1950s were the village's dominant family:

> The conduct of the two brothers in governing the village was harsh but not ruthless; only two cases of major violence perpetrated by the Samads were reported to me. The first involved a peasant cultivator who had urgent business with Mustafa Samad and pursued him persistently, causing Mustafa to lose his temper and beat him. This incident accidentally led to the man's death, but the issue was settled privately by Mustafa and was never discussed by the villagers with outsiders, a practice quite common in Egyptian villages. A second case involved the accidental shooting of a woman by a member of the Samad family. Again, no official investigation followed the incident, and Mustafa settled the matter with the woman's family. The only other use of violence attributed to the Samad's government involved the beating, intimidation, and blackmail of villagers who caused problems or dared challenge the Samads' authority.[25]

Harik's account of the village he calls "Shubra al-Jadida" is the most thorough study that was written of Egyptian rural political life in the 1950s and 1960s. But remembering the report against Ahmad Hasan, one begins to wonder how many more cases of "harsh but not ruthless" behavior, privately settled "accidents," and routine violence against those who "caused problems" would need to be uncovered for all this to merit proper consideration as belonging to the book's central concern, described as "the structures of power in the community."[26] By the time the author arrived in Shubra in the late 1960s the Samad family had been displaced by another powerful landowning family, the Kuras. The book mentions in passing that one of the Kura men was "given to violent expressions of his feelings" and that the two lieutenants on whom they relied "for contact with villagers" were "known for their short tempers."[27] But the question of a culture of fear or the use of violence is simply not raised.

The failure to examine the question of political violence against the poor in American academic writing on rural Egypt was not merely a matter of oversight or neglect. Rather, as the rest of this chapter will argue, the literature generally constructed its object of study in such a way that any evidence of such violence, given its elusive nature, was inevitably discounted, or translated into something else. There are several ways in which this occurred, which I will illustrate through a reading of the two major American works analyzing the period of Nasserist intervention in the countryside, James Mayfield's *Rural Politics in Nasser's Egypt* (1971) and Harik's *The Political Mobilization of Peasants.* I have chosen these two works because they deal with the period in which the reports of the Higher Committee for the Liquidation of Feudalism were compiled, and will enable us to consider in more detail our understanding of rural violence in that critical period. There were some important case studies of rural Egypt in later periods, such as Adams's study of agrarian poverty and political life in two Egyptian villages, and Hopkins's detailed analysis of the transformation of labor relations in the Upper Egyptian village of Musha.[28] In the late 1970s the demand for migrant labor in the Gulf and the construction boom in Cairo made it possible for the rural poor to escape the countryside in unprecedented numbers, creating a seasonal shortage of agricultural labor, a rise in wages (although the figures here are ambiguous), and a burst of rural construction and other economic activity as the migrants returned to the villages with their savings.[29] These sharp, though short-lived, changes did not end underlying patterns of exploitation or the forms of violence they may involve (although the question of violence was still not explicitly addressed in the more recent studies). Nevertheless, the situation described by Adams, Hopkins and Commander and in other later works is clearly different from the 1960s, and is not directly discussed in this chapter.[30]

Mayfield's *Rural Politics in Nasser's Egypt* is a study of the Arab Socialist Union, the single political party set up in 1962 as part of the process of state-capitalist intervention in the countryside, and of the "psychological barriers" that this process encountered in the form of the Egyptian peasant's "personality and culture." Continuing a long tradition of colonial writing on rural Egypt, mixed with more recent American theorizing on culture and personality, the book translates fragmentary evidence of political violence into the symptoms of a cultural psychopathology.

The book explains the peasant personality as an unstable mixture of violence and submissiveness. The submissiveness is said to be created by the peasant's general inability to comprehend the forces shaping his life, and by the way he raises his children. "The main objective of child training," we are told, "is to cultivate a docile and yielding disposition." The child learns to cherish authority, being discouraged from "independent thinking" by the "feelings of uneasiness or anxiety that may develop in a person making a decision outside the accepted framework." The inevitable resentment toward superiors of the peasant, trained from childhood "to obey without questioning," "can be relieved only on inferiors—even if it is only the village animals." Thus an inbred submissiveness in turn breeds violence. "When a complaint does occur, it is likely to be in the form of an emotional protest, or even in the form of violent behavior. With rare exception there is little training in the kind of pragmatic give-and-take that a democratic polity requires."[31]

The violence lying beneath the peasant's submissive surface explains other psychological traits, such as what the American visitor experiences as the peasant's "excessive" politeness and generosity. The hospitality and generosity of the Arab "ward off expected aggression," explains Mayfield, quoting the Princeton sociologist Morroe Berger, whose own views have a genealogy explored in the previous chapter.

> One has the feeling, indeed, that the hostility that becomes overt aggression is so uncontrollable that such measures as excessive politeness (a form of avoidance) or hospitality (a form of ingratiation in a situation where intimacy cannot be avoided) are at times absolutely necessary if social life is to be maintained at all.[32]

Given this risk of an uncontrollable aggression threatening the very possibility of social life, the peasant "expects the superior to be strict and firm," Mayfield says. "This attitude is often forgotten by bureaucrats and government workers who try to be friendly and kindhearted. Such behavior immediately creates distrust, since they are not playing the role the peasant expects of them."[33] If peasants seem distrustful of authority, in other words, it is because they are not getting enough of it.

The peasant's inbred desire for authority produces not only a spasmodic violence but also a permanent dishonesty of character, termed the "*fahlawi* personality." The *fahlawi* is a peasant skilled in "deception and trickery," who adapts himself according to the situation. He is sycophantic toward his employer, "kissing his hand and caressing him with flattering words," but as soon as the employer's back is turned the *fahlawi* "satisfies his ego and frustration" by making him the butt of his jokes. Given this dishonesty and the fact that "superficiality is the accepted behavior," the *fahlawi* peasant cannot be trusted as an employee. He has a "wondrous" ability to evade work and responsibility, to find "the 'shortcut' way of doing things," and to "finish his job quickly" without seeing to "the 'finishing touches.' " The *fahlawi*'s dishonesty even explains evidence that seems to contradict these racial stereotypes. When the author makes the surprising discovery that many villagers with whom he talked desired a modern education for their children, he interprets this as a sign of the *fahlawi*'s ability "to perceive what he must do, say and believe in order to be accepted and therefore not bothered" rather than a serious desire for the advantages of schooling.[34]

The author cautions us that not every rural Egyptian is necessarily a *fahlawi*. The more general characteristics of the peasant's psyche include "the obstinate conservatism and parochialism, the suspicion and mistrust, the general apathy and unconcern," together with his "hopelessly avaricious" preoccupation with just two objects of desire, "the acquisition of land and money," a preoccupation "by which his whole personality is twisted." The greed and suspicion combine in the peasant personality to produce "that frantic jealousy which, from passionate and personal causes in the villages, saps the vitality of private enterprises and government institutions, and makes mutual confidence and cooperation almost impossible."[35]

The reasons for the failure of policies of rural modernization already seem clear. But the flaws in the peasant personality will cause him not just to weaken the vitality of capitalist development, but to reject the very authority of landowners, agricultural experts, and the state. In compensation for his "feelings of inadequacy" the peasant develops an immense egoism, visible in "the tendency to exaggerate one's self-importance, abilities, and control of the situation." The peasant ego is enhanced by making "private attacks on the governor, the landlord, or the village doctor" and expressing "indignation toward anyone or anything that emphasizes difference in status." While outwardly respectful toward his superiors, "inwardly he rejects their authority. This feeling can be noted in conversations among the fellahin about the young agricultural engineers who wear 'the western suits' and about whom the *fahlawi* will say *fulan ʿamil rayyis* ('such a person acts like a boss')."[36] The end result of this pathology of submissiveness, violence, distrust, greed, and exaggerated egoism is that the rural Egyptian "does not look upon government authority as necessary to society."[37] The state therefore faces in an acute fashion the problem confronting all "newly emerging nations": how to develop among these abnormal personalities "a deep and unambiguous sense of identity with the national government." The name for this problem is invoked in the book's subtitle, "A Quest for Legitimacy," which is defined as "the process of inculcating and deepening the belief among members of a society that the present political institutions, procedures and ideals 'are right, are good, and are appropriate.' "[38]

The traits of character described in *Rural Politics in Nasser's Egypt* are in most cases simply an accumulation of earlier Orientalist lore, which is a major source for the book's observations.[39] This lore generalizes to an absurd degree, and tells us far more about the political frustrations and desires of those involved in organizing the transformation of Egyptian landholding and agriculture over the preceding century than about the particular experiences of Egyptian villagers. (With his reputation established by this book, over the following quarter century Mayfield became a leading academic consultant on rural Egyptian politics, hired continuously by the U.S. Agency for International Development.) Nevertheless, texts of this sort can be made, despite themselves, to reveal something of that experience. What appear to the outsider as patterns of docility and dissimulation, of distrust and disrespect for authority, of conservatism and suspicion, can be read as the characteristic symptoms of a culture of fear. Forms of coercion that leave no explicit trace of themselves may nevertheless reveal themselves to strangers through negative signs: silence, avoidance, extreme formality, and outward submissiveness.[40] As I suggested at the start of this chapter, there is no way to establish the truth of these signs, for they are marks left by what is missing. But a writing addressed to the question of "personality and culture" commits itself in advance to interpreting them at face value, as inbred features of the peasant "character." This inevitably transforms what may be the fragmentary evidence of everyday coercion into the symptoms of a cultural pathology. In fact, an "avaricious" preoccupation with acquiring land and money might actually be a sign of poverty; "indignation" at differences in social status might indicate the harshness of the inequality; an unwillingness to "finish the job" might express the alienation of those coerced into producing for others' consumption at the expense of their own needs; the view that government is "unnecessary to society" might accurately reflect the way its police and army help suppress all fundamental attempts to improve things. But instead of pursuing such questions, all these marks of violence are turned into the psychological defects of its victims, and the violence disappears from view.

Iliya Harik's *The Political Mobilization of Peasants* criticizes the psychological focus of works such as Mayfield's. It covers the same period in Egyptian politics but studies an individual village and concentrates "on behavior rather than personal characteristics" in order to uncover the local power network that implements development plans and shapes their success. Before addressing the somewhat different problems presented by this approach, I will situate the book's discussion more closely within the politics of the period. "Shubra" is located in Buhaira Province, whose governor, Wagih ʿAbaza, was a close ally of the Egyptian prime minister of 1964–65, ʿAli Sabri. In March 1965 ʿAli Sabri took over as secretary-general of the country's single political party, the Arab Socialist Union (ASU), and with the help of men like ʿAbaza began reorganizing it as an instrument of mobilization and political surveillance that would simultaneously co-opt or neutralize the left and undermine the power of large landowners and provincial bureaucrats. When Harik arrived in Buhaira early in 1967 he was accompanied by the district secretary of the ASU and a public relations official from the Ministry of Agrarian Reform. With their help he chose as his research site a village where the new organizations for peasant mobilization had successfully been set up. He also selected a village that was not "strife-ridden," arguing that endemic strife is usually caused by conflict between family groups and can therefore interfere with "normal change processes."[41] For both these reasons, the chosen village turned out to be a model of the success of the new policies of ʿAli Sabri and Wagih ʿAbaza, at least at first.

During the 1950s, Harik found, the control of the village by the Samad family, some of whose methods of violence I described above, had been weakened. Although their own estates had not been subject to the 1952 reforms, land they had leased from an absentee owner, a prince of the royal family, had been confiscated and distributed among small tenants. The Samads found their political position challenged by the only other large landowners resident in the village, the Kuras. The two Kura brothers and their nephew were from a merchant family originally involved in the cotton business. They lived outside the village itself in a large compound on the family estate, land their father had purchased in the village around 1913. As businessmen and politicians they were well connected with the new regime in Cairo, one of the brothers serving as an executive in a nationalized textile company in Tanta and later as a representative in the National Assembly. Thanks to the regime's 1952 reforms the Kuras had become the village's largest landowners, and by 1960 they had used their political connections and their increased influence within the village to replace the Samads as its dominant family. These changes were typical of the way larger rural landowners and the managers of state-owned enterprises transformed themselves during the dozen years after 1952 into an emergent Egyptian ruling class. It was the consolidation of the political and economic power of this class that the ASU mobilization program attempted to undermine in the years 1965–67. In Shubra, Sayid Kura was replaced as head of the village council by a twenty-eight-year-old party activist from Alexandria, who used evidence of the Kuras' mishandling of council funds and property, together with numerous village improvement projects, an active youth organization, and close surveillance of more militant peasants, to win the political support of small landowners in the village and isolate the Kuras.

This was the situation witnessed by Harik in the spring of 1967. By then, however, the mobilization policies were already being slowed down by conservative forces within the regime. They were brought to a halt by the Israeli invasion in the war of that summer, which also cut short Harik's fieldwork in the village after just three and a half months. When he returned for another stay the following summer, he found the party youth organizations had been banned after workers and students had led large antigovernment riots, the young head of the Shubra village council was being transferred elsewhere, and new council elections were under way. With organized campaigning prohibited and only seven hundred villagers voting (out of a population of more than six thousand), the Kuras regained their political control. These developments paralleled those in the country as a whole: the state managerial class and their rural allies used the military and political defeat of 1967, the economic crisis it accelerated (Suez Canal fees, Sinai oil, military equipment, tourist revenue, and potential U.S. economic aid had all been lost), and the resulting pressure upon the regime to begin accommodating itself within American regional interests, to reassert their influence over government policy. The Higher Committee for the Liquidation of Feudalism was disbanded, the lands confiscated from large owners like Ahmad Hasan ʿAbdun were restored, and, following Nasser's death in 1970, the more populist and pro-Soviet political faction led by ʿAli Sabri was defeated by a faction led by the champion of state and large landowning interests and the future symbol of the country's reintegration into the North's global economic circuits, Anwar Sadat.

Part of the value of Harik's account is that he was the only scholar to have captured some of these struggles as they occurred and to have illuminated their local complexion. Despite its obvious improvement over Mayfield's psychological and cultural approach, however, the book exemplifies the problems of the literature of the late 1960s and 1970s on political development. There are three conventions of the literature that I will analyze. Rather than transforming the symptoms of violence against the poor into a cultural pathology in the manner of Mayfield, these conventions tended to exclude them altogether.

First, there is the question of theme. In any work of political analysis, the account must invoke a larger political logic that particular events are then arranged to illustrate. The logic invoked and illustrated in *The Political Mobilization of Peasants* is a familiar one for American political analyses of this period, "the phenomenon of change." Change is conceived in common Weberian vocabulary as the modernizing process of rationalization, initiated by the national government. The regime in Cairo imposed "new normative rules" on the village, it is said, which brought about "the rationalization of its economic and political management" and a corresponding development in the villagers themselves of "new capacities and attributes." The end result is described as "village pluralism."[42]

This kind of narrative of the coming of modernity has been frequently criticized, and perhaps Harik himself would later have said certain things differently—although most of the assumptions of modernization theory were to come back into circulation in the 1980s and 1990s under the rubric of globalization.[43] I do not intend to repeat the criticisms here, but rather to focus on those aspects that seem to elide the question of violence. A first problem with the narrative of change is the process of abstraction it involves. To put it simply, to make events from an individual village portray a phenomenon as abstract as "change," a lot of detail must be eliminated from the picture—details that may provide the very clues through which an elusive political violence is revealed. Exactly what gets eliminated depends upon how the logic of change is conceived. Like most such literature, *The Political Mobilization of Peasants* thinks of change as a centralized force intervening in the village from outside. "In Shubra," the book explains, "the major forces that had set in motion the processes of change came from outside the community, namely, the national government."[44] The forces of change are more or less synonymous with a central power, the state, which imposes itself on a resistant periphery.

What this conception excludes, on the one hand, is the possibility of thinking of power as something local in construction; that is, drawing upon and shaped by larger logics, but built out of the practical relations between farmers and laborers, landowners and middlemen, bureaucrats and merchants, men and women. The fields that villagers own or rent, labor in or supervise, sell or seize control of, are the crucial sites for constructing and contesting rural power relations—which is why almost every account of violence in the report on Ahmad Hasan ʿAbdun mentions fields in one way or another. "Shubra," on the other hand, appears to be a village without fields. For all the book's richness of information about village life, from the details of people's travel habits to the closely observed conduct of a local election, one closes *The Political Mobilization of Peasants* without ever having seen a field, or learning about the day-to-day relations between the various groups for whom in different ways the fields are the center of their lives, or about the other forces—technical, animal, agricultural, or hydraulic—in relation to which those lives are lived.[45]

Seen from the perspective of the fields, on the other hand, the state becomes a more complex set of relations. These no longer appear primarily in the form of a central power intervening to initiate change, but as local practices of regulation, policing, and coercion that sustain a certain level of inequality (not just in the control of the land but in a policy of rural pricing and taxation, for example, that takes from the poor and gives to the rich).[46] The programs of change, from this point of view, appear not as a modernizing logic but as temporary interventions, which occur in reaction to crises in the local construction of power and are themselves a site of struggle and reversal. The temporary, reactive, and uncertain nature of these interventions cannot emerge from a narrative that seems to generalize such moments, under the abstract name of "change," into the unfolding of a unilinear history.

The mid-1960s, as I have already suggested, were years of uncertainty and crisis, particularly in the countryside. A postcolonial bourgeoisie had emerged as the dominant force in both the countryside and the nationalized economic activities of the city, but had not been able to consolidate its control over the apparatus of government or force upon it the shift, necessary for that consolidation, from dependence on the Soviet Union to dependence on the United States. Even before the disaster of the June 1967 war an economic crisis had set in, as hard currency reserves dried up, growth rates came to a halt, the United States suspended food aid, and the cost of living jumped more than 50 percent in four years. The rural poor were badly hit by the crisis and paid for it in part with their own wages, which were already well below the poverty level and dropped a further 10 percent in real terms between 1965 and 1967.[47] Public protests, marches, and hunger strikes were organized in the provinces, particularly in the Delta around large towns like Disuq, Damietta, Kafr al-Shaykh, and Damanhur, the latter being the market town just a few miles from Shubra. In Damietta in 1965 an incident between local fishermen and the police sparked a large protest, in which people marched on the police station and were met with gunfire. Peasants, students, and the unemployed joined in, overturning cars and trucks as barricades, throwing missiles, and ransacking government offices and food cooperatives, until the central authorities intervened and placed the area under martial law.[48] It was incidents of this sort that persuaded the regime to launch its program of party mobilization, which was intended to divert discontent away from the government and at the same time turn the party into an apparatus of local surveillance.

The narrative of "change," focusing on initiatives from the center and abstracting them into a story of development, inevitably tends to overlook the concrete political struggles in which political and economic control is contested or reaffirmed, as well as the forms of coercion and violence this involves. Power is not simply a centralized force seeking local allies as it extends out from the political center but is constructed locally, whatever the wider connections involved. The so-called mobilizing initiatives from the center occurred in response to struggles for specific changes at the local level. The center did not initiate change, but tried to channel local forces into activities that would extend rather than further threaten the weakening influence of the regime.

The adverse consequences of such central intervention can further illustrate this point. The local forces the government attempted to co-opt would inevitably overflow the new channels and require further diversion or supervision. This was quickly demonstrated by the famous incident in the Delta village of Kamshish, which is retold in the first chapter of Ansari's book and can be briefly summarized. Salah al-Din Husain, a villager from Kamshish who had been seized and then released again in the military-ordered arrest of thousands of political activists in the summer of 1965,[49] was one of those co-opted by the mobilization program onto the new ASU committee in his village. He used this position to renew an old campaign from the 1950s against the political power of the landowning family that dominated the village. The government's response was to have Salah Husain immediately placed under surveillance. Investigators discovered that he was the leader of a group of "communists" in his village, who were holding meetings among the peasants at which they "exploited the hatred of the village inhabitants" toward the large landowners and called for "the collectivization of agriculture and the abolition of private property." Two party officials were sent to Kamshish, a surveillance report mentions, to hold a public meeting at which they explained the government's idea of socialism. But Salah Husain "insisted after the conclusion of the discussion in telling the peasants that our socialism is influenced by

Marxist thought." He was creating "dangerous divisions" among party members in the village, the report concludes, and was causing a threat to the country's "internal security."[50] It was such local threats rather than any process of development, as Harik and others would have it, that explains the central government's initiatives.

The following month, April 1966, Salah Husain was shot dead in the village, and his murder was attributed to the large landowners he had denounced. Unlike the killings attributed to Ahmad Hasan ʿAbdun, with whose story we began, Salah Husain's death quickly gained attention beyond the village.[51] Party officials and journals took up his case, and the government was forced to respond. President Nasser visited Kamshish and promised an investigation, but once again the government tried to divert popular pressure away from fundamental change and into support for the regime. Instead of allowing ʿAli Sabri and ASU activists to continue investigating the power of large landowners, Nasser set up the Higher Committee for the Liquidation of Feudalism and placed it in the trustworthy hands of his military chief, Field Marshal ʿAbd al-Hakim ʿAmir. As I mentioned earlier, ʿAmir limited the committee's investigations to the few hundred families that had been subject to the original 1952 land reform. The problem was thus defined narrowly as the survival of individual "feudalists," meaning remnants of the old regime, rather than as the power of a landowning class nurtured by the new regime. Feudalism could be portrayed as an isolated obstacle to the larger process of development, obscuring once again the more systematic and local forms of coercion out of which everyday domination is built.

The case of Kamshish illustrates how complex, uncertain, and violent can be the struggles in which political control is locally constructed. It also illustrates how the literature on political development, by abstracting such events into the story of how a process of change encounters local obstacles, imitates the language of the regime—a language incorporated into such institutions as the Higher Committee for the Liquidation of Feudalism. The limitation is unsurprising, given that for the writers on development "change" is almost synonymous with the exercise of central power. We cannot expect, therefore, that literature of this sort might take as its focus the kinds of everyday coercion against which the villagers of Kamshish campaigned.

The second narrative technique that tends to elide the question of violence is to construct the story at the local level as an account of interacting individuals. The analysis of village politics, argues Harik, "has to focus on individuals rather than on social classes," a focus that is again a convention of such accounts.[52] One examines the alliances individuals form, the strategies they pursue, and the dominations they attempt. The picture that emerges in the case of Shubra is of a "pluralistic" balance of competing village alliances, in which individual allegiances continually shift, rather than any domination of the village by a "power elite."[53] We should note, however, that the individuality taken as the starting point of such analyses is always itself politically constructed. It is a position created out of a certain arrangement of social relations, including relations of subordination and domination. To take the individual as one's starting point renders these relations invisible, and obscures the forms of coercion on which they may depend. In a village such as Shubra, the most significant such relations will be the differing relationship to the land. Although *The Political Mobilization of Peasants* argues that "there is very little social differentiation among the villagers of Shubra" and gives no precise figures, the book provides sufficient information to enable us to outline the different kinds of individuality that social relations in Shubra construct.[54]

Broadly speaking, social relations in Shubra place its inhabitants—or at least its adult males, for women and children are subject to additional forms of subordination about which the book tells us nothing—in one of four different positions. About 40 percent of them, having no land of their own, are employed by others and live in severe poverty. Most sell their labor to middlemen who supply agricultural laborers to village landowners or provide work gangs for government irrigation projects out in the desert; others are employed as guards, servants, office boys, vendors, and itinerant artisans.[55] Their average income is E£3 a month, or E£36 a year if they are fortunate enough to find work all year round.[56] In 1967, to sustain an average family of two adults and 3.25 children at the poverty line cost E£148 per year, or more than four times the annual income of the fully employed landless villager.[57]

A second class of villagers, slightly larger than the first, consists of those with access to small plots of land, either owned or rented.[58] All of them are beneficiaries, directly or indirectly, of the 1952 land reform and farm an average of 2.5 acres each.[59] This provides each farmer with a net income of about E£200 a year, more than five and a half times the income of the landless peasant and enough to keep an average family adequately above the poverty line.[60] With a cultivated area of 3,559 acres, the village has enough land to give every adult male 2.5 acres of his own and thus end the desperate poverty of the landless (indeed, there would still be a few hundred acres surplus after such a distribution). A limit of 2.5 acres would be comparable to the limit of three *chia* (2.76 Egyptian acres) imposed in the early 1950s by two of the most successful land reform programs in the Third World, those of Taiwan and South Korea, which I discuss in chapter 7.[61] But with the Egyptian government allowing private estates of up to one hundred acres per family, the remaining land in Shubra was concentrated in the hands of a few dozen large owners.

Possessing an average of about twenty acres, these landowners together seem to constitute what one might identify as the third and fourth social classes. Samir Amin's analysis of agrarian class relations in Egypt divides such landowners into "rich peasants" (owners of five to twenty acres) and "rural capitalists" (over twenty acres).[62] This is a convenient shorthand, although I prefer the term "farmer" to "peasant" and, as I explain in chapter 8, I think we should be careful in assuming we know what we mean by "capitalists." We need to link with the latter the large shopkeepers and the middlemen, who, as we will see, play a vital role in the exploitation of the poor but whose numbers or place in the village are not described. It also needs to be said that no clear boundary separates the "rich farmers" from the wealthier of the small farmers, and in fact in the period of party mobilization it was this uncertain boundary that became the site of the shifting political allegiances that Harik labels pluralism. However, the relationship between the handful of largest landowners—the Kuras, the Samads, and about four absentee owners—and those with little or no access to land is quite clear. The three Kura men, for example, had a registered holding of 136 acres.[63] Leaving aside the question whether they had unregistered holdings and their significant income from other sources, their land holding gave each of them an annual income from farming alone of at least E£3,600, or one hundred times the earnings of a landless villager.[64]

To be an individual in such a village economy means to be already situated in a set of coercive relations. For the landless 40 percent it means being positioned as a person living with poverty, malnutrition and a desperate need for work—all of which constitute forms of coercion, invisible to a narrative that focuses on interacting individuals. To illustrate the coercive power of these social relations, we can examine the story of an effort to unionize Shubra's agricultural laborers. As part of its attempt to reduce profiteering in the countryside, in 1966 the ASU helped landless laborers in Shubra establish a labor union to replace the system of labor contractors. Instead of selling their labor at a rate below market price to a middleman, who then sold it to government land reclamation projects or agricultural cooperatives at a profit, the laborers' own representative was to deal directly with the employer. Three laborers from the village were trained by the party as union leaders, and were shown how "official and semi-official government agencies exploited them no less than did landlords."[65] Despite this outside assistance the effort seems to have failed, at least as regards the village's largest employer, the government-run cooperative. The workers needed to be paid every day in order to feed themselves and survive, but the cooperative paid wages through a central bureaucracy only once every two weeks. Under the old system, labor contractors possessed sufficient capital to advance the workers their pay on a daily basis (and also no doubt to provide small loans to cover medical, marital, or other exceptional expenses that wages well below the poverty level can never cover, thereby creating a typical relationship of debt bondage).[66] The new union had no resources from which to make such advances. The local leadership of the cooperative, which represented the small landowners of the village and was opposed to unionization, refused to advance the union the necessary credit from cooperative funds, and so the attempt to eliminate the middlemen failed.[67]

The book suggests that we interpret this dispute "without preconceived ideas of social class." The two parties involved have "similar humble backgrounds," it is said, and we should explain their conflict simply as "a contest situation in the context of incompatible interests."[68] It should be read, that is, as one more example of interacting individuals forming competing alliances in a system of village pluralism. In fact the parties' backgrounds appear similar only when compared to an outsider or to the very largest landowners. As we just saw, the small farmers who constitute the membership of the cooperative in fact enjoy an average income more than five and a half times that of landless laborers (and the leaders of the cooperative are wealthier than the average member). Moreover, their own relative prosperity depends on maintaining the low wages of the laborers they employ on their farms, which is why they support their forcible exploitation by middlemen (who form a third, but unanalyzed, party to the conflict). It is precisely these kinds of coercive relationship that an analysis of social relations can illuminate, and whose form of everyday violence the "focus on individuals" eliminates from view.

The third and final narrative technique to examine is the positioning of the author. Like most social science literature, *The Political Mobilization of Peasants* situates its author in the position of an objective outsider, disconnected from the object he describes.[69] My concern with this convention, needless to say, is not to question the writer's integrity, but to examine the means by which the village of Shubra is set up as an object apart from the narrative and its author, and the effect of this on the representation of violence.

An American scholar visiting an Egyptian village is clearly an outsider, but the outsider can also constitute a position within the village. The Kuras are outsiders, set apart by the distance of their family compound from the rest of the village, their political connections, and their large estate, yet these same factors also situate them within the village. The young party activist brought in from Alexandria as the new mayor of Shubra is another sort of outsider situated in a particular way within, as are the district officials of the ASU to whom he submits his regular surveillance reports.[70] It was these officials, in turn, who introduced the author to the village, and their close intervention in the villagers' affairs was the context in which he began his observation of their political behavior and administered to them his questionnaire. Such circumstances inevitably situated the author within the complex political struggles of the village.

One can get a sense of the author's situation from the book's account of accusations of corruption in the village cooperatives. In the case of one cooperative, villagers made "allegations of fraud and profiteering against the clerks, sometimes charging the board with complicity."[71] With another, a group of villagers claimed that its leader, ʿAli al-Shawi, appropriated cooperative resources for his personal use.

> Specifically, they claimed that he had sprayed his clover by using cooperative spraying machines free of charge and that he offered to spray his neighbors' fields at a low rate. They also charged ʿAli's brother with having cut down trees belonging to the cooperative and with using the cooperative's tractor to transport them to the family compound, where they were used in constructing a roof. They accused another board member, Yasin, with complicity from the board, of selling a waterwheel that belonged to the cooperative.[72]

An investigating committee set up by the provincial governor found the board guilty of these offences, but was unable to find sufficient evidence to establish a number of other charges. The author intervenes at this point in his own narrative, speaking in the first person, to describe the governor's report as "clearly biased."[73] He explains the accusations as the product of "a community suspicious of holders of public office" and argues that the board members lacked "the tenacity to withstand the pressures and slights to which public servants are usually subjected" in such a community. This explanation happens to reflect exactly the views of the board members themselves. "People are not appreciative," one of them complained to the author. "They are quite suspicious of a person in office. If a board member repairs the ceiling of his house, buys a water buffalo, or improves his land, they think he is using public funds of the cooperative for personal advantage." Such individuals were "oversensitive," the author concludes. "Criticism and suspicion of their record came only from a militant few."[74]

On the other hand, given the author's situation, we learn little about these "militant few." The accusations against the cooperative came from a group led by "a tractor driver in need of a job, having been laid off from the Kura farm."[75] But we discover nothing about, say, his treatment as an employee, the reasons he was fired, the poverty he may suffer, or the prospects for such a "militant" of ever finding other employment. The focus of the study is on the village elite (even though they too constitute, of course, only "a few"), and inevitably it is through their eyes that the author sees the village. Still more reflective of the author's situation in the village is the exclusion from the study of women. "Because I observed no involvement on the part of women in the public affairs of the community," the author explains, "and because of practical research limitations, women were not included in the survey."[76] What is termed a question of practical research limitations is actually the theoretical issue of the author's status as an outsider and a male. One consequence of this status is the researcher's conception of politics as "public affairs," meaning activities that are open to the observation of a visiting stranger. The problem in both these cases lies not in the author's failure to report the views of the unemployed or to gain access to the women's realm. Given his situation in the village, this was probably inevitable. It lies in our willingness to accept an account that says almost nothing about the poor and excludes all reference to the experience of women as a picture of "the structures of power in the community."[77] Once again one must wonder, given the exclusions, how any evidence of the experience of violence among these groups could find its way into the picture.

There is a further aspect to the method of positioning the author in relation to his object. To establish the objectness of the village, and thereby the author's separation from it, the village has to be constructed as something object-like, available to external observation. This means construing it as a system of behaviors, something visible to an observer. Its visibility is contrasted to the invisibility of ideas, which are converted into visible form by assuming them to consist merely of individual attitudes and recording these in a questionnaire. Behavioralism is a more recent form of the positivism that animated the cartographers conducting the cadastral survey at the start of the twentieth century. Its use in political analysis was criticized well before Harik's study was written (although such criticisms often end up presenting the same material/mental dualism in more sophisticated form).[78] My purpose here is to relate this issue to the representation of violence. For reasons I will try to explain, such attempts at representation can never capture a culture of fear.

First, coercion may be articulated in the form of practices that can be reduced neither to observable behavior nor to individual opinions accessible by questionnaire. For example, people in Shubra share a "cultural norm of dignity and self-respect," we are told, expressed not simply in personal attitudes but in a system of deferential practices, appropriate behaviors, and patterns of modesty.[79] Such practices can operate as a subtle force of coercion, by which dominant families exercise what Bourdieu calls "symbolic violence"—those forms of obligation and compulsion that are never recognized as coercive but are experienced as generosity, piety, personal loyalty, or self-respect.[80] The local elections of 1968 in Shubra were governed by such expectations, which impeded active campaigning and helped ensure the victory of the Kuras, thanks to their large accumulation of credit (Bourdieu's "symbolic capital") in the system of cultural coercion. This invisible kind of coercion cannot be understood from an observation of the behavior involved, which will appear simply as politeness or decorum. Nor can it be revealed by a survey of attitudes, since the essence of symbolic violence is that it is never recognized as such, but is experienced as a system of morality.

Second, attitudes themselves can express far more than they actually say, particularly in the case of those living within the coercive constraints of poverty or political oppression. Although *The Political Mobilization of Peasants* reports little of the views of poorer villagers, there is much to be read from what they tell us. The book reproduces part of the transcript of an interview with a fifty-five-year-old farmer, ʿAbd al-Mawla. It begins as the author poses question number eight from his survey, concerning the activities in the village of the ASU Leadership Group.

> "I don't know anything about them."
>
> "You mean you have never heard of them?"
>
> "I have, but I do not know anything about them. I just mind my own business."
>
> "How did you hear about them?"
>
> "From my children." He paused for a moment and then said, "I am told they go to meetings and talk politics. They want to appear like big people."
>
> "You don't think this is right for them to do?"

"A peasant should not mix with such things. This is the big people's job. These men have left their fields unattended and are going around doing things that are none of their business."

We changed the subject and talked about village problems.

"There are no problems," he said.

"We just need a bakery," he added. "Not much grain these days in the village, and people baking at home are causing fires."

"You think you can do something about it?"

"No, I am a poor man and nobody listens to a poor man."[81]

Answers of this sort reveal little about "attitudes," and therefore seem to support conclusions about the absence of political consciousness among the poor. But these statements reveal several things that they do not consciously say. First there is the evident apprehension. ʿAbd al-Mawla "was courteous though ill at ease" during the interview, we are told, and each of his answers begins in the negative and expresses an unwillingness to speak: "I don't know anything about them"; "There are no problems." When he does consent to speak, his answers express more than anything else a sense of powerlessness: "I just mind my own business"; "A peasant should not mix with such things"; "Nobody listens to a poor man." We cannot gauge from this brief transcript the degree of apprehension or fear, the extent of powerlessness or its causes, or the local forms of violence of which these words might be an indirect expression. What we can judge, however, is that a culture of fear will never emerge from the measurement of attitudes.

A connection emerges, therefore, between the methods of analysis required by the stance of objectivity and the disappearance of any sign of violence. On the one hand, the writer's position as an outsider within the village makes his writing tend to portray the experience of the wealthier male landowner at the expense of the experience of women or the poor. On the other hand, the convention of reducing meanings to those ideas available to individual villagers and expressible in the form of attitudes, so that they may be collected from questionnaires or interviews, tends to exclude the possibility of representing the experience of violence. Those who live intolerable lives, coping with poverty, unemployment, hunger, and other, more direct forms of coercion, must somehow express their condition and yet may be unable to find the opportunity, the courage, or the language to do so. These are conditions that may express themselves not in attitudes or accounts of observable events, but in silences, an unwillingness to respond, or the sheer inability to narrate. None of this can be explored by the conventional methods of political analysis found in the works on rural Egypt.

A close reading of some of the American literature on rural politics in Nasserist Egypt has shown how the kind of narrative a particular work adopts can determine whether, and in what way, the question of rural violence is represented. An account of cultural or psychological obstacles to development, a narrative of change, an analysis of interacting individuals, and the construction of an objective view of political behavior and attitudes can in each case transform what evidence there may be of violence into some other pathology, or render its effects invisible. This kind of writing contrasts starkly with the report on the violence of Ahmad Hasan ʿAbdun. The report is an isolated document, the by-product of an attempt to dissipate broader forms of popular discontent, accidentally preserved in the archives. There is no need to suppose that its story is representative of agrarian relations in Egypt in that period, or even reliable evidence for the particular case it records. But the report does have an important use. Its unsettling details challenge us to reexamine the way Western scholars have represented rural political life in Egypt during the crucial struggles of the 1960s, and to question the almost total absence of any sign of, and certainly any investigation of, local violence against the poor.

6 Heritage and Violence

One of the odd things about the arrival of the era of the modern nation-state was that for a state to prove that it was modern, it helped if it could also prove that it was ancient. A nation that wanted to show that it was up-to-date and deserved a place among the company of modern states needed, among other things, to produce a past. This past was not just a piece of symbolic equipment, like a flag or an anthem, with which to organize political allegiance and demonstrate a distinct identity. As many recent studies of nationalism point out, deciding on a common past was critical to the process of making a particular mixture of people into a coherent nation.[1]

The idea of the nation presents a way of living the experience of social relations by imagining them to extend back over a continuous period of time. The political community can then understand its present historically. The projection into the past may help make the present seem natural, disguising some of the arbitrariness, injustice, and coercion on which it depends. Historical thinking achieves this not just by projecting a past, but by organizing that past as the life of a self-directing object, the "nation" or "society." Contemporary political arrangements acquire a degree of inevitability by appearing as the genetic destiny of this historical being.

Recent writings on nationalism have also pointed out that to produce a past a nation-state had to produce a place. If making the nation depended on extending present social relations back through time, this could only be done by defining their geographical boundaries. Benedict Anderson argues that the idea of the nation came about when modern forms of writing enabled the social worlds of individual citizens to expand. Innovations such as the modern novel and newspaper made it possible for people to imagine unknown others as members of the same community.[2] Yet in many parts of the world, as Anderson also acknowledges, the idea of the nation required people not only to expand their sense of community in new ways, but in equally novel ways to constrict it. People's sense of religious community or tribal cognation, their networks of trade and migration, communities of learning and law, and patterns of imperial power and allegiance were in many places much more diverse than the narrow boundaries of modern nation-states. Ernest Renan famously remarked that the idea of the nation required that people learn to forget certain aspects of their past.[3] Many people also had to learn to forget, or at least to reconsider, their sense of place. They were supposed to reduce the significance of those interconnections, exchanges, genealogies, hegemonies, moral systems, and migrations that defined a social landscape whose horizons reached beyond what became the boundaries of the nation, or even to forget their existence altogether.[4]

Until the late nineteenth century, those in power in Cairo did not consider themselves to be ruling over an object that corresponds to the twentieth-century nation-state known by the name of Egypt. In the 1930s, a British historian of colonial India popularized the view of Mehmed Ali, the Ottoman governor of Cairo in the first half of the preceding century, as "the founder of modern Egypt."[5] Yet Mehmed Ali saw himself as a provincial governor within the Ottoman Empire, not as the ruler of a political entity defined by its geographic body. He undertook a remarkable program of industrialization and military expansion, colonized the Sudan, and took control of Ottoman provinces in Arabia, Palestine, and Syria. As Khaled Fahmy shows, however, these developments were not organized and undertaken as a proto-nationalist project to build a territorially imagined "modern Egypt," but were an attempt to remake, from the province of Cairo, the Ottoman order.[6] Politics was imagined and undertaken as a world of expanding imperial authority, not of territorially bounded nation-states. The particular geographic state that began to emerge in the colonial period, it follows, was one of several possible outcomes of this imperial history.[7]

The relatively recent formation of the national state is obscured by the English words routinely used to translate Arabic place-names from the nineteenth century. Ottoman provinces were generally referred to by the name of the city that ruled them.[8] Mehmed Ali was the governor of the province of Misr, or Cairo. The term suggested not the city alone but the city and its country, meaning the hinterland of towns and villages that supported it, politically and materially. This meaning was also invoked with phrases such as "the Cairo region" and "Cairo country."[9] From the later nineteenth century, however, the word Cairo *(misr)* also came to be used by extension to describe a new object, the territorial state. Phrases like "the country of Cairo" *(bilad misr)* were shortened to just *misr,* and the word came to be used interchangeably for the city and the country. Modern scholars, accustomed to thinking of all history as the history of nation-states, began to write anachronistically of the Ottoman province of "Egypt" (instead of Cairo). The term Egypt had come to refer to a spatial unit identified by geographical boundaries. The older phrases did not picture a territorial object but referred to the place in terms of a relationship—the connection between a city and hinterland.

One might suppose that the Lower Nile valley, compared to many other parts of the world, offered a well-defined geography and history within which to imagine a self-contained society. It should have been relatively easy to picture Egypt as a self-sufficient nation, to minimize the wider relations people may have had with other regions, and to give its particular mixture of communities a singular and self-contained past. The survival of monuments from more than five thousand years before, indeed the powerful image of what we call "ancient Egypt" as the cradle of civilization, would seem to offer modern Egyptian nationalism a neat and uncontroversial way to lay together superincumbent images of people, place, and past.

Yet constructing the past is never so straightforward. In the first place, ancient monuments do not automatically belong to one's own past. As someone from England, I can admire the imaginative power and ancient precision of Stonehenge, but I cannot feel those stones as part of my own past. In order to belong to one's history, monuments must connect with some aspect of one's social identity. Something similar seems to be true of the way the monuments of ancient Egypt figure in the politics of Egyptian nationalism. Periodically an effort was made to present the Pharaonic past as a source of modern Egyptian national identity. The idea that modern Egypt is a society whose ancestry goes back in a continuous line to a Pharaonic beginning is also the view of the nation's history found in Egyptian school textbooks.[10] However, such uses of the past have generally been of limited political use in the country's modern politics.

The most sustained effort to invoke the glories of ancient Egypt as the source of modern Egyptian identity came in the second quarter of the twentieth century, following the discovery of Tutankhamen's tomb in the Valley of the Kings, near Luxor, in 1922. When the British archaeologist Howard Carter unearthed the riches of the first royal tomb to be found intact in modern times, the event attracted worldwide attention. The discovery coincided with Egypt's winning partial independence from the British military occupation established in 1882, and provided the new nationalist government with a powerful expression of the nation's identity. The government refused to allow the British archaeologists to take possession of 50 percent of the discovered treasure, the practice followed with earlier finds.[11] Its determination to keep control of the treasure provided a useful demonstration of the government's newly acquired authority. Yet in the years following this event, the Pharaonic past played only a subordinate and diminishing role in Egyptian nationalism.

In architecture, a neo-Pharaonic style came briefly into fashion, but its importance lasted less than a decade.[12] For a few more years, a group of conservative writers with cultural ties to Europe continued to insist on the significance of the nation's Pharaonic origins. But they did so as part of an argument against northern Europeans who insisted on the Oriental and therefore backward character of Egypt, and against local intellectuals who insisted on the exclusively Islamic character of their society. The writers' concern was to show that Egypt was a modern, Western nation, a view to be proven by the fact that the West's own past lay within Egypt. The significance of the past for these writers was not so much that it gave the nation a distinct and authentic identity, but that it showed that the nation belonged to the larger community of the West, and was therefore modern. The role of the past, in Dirks's phrase, was to serve as a sign of the modern.[13]

In the same period a right-wing populist party, Young Egypt (Misr al-Fatah), began to emphasize the importance of the Pharaonic past, finding there an expression of its belief in leader worship, militarism, and an Egyptian imperialism stretching from the Mediterranean to the equator. This too was short-lived. By the 1930s most political argument in Egypt had reverted to themes that connected more readily with people's everyday experience and self-conception, principally the themes of Islam, Arabism, and anti-imperialism.[14] These political identifications did not necessarily refer to the confines of the Nile valley, and gave local politics a much wider resonance than a purely Egyptian nationalism.

The difficulties and ambiguities in the production of the nation's past can be more fully understood if one shifts one's attention from the history of nationalism, as it is conventionally written, to the political process that I call making the nation. I find it useful here to think in terms of Bhabha's distinction between the nation as pedagogy and the nation as performance.[15] The history of nationalism reconstructs the more or less coherent story of how the nation emerges as a pedagogical object. It pieces together the official nation that is invoked in the ideology of political parties, the propaganda of government programs, the imagery of a national film industry, the rhetoric of school textbooks, the memoirs of public officials, and the news reporting and opinion making of the mass media. These sources constitute the formal archive examined by any standard history of the emergence of twentieth-century Egyptian nationalism.[16] What such an account generally overlooks is the more mundane and uncertain process of producing the nation. I have in mind the variety of efforts, projects, encounters, and struggles in which the nation and its modern identity are staged and performed. The difference between performance and pedagogy is not a question of looking at the practical realm rather than a realm of ideas, or the local rather than the national. Both pedagogy and performance involve the making of meaning, and both take place in particular sites among particular parties. What is different about making the nation is that it always involves the question of otherness.

In the nation as pedagogy, the emergence of the national community is understood as the history of a self that comes to awareness, or of a people that begins to imagine its peoplehood. History is written to describe the growing self-awareness or imagination of a collective subject. This imagination takes the form of a gradual revealing of the collective subject to itself, a revelation shaped by those powers of communication, reason, and consciousness that define our understanding of an emergent self. There is no encounter with otherness, except as part of the general discovery of a world beyond the self. In the performative making of the nation, on the other hand, otherness plays a constitutive role. The nation is made not out of a process of self-awareness, but out of encounters in which this self is to be made out of others; or rather, is to be made by making-other. The nation is made out of projects in which the identity of the community as a modern nation can be realized only by distinguishing what belongs to the nation from what does not, and by performing this distinction in particular encounters. Unlike conventional accounts of the emergence of the nation as pedagogy, our understanding of such encounters cannot be governed by the consciousness of a collective subject that produces the meaning of the nation; this collective subject, the nation, is not the author of the performance, only its occasional effect. Moreover, one can bring into view the forms of difficulty, uncertainty, violence, and subversion that the production of the nation may involve.

In Egypt, one of the most important figures in this process of making the self through making-other is the figure of the peasant. In the preceding two chapters I examined a variety of mostly foreign representations of the peasant. The new national elite within Egypt developed a more complex relationship to the countryside, a theme that figured prominently in early nationalist fiction, film, and political argument. This chapter takes two interconnected episodes from twentieth-century Egypt, both concerned with the politics of national identity and cultural heritage, and both involving the lives of a local village community. One is a campaign launched in the 1940s to define and preserve a national cultural heritage, pursued through a struggle to create a national architecture based on the vernacular forms of the Egyptian village. The other is a dispute over the protection and presentation of the heritage of ancient Egypt, in particular the Theban Necropolis near Luxor where Howard Carter earlier unearthed the treasures of King Tutankhamen. In 1945 these two different efforts to produce and defend a national heritage came together in the plans to demolish and rebuild a village in southern Egypt. In the 1990s, more than half a century later, the village remained the site of an unresolved struggle over the country's national heritage.

MAKING THE NATION

In 1945 the Antiquities Department of the Egyptian government commissioned the Cairo architect Hassan Fathy to design and build a village to rehouse the inhabitants of the village of Gurna. The village lay on the west bank of the river Nile opposite the town of Luxor, four hundred miles south of Cairo, adjacent to Shahhat's village of Buʿairat, which we were introduced to in chapter 4. It consisted of a group of hamlets stacked along the desert escarpment at the valley's edge, amid the ancient rock-cut tombs and funerary temples known as the Theban Necropolis. A year or two earlier the Department of Antiquities had been embarrassed by the removal of an entire wall of one of the ancient tombs under its guard. It blamed the local inhabitants for the theft and decided they should be removed from the hillside and housed in a new village, to be built amid the sugarcane fields of the valley below.

Hassan Fathy was a visionary architect. In Gurna he pioneered the adoption of what later came to be known as "appropriate technology." Believing in the value and virtue of vernacular building methods, he rejected the use of reinforced concrete and mass-produced red brick—materials that were already becoming the standard in public housing projects—and insisted on building with handmade bricks produced in the local manner from mud, mixed with straw and dried in the sun. Mud brick was more affordable, he argued, especially if the villagers themselves were allowed to participate in the building, making their own bricks out of local earth, and provided better insulation against the heat of summer. It was also more aesthetically pleasing, he believed, especially when used not just for walls but also for roofs, which could be made to support themselves in the form of elegant vaults and domes. Fathy built New Gurna as a model village to demonstrate the affordability and beauty of this vernacular peasant architecture. He intended it as a prototype, not only for other public housing projects in Egypt, but for the development of an Egyptian national style.[17]

New Gurna became internationally famous. Its construction announced the rejection of modernism in architecture and the desire to reappropriate the styles and materials of an indigenous national heritage. The building of the model village also marked, as Kees van der Spek notes, the moment of this vernacular style's untimely death.[18] The government purchased fifty acres of sugarcane land in 1945, a dike was built to keep out the irrigation water, and the construction of the village proceeded over the following three winters. In 1948, with only a fifth of the village completed, Fathy was forced to abandon the project, partly because of bickering between government departments, but mostly because one night that winter men from the old hamlets of Gurna, whose families opposed the planned eviction and resettlement, cut the dike and flooded the low-lying village.

Fathy's account of these events, published twenty years later, expresses his disappointment at the failure of his plans "to revive the peasant's faith in his own culture" and his bitterness toward the "suspicious and strict" inhabitants of Gurna who had refused to cooperate and "were not able to put into words even their material requirements in housing."[19] It is easy to criticize Fathy today, whether for his paternalism toward villagers who stood in the way of his architectural vision, or for the cosmopolitanism that led him to propagate this vision in widely admired books published in English and French but cut him off from those who preferred to read in Arabic.[20] My concern here is not with Hassan Fathy, however, but with those events in the 1940s in Gurna, where the attempt to reappropriate and preserve an Egyptian vernacular was simultaneously born and destroyed. It is this relationship between culture and destruction, between national heritage and its subversion, that I am going to explore. Why did the manufacture of the modern vernacular, the attempt to revive or preserve a peasant culture, as well as the protection of a more ancient, archaeological past, seem to depend upon a relationship of force and a structure of antagonism? Is there something larger one can learn from the fact that the birth of a national heritage movement in New Gurna based upon the building methods of peasant architecture was also the moment of its violent demise?

The history of Hassan Fathy's vernacular model village intersects with a continuing effort to present and preserve a different national heritage, the monuments of ancient Egypt. Fifty years later, toward the close of the twentieth century, the road past New Gurna was filled with tourist buses, which stopped beyond the village at the Colossi of Memnon before proceeding to the Valley of the Kings and other ancient sites. None of the buses ever stopped at the model village, which was barely visible behind the police inspection points and tourist signs that lined the main road. "The Village," as locals still referred to the place, was a thriving community, but Fathy's houses were by now overlaid with additions and extra floors (to the extent that domed roofs allowed), or in many cases pulled down. Fathy's village school, whose domed roof had collapsed from neglect, was demolished by the Ministry of Education in the late 1980s and replaced with a larger school built according to the ministry's uniform design for all schools, with a reinforced concrete frame and manufactured brick. The handmade mud bricks of the original school were used as rubble to make the new building's driveway.

One thing, however, survived intact after more than fifty years: the unfulfilled desire to evict the inhabitants of the old village of Gurna. After several intervening failures, between 1992 and 1994 new plans were drawn up, as part of a master plan for Luxor funded by the United States Agency for International Development (USAID), to depopulate the seven or eight hamlets on the Gurna escarpment, from Sawalim in the north to Gurnat Marʿi in the south, as well as the neighboring hamlet of Medinat Habu (the home of Critchfield's Shahhat).[21] Over the following four years new villages again were built, this time located in the desert five to ten kilometers north of old Gurna, and again the households of Gurna largely refused to move and see their village demolished. On January 17, 1998, after several earlier skirmishes, a government bulldozer accompanied by two truckloads of armed police moved into Gurna to carry out demolitions. A group of about three hundred villagers gathered, later swelling to several thousand, and drove the police back with stones, pushing their bulldozer into a canal. The police opened fire on the villagers with automatic rifles, killing four and leaving more than twenty injured.[22] This incident set back the relocation plans, but by the end of the same year the head of Luxor City Council, Major General Selmi Selim, confirmed that the plans to depopulate "nine shanty areas known as Old Gurna" would go ahead, as part of a vision to turn the area into "an open air museum and cultural preserve."[23] As he explained to the press, "You can't afford to have this heritage wasted because of informal houses being built in an uncivilized manner."[24]

The major general's understanding of "heritage" was very different from Hassan Fathy's. Fathy had never succeeded in persuading the Egyptian government that it had anything to learn from the peasant. His conviction that a modern, national style, as well as solutions to the practical problems of modernity, could be found in the ways villagers had traditionally done things had no place in official visions of technical development and a tourist-based heritage industry. Yet for all their differences, the two perhaps had something in common. The major general's use of the term "uncivilized" to justify the evictions echoed the earlier language of Hassan Fathy. Fathy's account of the events of the 1940s tells the history of planning and building New Gurna as a story of the progress of culture and intelligence, impeded by the ignorance and lawlessness of the natives. The families of Gurna lived mostly as tomb robbers, Fathy said (an accusation to which I will come back), and it was to preserve this lawless way of life that they sabotaged his project. (In the plans for the model village there were to be several public buildings, including a theater and an exhibition hall, intended to create the kind of public spirit that Fathy felt was missing in ordinary villages; but there was also to be another kind of building not usually found in villages, a police station.) This violence and lawlessness provided the pretext for building the new village. It was only by addressing the problems of the ignorance of the peasant and the absence of civilization that an architect interested in a program to create a modern, peasant vernacular could find an opportunity to work. There had to be some lack, something missing from the peasant, for even a sympathetic modernizer to transform his house into a national style.

I want to begin my analysis of Fathy's project by recalling what seems a minor episode in his account, an event he refers to as the malaria epidemic of 1947. He notes in passing that the epidemic "killed about a third of Gurna's inhabitants," but concentrates more on the restrictions imposed on travel from Cairo and other delays the epidemic caused to his project.[25] It seems startling today that Fathy would not discuss any larger objections to uprooting a community in the midst of such suffering. But in fact there is more to this oversight. Writing twenty years later, Fathy had collapsed together two epidemics. And these events were not just an obstacle to his plans, but the source of the political circumstances that made them possible.

The 1947 epidemic was actually an outbreak of cholera, not malaria, and affected mostly Lower Egypt, although restrictions were placed on travel to and from the south (Fathy helped the villagers in Gurna to sterilize their wells as a measure against any local outbreak). But a few years earlier, in 1942–45, an epidemic of malaria had occurred in the Luxor region, the outbreak of gambiae malaria, the disease's most lethal form, that I discussed in chapter 1. Brought from the south by recent irrigation work designed to increase the sugarcane plantations, as I mentioned, and by increased wartime traffic with Sudan, it was this earlier epidemic, along with the famine that resulted from wartime food shortages and men too sick to harvest the wheat crop or earn wages cutting cane, that killed more than a third of the people in the Gurna region.[26] Among the 100,000 to 200,000 people who died in the south, the heaviest casualties were in Gurna and other sugarcane plantations, where perennial irrigation enabled the gambiae mosquito to reproduce. It was the manager of the plantation neighboring the Gurna sugar estate who estimated in May 1944 that 80 to 90 percent of the local population had contracted the disease, and the doctor in the nearest town on the west bank, Armant, who reported 80 to 90 deaths a day.[27] Hassan Fathy arrived in Gurna only a few months after the last gambiae mosquito was killed, before the survivors in the local villages had even gathered another harvest.

The gambiae malaria epidemic, as we saw in chapter 1, provoked a political crisis in Cairo. Opposition politicians blamed the large number of deaths on the poverty of the Luxor region and the rest of the extreme south, where a handful of owners controlled most of the land in sugar plantations of thousands of acres each, and the majority of the population was landless and worked for starvation wages. A deputy in parliament argued that living conditions in the Soviet Union were far better. The ruling Wafd party, which expressed the interests of large landowners, was anxious to defuse this radical threat to the principle of landownership. It argued that the cause of the epidemic was not poverty and inequality but the unsanitary living conditions in the villages. Instead of land reform and the redistribution of wealth, it supported a plan to demolish the country's villages and replace them with well-ventilated, sanitary, and attractive model villages.[28]

The idea of solving the problems of the countryside by replacing village housing with model villages had been promoted by a new generation of sociologists, educators, medical experts, and architects.[29] In 1933 the Royal Agricultural Society built a model *'izba* (housing complex) on its estate at Bahtim, near Cairo, and in 1940 gave Hassan Fathy his first large architectural commission, to build a second *'izba* at the same site.[30] Henry Ayrout, whose father and brothers were architects practicing in Cairo, promoted the rebuilding of the country's villages in his study of the Egyptian peasant, *Moeurs et coutumes des fellahs* (Paris, 1938), which was republished in Cairo in French and Arabic editions in 1942 and English in 1945.[31] In 1941 the Cairo architectural review *al-'Imara* launched a campaign for village reconstruction and published a plan for a model village.[32] None of these proposals received government funding, until the political crisis of 1944–45, when Hassan Fathy was invited by the Antiquities Department to construct his model village at Gurna.

The government purchased the fifty acres of sugarcane land from Boulos Hanna Pasha, who owned thousands of acres in the Gurna region and was one of the largest landowners in Upper Egypt. The fifty acres were to provide space for the village with its generously proportioned houses and its numerous public buildings, a freshwater pond for swimming (to keep children from the canals, where they contracted schistosomiasis), and a public park for recreation—but not a single acre on which to grow food. Unable to consider the dangerous question of villagers' rights to agricultural land, Fathy helped establish a textile workshop, employing twenty child weavers, to provide some income for the village. A visiting government official noticed that the children in the workshop "looked thin and hungry," and suggested that they be given a bowl of lentil soup every day. "It was a sensible and practical suggestion," Fathy admits. But no money could be found to provide the food.[33] The solutions Fathy pursued were architectural and did not address questions of landownership. This was not seen, however, as a limitation. Fathy saw his village as a pilot project launching a "National Program for Rural Reconstruction" that would lead "to the complete regeneration of the Egyptian countryside through rebuilding its villages."[34]

This approach to social problems was founded on the belief that the recovery of a vernacular national heritage—a heritage that was pure and undebased, and thus clean and sanitary—would provide a means to the recovery of social energy, health, and purpose. Such thinking went beyond the architectural politics of the later nineteenth century, expressed in the rebuilding of Cairo and other large towns and the construction of workers' housing on agricultural estates as rectilinear, visually organized spaces.[35] Planning and rebuilding would now lead to the construction of new peasant selves. At the same time it offered an alternative to impractical and controversial proposals that threatened the social order of landownership. Fathy was a farsighted individual, devoted to the new possibilities of planning and architecture, not just for their end results, but as a process. He insisted on the participation of villagers in the design—a novel idea—and believed the very process of planning would be the means for them to recover their lost individuality (about which Ayrout had written), through developing their power to make decisions. They would develop into subjects of the nation by discovering, in the rebuilding of their heritage, the ability to think for themselves. "Ideally," Fathy wrote, "if the village were to take three years to build, the designing should go on for two years and eleven months."[36]

This was a radical view of the possibilities for peasant initiative and peasant culture. The limitation we can now see—the inability to consider that villagers might prefer to stay in the houses they had already designed and built themselves—reflected the new hubris of planning. Fathy prided himself on the fact that in New Gurna, a village intended to house seven thousand people, every house was to be individually designed. Yet this desire embodied a contradiction, the oxymoron of planned individuality. What was distinctive in village housing was precisely that villages never planned their houses as finished objects. They built them to grow with the households and activities they housed, expanding and subdividing them, adding and removing extra floors, turning rooms into workshops, stables, or storefronts, over years or generations. The irregular streets and interlocking houses that Fathy designed for New Gurna expressed his attempt to recreate the way the villagers' "customs and taboos, their friendships and their disputes [were] intimately integrated into the topography, into every wall and beam of the village."[37] But to produce this irregularity as something planned in advance, the houses had to be placed tightly together, so that streets could twist and interlocking relationships find expression in the village's topography. As a result, the planning provided no space for the houses to be later expanded or reorganized.

Fathy's attitudes toward problems of peasant initiative also expressed the fact that he himself was from the landowning class (his father was the owner of one or more estates) and indeed was something of a royalist, with admirers and supporters among the Egyptian royal family, including the sisters of King Farouk.[38] His architectural commissions came from the same milieu, for only large institutions or wealthy individuals could afford the luxury of architecture. Before receiving the commission to build the village of New Gurna, he designed the model farm for the Royal Agricultural Society (1941) and a headquarters at the Red Sea port of Safaga for the Anglo-American-controlled Chilean Nitrate Company (1942), two institutions supporting large-scale farming. Most of his other architectural designs in this period were country houses for the proprietors of large agricultural estates.[39]

If Fathy saw the villagers of Gurna as unable "to put into words even their material requirements in housing," when one puts his project into a larger social context it is the architect who is perhaps not able to put into words its material basis. The sugar plantations of the Gurna region had originally been village land. As we saw in chapter 2, from the mid-nineteenth century the ruling household in Cairo began to take over village land, paying little or no compensation, as new irrigation schemes made it possible to channel the annual Nile flood and plant the sugarcane crop year-round. After the country's Ottoman Turkish ruling household was declared bankrupt by its British and French bankers in 1875 and the British army invaded and occupied Egypt, the foreign bankers managed the estates and then auctioned them off, not returning them to the original village owners but selling them to barons like Boulos Hanna and Ahmad ʿAbbud. In 1908, when the bankers auctioned the former viceregal estates near Gurna, local villagers discovered that their land and even their houses were to become the property of the new plantation owners. When the bailiffs later came to evict the villagers, in one reported instance, they met resistance. Fifteen members of the eviction force were injured, and fifty-seven villagers were arrested, one of who died in custody.[40] So when the government neglected to provide New Gurna with land to grow its own food, or even bowls of lentil soup for child workers, this was not an insignificant oversight. It was the continuation of a process of expropriation constructed and reconstructed over the preceding hundred years through the depredations of a ruling elite and their European bankers. And it was to counter the new challenges to this coercive order, following the malaria epidemic of 1942–45, that men were dreaming up plans for model villages and Fathy was proclaiming the architect's unique ability "to revive the peasant's faith in his own culture."[41]

In projects of this sort one sees the difficulties of making the nation. To perform the nation, groups must be included by first declaring them excluded for their lack of civilization, villages destroyed in order to preserve them, pasts declared lost so that they may be recovered. Fathy wanted to "revive" an indigenous culture as a means of developing an Egyptian national heritage. To perform this revival, he needed the people of Gurna. Yet he needed them as a people outside the nation, whose removal would help bring the nation and its past into being. The Gurnawis were to be treated as ignorant, uncivilized, and incapable of preserving their own architectural heritage. Only by seeing them in this way would the architect have an opportunity to intervene, presenting himself as the rediscoverer of a local heritage that the locals themselves no longer recognized or knew how to value. As the spokesman bringing this heritage into national politics, the architect would enable the past to speak and play its role in giving the modern nation its character.

The people of Gurna could enter into national politics only by submitting to an act of violence. To preserve their heritage, the architect first had to destroy it. Old Gurna was to be pulled down and rebuilt—and not just because it was built over antiquities, for if the project succeeded, Fathy hoped that every other village of Egypt would also be demolished and rebuilt (a proposal later taken up by the United States development program in Egypt).[42] The preservation of the past required its destruction so that the past could be rebuilt. Likewise, the performing of the nation required that every one of its rural inhabitants be declared outside the nation, uncivilized and unhygienic, so that in rendering them civilized and clean, the nation could be made.

When Fathy first visited one of his family's own large farms, near Talkha in the Nile Delta, "it was a terrible experience," he reports. "I had had no idea until then of the horrible squalor and ugliness amid which the peasants on a farm lived. I saw a collection of mud huts, low, dark, and dirty, with no windows, no latrines, no clean water, cattle living practically in the same room with people; there was not the remotest connection with the idyllic countryside of my imagination."[43] Fathy persuaded his parents to rebuild the workers' housing, or *ʿizba*. As he embarked on this and subsequent projects, however, he discovered two difficulties, one aesthetic and one practical. It was the solution to this dual difficulty that was to define the style of building for which he became famous. The genealogy of the solution is important, because it involves a series of interlocking elements over which Fathy had no control. These illuminate the complexities of turning to the peasant, or to the ideal countryside of the imagination, in the attempt to solve national problems and define a national style.

The aesthetic problem was that Fathy was unable to discover a model for the vernacular form he sought to revive in any of the villages he was rebuilding, or any other village he visited in Egypt. The idyllic countryside of his imagination existed nowhere. The practical difficulty was that Egypt was without forests and had no commercial supplies of lumber, which Fathy needed to build the roofs of his mud-brick structures. In 1941, when building the model farm for the Royal Agricultural Society at Bahtim, the difficulty became acute, because the project included large granaries whose roofs spanned a greater width than those of the ordinary workers' housing. To solve the problem Fathy attempted to build the granary roofs without lumber in the form of vaults and domes, employing the same mud bricks used for the walls. The vaults were intended to support themselves using the principle of the arch, and in turn carry the weight of the domes. This complex method was unsuccessful, however, and the domes collapsed.[44]

Hassan Fathy's brother, ʿAli, who worked as an engineer on the Aswan Dam, helped him overcome the problem. He invited him to come and visit the village of Gharb Aswan, near the dam, where Fathy finally found houses whose roofs included large mud-brick vaults. Gharb Aswan, he wrote,

> was a new world for me, a whole village of spacious, lovely, clean, and harmonious houses each more beautiful than the next. There was nothing else like it in Egypt; a village from some dream country . . . whose architecture had been preserved for centuries uncontaminated by foreign influences. . . . Not a trace of the miserly huddle of the usual Egyptian village, but house after house, tall, easy, roofed cleanly with a brick vault. . . . I realized that I was looking at the living survivor of traditional Egyptian architecture.[45]

Fathy recruited a master mason from the village, ʿAlaa al-Din Mustafa, who showed him the method of building vaults and worked with him on New Gurna and several of his subsequent projects. The mud-brick vault and dome henceforth defined Fathy's Egyptian vernacular. At the same time, he believed, by eliminating the use of expensive timber, these methods provided a means of building "an architecture for the poor."

There were problems with Fathy's solutions on both counts, the aesthetic and the practical. On the aesthetic side, Gharb Aswan was a Nubian village, and its houses were built in the distinctive style of the Kanuzi, one of the two main Nubian linguistic and cultural groups. Fathy chose to see this style as the survival of a pure Egyptian architecture, "uncontaminated by foreign influences." The Egyptian government did not recognize the Nubians, whose country spanned the modern border between Egypt and Sudan, as a distinct people or ethnicity, so Fathy's view of Nubian cultures as Egyptian was in accord with official opinion, even if the Kanuzi themselves might not have considered their heritage Egyptian. Still, it was ironic—and instructive—that only among a people whose language, culture, and history were all different from those said to define modern Egypt could Fathy find an Egypt uncontaminated by the foreign.[46] The point is not to discredit Fathy's desire for a vernacular Egyptian architecture, but to acknowledge its complex and heterogenous origins.

More of an obstacle to the success of this new aesthetic was that in both Egypt and Nubia domes carried a rather different connotation in vernacular architecture than the meaning Fathy wanted to give them. They were traditionally used only for the roofs of mosques, churches, and tombs. While this association may not have been especially resonant for a cosmopolitan Cairo architect trained in the modernist style, in rural Egypt, especially in the south, domes were used everywhere for the small roofs of saints' tombs, and never for the building of houses. Despite what many agreed was the powerful simplicity and beauty of Fathy's designs, he could never erase the existing significance of domes in the countryside, which transformed his own designs into an inappropriate confusion of sacred and domestic styles.

On the practical side, vaults and domes were a solution to a problem that for most villagers in Egypt did not exist. Fathy found timber expensive—and calculated elaborate mud-brick roofs to be more affordable—because he was obliged to purchase it commercially. For the farm at Bahtim he was building an entire model hamlet, and in particular the large granaries to store the landowner's grain, something ordinary villagers never had the luxury of needing, so he required timber in large amounts. Egypt imported its commercial timber from Romania. The Second World War cut off these supplies and caused the British army to requisition materials already in the country. The resulting timber shortage obliged Fathy to turn to the more complicated alternative of vaults, which required large quantities of mud brick and the labor of skilled masons.

In Gurna and other parts of Upper Egypt there was a local method of vaulting using a technique known as *tuuf,* which was simpler and less expensive than Fathy's method.[47] But this was used only in exceptional circumstances, such as where termites were present, and Fathy seems not to have learned of its existence. In most cases villagers made flat roofs from the trunks of locally grown date palms, overlaid with palm stalks and mud plaster. Unlike Fathy, they had no need to purchase commercial supplies of wood. They built their houses themselves, and when it was time to build or extend a house another palm tree could always be found, usually one of the villager's own. Palms, as it happens, are male or female, and only the latter produce fruit. Just one male tree was needed to fertilize every fifteen or twenty females, so the other males could be cut for timber.[48] Thanks to the reproductive mechanisms of the date palm, for the villager, unlike the architect, there was no timber shortage, and thus no need for the complexities of domes.

For reasons both aesthetic and practical, Fathy's mud-brick domes and vaults never caught on, except among a small group of his students and friends. The use of mud brick for any kind of architecture, moreover, was never supported by Egyptian officialdom or the architectural profession, and large building contractors like Osman Ahmed Osman lobbied successfully against Fathy's ideas. Villagers continued to build their own houses with mud brick walls. But even these gradually gave way to the use of baked red brick and concrete. Curiously, the elements that were bringing about the demise of this local heritage were the same developments that had enabled Fathy to discover his distinctive style—large-scale agriculture, and the Aswan Dam.

By the end of the 1960s, two decades after the building of New Gurna, the government had taken the place of large landowners in deciding what to grow and had constructed a second dam at Aswan. The High Dam ended the annual flooding of the Nile and enabled the authorities to extend the cultivation of sugarcane, which displaced the growing of wheat. Villagers no longer had the long weeks of the Nile flood, which in the past provided time for the laborious work of brick making and communal house building. Many no longer had their own wheat to provide the straw needed for bricks and plaster. For both these reasons, building with mud brick began to lose its advantages over the faster method of building with reinforced concrete.

Thanks to the dam, moreover, even the mud itself was less and less available. The fields were no longer flooded, there was no longer an annual deposit of Nile silt, and no longer any renewal of the alluvial mud out of which mud-brick houses were built. Before the High Dam, the Nile carried some 124 million tons of sediment to the sea each year, depositing nearly ten million tons on the flood plain. After the dam, 98 percent of that sediment remained behind the dam.[49] By the 1980s the government was forced to ban the use of alluvial mud for brick making, to protect agricultural land. Fathy's celebration of a vernacular based on centuries of accumulation of local mud was launched at precisely the moment when (and for reasons connected with the fact that) the mud for the first time in history was no longer in supply.

If the irrigation works at Aswan caused mud-brick building to gradually disappear, ironically they had also played an unnoticed role in Fathy's production of an Egyptian vernacular. Gharb Aswan, the village in which Fathy discovered an Egyptian architecture "preserved for centuries," was in fact a modern village. It was built at the turn of the century to house people from the Nubian villages to the south, which were submerged by the reservoir created by the first Aswan Dam.[50] The dam had given Fathy the opportunity to build his vernacular village, by creating first the estates and then the epidemics that brought the politics of rural reconstruction into being. These irrigation works had simultaneously destroyed the country of Nubia, whose rebuilt houses were the inspiration for his Egyptian vernacular. The nation, and its heritage, must be made out of the material lives of others. In doing so, however, it incorporates processes and materials whose use and meaning it does not entirely control.

THE PERFORMANCE OF THE PAST

Fifty years later the government was still trying to evict the population of old Gurna, and still describing them as lawless and unhygienic. To the old arguments about tomb robbing, official statements in the 1990s now added the claim that their "living conditions are poor, unhygienic, and spoil the view," and that the presence of this large population in what was now recognized by UNESCO as a World Heritage Site prevented its archaeological preservation and its development as an "open air museum."[51]

The issues were still those of heritage and civilization. But by the close of the twentieth century, Hassan Fathy's vision of a national culture inspired by the revival of peasant initiative and know-how had disappeared, along with most of the houses of his model village. Instead the government planned an open-air museum, in which the role of the peasant, as we will see, was rather smaller. The development plans of the 1980s and 1990s are discussed more fully in the final section of this book. But the plans for the development of tourism and national heritage in Gurna can provide an introduction to these issues, as well as a contrast with the peasant politics of an earlier period.

In 1982 the World Bank hired the U.S. consulting firm Arthur D. Little to draw up a program for increasing tourism revenue in Luxor (the same firm had been hired to do a similar study in 1953).[52] The consultants revived the proposal for the depopulation of Gurna, along with Hassan Fathy's scheme to set up a cooperative to improve the quality of locally made souvenirs. With the local population removed, the increase in tourism revenue was to come from better "visitor management" and improved infrastructure to enable the development of luxury hotels and Nile cruise ships. Since there was a limit to the number of tourists who could be squeezed each hour in and out of King Tutankhamen's tomb, income growth was to come partly from a shift toward wealthier tourists. The government proceeded to spend $60 million on these improvements, more than half of it borrowed from the World Bank to pay for foreign consultants and contractors.[53]

These investments made possible a rapid growth in tourism. From 1982 to 1992 the number of visitors to Egypt and their estimated expenditures more than doubled (although attacks by Islamic militants caused numbers to dip again in the 1990s).[54] In Luxor most of the growth, as planned, was in luxury hotels and cruise ships. Across the river in Gurna, those who had established small hotels or other tourist enterprises before the development ban was imposed did well. They typically put their profits into importing small air-conditioned tour buses from Germany and Japan, or buying land and putting up apartment buildings in Luxor. For many villagers, however, there was almost no way of breaking into the tourist business, except for those who found unskilled work on the cruise ships at below-subsistence wages. A few dozen young men did better by finding a foreign tourist to marry—usually a much older woman, who might visit each winter for a few weeks and with luck was wealthy enough to set the husband up in business. One woman, an enterprising California divorcée named Happy, began to build a small hotel on the edge of the desert south of the Theban Necropolis.[55] The building was stopped by the authorities, of course, and after six years and many payments to persuade the officials to allow construction to proceed the hotel was still not quite finished. Most of the husbands settled for something less, such as an imported car to run as a tourist taxi. Cruising past those working in the sugarcane fields in their air-conditioned Peugeots, these young men seemed to underline the separation of the tourist world from the village.

The World Bank's program was designed to increase this separation. Arthur D. Little, Inc., conducted a survey of tourists' experiences in Luxor and reported, as they had in their 1953 study, that the biggest problem concerned the visitors' contact with the local population. Tourists complained of being bothered continually by people trying to take them somewhere or sell them something. The consultants recommended that no further peddlers' licenses be issued.

More significantly, the visitor management scheme they devised was planned to minimize unregulated contact with the tourists and increase their physical separation from the local community. Separate river ferry and bus facilities were developed to isolate the movement of tourists from local traffic. An enclosed visitor center with its own restaurant and shops was to be built to enclose the tourists waiting for transportation. In a village adjacent to Gurna the plans called for an elevated walkway to be erected through the middle of the hamlet, so that tourists could cross from the bus parking lot to the Pharaonic temple without touching the village itself.

Enclave tourism, as this kind of arrangement is called, had become the typical pattern of tourist development in regions outside Europe and North America. It appeared to be required by the increasing disparity between the wealth of the tourists and the poverty of those whose countries they visited. The Egyptian Ministry of Tourism appealed to foreign capitalists considering putting money into hotels or other tourist enterprises in Egypt with the claim that investors were "enjoying outstanding profits in the tourism field," thanks to the easy repatriation of those profits and to "labor costs that are more than competitive on a world-wide scale."[56] In the late 1980s the ministry calculated that each tourist spent on average $100 a day in Egypt, which was more than most hotel employees earned in a month. A decade later the disparity was far greater.[57] The difference in wealth was so pronounced that the tourists' enjoyment could only be secured by their physical separation from the host community.

There was a further reason for the creation of enclave tourism. As the industry became concentrated in the hands of luxury hotels under the management of U.S.- or European-based international chains, along with half a dozen large Egyptian entrepreneurs, the hotel managers sought to increase their profits by containing more tourist expenditure within their own establishments.[58] The grand Egyptian hotels that used to provide little more than spacious accommodations and an elegant dining room were replaced by hotel complexes that offered three or four different restaurants and cuisines, several bars, shopping arcades, a swimming pool and fitness club, cruises and excursions, business facilities, and evening lectures and entertainment. The Nile cruise ships and the walled "tourist villages" popular where space was plentiful, such as the Red Sea coast, were even more self-contained.

In chapter 2 we encountered a different kind of walled village, the *'izba* or housing complex built for the workers on large agricultural estates. There is no similarity between the two kinds of enclosures, except this: both represent methods to contain a population, to establish a local zone of sovereignty where external forms of law, exchange, or movement might not apply. In a later chapter we will consider how what is called capitalism or the market adopts many different strategies to build enclosures or enclaves of this sort.

If the *'izba* was built to keep the peasants in, the enclave hotel was built to keep them out. The local population, except for a small elite, was excluded by the prices charged and the guards posted at the gate. To enter particular areas, such as the swimming pool or gambling casino, a foreign passport might be required. The result was a system of almost total segregation. Most Luxor tourists found themselves living, eating, and sleeping in their enclave hotels, traveling in separate air-conditioned taxis and buses, and going to separate entertainments. The few occasions in which organized tourists encountered the local street, whether half an hour set aside for shopping in the Luxor bazaar or a five-minute walk from the cruise ship to an archaeological site through a strip of village, became frenzied scenes in which local peddlers, merchants, and entrepreneurs tried to secure some small share of the tourist business.

The segregation was further encouraged by government and World Bank policy. In the 1980s the World Bank directed Egyptian public funds into building the infrastructure for tourist development. In the 1990s the World Bank pushed for the profits from this public investment to be switched into private Egyptian and foreign hands. Supported by a former IMF employee and banker–turned–minister of tourism, Fu'ad Sultan, in 1992 the World Bank paid the consultants Coopers and Lybrand Deloitte to draw up plans to sell off the country's luxury hotels, which, although managed by international hotel chains, were still owned by the state.[59] The hotels were highly profitable, providing returns of up to 50 percent of revenue or more. As the consultants acknowledged, the investors enjoyed prospects for windfall profits from the future resale of undervalued properties.[60]

Whatever the windfall, the increased control of Luxor tourism by outside capital had two likely consequences. First, it would send not just the profits from tourism abroad, but tourist expenditure in general. Increasing international integration of the tourist industry decreases the proportion of tourist expenditure that remains in the host country or region.[61] The integration of the hotel industry was accompanied in the 1990s by that of the foreign tour operators.[62] Second, as those who purchased these assets increased the pressure on local managers to build their share of a limited market, the process of segregating the tourists within their luxury enclaves would intensify. For the young men of Gurna and neighboring villages seeking employment, both developments were likely to decrease the proportion of tourism income available to the local community.

Yet even as the process of segregation developed, the lives of the local community were increasingly affected by the tourist presence. Because of the kind of industry tourism is, its development involves more than a simple process of segregation. A conventional industry, whether based in manufacturing or agriculture, involves organizing people to produce. Mass production relies upon all the well-known methods of recruiting and disciplining a workforce, organizing their use of time, their movement, and their arrangement in physical space, and developing systems of instruction, supervision, and management. Mass tourism, by contrast, involves organizing people to consume. It relies upon similar methods of managing flows and timetables, arranging physical space, and instructing and supervising, to maximize the process of consumption.

Tourism is an industry of consumption, and the consumption not of individual goods but of a more complex commodity, experiences. No object of modern consumption is ever just a thing. The purchase of food, clothing, or cars is always the purchase of a certain taste, lifestyle, or experience. One pays not just for the thing but for what it signifies. With tourism, this consumption of what things signify is taken to the extreme. The tourist industry sells not individual objects of signification but entire worlds of experience and meaning.

In Luxor the tourism industry marketed the consumption of ancient Egypt. The experience was created out of the archaeological sites, but also by organizing the contemporary society to appear as a reflection and extension of the past. The 1982 World Bank report on visitor management explained that "the creation of an *overall environment* is needed on the West Bank in order for Luxor to reach its full market potential."[63] This meant turning Gurna into an "open air museum," its population moved out, and its houses destroyed. A few houses were to be left standing as examples of local architecture, and used to house artisans and craftsmen producing tourist artifacts.

The new plans to evict the population of Gurna were formalized in a study carried out between 1992 and 1994. The new relocation site, first identified and surveyed in the 1950s, lay several kilometers to the north. Adopting themes first articulated by Hassan Fathy and subsequently transformed into standard development practice, the Terms of Reference for the relocation study, funded by USAID, emphasized the need for detailed architectural, social, and cultural surveys of the old village and "community participation" in the planning. The former now involved the making of an ethnographic film about the community that was to be removed, while "community participation" was reduced to constructing plywood model houses in three sizes, which villagers could visit to select their house design.[64] Several hundred villagers, in most cases those who were able to exchange one old house for several new ones, agreed to move to the new settlements, leading to extreme overcrowding (since 1978 the government had banned further building in old Gurna). So only a few dozen old houses were available for demolition. When the government tried to force other villagers to move, the result more than once was resistance, culminating in the riot and shootings of January 1998.

The World Bank, USAID, and the Egyptian Government spent tens of millions of dollars during the 1990s alone planning and attempting once again the eviction of the people of Gurna.[65] Despite this large employment of architects, planners, ethnographers, bureaucrats, and bulldozers, there was little investigation of the actual need for the evictions or their possible impact. While there were studies of the aesthetics and culture of old Gurna, there was to be no investigation of the actual problems these people were said to be creating, which might put in question the need for the evictions and for the employment of so much expertise.

The alleged problems can be briefly examined. First, it was said, the people of Gurna were tomb robbers, an accusation repeated so often that even many critics of the eviction assumed it to be true. The image of tomb robbers was a standard element in national media representations of Gurna, from Shadi ʿAbd al-Salam's famous film of 1969, *al-Mumiya* (The Mummy), to a popular television serial aired during the middle of theses events in 1996–97, *Hilm al-janubi* (The Southerner's Dream), whose plot turned on the conflict between an evil tomb robber in the Luxor area and an educated hero who sought to defend and rediscover Egypt's heritage.[66] Occasionally the government reinforced these images by staging a raid on a Gurna house. In 1996 Muhammad al-Adhim, sixty-three years old, came home to find that the authorities had discovered a tomb cut into the rock behind the wall of his late great-grandmother's bedroom. The tomb was just an empty tunnel, but this did not stop the authorities from arresting the old man, who worked as an assistant in a local dentist's office, and making a public example of him. "I am completely stunned. I never knew there was a tunnel," he said. "I think the tourist authority just made a balloon to attract foreigners. Tomorrow they will say these slippers I am wearing came from Ramses II." Tomb robbers, he pointed out, were supposed to make lots of money. "But can you tell me where is my Mercedes, where is my six-storey house?"[67]

Over some two hundred years certain households in Gurna formed a small part of the international network that moved the treasures of ancient Egypt to the great museums and private collections of Europe and North America. It is curious that we now look back on the Gurnawis as tomb robbers, but still find it difficult to describe the British Museum in London or the Metropolitan Museum in New York as collections of stolen goods.[68] An illicit trade in Egyptian antiquities still continued, driven by the demand from private collectors in the West. Occasionally these trading rings were broken, however, and news reports showed that the sources of stolen goods were invariably storerooms under the control of the government, dozens of which were dotted around the country, holding as many as a million pieces.[69] These problems might have best been addressed by measures such as better pay and training for local employees of the antiquities authority, more secure storerooms, and a more vigorous international campaign against the American and European dealers. In 1970 UNESCO adopted a convention to prohibit and prevent the international trade in stolen art and antiquities. Thirty years later, Britain, Germany, Switzerland, Japan, and several other countries that played an important role in the illegal trade had not ratified the convention.[70] Enforcement was so weak that Interpol estimated that 90 to 95 percent of stolen artifacts were never recovered.[71] Attempts to get the United States and other leading importers of stolen antiquities to pass domestic legislation to prevent the trade were also unsuccessful.[72] It was easier to demand the eviction of villagers from a hillside in southern Egypt than to investigate how the trade in antiquities was actually organized and run and to collaborate on measures against international dealers and buyers. Development agencies, architects, planners, and academics could then repeat without evidence the claim that Gurnawis were tomb robbers.

Second, it was argued, whether or not they were robbing its tombs, the villagers of Gurna were damaging the Theban Necropolis by their very presence. The wastewater from the Gurna houses was damaging the tombs, the authorities claimed, and houses built over tombs "spoiled the view" and prevented the development of tourism.

Again, it is not clear what the evidence was for these claims. The hamlets of Gurna were not allowed to have running water or to dig wells. They had to fetch all the water they needed in wheeled oil drums pulled by donkey. The only running water on the Theban hillside was in the accommodations of the European archaeological missions. Although moisture damage was a serious problem, there was no geological survey of the Gurna site, with its alternating layers of limestone and shale, to assess the impact of habitation (versus, for example, the impact of the general raising of the water table and humidity levels since the building of the Aswan High Dam), or to identify which locations could support human occupation without damage to the tombs.[73] Once again, despite the millions of dollars spent on outside consultants, these basic studies had not been done. Nor was any effort made to consider less disruptive solutions to the problem of wastewater.

Detailed information was available, on the other hand, about the damage that tourists were doing, and especially the damage done by tourists' wastewater. If a tomb in the Theban Necropolis was occupied by twelve visitors, in one hour their sweat increased the relative humidity by 5 percent. At the peak of the tourist season, up to 4,500 tourists visited the Necropolis every hour. More than one-third of them, between 1,500 and 2,000, visited the three most popular tombs, causing the humidity in them to increase by up to 100 percent, a level at which one-fifth of the wall painting can be lost.[74] Although villagers could be denied running water to reduce the problem of wastewater, there appeared to be no equivalent way to stop tourists from sweating. The master plan for Luxor, of which the depopulation of Gurna was a part, envisioned quadrupling the number of tourists within twenty years, from one million each year to four million. Every one of those three million extra visitors would want to squeeze themselves, dripping with perspiration, into and out of the tombs of Gurna. Far from eliminating the problem of wastewater, the plans for Gurna were going to add to it significantly.

As for access to the ancient tombs, although a handful of them had houses built over their entrances, there were many hundreds of others that were not concealed by houses yet were not opened up to tourism. Some of these were used by the authorities for other purposes, such as storerooms. The tombs concealed by the houses the authorities wanted to demolish were arguably better off than all the rest. Although tombs of no archaeological significance were often simply cavelike extensions of the house built against them, the few of archaeological merit were closed off from the house itself and controlled by the antiquities department. Moreover, the relationship between household and tomb may represent a more historically interesting aspect of the local heritage than many of the empty tombs cleared out and opened up as tourist sites. Indeed, one or two archaeologists working in the area had started to dig not in uncleared tombs but in the piles of debris cleared out by earlier excavations. Earlier excavators were interested only in Pharaonic treasure, or at most in the art and artifacts of the Pharaonic period. Yet many of the tombs came to serve as human habitations over subsequent centuries, and the debris of earlier excavations contains rich evidence of this long period of Coptic and early Islamic local life. The communities living among the tombs today may date back a mere four or five hundred years. But as van der Spek argues, the relationship they represent between a dead past and a living community is part of the history of the Theban Necropolis.[75]

In 1981 half a million tourists visited Luxor and each stayed for an average of only 2.1 nights. By the 1990s the number of visitors in a good year was more than double that, but the length of stay had declined to an average of less than one night.[76] The local tourist industry had less than twenty-four hours within which to maximize the tourist's consumption. This required a meticulous planning of meals, drinks, sleeping, and entertainment, as well as the requisite trips to Karnak and Luxor temples, the sound and light show, the felucca ride, a visit to the Luxor bazaar, plus trips to King Tutankhamen's tomb and other sundry tombs and temples of the Theban Necropolis across the river.

This mass production of experience produced a curious common interest between tourism's overorganized heritage consumers and some of the local community. In the 1982 World Bank survey, alongside the complaint about the behavior of peddlers and local merchants, the most frequent tourist request was for more meaningful contact with the local population. Many tourists to Luxor were anxious to escape the routine and meet "real Egyptians." Many of the local population, interested in diverting tourist expenditure back toward their own needs, were keen to help. Zaynab, for example, had a house directly in front of a parking area for tour buses. Her children would hang around the buses, out of sight of the tour guides, and catch the eye of tourists lagging behind the main group as it headed off toward the temple. They then invited them into the house to watch their mother baking bread at the earthen oven. The children expected a tip of a pound or so, and some of the tourists even offered money to their mother.

The mass consumption of heritage included countless small encounters of this sort, in which the logics of exclusion, impoverishment, and eviction were briefly suspended. Such events operated like a local ecotourism, almost invisible to the large-scale tourist industry, performing, like Zaynab's children, behind its back, yet for many individual tourists often representing the highlight of their day, far more memorable than all that sweaty Theban heritage. These encounters very occasionally developed into longer exchanges, including the foreign women who as tourists found a part-time husband in the village. None of this was necessarily an ecotourism to celebrate, for it was usually constructed on considerable inequalities and misunderstandings. But it does remind us that the manufacture and consumption of heritage produced encounters beyond the control of heritage managers, where the act of consumption briefly undermined the place of things in the heritage system.

Let me conclude by bringing the question of tourism and the heritage industry back to the issue of producing the nation. In November 1996, the heads of more than seventy Gurna households threatened with eviction and the demolition of their homes signed a petition to the authorities. "We the people of Gurna," it stated,

> . . . have become threatened in our homes, we have become agonized with fear, while our houses are demolished above our heads and we are driven from our homeland. Sirs, you know the feelings suffered by the refugee driven from his home, the exile from his land, the person who becomes a stranger in his own country. We have begun to wonder whether we are Egyptians.

The petition describes the fear and violence of relocation, connecting it to other, more brutal expulsions of a sort that Egyptians in recent history have not had to face. The villagers then invoke for themselves the idea of the nation, asking the question "whether we are Egyptians." This simple question opens up the contradictions of nation making. Their eviction has been justified as a project of producing the nation. To preserve the heritage of the nation, and to turn those portrayed as lawless and uneducated into honest citizens of the state, they must be expelled from their homes. To produce the nation requires an act of violence, and in revealing this violence its victims bring to light the forces and instabilities that nation making brings into play. The petition continues:

> The pretext for all this is that we damage and do harm to tourism and that we threaten the safety of the monuments. We do not understand who has fabricated these rumors. We come from the monuments and by the monuments we exist. Our livelihood is from tourism. We have no source of sustenance beyond God except for our work with tourism. . . . We are married to the tourists. [77]

Against the popular official portrayal of them as backward, unclean, ignorant, and an obstacle to the development of a modern heritage site, they declare "we are married to the tourists." Both a metaphor for their close involvement with the tourist industry, and a reference to the fact that foreign women have in fact married local men, this claim gently but insistently subverts the official rhetoric.

Given that the authorities had been periodically attempting to evict the people of Gurna for more than five decades, and now had on their side all the resources of bulldozers, armed police forces, tourism investors, and U.S. and World Bank consultants, it is important to take seriously the power to subvert the violent plans of the heritage industry. This subversion, I have argued, was not the pure resistance of an indigenous community opposed to the plans of the authorities. It was a subversion that operated within, and opened up to view, the contradictions of the projects of heritage and nation making. The manufacturing of a national heritage attempted to divide the world into consumers of tradition and the dead, depopulated heritage they were to consume. But on numerous levels and in multiple ways, neither the consumers nor those facing eviction agreed to this program. And in their minor acts of disruption, they brought its hidden violence into view.

III

FIXING THE ECONOMY

7 The Object of Development

Open almost any study of Egypt produced by an American or international development agency and you are likely to find it starting with the same simple image. The question of Egypt's economic development is almost invariably introduced as a problem of geography versus demography, pictured by describing the narrow valley of the Nile River, surrounded by desert, crowded with rapidly multiplying millions of inhabitants.

A 1980 World Bank report on Egypt provides a typical example. "The geographical and demographic characteristics of Egypt delineate its basic economic problem," the report begins.

> Although the country contains about 386,000 square miles, . . . only a narrow strip in the Nile Valley and its Delta is usable. This area of 15,000 square miles—less than 4 percent of the land—is but an elongated oasis in the midst of desert. Without the Nile, which flows through Egypt for about a thousand miles without being joined by a single tributary, the country would be part of the Sahara. Crammed into the habitable area is 98 percent of the population . . . . The population has been growing rapidly and is estimated to have doubled since 1947.[1]

The visual simplicity of the image, spread out like a map before the reader's eye, combines with the arithmetical certainty of population figures, surface areas, and growth rates to lay down the logic of the analysis to follow: "One of the world's oldest agricultural economies," a report written for the United States Agency for International Development (USAID) begins,

> Egypt depends upon the fruits of the narrow ribbon of cultivated land adjacent to the Nile and to that river's rich fan-shaped delta. For more than 5,000 years agriculture has sustained Egypt. During the first half of this century, however, . . . the growth of agriculture failed to keep up

> with the needs of a population which doubled, then nearly tripled. It is a matter of simple arithmetic . . . [2]

The popularity of this image of space and numbers is summed up in the World Bank report. "These two themes—the relatively fixed amount of usable land and the rapid growth of the population—will be seen as leitmotifs in the discussion of Egypt's economic problems."[3]

Fields of analysis often develop a convention for introducing their object. Such tropes come to seem too obvious and straightforward to question. The somewhat poetic imagery favored by writings on Egyptian development seldom lasts beyond the opening paragraph, and the text moves quickly on to the serious business of social or economic argument. Yet the visual imagery of an opening paragraph can establish the entire relationship between the textual analysis and its object. Such relationships are never simple. Objects of analysis do not occur as natural phenomena, but are partly formed by the discourse that describes them. The more natural the object appears, the less obvious this discursive manufacture will be.

The description that invariably begins the study of Egypt's economic development forms its object in two respects. In the first place, the topographic image of the river, the desert surrounding it, and the population jammed within its banks defines the object to be analyzed in terms of the tangible limits of nature, physical space, and human reproduction. These apparently natural boundaries shape the kinds of solutions that will follow: a more scientific management of resources, and new technologies to overcome their natural limits. The world is divided into nature and science, the material and the technological, a realm of objects and a realm of ideas. Yet the apparent naturalness of the imagery is misleading. The assumptions and figures on which it is based can be examined and reinterpreted to reveal a very different picture. The limits of this alternative picture are not those of geography and nature but of powerlessness and social inequality. What appears as nature is already shaped by forms of power, technology, expertise, and privilege. The alternative solutions that follow are not just technological and managerial, but social and political.

In the second place, the naturalness of the topographic image, so easily pictured, sets up the object of development as just that—an object, out there, not a part of the study but external to it. The discourse of international development constitutes itself in this way as an expertise and intelligence that stands completely apart from the country and the people it describes. Much of this intelligence is generated by organizations such as the

World Bank and USAID, which came to play a powerful economic and political role within countries like Egypt. International development has a special need to overlook this internal involvement in the places and problems it analyzes, and present itself instead as an external intelligence that stands outside the objects it describes. The geographical realism with which Egypt is so often introduced helps establish this deceptively simple relationship.

Earlier chapters of this book have discussed a series of projects and forces that configured the Egyptian countryside in the nineteenth and twentieth centuries, including the estate system and the law of property, irrigation works and epidemic disease, artificial fertilizer and industrial crops, the manufacture of heritage, and the importation of social science. The final part of the book turns to the end of the twentieth century.

In 1973–74 the government of Egypt announced an "open door" economic policy *(infitah)*, after almost two decades of close regulation of foreign investment and imports. The government's ownership, funding, and management of large industry, trade, construction, and finance was now to be complemented by foreign and local private sector initiatives, often in partnership with state banks and enterprises. The significance of this change in policy should not be exaggerated. Economic relations had been formatted as a mix of government and so-called private processes since at least the creation of modern landed property, law, irrigation works, railways, policing, hygiene, and other networks in the nineteenth century, as we saw in chapter 2, and this formatting had gone through numerous crises and adjustments. The reforms of the last quarter of the twentieth century represented another series of adjustments, rather than any simple shift from "the state" to "the private sector" or, as it came to be known, "the market."

One important part of this reformatting was the new role played in Egypt by the three Washington-based political agencies increasingly active across the postcolonial world, the International Monetary Fund, the World Bank, and USAID. These public sector agencies formed alliances with U.S. and other Western banks, corporations, government treasuries, and foreign ministries, and with a variety of forces within Egypt, both official and unofficial. They also met with resistance in Egypt, official and unofficial, and were seldom able simply to impose new policies, still less to control the outcome when their interventions were successful. Where they did achieve results, however, was in their monopoly of expertise.

The final three chapters examine this expertise and its place in Egyptian politics. The current chapter examines the reforms of the 1970s and 1980s, and the way these were formatted as solutions to the problems of geography and nature in terms of which Egypt was always defined. Chapters 8 and 9 look at the crisis that followed at the end of the 1980s, and the remaking of the economy in the economic reforms of the 1990s.

TOO MANY PEOPLE?

We can start with the common image of overpopulation and land shortage. Whenever you hear the word "overpopulation," Susan George suggests, "you should reach, if not for your revolver, at least for your calculator."[4] It is seldom clear, as she points out, to what the prefix "over" refers. What is the norm or the comparison to which it relates? "Egypt has the largest population . . . in the Middle East," noted the World Bank report *Trends in Developing Economies* in 1989: "Its 52 million people are crowded into the Nile delta and valley . . . with a density higher than that of Bangladesh or Indonesia."[5] Why Bangladesh and Indonesia? The World Bank might equally have mentioned Belgium, say, or South Korea, where population densities were respectively three and four times higher than Indonesia—but where the comparison would have had a less negative implication.

It is true that Egypt's level of agricultural population per hectare of arable land was similar to that of Bangladesh, and about double that of Indonesia.[6] But this comparison is misleading, for arable land in Egypt is vastly more productive. It was estimated in 1986 that Egyptian agricultural output per hectare was more than three times that of both Bangladesh and Indonesia.[7] So it is not clear that Egypt was overpopulated in relation to either of these countries.

Perhaps it would be more realistic to gauge Egypt's land shortage by comparing it not with poorer countries but with places that had a similar total population and per capita gross national product, combined with far greater areas of cultivated land. The Philippines and Thailand were the two closest examples in population size and GNP and had cultivated areas three times and eight times that of Egypt, respectively.[8] Yet despite having far less land to farm, Egypt's agricultural population produced more crops per person than either of these countries. Egyptian agricultural output per worker was perhaps 8 percent higher than that of the Philippines and 73 percent higher than that of Thailand.[9]

Despite the visual power of the image of more than 50 million Egyptians crowded into the valley of the Nile, there is no prima facie evidence for the assumption that this population was too large for its cultivable area. Perhaps it might be argued in more general terms that the world's population is too large in relation to the earth's limited resources.[10] In that case, however, there is no reason to single out Egyptians. On the contrary, Egyptians made very modest demands on the world's resources (measured in terms of energy consumption per capita) compared with inhabitants of Western Europe, Japan, and North America. One inhabitant of the United Kingdom, for example, required more of the world's energy per year than six Egyptians, and one American was more expensive in energy terms than a dozen Egyptians.[11] So it can hardly be the latter who were threatening the world's limited resources.

Perhaps it can be agreed that having more than fifty million inhabitants did not necessarily make Egypt "overpopulated." Development experts might insist, however, that the problem was not the size of Egypt's population but the rate at which it was growing. A report in 1976 by the United States Department of Agriculture asserted that the country's "exploding population is the most serious problem facing Egypt today."[12] The rapid growth in population appeared to have outstripped the country's ability to feed itself, and in 1974 Egypt became a net importer of agricultural commodities. By the 1980s food accounted for almost 30 percent of Egypt's merchandise imports, a higher proportion than for all except one of the one hundred countries for which figures were available.[13] It would appear from these figures that the case for an imbalance between population figures and agricultural resources had been established after all. But before accepting this conclusion we should reach, once again, for the calculator.

NOT ENOUGH FOOD?

Between 1965 and 1980, according to World Bank tables, the population of Egypt grew at an annual rate of 2.1 percent. Yet during the same period, the World Bank also shows, agricultural production grew at the even faster rate of 2.7 percent a year. During the 1980s, when the population growth rate increased to 2.4 percent a year, agricultural growth continued to keep ahead.[14] In 1991, food production per capita was 17 percent higher than at the start of the previous decade.[15] So it is not true that the population was growing faster than the country's ability to feed itself.

If this is the case, then why did the country have to import ever increasing amounts of food? The answer is to be found by looking at the kinds of food being eaten, and at who got to eat it.

Official statistics suggest that Egyptians were consuming relatively large amounts of food. The World Bank ranked Egypt as a "low income" country in the 1980s, yet the country's daily calorie supply per capita was estimated to be higher than all except one of the "lower middle-income" countries, and indeed higher than a majority of the world's upper-middle and high-income countries.[16] The daily protein supply per capita also exceeded the level of most middle-income countries and rivaled that of many high-income countries.[17] Despite these figures, Egyptians suffered from high rates of undernutrition. A 1988 survey found that 29 percent of children suffered from mild undernutrition and another 31 percent from moderate or severe undernutrition.[18] Between 1978 and 1986 the prevalence of acute undernutrition may have more than doubled.[19] A study of anemia (probably caused by the interaction of malnutrition and infection) in Cairo found the condition in 80 percent of children under two years old and in 90 percent of pregnant women,[20] rates that the World Bank described as "alarmingly high."[21] Clearly the high figures for calorie and protein supply per capita did not reflect the actual distribution or consumption of food.

What the calorie figures probably reflected was high levels of food consumption among the better off, a shift in what they consumed toward more expensive foods, especially meat, and the diversion of food supplies from humans to animals. A World Bank study of agricultural pricing policy in Egypt in the 1980s noted that there was a very high variation in the value of food consumed between rich and poor, which it attributed to the low per capita level of income and its unequal distribution.[22] This inequality was already increasing from 1964/65 to 1974/75: in the countryside the share of household expenditure of the lowest 20 percent of households decreased from 7 to less than 6 percent in that decade, while in urban areas the share of the top 20 percent of households increased from 47 to 51 percent.[23] During the brief oil boom from the late 1970s to the mid-1980s, the income of the poor improved and the gap between low- and middle-income families may have narrowed. But the wealthiest 5 percent increased their income share between 1974/75 and 1981/82 from 22 percent to 25 percent in the case of rural households and to 29 percent in the case of urban.[24] In the late 1980s, as USAID and the International Monetary Fund (IMF) finally succeeded in imposing restructuring policies that removed price subsidies, increased unemployment, and brought economic recession, the degree of inequality almost certainly increased. A 1992 report on Egypt for USAID made clear that under these policies "losers necessarily outnumber winners." While arguing that the increased poverty for the majority would occur only in the short term, the report admitted that there was no indication of any significant progress toward the long-term benefits this poverty was believed to bring.[25]

Increasing wealth, together with increasing numbers of resident foreigners and tourists, led to a large increase in the demand for meat and other animal products, which were "chiefly consumed by tourists and other non-Egyptians, plus middle- and upper-class urban residents."[26] A 1981/82 household survey showed that the richest 25 percent consumed more than three times as much chicken and beef as the poorest 25 percent.[27] In the subsequent oil-boom years, income growth together with extensive U.S. and Egyptian government subsidies encouraged a broader switch from diets based on legumes and maize (corn) to less healthy diets of wheat and meat products. From 1970 to 1980, while crop production grew in real value by 17 percent, livestock production grew almost twice as much, by 32 percent.[28] In the following seven years crop production grew by 10 percent, but livestock production by almost 50 percent.[29] To produce one kilogram of red meat requires ten kilograms of cereals, so feeding these animals required a large and costly diversion of staple food supplies from human to animal consumption.[30]

FODDER FOR PEACE

It was this switch to meat consumption, rather than the increase in population, that required the dramatic increase in imports of food, particularly grains. Between 1966 and 1988 the population of Egypt grew by 75 percent. In the same period, the domestic production of grains increased by 77 percent but total grain consumption increased by 148 percent, or almost twice the rate of population increase.[31] Egypt began to import large and ever increasing quantities of grain, becoming the world's third biggest importer after Japan and China. A small proportion of the increase in imports reflected an increase in per capita human consumption, which grew by 12 percent in this twenty-two-year period. But the bulk of the new imports was required to cover the increasing use of grains to feed animals. Grain imports grew by 5.9 million metric tons between 1966 and 1988, to cover an estimated increase in nonfood consumption of grains (mostly animal feed, but also seed use and wastage) of 5.3 million tons, or 268 percent (see fig. 2).[32]

The dependence on grain imports after 1974 was caused not by population growth, which lagged behind the growth of domestic grain production, but by a shift to the consumption of meat. This shift was obscured, however, by the way different grains were used. Rather than importing animal feed directly, Egypt diverted domestic production from human to animal consumption. Human consumption of maize (corn) and other coarse grains (barley, sorghum) dropped from 53 percent in 1966 to 6 percent in 1988.[33] Human supplies were made up with imports, largely of wheat for

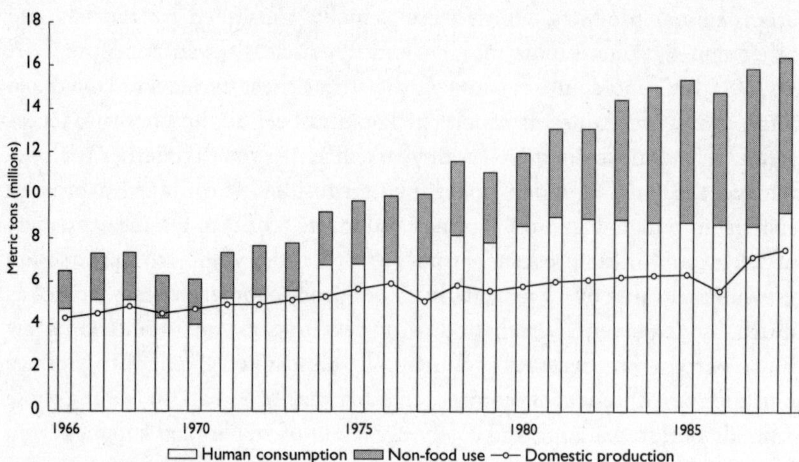

Figure 2. Supply and consumption of grains in Egypt, 1966–90. Source: Calculated from USAID, *Status Report* (Cairo, 1989).

bread making. So it appeared as though the imports were required not to feed animals supplying the increased demand for meat, but because the people needed more bread. USAID supported the shift to meat consumption among the better off by financing at reduced interest rates more than three billion dollars worth of Egyptian grain purchases from the United States between 1975 and 1988, making Egypt the world's largest importer of subsidized grains. Yet the agency claimed that the purpose of these subsidies was "to help the poor."[34]

Subsidized American loans financed only a part of the grain imports. The rest required further borrowing, contributing to a total external debt that in 1989 reached $51.5 billion, a figure surpassed that year by only five other countries. Whereas the debt levels of the other five heavily indebted countries ranged between 22 and 95 percent of gross national product, Egypt's debt amounted to 165 percent of its GNP.[35] Egypt began to default on the debt and required large loans just to keep up payments on its earlier loans. To address this crisis, the United States used the pretext of Egyptian support in 1990–91 for a war against Iraq to write off Egypt's $7 billion military debt and to arrange for a relaxation of the remaining $28 billion of long-term bilateral debt, half of which was written off and half rescheduled.[36] As a condition of this refinancing, the United States insisted on a further shift toward export crops, away from staple foods, to produce more hard currency to pay the debts.

The transformation in food consumption habits affected not only agricultural imports and the balance of payments, but also domestic agriculture. By the 1980s it was no longer accurate to write that Egyptian capitalist agriculture "still is to a large extent the cultivation of cotton."[37] In terms of the commitment of land and labor, the priority was now the production of meat, poultry, and dairy products. In 1989 cotton occupied only about one million of Egypt's six million acres.[38] The other major industrial crop, sugarcane, occupied a little over a quarter of a million acres. Of the remaining four and three-quarter million acres, more than half was used to grow animal fodder—principally Egyptian clover (berseem) in the winter and maize and sorghum in the summer and autumn.[39] Egypt was now growing more food for animals to consume than for humans.

The shift to the production of meat and other animal products (which was accompanied by an increased production of other more expensive, nonstaple agricultural products, particularly fruit and vegetables) had two principal causes. First, as the World Bank put it, "effective demand has been modified by a change in income distribution."[40] In other words, the growing disparity in income between rich and poor enabled the better off to divert the country's resources from the production of staples to the production of luxury items. Second, the Egyptian government, supported by the large American loans already mentioned (called "Food For Peace"), encouraged this diversion by subsidizing the import of staples for consumers, heavily taxing the production of staples by farmers, and subsidizing the production of meat, poultry, and dairy products.[41] Livestock raising was particularly concentrated on large farms, those over ten acres, where there were three to four times as many cattle per acre as on farms of one to ten acres.[42] Yet government food policy forced even the smallest farmers to shift from self-provisioning to the production of animal products and to rely increasingly on subsidized imported flour for their staple diet.

The image of a vast population packed within a limited agricultural area and increasing in size at a rate that outpaced its ability to feed itself is therefore quite misleading. The growth in agricultural production was always ahead of population growth. Egypt's food problem was the result not of too many people occupying too little land, but of the power of a certain part of that population, supported by the prevailing domestic and international regime, to shift the country's resources from staple foods to more expensive items of consumption.

Population growth rates of over 2.5 percent a year, some might argue, were nevertheless still very high. Surely it would have been better to produce fewer children and more buffaloes, cows, and chickens—as in fact a

1990 family planning initiative proposed. But this depends on one's point of view. Such a proposal would probably have seemed reasonable to an upper-class or middle-class family in Cairo, and indeed the birth rate among such families was already much lower. But to a rural family or among the urban poor it might seem far less reasonable.

In a social world where daughters leave their parents' family at marriage to join their husbands' households, and where there is virtually no system of social security to support parents when they become too old or sick to work, it can be argued that to desire a minimum of two surviving male children was not excessive. According to figures for 1980, in rural Upper Egypt, the poorest part of the country and the region with the highest fertility rate, women gave birth to an average of 7.5 children during their childbearing years. But almost one in three of their children (2.7 out of the 7.5) died in childhood.[43] Under these circumstances, if the parents' aim was to ensure that at least two sons survived to support them in later life, then 7.5 children was not an unreasonable birth rate. After 1980 infant deaths were reduced, thanks largely to a simple treatment for diarrhea, and women began to have smaller families.[44]

These women were unlikely to attribute their economic problems to population growth, as did the World Bank. Far more serious, perhaps, was the insecurity of their futures, their meager share of local, national, and global resources, and the political and economic powerlessness that prevented them from altering this condition. Any discussion of their situation would have to start from this question of power.

NOT ENOUGH LAND?

The effect the pictorial framework has on the analysis it introduces can be seen by turning to the question that is central to the problem of rural poverty and powerlessness, that of land distribution. The image of a narrow strip of fertile land crammed with so many millions of inhabitants enabled most contemporary analyses of Egyptian economic development to move very quickly past the problem of access to land. With so many people occupying so little space, the problem appeared to be already explained. "The present picture is not bright," concluded a study for USAID in 1976 discussing the economic status of the farmer, "mainly because there is just not enough land to go around. The average size of a holding is two feddans [acres], 94 percent of all owners have less than 5 feddans each, and only 0.2 percent have at least 50 feddans each."[45]

This picture of a countryside made up of millions of tiny parcels of land suggested once again that if Egyptian farmers were finding things difficult, it was because there were just too many of them for the space available. As before, however, we should ignore the image and check the figures.

First of all, holdings of less than five acres are not as small as they may seem. With Egypt's fertile soils, year-round sunshine, and permanently available irrigation water, the country is like an open-air greenhouse in which high yields can be obtained from two or even three crops a year. A five-acre holding produces between ten and fifteen acres of crops a year. In fact five acres is reckoned to be the maximum size for a family farm—the maximum area a family of five can cultivate on its own, working full time, without hired labor.[46] The minimum farm size required for such a family to feed itself, assuming an annual consumption of 250 kilograms of grains (or equivalent) per head and a state tax of 30 percent of production, was estimated in 1982 to be 0.8 feddan (acre), or just over 19 qirats (1 feddan = 24 qirats).[47] Given the increase in yields in the 1980s, the minimum area required by 1988 was only 0.625 feddan, or 15 qirats.

The USAID report mentioned that 94 percent of landholdings were smaller than five acres, the limit of a family farm. What it failed to mention was that the remaining 6 percent of landholders, with holdings from five acres up to the legal limit of fifty acres per individual or one hundred acres per family with dependent children, controlled 33 percent of the country's agricultural area.[48] From the mid-1970s, moreover, these large landholdings increased in number. By 1982 they represented 10 percent of holdings and controlled 47.5 percent of the country's cultivated area.[49]

The official figures, furthermore, underrepresented the concentration of landholding, for they were based on village land registers. Studies of landholding in individual villages frequently revealed a much greater concentration of ownership, as I discussed in chapter 5, with the largest farms being registered under several different names to stay within the legal limit. The official limits also did not apply to the large holdings of agribusiness corporations. In the 1980s, for example, Bechtel International Agribusiness Division managed a ten-thousand-acre estate in Nubariyya owned by a Gulf investor,[50] and the Delta Sugar Company, a joint venture of the Egyptian state sugar company and a group of Egyptian and international banks, owned a forty-thousand-acre estate on irrigated land in the north-central Delta.[51]

Even if one ignores these additional forms of landholding, the official figures still represented a large concentration of land in relatively few hands. The limit of fifty to one hundred acres should be compared with the limit of about 2.5 to seven acres (one to three hectares) achieved in the 1940s and 1950s by the land reform programs of Japan, Taiwan, and South Korea.[52] In Korea, less than 20 percent of the land in 1975 was held in farms of two hectares or more (approximately five acres), while in Egypt almost half the land (47.5 percent) was in holdings above this limit.[53] On the other hand, almost one-third of landholders in Egypt (32.3 percent) had holdings under one acre, amounting to only 6 percent of the agricultural area.[54] In addition, a significant but unmeasured proportion of the agricultural workforce, which totaled 4.3 million workers in 1985,[55] remained without any land at all.

If Egypt were to carry out land reform measures comparable to those of Japan, South Korea, and Taiwan, the problem of landlessness and near landlessness would be eliminated.[56] By placing the ceiling on landholding at three acres (an area several times the minimum required to feed a family), at least 2.6 million acres of land would be available for redistribution.[57] If distributed to the landless and near landless, no agricultural household in Egypt would have less than the fifteen qirats required to feed itself. Total agricultural production would also be likely to increase, as there is ample evidence that small farmers produce larger yields per acre than large farmers.[58] East Asia also provided a model for financing such a redistribution. In the Taiwanese land reform of 1953, the government compensated large owners through a concurrent privatization program, giving them shares in the Taiwan Cement Corporation and other state-owned industries inherited from the Japanese occupation.[59] In the 1990s Egypt launched a program to privatize state-owned enterprises, including several cement companies. The distribution of shares in this property offered a straightforward method of paying compensation for the redistribution of land in the countryside.

The discussion of landholding in Egypt usually ignores the large proportion of land held in amounts over five acres, and refers to such holdings as merely "medium" sized. Only owners of more than fifty acres are labeled "large." The fifty-acre threshold, incorporated into the 1961 land reform law, was the definition of large landowner formulated in 1894 by the British consul-general in Egypt, Lord Cromer, in accordance with British political and fiscal interests.[60] It takes no account of the contemporary interests of most Egyptian farmers. Nor does its continued use reflect the fact that crop yields increased by a factor of 4.5 over the one hundred years after the British occupation.[61] A 50-acre farm in 1982 produced as much as a 225-acre farm of the 1880s, or perhaps a 450-acre farm if one took into account the spread of perennial irrigation and double and triple cropping. From 1982 to 1999, moreover, yields of wheat, the major food crop, grew by another 80 percent, further increasing the output of large farms.[62]

The redistribution of agricultural land also offered a way to create non-agricultural livelihoods in the countryside and provincial towns. Increasing the number and assets of small farming households would generate three kinds of local economic linkage.[63] It would increase demand, first, for locally made agricultural inputs (ploughs, hand tools, draft animals, carts, threshing machines, and small irrigation pumps); second, for consumer goods made and serviced by local industry (furniture, building materials, basic appliances and electronics) rather than luxuries imported from abroad; and third, for a variety of local processing industries for food and textile crops, such as small wheat and rice mills, sugarcane processing, and textile looms. Compared to the large-scale, capital-intensive industry favored by the state and international financial institutions, small-scale processing industries based on intermediate technology had two advantages. They typically produced a less refined and more nutritious product, such as brown sugar or whole-grain flour. And they employed more people and produced goods at lower overall cost.[64]

The redistribution of agricultural land offered a workable and proven means of creating sustainable rural livelihoods.[65] Over the following decade, in other parts of the world land reform was "back on the agenda," the U. N. Food and Agriculture Organization reported, mainly because rural populations put it there. The Chiapas rebellion in Mexico, the invasions of land seekers in Malawi and Zimbabwe, the Movimento Sem Terra in Brazil, the demand for restitution of property taken by the apartheid regime in South Africa, and the success of the 1990s land reform in the Philippines, all contributed to this new pressure to recognize the importance of land rights for small farmers.[66] But in official studies of the obstacles to Egypt's further economic development, the question of additional land reform was simply never raised. USAID refused to support detailed independent proposals for land reform and instead, as we will see, helped to introduce a "free market" program for rural Egypt that began to undo earlier reforms and consolidate land into larger farms.[67] Thanks to the powerful image of millions of Egyptian peasants squeezed into a narrow river valley, it seemed natural to assume that landholdings were already smaller than was practicable and that other sorts of solutions were required.

HIGH-PAYOFF INPUTS

Once the problems Egypt faces were defined as natural rather than political, questions of social inequality and powerlessness disappeared into the background. The analysis could then focus instead on how to overcome these "natural" limits of geography and demography. In the 1980s the international development industry in Egypt proposed and funded two complementary methods for the solution of Egypt's problems, the technological and the managerial. One required large capital resources from the West, the other its expertise. "The development problem is essentially a question of the quantity, quality and proportion of resources to be devoted to development on the one hand," according to a World Bank report on Egypt that laid out an agenda for the 1980s and 1990s, "and to economic management on the other."[68] The productive limits set by nature, in other words, would be overcome by the forces of technology, while existing natural resources would be made more productive by more rational and efficient management—in particular by dismantling the bureaucracy of the Egyptian state and recasting its power in the form of "market forces."

The timeless image of the Nile River and its inhabitants often introduces a certain construction of history, from which follows the need for technological rather than political solutions. The geographical determinism of the image implies an agricultural order that remains in essential ways unchanged since antiquity. Only recently, it seems, has this ancient world discovered the West—or its synonym, "the twentieth century." This relationship between nature and an unchanging history was expressed in one of the passages already quoted from a USAID report: "One of the world's oldest agricultural economies, Egypt depends upon the fruits of the narrow ribbon of cultivated land adjacent to the Nile and to that river's rich fan-shaped delta. For more than 5,000 years agriculture has sustained Egypt."[69] A similar theme, and similar words, are found introducing an earlier report for USAID. "The Nile Delta and its lifeline, the Nile River Valley extending southward some 600 miles, is one of the oldest agricultural areas of the world, having been under continuous cultivation for at least 5,000 years." With this in mind we are ready to accept a few lines further down the strange idea that, "In many respects, Egypt entered the twentieth century after the 1952 Revolution."[70] A 1977 USAID report stated baldly that "The transformation of the Egyptian village started twenty five years ago with the agrarian reform measures."[71] In the same years, as we saw in chapter 4, Richard Critchfield was writing the same thing in his Ford Foundation–funded study, *Shahhat,* after which he was hired by USAID as an expert on rural development.

The implication of these statements and images—that until the latter half of the twentieth century life in the Nile valley had remained essentially unchanged for centuries, if not millennia—is of course highly misleading. As earlier chapters have stressed, it ignores hundreds of years of far-reaching economic and political changes, such as the growth in the Middle Ages and subsequent decline of a network of world trade passing through the Nile valley, or the consolidation in the nineteenth century of a system of export-oriented agricultural production based on irrigation works and private landownership, all of which involved transformations in Egyptian villages as important as the land reforms and irrigation schemes of the mid-twentieth century. Ignoring such developments creates the reassuring impression that the poverty of the Nile valley is the traditional poverty of a peasantry that has not yet or has only recently joined the "twentieth century," rather than very much a product of the political and economic forces of that century.

This image of a traditional rural world implies a static agricultural system that cannot change itself. If Egypt "is to fully enter the modern world," a report for USAID in 1976 explained, the impetus and the means must come from outside.[72] These external forces must carry out not simply adjustments to the existing system but what the World Bank in 1980 called a "qualitative transformation" of Egyptian agriculture.[73] New capital investment, new irrigation methods, improved seed varieties, mechanization, and the switch to export crops such as vegetables and cut flowers to bring in the foreign capital required to finance such technologies were the principal means to achieve this transformation.

USAID's Agricultural Mechanization Project, which ran from 1979 to 1987, used just this image of a "traditional" agricultural system to justify technological solutions to the problems of rural Egypt. The project's aim was to encourage the mechanization of Egyptian farming by purchasing agricultural machinery from the United States for field trials and demonstration programs in Egypt, financing the construction of service centers for the machinery, and sending Egyptians to the United States and other countries for training in "the techniques of technology transfer."[74] USAID awarded the $38 million contract for this to Louis Berger International of East Orange, New Jersey. In their final report, the contractors explained the "underlying philosophy" of the mechanization program. "To ensure that the project serves the purposes of development, it is necessary to relate mechanization to development theory so that mechanization does not conflict with, but rather is supportive of, development objectives."[75]

To supply the kind of theory that would ensure "the purposes of development" were served, they drew on the ideas of Theodore Schultz, whose *Transforming Traditional Agriculture* (1964) was an early classic in the field of economic development. Schultz argued that farmers in "traditional" agriculture make efficient use of their resources within the limits of the expertise and technology available to them. Through long years of trial and error, he claimed, they have eliminated inefficiencies and wastage and reached "a particular type of equilibrium" in which the agricultural economy is "incapable of growth except at high cost." Only the large-scale introduction of new technology and capital from outside this equilibrium can enable the farmer "to transform the traditional agriculture of his forebears."[76] "In other words," Louis Berger International explained, "the continued investment in traditional inputs will produce very little in terms of an additional income stream. Consequently, the transformation from traditional agriculture is an investment problem dependent on a flow of new high-payoff inputs: the inputs of scientific agriculture."[77] There has probably never been a "traditional" agriculture resembling Schultz's description. Certainly no such system has existed in Egypt in recent historical memory, still less in the 1980s when Louis Berger International arrived there from New Jersey. What was missing most of all from Schultz's account of individual farmers making rational decisions to maximize their income, as an anthropologist's critique points out, was any concept of social and economic inequality.[78]

Schultz tested his theory using evidence from studies of a Guatemalan village by Sol Tax (1953) and a village in north India by David Hopper (1957).[79] The Guatemalan village was involved mostly in trade rather than the production of food for local consumption, so it was hardly "typical of a large class of poor agricultural communities," as Schultz claimed.[80] The Indian village yielded evidence that the proportion of land and other resources allocated to various crops corresponded closely to their relative market prices, so that altering the allocation of inputs would not significantly increase the farmers' income.[81] But this analysis paid no attention to inequality and the difference that poverty makes. "Severely impoverished individuals," Hill notes, "who exist in all communities, . . . are necessarily inefficient if only because they lack the resources to set themselves to work effectively."[82] For example, poor farmers in Egypt usually cannot afford sufficient fertilizer for their crops and may get lower yields as a result. The most "efficient" allocation of resources in Schultz's terms, Hill points out, would allocate no land at all to the poorest farmers.

Despite the lack of firm evidence for Schultz's rather dated argument, it supplied the "philosophy" to justify American funding for the mechanization of Egyptian agriculture. Mechanization was also funded by the World Bank and by the Japanese Agency for International Cooperation.[83] These external funds required large additional contributions from the Egyptian government, which was already paying for mechanization by providing farmers with subsidized loans and fuel. Consultants hired by USAID claimed that this "high-payoff" solution to Egypt's problems would shorten the interval between crops and increase crop yields by as much as 55 percent.[84] This claim contradicted the evidence from other countries, which suggested that higher crop yields occur with mechanization only in exceptional cases, and certainly not under conditions of intensive land use as in Egypt.[85] It also contradicted existing experience in Egypt, where, as Alan Richards reported, there was "no evidence that tractor farms have higher yields or cropping intensities than unmechanized farms."[86] A subsequent study showed that indeed no increase in yields had occurred.[87]

The demand for mechanization had intensified among large landowners in the later 1970s, due to a supposed shortage of agricultural labor that lasted into the early 1980s. This "shortage" took the form of a temporary rise in the wages of male agricultural laborers, particularly in regions close to large cities, caused by the higher wages available for urban construction work during the building boom of that period and by labor migration to the oil-rich countries of the Gulf.[88] Agricultural wages, having averaged only one-third of the average real wage for all economic sectors during the first half of the 1970s, for a while began to catch up with urban wages. Large farmers, given the artificially low prices they received for their crops, were unable or unwilling to pay the higher wages. The larger cause of the labor "shortage," in other words, was the unequal distribution of land into large farms requiring hired labor (small farms use mostly family or cooperative labor) and the low agricultural prices imposed by the state. Rather than addressing these problems, however, the government, large farmers, and international development agencies turned to the high-payoff program of mechanization. The high payoffs did not take the form of increased yields, as we have seen, but of higher profits to the new machine owners and their importing agents and foreign manufacturers. The demand for rural male labor was reduced once again, and the inequalities between agricultural laborers and landowners were kept in place. It is these inequalities that mechanization and other "high-payoff" inputs consolidate, and that accounts of the Nile valley and the need to transform its "traditional" agriculture keep from view.

DECENTRALIZATION AND THE MARKET

There is a second dimension to rural inequality in Egypt, and a second aspect to the historical image of the Nile valley that tends to naturalize it. The rural poor suffered not only from local inequalities in distribution of land and other resources, but also from the inequality of central government policies that transferred wealth from the rural population to the state. The state had come to play a major role not just in maintaining inequality, but in producing it. This is a political question, requiring an analysis of the networks of power and privilege that pass through the state and tap into the wealth it appropriates. International development, with its naturalized images of the Nile valley and its limited resources, depoliticizes this issue and transforms it into a question of the proper management of resources. The solutions that follow are those that are supposed to increase efficiency: decentralizing the state and reconfiguring some of its networks and powers as forces of "the market."

Before 1952 it was mostly the institution of large landowning that extracted wealth from the farming population and transferred it elsewhere. The 1952 land reforms preserved significant landholding inequalities, but placed a majority of farmers directly under the control of the central government and its compulsory cropping requirements, requisitions, and price policies. Even if one takes into account state investment in irrigation and the subsidizing of farm inputs, the net effect of government policies between 1960 and 1985 was estimated to appropriate 35 percent of agricultural GDP.[89] Small farmers, moreover, suffered more than larger landowners, as the latter had greater opportunity to invest in more profitable areas such as fruit, vegetable, and dairy farming. After 1974 the government began to relax the compulsory cropping and price fixing policies, and after 1986 to abolish them. But the changes were carried out in a way that benefited primarily larger landowners. Smallholders continued to be disproportionately involved in cotton, rice, and sugarcane production, where fixed prices and compulsory deliveries to the state were the last to be relaxed. To complete the reversal of the 1952 reforms, in 1992 the government moved to abolish the security of tenant farmers, reestablishing the "free market" in agricultural land and causing hundreds of thousands of small farmers to be faced with the risk of eviction (see chapter 8).

The system for appropriating wealth from the countryside needs to be examined as a political process, in which changing state policies have reflected a complex of dominant (although not always coherent) social interests—those of the state managers and bureaucrats, the growing government-supported private sector, and larger rural landowners. The image of the Nile valley, its population, and a five-thousand-year-old agriculture makes it possible to ascribe this appropriation instead to a "tradition" of "strong central government" determined by the very geography of the Nile valley and stretching back to Pharaonic times. Thus the coordinator of a USAID-funded program at Eastern Kentucky University providing management training to Egyptian local government officials explained, "For centuries Egypt has been governed as a political system with a highly centralized decision making process. Although there have been a few minor exceptions, this statement is valid for the period since the unification of Upper and Lower Egypt was accomplished late in the fourth millennium B.C.—i.e. for at least the past 5 thousand years."[90] Drawing on familiar imagery, the author went on to explain this centralized power in geographical and demographic terms. "Integral to the question of administrative structure of the Arab Republic of Egypt is its principal social and economic problem—over-population—and the Nile River. Although the land mass area of the ARE includes 386,000 square miles, over 96 percent of the population resides on the 4 percent of the land area adjacent to the Nile valley and its delta."[91] Depoliticized in this way, the state's role in agriculture ceased to be a question of power and control over people's resources and lives. It became instead a problem of management. The intervention of the state has resulted in "disequilibrium," it was said.[92] The language of neo-Ricardian economics was employed to imagine a naturally achieved balance between forces of agricultural supply and demand, a balance called "the market." The market is a simple image for picturing the relations between farmers, laborers, landowners, state officials, international agribusinesses, and consumers, an image that reduces these interrelated but very unequal concentrations of power into nominally equivalent buyers and sellers, and represents the inequality between them as the market's equilibrium. Building this imagined equilibrium, which has never existed in two centuries of modern Egyptian agriculture except as a sequence of dispossessions, food shortages, monopolies, minor revolts, violent repressions, and urgent demands for state intervention, was the aim of the process of "structural adjustment."

To begin creating such an equilibrium, alongside the supply of "high-payoff inputs," USAID began to promote in rural Egypt a gradual reorganization of the role of the state, under the slogans of "decentralization" and "privatization." USAID even talked of encouraging "democracy and pluralism" in the provinces by increasing the role of local officials and involving the country's elected village councils.[93] To weaken the power of the central bureaucracy might have been a positive step for rural Egyptians, but the actual political outcome would depend on the distribution of resources and power at the provincial, district, and village levels to which authority and funds were transferred. Local government or the private sector is not necessarily more democratic, or even more efficient, than central government. Popular village councils, if they had any role at all, were frequently controlled by powerful village landowners and local officials, largely for their own benefit. Decentralization was likely to do no more than shift exploitation from one agency to another.

A review of decentralization projects in eight different villages found that funds had gone to improvements in infrastructure and to income-producing projects such as the purchase of milk refrigeration units; animal husbandry; poultry, bee, and silkworm raising; date packaging; olive canning; carpentry and furniture making; and the purchase of trucks, tractors, and taxis. The report, written for USAID, noted that "naturally, not all villagers have savings that enable them to invest" in these projects, and therefore the profits accrued to those in "middle to upper bracket income groups more than poor folks."[94] An olive pickling and canning project in a village in Fayyum, for example, provided employment for two hundred villagers but served the marketing needs of just five wealthy farmers, for only wealthy farmers could afford to grow olive trees. Likewise, "only the wealthy villagers can hope to raise bees, because the economic success of such an enterprise requires raising at least 20 beehives, which is a large investment. Village officials such as agronomists often enter into partnership with such farmers and undertake such projects on their own."[95] In other words, when they transferred resources to an existing system of inequality, decentralization and privatization were liable to reinforce that inequality. The profits went to large farmers and local state officials, and the poor received at best only certain opportunities for wage labor. The USAID report acknowledged that "the better off, the more educated and expert officials benefit more than ordinary villagers," but argued that this was "developmentally advisable."[96] "It would be remiss to call such a phenomenon exploitation simply because the better-off can benefit more," the report argued. Exploitation in rural Egypt existed only "before 1952 where cultivators were given survival wages or shares by owners." The relationship between rural capitalists and wage earners was termed instead "differential advantage," meaning "the variable ability of individuals or groups to make better use and reap greater benefits than others from available opportunities."[97] A sure way to "reap greater benefits" from an investment, of course, is to pay lower wages to those one employs. This "ability" was based on a distribution of land that left many villagers with no resources besides their labor, in the absence of a minimum wage, and under a system of patronage, policing, and surveillance in rural Egypt that prevented "poor folks" from protesting against or organizing to change their condition. Even when exploitation was shifted from state to local or private means and renamed "differential advantage," it remained a politically constructed system of inequality—which decentralization and privatization programs would only reinforce.

The reinforcement of inequalities in the name of improved "management" of resources and of "removing constraints to the operation of market forces" can be seen in another major strategy for reducing the role of the state. This was what the development industry called "cost recovery" in the provision of government services.[98]

Cost recovery was a euphemism for transforming healthcare, schooling, and other public services into private, fee-based institutions as in the United States. In education, for example, USAID pushed for the introduction of private schooling in Egypt at the secondary and university level and, on a more modest level, for a scheme to sell advertising space on the covers of school exercise books.[99] In healthcare, for which USAID budgeted only $246 million from 1975 to 1989, representing 1.6 percent of total nonmilitary assistance to Egypt, the sum of $95 million (almost 40 percent of the health budget) was scheduled for privatization programs. With technical assistance from the consulting firm of Emery Associates / Taylor Associates, USAID's aim was to "establish a sound financial structure for the health sector emphasizing cost recovery systems." The programs involved pushing the Egyptian government to implement "policy changes to allow a fee structure for curative care" and "to convert selected hospitals and clinics to fees-for-service facilities."[100] One of the advantages of selective private healthcare is its increased dependence on imported U.S. drugs and equipment. It is worth noting that even under the existing system of public financing for healthcare and schooling, Egyptians spent large personal sums on health and education. The percentage of total household consumption expenses spent on medical care in Egypt (14 percent) was already second highest in the world, after Switzerland, and equal with that of U.S., and the percentage spent on education (11 percent) was the third highest in the world, after Canada and Singapore.[101]

Privatizing healthcare, schooling, and other social services does not inherently create a "sound financial structure." What it does do is transfer the source of funding from government revenue, to which people contribute according to their means, to fees or insurance premiums, for which the poor must pay as much as the rich. This creates or reinforces an unequal access to healthcare and schooling. Privileged levels of education and health become, in turn, a mechanism for transferring wider social privilege from one generation to the next.

The rhetoric of management, financial soundness, and market forces depoliticized these complex issues. Programs for decentralization and cost recovery transformed questions of social inequality and powerlessness into issues of efficiency and control—in the same way that agricultural mechanization programs transformed the question of inadequate wages and landlessness into issues of technological efficiency. The underlying political issues people faced could be ignored, because the naturalized imagery of the Nile and its population had reduced the topic to questions of natural resources and their more efficient control. It never had to be asked at whose cost efficiencies were to be made, or in whose hands control was to be strengthened.

OBJECTS OF DEVELOPMENT

A final aspect of the geographical image of the Nile valley was the way it removed from sight the participation of development agencies in the dynamics of Egyptian political and economic life. By portraying the country and its problems as a picture, laid out before the mind's eye like a map, the image presented Egypt itself as something natural. The particular extent of space and population denoted by the name "Egypt" was represented as an empirical object, echoing the cadastral survey maps of the beginning of the century. Development literature reproduced the convention that Egypt exists as a sort of freestanding unit, lined up in physical space alongside a series of similar units. The workings of this unit—its economic functions, social interactions, and political processes—are understood as internal mechanisms. They constitute the unit's inside, to be distinguished from economic and political forces that may affect it from outside.

This convention of imagining countries as empirical objects is seldom recognized for what it is—a convention. The relations, forces, and movements that have shaped people's lives over the last several hundred years have never in fact been confined within the limits of nation-states, or respected their borders. The value of what people produce, the cost of what they consume, and the purchasing power of their currency are determined by global relationships of exchange. Movements of people and cultural commodities form international flows of tourists, television programs, information, migrant workers, refugees, technologies, and fashions. The strictly "national" identity of a population, an economy, a language, or a culture is an image that has had to be continually reinvented against the force of these wider relations and movements. This has always been the case, for the global interconnection of commodities, populations, languages, and ideas is far older than the modern invention of nation-states.

The apparent concreteness of a modern nation-state like Egypt, its appearance as a discrete object, is the result of recent methods of organizing social practice and representing it: constructing frontiers on roads and at airports, controlling the movement of people and goods across them, producing maps and history books for schools, compiling cadastral surveys, deploying mass armies and indoctrinating those conscripted into them, representing the nation-state in news broadcasts, international sports events, and tourist literature, establishing a national currency and language, and, not least, the discourse of "country studies" and national statistics of the American-based international development industry.

These essentially practical arrangements of language, imagery, space, and movement are mostly of very recent origin, as I explored in earlier chapters of this book.[102] We tend to think of them as processes that merely mark out and represent the nation-state, as though the nation-state itself had some prior reality. In fact the nation-state is an effect of all these everyday forms of regulation and representation, which set it up in the appearance of an empirical object. The geographical imagery of the Nile and its inhabitants that introduces so many studies of Egyptian development invokes and reproduces this effect.

MODEL ANSWERS

There are two consequences of the way economics takes for granted the nation-state as its object. The first is the illusion of the model. Portrayed as a freestanding entity rather than a particular position within a larger arrangement of transnational economic and political forces, an individual nation-state appears to be a functional unit—something akin to a car, say, or a mechanical pump—that can be compared with and used as a model for improving other such units. This supposed comparability is emphasized by the annual volumes of statistics produced by the World Bank and other international development agencies. Economic features of one state appear to be neatly transferable to other states, without regard for their different position in larger economic and historical networks.

The example of this in Egypt's case is the way agencies like the IMF and USAID began to promote the growth of exports as the solution to the country's economic problems. Egypt was to develop the export of winter vegetables and cut flowers to markets in Europe and the Gulf, along with textiles and possibly other light manufactured goods, in order to earn the hard currency to keep up interest payments on its foreign debts. The idea was that Egypt and similar countries should follow the path of the newly industrialized countries of East Asia—Singapore, Hong Kong, Taiwan, and South Korea.

This notion that solutions from East Asia provided a model for other Third World states was curious.[103] Egypt's merchandise exports in 1987 amounted to less than one-fifth of one percent of world trade. More than two-thirds of this merchandise consisted of oil, the supply of which was expected to decline in coming decades. To match the per capita level of exports of Singapore in the late 1980s, Egypt would have had to expand its exports to capture 23 percent of world trade—or significantly more than the merchandise exports of Japan and the United States combined.[104] Even the far more modest goal of matching South Korea, whose exports were worth $1,120 per capita in 1987, would have required Egypt to capture 2.35 percent of world trade. This would involve a forty-fold increase in nonoil exports, from an annual level at that time of about $1.25 billion to more than $52 billion.[105]

There was no evidence that Europe's demand for airlifted shipments of Egyptian cut flowers and winter tomatoes might grow by even a fraction of this amount. In the absence of the kind of far-reaching land reform carried out in South Korea, there was also no evidence that such export policies would be of any benefit to the landless and near-landless majority of rural Egyptians.[106] In fact other cases of agro-export policies suggest the opposite. For example, Brazil, which was "a stunning success as measured by investment in agrofood production and exports," was also "a nightmare of evictions from the land, displacement of local food systems, hunger, and social unrest."[107] Finally, as Streeten and others noted, this export-oriented solution was supposed to occur not during a period of enormous regional and global demand, such as that generated by Japanese growth and the Vietnam war during the period when the East Asian economies began to expand, but in a period of economic retrenchment during the 1980s, a period when a dozen or more large Third World countries were adopting similar remedies and competing for the same limited market.[108] In fact, Adelman's economic modeling suggested that in the situation of depressed world trade an alternative policy of transferring wealth to medium and small farmers (via land reform, infrastructural investment, and higher producer prices) to stimulate rural employment and consumption would result in higher rates of growth and larger exports than export-led policies.[109] It would also produce a substantial redistribution of income from rich to poor.

There is a second consequence of the way the imagery of the Nile valley and its people—and the larger discourse of development—constitute Egypt as a self-contained object. By setting out this sort of visual image of Egypt, the country is imagined as an object that exists apart from the discourse that describes it. The geographical metaphor that introduces the reports of an organization like USAID in Cairo evokes an entity "out there," Egypt, laid out like a map as the object of the organization's planning and knowledge. The organization itself, the metaphor suggests, is not an aspect of this object. It stands above the map of Egypt to measure and make plans, a rational center of expertise and policy making that forms no part of the object observed. USAID is not marked, so to speak, on the map.

Development discourse thus practices a self-deception—what Partha Chatterjee calls "a necessary self-deception," for without it development could not constitute itself.[110] Development is a discourse of rational planning. To plan effectively, it must grasp the object of its planning in its entirety. It must represent on the plans it draws up every significant aspect of the reality with which it is dealing. A miscalculation or omission may cause the missing factor to disrupt the execution of the plan. Its calculations must even include the political forces that will affect the process of execution itself.

This calculation has a limit, however, which is where the self-deception is required. As Chatterjee points out, the political forces that rational planning must calculate affect not only the execution of plans but the planning agency itself. An organization like USAID, which must imagine itself as a rational consciousness standing outside the country, is in fact a central element in configurations of power within the country. Yet as a discourse of external rationality, symbolized as the consciousness that unfolds Egypt as a map, the literature of development can never describe its own place in this configuration of power.

Consider the case of USAID's decentralization program, designed to reduce the role of the state and encourage "democracy and pluralism" by channeling development funds to private initiatives at the village and district level. The report quoted earlier suggested that among the principal beneficiaries of these funds were local government officials, state agricultural engineers, and other members of the state bureaucracy. The other main beneficiaries, wealthy farmers, often entered into partnership with such officials.[111] Far from encouraging a "private sector" in opposition to the state, such programs made the state an even more powerful source of funds and site of patronage. The new accumulations of wealth were never more than semiprivate, for they were parasitic on this strengthened state structure.

A similar process was described by Robert Springborg at the national level. He gave the example of one recipient of USAID funds, a man who was chair of the Foreign Relations Committee of the State Advisory Council (Majlis al-Shura). He was from a family long involved in Egyptian politics and business and had a personal wealth of several million pounds. USAID provided him with two sizable loans to purchase American irrigation equipment for large tracts of reclaimed land he owned, parts of which he sold off immediately after the equipment was installed. Springborg concludes that "a large proportion of USAID private sector assistance has been utilized by those well connected within the state apparatus to turn quick profits"—to the extent that even USAID economists in Cairo became disillusioned with the program of private sector loans.[112] In chapter 9 we will meet several other private entrepreneurs who grew rich from USAID programs, including one multimillionaire in his thirties who gave a new meaning to the American program of "cost recovery" in health care.

These examples illustrate the characteristic limits of development discourse. The major goal of USAID programs in Egypt was to develop what is termed the "private sector." The actual effect of these programs, however, was to strengthen the power of the state. This was not simply some fault in the design or execution of the programs. USAID itself is a state agency, a part of the "public sector," and therefore worked in liaison with the public sector in Egypt. By its very presence within the Egyptian public sector it strengthened the wealth and patronage resources of the state. USAID was thus part of the problem it wished to eradicate. Yet because the discourse of development must present itself as a rational, disinterested intelligence existing outside its object, USAID could not diagnose itself as an integral aspect of the problem.

OPPOSED TO SUBSIDIES?

This difficulty in seeing itself as a part of the scene reflected a much larger deception. The prevailing wisdom of organizations like the World Bank, the IMF, and USAID was that the problems of a country such as Egypt stemmed from the restrictions placed on the initiative and freedom of the private sector.[113] The program of "structural adjustment" these organizations attempted to impose on Egypt from the late 1970s, particularly following the 1985–86 collapse of oil prices, which left the country incapable of keeping up payments on its international debts, aimed to dismantle the system of state subsidies and controls and enable the private sector to flourish in the unrestricted freedom of "the market." Prices Egyptians paid to consume, or received for producing, food, fuel, and other goods were to reflect prices in the international market.

Yet it hardly needs pointing out that world prices for most major commodities are determined not by the free interplay of "private" market forces but by the monopolies or oligopolies organized by states and multinational corporations. Oil prices are determined not by the users of cars and electricity but by the ability of producer states to coordinate quotas and price levels. The price of raw sugar (a major Egyptian industrial crop), whose volatility was described as more than twice that of any other commodity monitored by the World Bank, is determined largely by U.S. and other government price support programs. Only about 14 percent of world production is freely traded on the market.[114] The international market for aluminum, one of the main heavy industries in Egypt, also operates under extensive state controls.

Perhaps the most significant example is the world grain market. One of the arguments against Egypt producing the staple foods it needed was that it could not compete in the world market against the low grain prices of American farmers. Yet these prices were the product of subsidies and market controls. American agriculture, operating under an imperative of constant growth, had come to be dominated by giant corporations that supplied the inputs to farming and processed and marketed its products. By the 1980s more than three-quarters of the American farm supply industry was controlled by just four firms. Six corporations, all but one of them privately owned, controlled 95 percent of U.S. wheat and corn exports and 85 percent of total world grain trade.[115] As Congressional investigations had shown, the monopolies these firms enjoyed enabled them to control the market and administer prices.[116] Squeezed by these monopolies on both ends, inputs and marketing, American farmers found themselves having to grow ever larger quantities of crops merely to survive, investing constantly in new technologies and getting increasingly into debt. Since the 1930s, this accelerating treadmill had put more than two-thirds of the country's farms out of existence—and continued to ruin them in the present.[117]

To mitigate the system's effects, the state introduced large subsidies, starting with the price supports and crop controls of the New Deal programs, followed by the subsidized exports of the postwar Marshall Plan, the Public Law 480 program (which financed up to 58 percent of U.S. grain exports during the 1950s and 1960s), and President Nixon's 1972 New Economic Policy (which further subsidized exports, and boosted prices by paying farmers to take 62 million acres out of production, an area equal to ten times the total cultivated area of Egypt). As a result of these policies, by

1982 American grain was being sold at prices 40 percent below estimated average production costs, and keeping farmers afloat was costing $12 billion a year in state subsidies.[118] Despite the low producer prices, moreover, consumer prices remained so high that 40 million Americans required government subsidies to purchase food, costing a further $27 billion a year in federal funds.[119] Government export subsidies paid for middle- and upper-class consumers in non-Western countries to shift to a meat-centered diet and thus expand the market for American feed grains.[120] By the 1990s this system was collapsing. The United States and the European Union could no longer afford the ever increasing levels of state subsidy, new Third World agricultural exporters were cutting into the dominant countries' market share, and transnational agro-industries were finding some of the restrictions on free trade an impediment to further growth and globalization. Short-term solutions were sought in a reorientation of trade into regional market blocs and a shift from price supports to income supports (which do not encourage excessive surplus). But following the U.S. Freedom to Farm Act of 1996, federal payments to farmers continued to rise, reaching an annual $23 billion—twice the level of 1982—by 1999.[121] There was no evidence of a long-term solution or an end to state subsidies and controls. As we have seen, the largest site in the world to be incorporated into this system of state-subsidized American farming was Egypt. The arm of the state that has organized this incorporation was USAID.

The self-deception of USAID discourse was not just that it set up an object called Egypt in which it could not recognize its own internal role. It is that this supposed object was caught up in a much larger configuration of power, a network of monopolies and subsidies misleadingly named the world "market," of which USAID itself was but a subsidiary arm. An agency devoting itself to the cause of dismantling subsidies and promoting the "private" sector was itself an element in the most powerful system of state subsidy in the world.

USAID's role as a source of subsidies to American agriculture and industry can be seen by examining how it spent the $15 billion budget for "economic assistance" to Egypt from the start of its operations there in 1974–75 up to 1989 (see fig. 3). Almost every penny of this amount, it can be shown, was actually allocated to American corporations. Just over half the total, first of all, represents money spent by Egypt to purchase goods from the United States. The Public Law 480 Food Aid program and the Commodity Import Program, totaling about $7.7 billion up to 1989, enabled Egypt to purchase grain, other agricultural commodities, agricultural and industrial equipment, and other U.S. imports.[122] Egypt paid for about

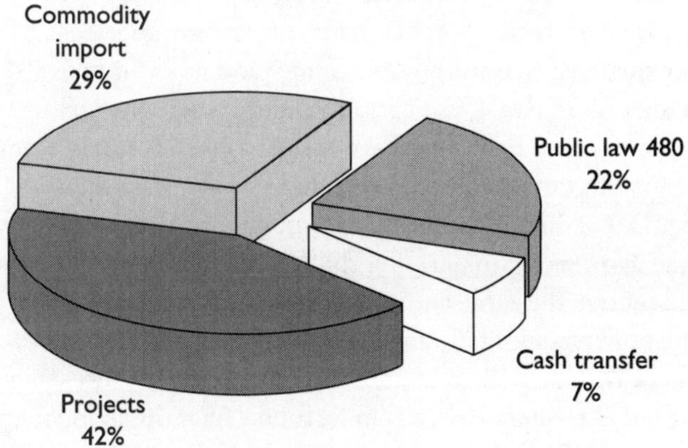

Figure 3. U.S. economic assistance to Egypt, 1975–89. Source: USAID, *Status Report* (Cairo, 1989).

half the commodities in dollars, with the United States providing low-interest long-term credit. The other half were paid for immediately or on short-term credit, but in Egyptian pounds.[123]

A further $1 billion of the total aid was also paid directly to the United States, this part by the U.S. government itself, in the form of so-called Cash Transfers used to keep up payments on Egypt's military debt. United States law stipulated that all aid except food must be stopped to a country that falls more than a year behind in military debt repayments, as Egypt began to do in the winter of 1983–84.[124] The U.S. government responded to this threatened collapse of the system of subsidies to its own private sector by converting all subsequent military loans to grants, allocating the bulk of those grants for progress payments to itself on earlier Egyptian arms purchases, and instructing USAID in the meantime to circumvent the law by setting aside about $100 million a year from economic development funds as Cash Transfers, to be deposited in the Federal Reserve Bank of New York and then returned to Washington as Egypt's monthly interest payments on its military debt.[125] When this illegal diversion of economic development funds for military purposes was discovered by Congress (thanks to the leak of a USAID cable to the *Washington Post*), the aid agency denied it was happening—but continued the practice. The law, an agency lawyer later admitted, "was an academic question, since actual CT [Cash Transfer] expenditures were untraceable."[126]

In 1987, when new accounting rules finally revealed the illegal diversion of funds, the U.S. government reversed itself and argued that such military use of economic aid was legal, on the grounds that 1) military debts, once incurred, became an "economic" and not a "military" question, and 2) in the case of Israel, Congress routinely repaid the U.S. Treasury Israel's annual military debt out of economic assistance funds. Congress rejected the first argument, pointing out that by paying Egypt's past military debts USAID was directly ensuring the supply of current military aid, and rejected the assumption underlying the second argument, that other countries could receive the same exemption from U.S. law enjoyed by Israel, as a gross misunderstanding of "the realities of this Congress and what happens up here with respect to Israel."[127] USAID agreed, once again, to stop paying Egyptian military debts from its funds—but the following year was already asking to have the new accounting rules relaxed. In 1990, following the Iraqi invasion of Kuwait and further Egyptian debt defaults, the U.S. government wiped out Egypt's entire $7.1 billion military debt, using Egypt's political support for a war against Iraq to overcome Congressional opposition.[128]

Thus a total of $8.7 billion, or 58 percent of all U.S. economic assistance, was spent directly in the United States rather than on development projects in Egypt, and most of this "American aid" in fact represents money paid by Egypt to America.

The remaining 42 percent of U.S. economic assistance funds to Egypt, totaling $6.3 billion, were earmarked for development projects within the country (see fig. 4). Yet none of this money was transferred directly to Egypt. The entire amount, as far as one can tell, was spent in the United States, or on American contractors in Egypt. The major recipients of the funds were large American manufacturing, construction, and consulting firms. More than $1 billion went to corporations like General Electric, Westinghouse, and Overseas Bechtel to purchase thermal power turbines and electricity distribution systems. More than $1.5 billion went to U.S. engineering and construction firms to build sewage networks and drinking water plants. Three hundred million dollars went to American Telephone and Telegraph and other U.S. communications companies to supply telephone equipment for Cairo and Alexandria. More than $200 million went to Ferguson International of Cleveland, Ohio, and other U.S. firms for the construction of two cement plants. American agribusiness and engineering firms received multimillion dollar contracts to supply grain silos and fats storage facilities for the country's expanded U.S. food imports. Dredging and earth-moving equipment was purchased from firms like Caterpillar,

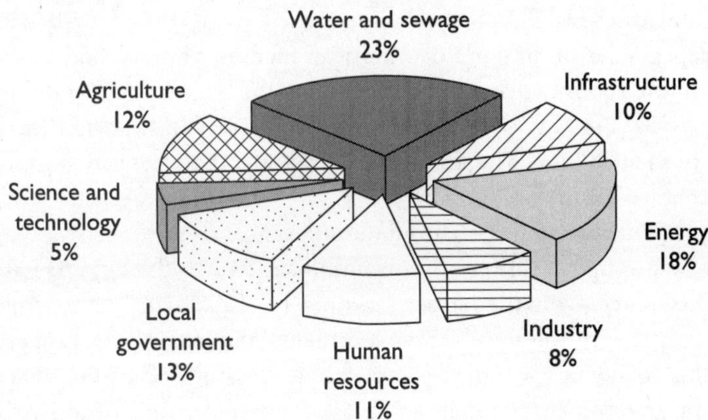

Figure 4. USAID projects by sector, 1975–89. Source: USAID, *Status Report* (Cairo, 1989).

John Deere, and International Harvester. Westinghouse Health Systems received tens of millions of dollars to improve rural and urban "health delivery." And hundreds of millions of dollars went to American universities and research institutes to provide training in agricultural sciences, management, and technology transfer.[129]

Many of these projects also required local payments within Egypt in Egyptian pounds. In 1988 such local implementation costs were said to amount to about E£200 million annually, equivalent then to just over $100 million, or about 10 percent of annual U.S. dollar aid for development projects.[130] But such payments were not made from U.S. dollar funds. Instead, local currency funds paid by the Egyptian government to purchase American imports under the Commodity Import Program, mentioned above, were used by USAID in Cairo to pay for all local costs. In other words, the local implementation expenses of development projects (and even the local operating costs of the USAID mission in Cairo) were paid by the Egyptian government, in exchange for commodities imported from the United States.[131]

Many millions of Egyptians, needless to say, benefited from this economic assistance, at least in the short term. The supply of power stations, sewage networks, telephone exchanges, and drinking-water plants improved the deteriorated physical fabric, especially in the two metropolises of Cairo and Alexandria, which had been overwhelmed by migration from the countryside following the failure to redistribute a better share of income among the rural population. At the same time, the aid program exacerbated basic problems in the distribution of wealth and political power, and as several Egyptian scholars argued, came at the price of a crippling dependence on imports of American food, machinery, and technology.[132] In the 1980s the United States became the largest supplier of Egyptian imports, and by 1988 the country's imports from America had reached E£1.94 billion. The following year, 1989, they jumped more than 50 percent, to E£2.93 billion.[133]

This dependence, and the astronomical levels of debt it caused, gave the United States a powerful position of influence within the Egyptian state. USAID conducted what it termed "cabinet-level dialogue" on macroeconomic policy with the Egyptian government. At times, USAID reported, when this "dialogue" was not "completely successful"—meaning that the Egyptian government rejected or delayed implementing American demands—"annual releases of funds have been delayed."[134] Acquiring at every level of the Egyptian bureaucracy this sort of "policy leverage," as it was called, became the principal criterion according to which USAID development projects in Egypt were evaluated.[135] And all this was achieved by a program whose larger effect was to provide subsidies to the so-called private sector in the United States—both directly, by the purchase of billions of dollars of its products, and indirectly, by converting Egypt into a future U.S. market.[136]

OPPOSED TO THE STATE?

Thus USAID operated, more or less successfully, as a form of state support to the American corporate sector, while working in Egypt to dismantle state supports. None of this was explained in the discourse of USAID itself, which pretended to stand outside Egyptian politics, conducting merely a "dialogue" at the rational, detached level of "policy." Yet there is even more that was missing from the discourse of development on Egypt. The $15 billion of assistance between 1974 and 1989 represented only about one-half of U.S. aid to Egypt in that period. The other half consisted of economic assistance to the Egyptian military. From 1985 to 1990 total American aid to Egypt was more than $15 billion, half of which consisted of military aid.[137] The military aid was largely spent in the United States to purchase weapons, representing in those five years alone a further $7.5 billion of subsidies to U.S. industry. The United States excluded this aid from its figures for "economic assistance," however, and listed it separately as military aid.

So American aid, which described its aims in Egypt as the support of the private sector and "pluralism," in fact channeled half its funds (or more, if one includes the Cash Transfer payments with which America paid back to itself Egypt's military loans) directly into the most powerful sector of the state. The Egyptian military, with the support of American funds, developed into a major presence within the country's manufacturing, agriculture, construction, and consumption. Its arms industries, which received state subsidies but whose income went into military rather than national accounts, became the country's largest manufacturing sector, producing exports (mostly to Iraq) estimated to be worth about three times the total of all other nontextile manufactures.[138] The army also moved into civilian manufacturing, producing clothes, electrical appliances, construction goods, and pharmaceuticals. In 1986 it negotiated a contract with General Motors to manufacture passenger cars. Under pressure from the American Embassy, USAID pledged General Motors a $200 million subsidy from its aid budget. The project was abandoned for political and financial reasons, but later on the army began to assemble Jeep Cherokees from the Chrysler Corporation.[139]

Agriculture was another sector in which the military became a dominant presence, setting up dairy, poultry, and vegetable farms, fisheries, land reclamation projects, and food processing industries, particularly in meat, fruit, and vegetables. Its Food Security Division represented the largest agro-industrial enterprise in the country, producing in 1985–86 E£488 million worth of food, or almost one-fifth of the total value of Egyptian food production.[140] The military also played a leading role in the construction of bridges, roads, power lines, telephone systems, and other civilian infrastructure projects. All these activities provided plentiful opportunities for patronage and personal profit making. The Lockheed Corporation agreed in 1990 to pay a $1 million bribe to an Egyptian member of parliament, who used her influence to persuade the Egyptian military to purchase three of Lockheed's C-130 Hercules transport planes, giving an indication of some of the sums involved. (When Pentagon auditors discovered the bribe Lockheed promised not to pay it, but then paid it the following year, according to U.S. prosecutors, disguised as a "termination fee.")[141] The Ministry of Defense also began to build its own military cities, mostly around Cairo. Thirteen cities were built by 1986, each with a population of 150,000 to 250,000, complete with hospitals, shops, schools, and mosques, and a further ten were under construction.[142] Together with coastal resorts, tourist services, and elite training colleges, these developments transformed the professional officer class into what

Robert Springborg called "an almost entirely autonomous enclave of middle-class modernity in an increasingly impoverished and marginalized Third World economy."[143] Meanwhile, many from the most senior ranks, often equipped with diplomas in management from U.S. military colleges, moved on to enjoy the rents from senior positions in ministries, state-owned corporations, and local government.

These enclaves of privilege received substantial support from Egyptian public funds. Among the world's twenty or so lower-middle income countries, Egypt in 1987 came near the bottom of the list in the proportion of central government expenditure devoted to health and education (only Syria and Mexico spent proportionately less) and near the top in the proportion (20 percent) devoted to the military (only Syria, Jordan, North Yemen, and El Salvador spent proportionately more). At the same time, power and privilege on this scale would never have been possible without the multibillion dollar contributions of United States aid.

Despite its large presence in the Egyptian economy, the large proportion of government funds it consumed, and its even larger proportion of total American support, the military received almost no attention in the literature of organizations like USAID and the World Bank. Given the supposed objectives of developing the private sector and pluralism, the silence of this discourse is astonishing. The silence reflects the necessary limits of the discourse of development. A systematic inquiry into the economy and power of the Egyptian military would have revealed its relations to American military industries, to the system of state subsidies on which those industries depended, and thus to the larger object of American aid programs. In the same way, as I have suggested, a proper analysis of Egyptian agriculture examining the causes of the shift to meat production and the country's resulting shortages of food and growing indebtedness would have revealed the connections between these events and the crisis of American farming and the remedy of subsidized food exports. Such analyses would serve as a reminder that the discourse of development is situated within, not outside, such relationships.

That is the reason for the silence. Development discourse wishes to present itself as a detached center of rationality and intelligence. The relationship between West and non-West will be constructed in these terms. The West possesses the expertise, technology, and management skills that the non-West is lacking. This lack is what has caused the problems of the non-West. Questions of power and inequality, whether on the global level of international grain markets, state subsidies, and the arms trade, or the more local level of landholding, food supplies, and income distribution, will nowhere be discussed. To remain silent on such questions, in which its own existence is involved, development discourse needed an object that appeared to stand outside itself. What more natural object could there be, for such a purpose, than the image of a narrow river valley, hemmed in by the desert, crowded with rapidly multiplying millions of inhabitants?

8 The Market's Place

The dominant theme in the description of the rural Third World at the close of the twentieth century remains the story of its capitalist transformation. The theme was exemplified in rural Egypt, where the reform and removal of state controls through the program known as structural adjustment was intended to turn the land and its produce into market commodities and remake the countryside for the twenty-first century as a fully capitalist economy. There are several ways to critique this story of capitalism's advance. In the case of Egypt one can question how seriously some of the market reforms were applied, ask about the ways people resisted or evaded them, point to the increasing hardship and poverty they caused, attack them for reversing the 1952 land reform and other political achievements, and criticize their appropriateness for the way most households survive and make a living. What remains remarkably difficult, however, is to account for what was happening in the countryside in a way that not only questions the extent or desirability of the advance of market capitalism, but avoids telling it as the story of capitalism.

Let me return to the themes I introduced at the beginning of this book and recall why one might want to avoid telling capitalism's story. The power of the market economy reveals itself not only in the transforming of people's lives and livelihoods but in its influence over the way we think. It is one of those ideas that we seem able to grasp only in terms that the phenomenon itself dictates. There are many different ways to describe the nature of the market economy, yet every description carries a common assumption. It is variously said to be based upon principles of self-interest, profit making, the proper organization of pricing and other forms of information, the accumulation and reinvestment of capital, the separation of capital from the labor it exploits, and a continuous historical process of worldwide expansion and transformation. Different accounts may highlight or ignore different features from this list. But every attempt to describe the capitalist economy inevitably attempts to capture what distinguishes the market system from the nonmarket, or the capitalist mode of production from the noncapitalist. The distinction gives capitalism its identity.[1]

For capitalism to work as a structure of representation, that is, as a way of appearing to distribute phenomena in terms of a distinction between a real world and its meaning, it must have an identity. There must be some characteristic that is the essence of capitalism, some element of sameness, so that as it develops and expands one can recognize its occurrence through different material and temporal manifestations and hold together its story. One could call this the "homoficence" of capitalism: whatever the local variation, at some level capitalism always does the same thing, or has the same effect.[2] The sameness supplies the theme that enables the narrative to move forward. It provides a logic that becomes the source of historical movement and the motor of social transformations. In rural Egypt one can attribute the spread of free-market practices to the force of self-interest and individual economic freedom, once the restraints of state control and other noncapitalist arrangements are removed. Or, following a different conception of capitalism's essence, one can ascribe the changes to the power of Egyptian and international capital, driven by the need to accumulate and reproduce. Whichever way one tells the story, what is happening in rural Egypt, or anywhere else in the rural Third World, receives its logic and meaning from the movement of the principle of market capitalism.

This logic does not mean that there are no other factors at work. The narrative gives a place to all kinds of noncapitalist features. The countryside may contain what one thinks of as traditional practices or precapitalist social arrangements, which resist the spread of the market or even interact with it in some kind of transitional articulation. It may contain political forces that present obstacles to the spread of capitalism or corrupt its operation. People may have social values or cultural norms that differ from those of the market. What characterizes all these additional features, however, is that when they are placed within the larger story of capitalism they are determined by its logic. The narrative marks them as nonmarket factors, meaning that it defines their identity and significance in terms of what they are not. Their role is that of negative elements. They stand outside the principle of the market, as external, nondynamic, generally residual, mostly local factors. As the exterior of capitalism, moreover, although they may impede its progress or distort its path, they do not shape its essence. They play no part in defining its nature. The market economy is understood to be a universal form constituted only from its own internal logic. The local and residual features encountered in a place like rural Egypt do not affect its real nature.[3]

Since the capitalist economy is understood to be determined by its own inner logic, since it has an inside or essence that determines its nature, one thinks of it as its own sphere. It appears to be a self-contained space, distinct from other social spheres such as the household, the state, or the sphere of culture. During the past two centuries, the changing forms of capitalist economic discourse have defined this space in different ways. As I discussed in chapter 3, the classical political economists from the late eighteenth to the mid-nineteenth century did not refer to an object called the economy. Writers like David Ricardo described a regular motion of production, exchange, and consumption whose regularity derived from the natural cycle of the country's major commodity, wheat, and whose movement they called the market. Later in the nineteenth century, Leon Walras and the new science of economics turned the market into a mathematical abstraction, while Marx replaced it with a much broader conception of material production and exchange. It was only in the 1930s and 1940s that the modern idea of the economy appeared, reflecting the collapse of a colonial organization of power, knowledge, and exchange, and the rise of the national state as producer of statistical knowledge and custodian of the economic. In the last quarter of the twentieth century these conceptions began to shift again. In Anglo-American political discourse the market came to stand for a system of forces that the state claimed was independent of its management of the economy, setting limits that this management could not profitably transgress.[4]

The idea that market capitalism has a unitary and universal nature that is not determined by the local or nonmarket elements it encounters rests, therefore, not only on simple distinctions between capitalist and noncapitalist or market and nonmarket. These distinctions are part of more complex fields of practice that have established the measures, exclusions, and power relations that make possible the market or the economy as forms of technical and material organization. Academic disciplines, state institutions, international development organizations, and bodies of statistical and theoretical knowledge have all played roles in this process. The ideas of the economy and the market seem so matter-of-fact that they would appear as central categories in almost any discussion of the changes transforming the rural Third World. Yet when they are taken for granted they conceal more than they reveal. A study of contemporary rural Egypt that assumes the economy to be a universal and unproblematic object would overlook the political process of its creation, as well as the local history of this process in Egyptian politics that I outlined in chapter 3. What is more important, it would reproduce the assumption that the economy is its own freestanding sphere, determined by its own logic, and that the obstacles and resistances to the market economy encountered in the countryside must be grasped only as the subsidiary, reactive, and local responses to the universal story of capitalism.

There have been only a couple of studies of the ways in which villagers in Egypt relate to what we call the market, with many accounts treating the village in isolation. These studies describe the complexity of the social organization of marketing, which for any one village involves several different kinds of merchants and agents, numerous levels of trade ranging from the centralized to the very local, a variety of financial arrangements, and many alternative sites of exchange. They also stress the importance farmers attach to their personal relationship with merchants, because of the mutual trust on which exchanges often depend.[5] Such analyses provide an excellent corrective to the image of the market one finds among proponents of free-market reforms, which typically begin from an abstract model of exchange and mention what actually occurs, if at all, only as the failure of or deviation from this abstraction. They insist, however, that these complex local practices represent a certain level of development of "the market" in general, and that farmers are best understood as small capitalists. Even when farmers engage in an apparently nonmarket practice, such as growing food for their own consumption, they are calculating that this is a better use of resources than marketing their crops and purchasing food. They are therefore dealing with the market.

If one must decide whether small farmers are capitalist or noncapitalist, then capitalist seems the correct choice. It avoids attributing apparently nonmarket relations either to tradition and ignorance, as free-market reformers often do, or to a parallel mode of production, oriented toward subsistence, that somehow coexists amid all these complex involvements with a market system. Yet the effect of describing these local social forms as a variety of market capitalism is to reproduce the general narrative of capitalism. However complex the local variations, they must derive from some internal principle of capitalism—a principle so abstract it has no location, and is therefore assumed to be universal or global.

Another important way of addressing the variety of relations to the market has been to introduce the idea of "multiple capitalisms," or, more broadly, of "alternative modernities." Such an approach might emphasize the variety of local, regional, and global forces whose combination shapes the particular histories of capitalist globalization, producing different versions in different places. These formulations provide a less Eurocentric way of acknowledging the importance and variation of the non-European contexts of capitalism's development and can reveal the complex and multiple origins of what we too easily unify under the name of globalization. Yet the strength of this sort of approach also contains a weakness. On the one hand, the language of alternative modernities can suggest an almost infinite play of possibilities, with no rigorous sense of what, if anything, gives capitalist globalization what seems its phenomenal power of replication and expansion. On the other hand, the vocabulary of alternatives still implies a fundamentally singular capitalism underneath, modified by local circumstances into alternative forms. It is only in reference to this implied generic that such alternatives can be imagined and discussed.[6]

Is there another way to make sense of what is happening in places like the Egyptian countryside? Can one find a way to take this local complexity and variation and make it challenge the narrative of the market? Can one do so without positing the existence of a precapitalist or noncapitalist sphere, or even multiple capitalisms, positions that always reinvoke the universal nature of capitalism? To begin to do so, we have to stop asking whether rural Egypt is capitalist or not. We have to avoid the assumption that capitalism has an "is" and take more seriously the variations, disruptions, and dislocations that make each appearance of capitalism, despite the plans of the reformers, something different.

I propose to explore these questions by drawing on the experience of a rural community in southern Egypt in the 1990s.[7] There are several aspects of the village's experience I will discuss, but to give a focus to the account I want to look in particular at the question of wheat.

Wheat provides an appropriate theme for a critique of economic discourse. The classical political economists, as I mentioned in chapter 3, based their picture of the market as a natural process on the production cycle of wheat. Indeed David Ricardo wrote his seminal essay in political economy, the "Essay on Profits" of 1815, as part of a political debate about protecting the price of wheat.[8] A century later, between 1873 and 1935, the global expansion of the colonial powers coincided with large increases in the production of wheat and new ways of transporting it. Wheat became the first major commodity to develop a world market, with producers everywhere facing a single price.[9] Toward the end of the twentieth century wheat acquired a different significance, symbolizing a popular resistance to the global market. In Egypt and

Jordan and beyond the Arab world efforts to end national protection against the world market were marked by major riots protesting the increase in the price of bread. On January 18, 1977, when the Egyptian government announced it was accepting the demand of the International Monetary Fund (IMF) to eliminate food subsidies and doubling the price of bread, groups of workers, students, and the urban poor marched to the center of Cairo in protest. The demonstrations turned to riots and spread to Alexandria and nineteen smaller cities, where shops, government buildings, and police stations were attacked. The government brought the army into the streets to quell the protests by force but was able to restore order only two days later, when it rescinded the price increases. The government claimed that 77 people had died and 214 were wounded, but unofficial estimates were several times higher.[10] Two decades later, no discussion of the IMF reforms in Egypt could pass without reference to the bread riots of January 1977.[11]

Following this confrontation, as all the accounts of the Egyptian economic reforms relate, the government moved more slowly and surreptitiously toward the reintroduction of world market prices for wheat. Protection had begun in 1941 as a measure to counteract the food shortages and price inflation caused by the war and the associated fertilizer crisis, discussed in chapter 1. In 1966 the government introduced ration cards to control distribution after the United States cut off its supply of subsidized wheat. When nonmarket U.S. wheat returned in large amounts following Egypt's realignment with Washington in 1974, the ration system changed from a form of quantity control into a method of distributing almost unlimited supplies of highly subsidized bread.[12] From the mid-1980s, as the United States began to demand market prices for the wheat it had previously dumped (with the express aim of creating a future market), the Ministry of Supply started to increase the price and reduce the availability and quality of subsidized bread and flour. It also stopped issuing ration cards for children born after 1991. At the same time the Ministry of Agriculture began to introduce policies demanded by the United States to create an uncontrolled domestic market. The ministry claimed to have ended government control of all crop areas, quotas, and prices by 1987, except for rice, cotton, and sugarcane, and for all except sugarcane by 1992. The government also relaxed its control of marketing and processing. In the case of wheat, it reduced its share of domestic production to about 50 percent after 1992, and also allowed private companies to begin importing wheat flour.[13]

What was the experience of these changes in rural Egypt? The village from which I want to draw some observations is located in a sugarcane-producing region of Qina governorate. It lies about six kilometers from the town of Luxor on the other side of the Nile and on the periphery of its tourist industry.[14] Bread is the village's staple food, but in the 1990s it had no bakeries and almost none of its more than two thousand households bought bread already baked.[15] Instead they used wheat flour to make the large sourdough loaves known as *'aish shamshi,* leavened in the sun and baked in earthen ovens at home. The dozen or so largest landowners used only wheat from their own fields, but the rest depended in part or whole on sacks of purchased flour. As the government-subsidized domestic flour was made scarcer, more expensive, and of the worst quality, all except the poorest households came to depend increasingly on highly refined, mostly imported white flour purchased from local merchants at unregulated prices.

Many households with small landholdings dealt with these changes by growing increasing amounts of their own wheat, which they processed at one of the tiny, one-room village mills and used entirely for household bread making. Zaynab, for example, who owned twenty qirats (five-sixths of an acre) and used to produce little or no wheat, now grew it on more than half her land.[16] With eight children but no grown men to feed (her husband worked eleven months out of twelve at a poultry factory outside Alexandria), a strong yield would supply all her needs for the year. The Mahmud household farmed four acres and now used more than half the land for wheat, although with three married sons and their wives and children the crop would not quite supply their needs. Rather than run out of homegrown wheat, which makes bread of superior texture and taste, the women added a little white flour each time they baked. The village's largest landowner, Salim, who controlled more than 300 of its 2,750 acres, produced an enormous surplus of wheat, which he sold to grain merchants from Qina or other large towns. Unlike the smallholders, however, he had not increased his wheat acreage since the deregulation of the market, preferring (for reasons to be explored) to keep most of his land in sugarcane.

The Ministry of Agriculture produced statistics that reflected the increased production of wheat, at least among smallholders, and may have exaggerated it. The official figures for the country as a whole report that levels of wheat production stagnated at just under two million metric tons a year from the early 1970s until 1986, then suddenly doubled to more than four million tons by 1990 and increased to more than six million by 1998. The biggest percentage increase came in 1987, immediately following the removal of area restrictions, quotas, and fixed procurement prices, when production jumped by 40 percent in one year (see fig. 5). The ministry, the IMF, and the U.S. Agency for International Development

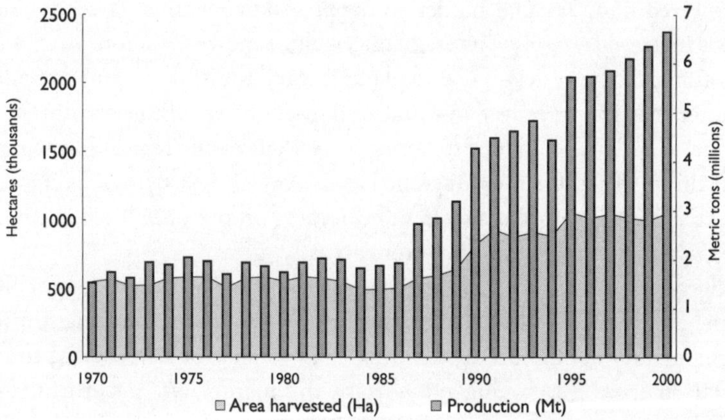

Figure 5. Wheat production in Egypt, 1970–2000. Source: FAO (http://apps.fao.org).

(USAID) regularly cited these figures as the best proof of the success of their program of free-market reforms.

While acknowledging that there was a significant increase in wheat production, one can point to two problems with this use of such figures. First, the system of compulsory cropping and low procurement prices in place before the 1987 reform, which particularly affected small farmers, gave them a strong incentive to disguise the size of their wheat yields. (The method of gathering agricultural statistics offered several opportunities for doing so. The census staff determined the area planted with a given crop in each village, "with the help of village administrative staff," simply by asking farmers what they had planted. They took field measurements for cotton, wheat, rice, and cane, measuring only half of each crop, and taking measurements only along the sides of existing survey parcels. They determined yields by asking the farmers again, and by eye estimates. Sample field measurements were made only in two villages in each district.)[17] Smallholders who were required to grow a quota of sugarcane or other commercial crops and sell them to the government at low prices also had good reason to divert part of their land to crops they could eat themselves, including wheat. At the very least they would ensure that any particularly poor soil was allocated to government crops, not those consumed at home. ("There's the government's sesame," ʿAmm Mahmud used to say, pointing to a barren patch of whitish soil that never produced anything.) These sorts of practices may well have increased during the 1980s, as procurement prices dropped in real terms, subsidized flour became harder to obtain, and consumer prices for other foods increased sharply. The stagnant yields of the years before 1987, which according to the official view made necessary the shift to an unregulated market, may in fact reflect, in whole or in part, the smallholders' unreported diversion of land and crops to better serve their own needs.[18] To the extent that this is the case, something one has no way of measuring, the impact of the free-market reforms may have been more on the statistics published by the state than on what farmers were actually growing.

Second, it is curious that those telling the story of Egyptian agriculture at the end of the twentieth century as one of successful movement toward a free market should produce as the best evidence of its progress the fact that farmers were moving not toward the market but toward increased self-provisioning and protection from the market.[19] The rationale for the deregulation of agriculture was that farmers would respond by growing more so-called high value crops, especially export crops such as cotton and vegetables, drawing themselves more fully into the national and transnational market economy and thereby increasing their own and the nation's income. This did not happen. In the six years following the 1987 deregulation the area planted with cotton, the two main vegetable crops (tomatoes and potatoes), and most other vegetables declined.[20] The value of agricultural exports fell sharply, and even a decade after deregulation had not yet recovered to prereform levels (see fig. 6). The area planted with grain and fodder crops serving mostly household production, on the other hand, remained steady, and in the case of two staple grains, wheat and rice, dramatically increased.[21] In the northern Delta, where rice replaces bread as the staple food, farmers planted so much of the crop that the government issued 250,000 fines and threatened farmers with imprisonment in an attempt to conserve water supplies for industrial and export crops.[22] Altogether, crops intended mostly for the farm household accounted for more than two-thirds of the crop area following the reforms.[23]

In the village itself several smallholders reported experimenting with growing vegetables for the market after the government controls were lifted, with mixed results. In 1988 Ahmad Hassan planted two qirats of aubergines and sold the crop for E£700, a good return.[24] The following year he planted six qirats, or a quarter of an acre, which was half his landholding. There was a shortage of irrigation water one month, the crop dried out, and his entire yield filled barely three baskets. He sold the crop for E£20. Others reported planting tomatoes and getting E£2 or E£3 per kilo, selling

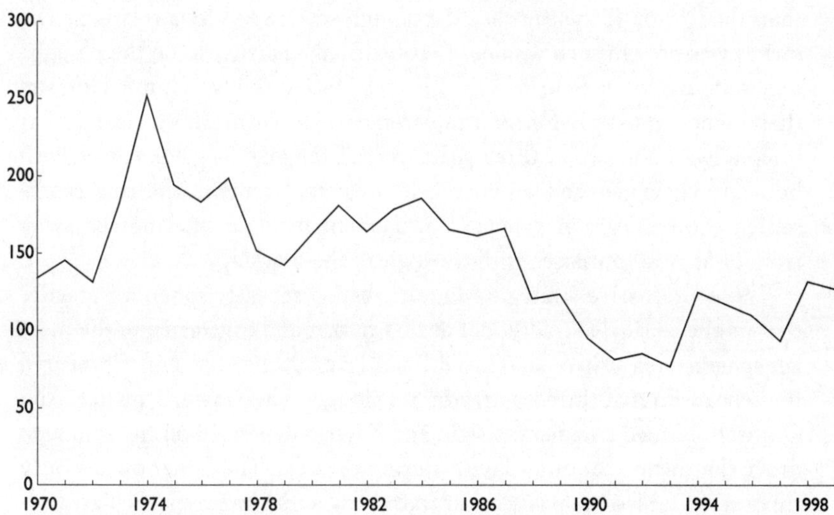

Figure 6. Index of value of Egyptian agricultural exports, 1970–99 (mean of period 1989–91 = 100). Source: FAO (http://apps.fao.org).

directly to a man with a truck who shipped them to the Rod al-Farag wholesale market in Cairo. Then came "ayyam Saddam," the 1990–91 Gulf crisis, when tourism collapsed and with it the price of vegetables. People were selling two or three kilos for just fifty piastres. Others told different disaster stories, while many more were unable even to consider taking such risks.

Instead farmers adopted other strategies to increase their income, but these often took them in different directions than the market. To prepare one of her strips of land for planting the 1996/97 crop of wheat, to begin with a simple example, Zaynab hired a distant cousin who used a wooden plough, drawn by a cow and its calf. During the eight years since she started farming her own land she had always hired tractors. By the end of the 1980s these had almost entirely replaced animal-drawn ploughs, a process encouraged by government subsidies and USAID programs to promote the importation of agricultural machinery.[25] The ending of subsidies, however, had removed some of the cost advantage of the tractor (E£1.50 to E£2 for a tractor to plough one qirat, compared to E£2.50 for the cow). Zaynab had also learned that animal-drawn ploughs produce a better yield, because they do not compact the soil as tractors do, especially when making tight turns at the ends of the narrow, elongated strips that small farmers own. Moreover, she talked the owners of neighboring plots into hiring the same plough and received a discount in return that made it cheaper than the tractor. (It helped that the plough was owned by a relative.) The owner was now in such demand that he hired a partner to do the ploughing, in return for one-third of the income. Machines have a limited life and their owners must pay for their replacement. The cow trains its own calf as it ploughs, and in two or three years the calf can take its place. Fueled with homegrown fodder and producing its own replacement, the cow represented another part of people's engagement in logics that moved away from or at cross-purposes with the logic of the market.

These alternative strategies do not create a separate sphere of practice that might be labeled traditional or nonmarket and contrasted to the market sphere. On a strip of land in a different part of the village, also prepared for wheat, Zaynab hired a tractor to plough. The tractor's owner, Abu Qumsan, farmed an adjacent strip and Zaynab depended on his son, who drove the tractor, for other favors during the year. The father owned only three acres, far less than any other tractor owner, so he was particularly dependent on renting out the tractor to work his neighbors' plots. Zaynab decided it would be prudent to maintain good relations with him by continuing to hire his tractor. Elsewhere in the village, to give a different example, farmers had begun to reintroduce the use of camels, particularly to carry the sugarcane crop. Like the animal plough, camels had been almost completely replaced by tractors over the previous decade. But then a number of young men from different hamlets in the village began to invest in camels. They used them to carry sugarcane in the mornings, then decked them with saddles and decorated cloths and took them to the ferry where tourists disembarked from Luxor to earn money offering rides through the village.

Sugarcane offers a more complex case of this imbrication, an example of the difficulty of distinguishing between market and nonmarket practices. The Mahmud household, with four acres and three married sons, while increasing their wheat crop to more than two acres, still kept one acre devoted to the year-round production of sugarcane. This was their only cash crop. The rest of the land grew maize and berseem (Egyptian clover) to feed the animals and onions, *mulukhiyya* (a soup green), and other small crops to feed the household. The cane provided the income to purchase seeds, diesel for the irrigation pump, and fertilizer they required for growing household crops. The acre of cane would earn between E£4,500 and E£5,000 from the government sugar factory. The factory paid part of this amount in advance, providing a cash loan early in the year on which the household now depended. This was a further reason why they kept the sugarcane—as a source of credit. If they switched to another crop they could not survive the growing season without the loan. They were involved in production for the market, but its purpose was to support the much larger system of self-provisioning. This was true for the village as a whole, and probably for the entire country. The pattern is the reverse of that described in the old debates on the articulation of modes of production, and far more complex. Rather than a subsistence sector surviving in support of capitalism, market crops, protected and promoted by the state, survived in support of self-provisioning.

Small and medium-sized farmers like the Mahmud household had no interest in extending the production of a market crop such as sugarcane beyond the needs of their household production precisely because of the expense and loss involved in getting it to the market.[26] They cut and stripped the cane themselves with the help of neighbors and relatives, but had to hire a tractor and cart to carry it across the village to the light railway line running to the mill in Armant, fifteen kilometers to the south, and had to hire a pair of men to load the railway wagons. For an acre of cane the tractor cost E£500, the loaders E£300. As Rajab Mahmud said, "the tractor takes our profit." The mill workers took some too, he swore, for when they weighed the cane at the factory they always cheated and recorded a lower weight for each farmer's wagons. Household crops, on the other hand, which they also cut themselves, were carried to the house on a donkey cart or by hand, or in a pickup truck rented for a few pounds if the field was farther away. No one else took their profit.

These same considerations produced a different logic for the handful of very large landowners, for whom sugarcane had comparatively low labor costs. Salim, for example, who grew more than a hundred acres of cane, hired teams of day laborers at E£5 each per day (in 1996/97) for the planting, weeding, and harvesting of all his crops. His sons and nephews helped to supervise the laborers working in different areas of the village, and he employed a handful of permanent workers to drive the tractors he owned and operate his irrigation pumps and other machinery. Since all his crops carried the cost of hired labor, sugarcane was no more expensive to grow than wheat, maize, or broad beans. In fact, its labor costs were much lower. The cane stayed in the ground for three to five years, reducing the cost of planting, and needed fertilizing only three times a year. Salim's crop was so large that its harvesting took five months, from late December until May. He employed wagon loaders continuously through this period, at a discount. He paid them only E£2 per ton of loaded cane, compared to the E£2.50 or E£3 that smallholders paid to hire loaders by the day, making his labor costs as much as 50 percent lower. Most important, villagers did much of his harvesting for free. Those with little or no land used the leaves of the cane, known as *gilwah,* as fodder for the household water buffalo. Mona, for example, who owned only a few qirats and rented several more to grow berseem, depended on the *gilwah* as an additional source of fodder. She helped harvest in the plots adjacent to her house and sent her sons to the plots on the far side of the same field. They did the difficult and physically dangerous work of cutting the cane and stripping its razor-sharp leaves without payment, or for a token amount, in exchange for taking the leaves, which had no market value. The interaction of paid and unpaid labor determined that the same crop that small farmers found the most costly to produce was for large landowners the cheapest. But the profits that led large owners to grow sugarcane rather than wheat depended upon a large supply of villagers with little or no land willing to do the most arduous work of all without payment.

I have been calling sugarcane a market crop, but this is misleading. The mill that bought the crop was owned by the government, which fixed the purchase price. Yet this is not the misleading part. If the government were to have privatized the Egyptian Sugar and Refining Company, the farmers would still have had little choice over to whom to sell their crop or at what price. The company owned the narrow-gauge railway, and there was no other easy way to transport the cane. Once it is cut the cane's moisture content and the sucrose proportion of the moisture rapidly decline, so it must reach the mill within hours. The crop takes eighteen months to grow when first planted and stays in the ground for at least two further nine-month cultivations, so farmers had no way to respond to the ups and downs of international sugar prices.

What is misleading is the very idea that there could be a free market in sugar. As a crop that requires the year-round sun of tropical or semitropical regions, and one whose harvesting cannot easily be mechanized, cane is the only staple food in the world whose cultivation and export are not dominated by the rich countries of the temperate zone. This anomaly was first overcome three hundred years ago by colonizing the Caribbean and enslaving Africans to grow cane there. (The sugarcane plantation was one of the earliest forms of industrial organization and discipline, as Sidney Mintz has shown, placing slave-based sugar manufacturing at the center of the emergence of capitalist production methods and the system of world trade.[27] The crop's history provides another reminder that the market has no essence, but always requires a changing variety of nonmarket methods at its core, sometimes including slavery.) When the United States and Europe lost control of their Caribbean dependencies in the mid-twentieth century, they responded by promoting the cultivation of sugar beet, an inferior crop that requires extensive use of chemical herbicides and had to be protected with price supports and import quotas. Surplus beet sugar was then dumped on the world market, depressing and destabilizing the price of cane sugar and costing its Third World producers billions of dollars each year in lost revenue.[28] In the second half of the 1990s European Union and American subsidies helped produce a global sugar glut five years in a row, pushing prices below production costs for all countries except Brazil.[29] The price of sugar in the United States included the hundreds of thousands of dollars the sugar industry paid each year buying votes in Congress in order to keep the subsidy system in place.[30]

Just as sugarcane cannot easily be understood as a market crop, neither can wheat. There is a similar difficulty in describing the movement of wheat outside the village as a market system. As with sugarcane, cotton, and other major crops, the agricultural policy reforms in Egypt were not able to deregulate the price of wheat. From 1992 private merchants were allowed to import wheat flour, ostensibly creating a free market in white flour. In practice, however, the reform replaced Egyptian government controls with a series of other restrictions and controls, running from the world market to the village merchant.

At the global level, the marketing of wheat was controlled by five or six international grain-trading corporations, most of them privately owned. Production prices depended on an extensive system of U.S. and European Union price supports, required to keep afloat their large and otherwise unprofitable commercial producers. The failure of large-scale commercial wheat production dates back more than a century, as I mentioned in the previous chapter, to the emergence of a global market in wheat between the 1870s and 1930s. As Harriet Friedmann has shown, the emergence of the market did not follow a logic one could describe simply as capitalist. It coincided with a global shift from large-scale commercial farming to the increasing production of wheat by family farms. Relying on their own unpaid labor, household producers were more efficient, flexible, and resilient than large farms using wage labor. (The territorial expansion of the United States, Canada, and other settler states in this period also encouraged, and heavily subsidized, the establishing of family farms.)[31] From the 1930s, as the crisis of large grain producers worsened, the United States and other governments began to introduce a system of price supports, which Washington extended after World War II into a program of subsidized grain exports that aimed to convert first Europeans and then parts of the Third

World into consumers of meat-based diets, which require much higher levels of grain production. In the 1970s and 1980s, as chapter 7 explained, the largest recipient of subsidized U.S. grain was Egypt, where cheap wheat imports helped depress farm incomes and diverted government spending to other sectors, especially the military.

In the United States and Western Europe, government subsidies kept wheat prices high to protect politically powerful producers. Total annual subsidies in U.S. agriculture reached about $29,000 for each farmer by the mid-1990s (or forty times Egypt's per capita GNP).[32] A separate system of support, using food coupons and welfare payments, made bread affordable for the poor.[33] In Egypt, where producers had no political power and a far greater proportion of the population could not afford the inflated prices of the world grain market, the government used subsidies differently, to keep consumer prices low. As was mentioned earlier, in the later 1980s the United States began to demand market prices for its wheat, forcing Egypt to embark on the program of agricultural policy reform. The government eliminated subsidies for most other goods, cut the quantity and quality of subsidized flour, and began adding corn flour to the wheat. Despite strong U.S. and IMF pressure to abolish bread subsidies entirely, however, the government was unable to eliminate the program. The private sector wheat market had to coexist with the system of government supply.

Farmers in the village were now caught in the resulting confusion. The Ministry of Agriculture claimed to have ended the system of area restrictions, quotas, and fixed procurement prices. The Ministry of Supply and Commerce, however, working with the local government authorities, still attempted to procure about 12 to 15 percent of local wheat production at a fixed price (E£100 per ardeb in 1996 and 1997).[34] The government-run land-reform cooperatives, which supplied seeds and fertilizer to beneficiaries of the 1952 land reform, demanded in return that the owners of each holding (the *nimra,* or original land-reform unit, which was legally indivisible but in practice usually shared among several second- or third-generation owners) sell to the government one ardeb (150 kilograms) of wheat. In the summer of 1996 a crisis erupted when the price of wheat on the commercial market rose much higher than the government's price and the Ministry of Supply was unable to obtain its wheat. The Qina governorate authorities responded by suspending development projects in any village that failed to supply its quota, forcing farmers to supply the missing wheat by purchasing it on the market, where prices jumped even higher. The authorities also reduced the supply of subsidized flour to each distributor. In Aswan governorate to the south, local authorities required that anyone seeking permits of any kind or other government assistance produce a document showing that they had supplied their quota of wheat. In at least one district this requirement was imposed on every village household, including those growing no wheat or even farming no land at all. To obtain the appropriate document, villagers had to pay the cooperative a sum covering the cost of purchasing wheat on the market to resell to the government. The authorities had banned the transport of wheat between governorates, so villages had to smuggle supplies through the desert to avoid the roadblocks and inspection points that now operated like international frontiers on the main roads.[35] The official accounts of Egypt's successful transition to a rural market economy did not discuss these unusual arrangements.[36]

There are further reasons why the movement of wheat outside the village did not resemble the model of a free market. The international cartel of grain-trading corporations that controlled world supplies was now copied within Egypt. A small group of merchants controlled the commercial importing of wheat flour and fixed the price.[37] Within the village itself, the commercial distribution of flour was also tending toward a local oligopoly. Three or four merchants in the village had official concessions to sell subsidized flour from the Ministry of Supply. Commercial sales of flour were now concentrated in the same hands. By far the biggest of these merchants was Hasan Qinawi, who with his brother Ibrahim inherited his father's village shop and transformed it in the mid-1990s into the dominant local business.

The history of this merchant household reflects the complexity of the changes that had been taking place. The Qinawi family was said to have its roots in the long-distance trade with the Sudan. Little of this trade—once an important activity of the village, which lies near the start of one of the old desert routes to the south—remained after the middle of the twentieth century.[38] The Qinawis' father made his living from a different long-distance trade that flourished in the region in the 1950s and 1960s, the supply of eggs by train to Cairo. Beginning as a middleman who went from door to door collecting eggs from the women who raised poultry, he later built a large hatchery, the remains of which four decades later still stood next to the family house. In the 1970s the poultry trade too was wiped out, partly by the decline of local grain production after the Aswan Dam made possible the extension of sugarcane cultivation, and partly by the rise of factory egg and poultry production in the north, subsidized with IMF loans and nonmarket U.S. feed grains. One of these giant poultry factories in the

Delta was where one or two of the Qinawis' poorer neighbors now found work, including the migrant husband of Zaynab.

The father survived the collapse of the local egg industry. He had become a general merchant and moneylender dealing especially in wheat and had opened a small shop built into the outer wall of his large house. Following the last round of land transfers in the 1960s, when the state sequestered land from some of those who had evaded or profited from the earlier reforms, he acquired fifty acres from an estate in a neighboring village. (Its owner was a local magnate who had managed the estate of Ahmed ʿAbbud, the sugar baron of chapter 1, and extended his own holdings after the 1952 land reform broke up ʿAbbud's six-thousand-acre property. In the 1960s this local magnate's own property was sequestrated and he moved abroad, returning a decade later after President Sadat reversed the final sequestrations. He now ran the estate, a large hotel across the river in Luxor, and several other operations from his home near Armant—the restored country house of ʿAbbud.) Qinawi was able to send his sons to study in the faculty of commerce at one of Cairo's large universities, an education useful less for what the sons were taught than for the connections they made with the sons of other merchant families in Cairo and throughout Upper Egypt. They returned home after their father's death, built a warehouse next to the mosque that faced the house (and which the father had built and recently renovated and enlarged), and turned his shop into the center of a large wholesale business, using their college merchant connections to ship in goods for all the smaller shopkeepers in the village. Within three years they had built a larger warehouse on the main road and another across the river in Luxor, and they were beginning to monopolize the supply of flour in the district, as well as certain supplies to the big tourist hotels, including a new brand of mineral water called Safi. (Safi was introduced by the food and beverages arm of the Egyptian military, the country's largest agribusiness operation, whose unpaid labor force represented another forced labor system within the so-called market.)

Most of the women who used to supply eggs to the father could no longer afford the factory-produced eggs. In the late 1980s the supply of nonmarket U.S. feed grains was cut as part of the program of agricultural price reforms. At the same time the government lifted a ban on imported frozen poultry, flooding the market with cheap supplies from the United States and the European Union, where subsidies had not been cut. Most of the country's commercial egg and poultry industry collapsed. The poultry population was cut in half between 1984 and 1989, and per capita egg consumption dropped from eighty eggs a year to fifty-three. Only the largest producers survived (including the one in the Delta that employed men from the village), building integrated operations with their own feed mills and distribution systems. By the early 1990s they formed a small cartel controlling prices and supply.[39] With more by-products from their own farming to use as animal feed, and unable to afford cartel prices, women in the village began to raise increasing numbers of their own poultry. Zaynab, for example, was raising at any one time a dozen or more pigeons, an equal number of chickens, and half a dozen ducks and geese, alongside the water buffalo and up to two dozen sheep and goats. Most farming households in the village raised a similar number and range of animals, although the poorer could not afford the buffalo while the wealthiest might have several buffalo and cows. Women sold surplus poultry and eggs among neighbors and at the weekly market in the neighboring village, where their numbers sometimes rivaled those of regular merchants selling vegetables, feed grains, and household supplies. Poultry raised at home also replaced beef purchased from the butcher for Thursday dinner, the one meat meal of the week for most households, many of whom could no longer afford to purchase meat following the reforms.[40]

This is the story of one merchant family and one village. Its usefulness is not for making any general point about the impact of market reforms but to argue against general points. It illustrates the great variety of factors at work in the attempt to introduce a market system, many of them incompatible with any abstract definition of a market. With poultry, as with wheat, the result of the market reforms was nothing like a market system. A similar debacle occurred with fertilizer: when the government ended its control over the supply of fertilizer in 1994, an oligopoly of three producers took over the supply and quadrupled the price, forcing the government to reassume control.[41] All these developments reflected not a failure to implement the reforms, but their interaction with existing networks and logics that resituated and transposed them.

I want to return one last time to the issue of bread. The market in flour could not function freely as a market, as we have seen, in part because for most people in Egypt bread is the staple food. The government had reduced or eliminated almost all other food subsidies, but could not end the supply of subsidized bread. In the village bread formed a large part of almost everyone's diet. Compared to the flat loaves of *'aish baladi* eaten in the towns, the thick *'aish shamshi* loaf produced in the villages of the south was extremely filling. For the poorest households it was almost the only food, taken with a cup of black tea at breakfast (the tea helped kill the appetite) and dipped in a bowl of *mulukhiyya* to give it moisture as the main meal.

The basic nourishment that bread could provide was the result of a major resource within the village, a resource that shaped the wheat market yet could not itself be marketed: the labor of bread making. The work women did in kneading and baking their bread and supplying fuel for the bread oven was one of the most important means of creating household wealth. Most women baked every four or five days, often working jointly with a sister-in-law, neighbor, or daughter kept home from school that day to share the labor of producing fifty or sixty loaves. The work was integrated with the other household labor of child rearing, laundry, cooking, and cleaning, and was closely connected with animal raising. Pats of buffalo dung, together with the remains of the maize or corn leaves used as animal fodder mixed with dung from the donkey, provided the main source of fuel for the bread oven. (Households needing extra supplies could spread a little dung on leaves in the lane outside the house, its smell provoking every passing donkey to provide some more.) Cardboard boxes, used school notebooks, and other forms of refuse in the village provided an additional source of fuel. Tourist groups from Luxor that visited the temple near Zaynab's house brought boxed lunches, whose packaging she had arranged to recycle in her oven. Dried scraps of bread from her table were never wasted, but carefully collected and fed to the poultry. Even the ashes from the bread oven were reused, as fertilizer in the fields.

This form of food production could not be reproduced commercially, given the market costs of fuel and labor, so *'aish shamshi* was not available for purchase. In the wealthiest landowning households, women who were spared some of the other chores of animal raising and collecting fodder still produced their own bread. Even the handful of younger, better-off women who lived in the small apartment buildings near the ferry, from where their husbands commuted to work as lawyers or pharmacists in Luxor, still usually returned to their mothers' homes in the village every few days to bake bread.

The system of self-provisioning would begin with the growing of wheat and the raising of domestic animals. No household was self-sufficient, for most lacked enough land to support themselves entirely, and those with large landholdings purchased tea, sugar, and other goods they could not grow. But self-provisioning involved far more than the resources represented by government figures for wheat production and numbers of farm animals. The village household produced its staple diet not only by raising crops and animals but by an intensive system of food manufacture. Neither the labor used to make bread nor the fuel was a market commodity. The same is true of the labor used in milking the buffalo and producing cheese, clarified butter, and other household milk products, or in preparing poultry to eat. This manufacturing system was probably the country's largest industry, at least in terms of the numbers it employed and the mouths it helped feed. Yet it had no official place in the government's program of agricultural reforms. Contemporary methods of estimating the country's gross domestic product (GDP) included some guess at the value of crops directly consumed by those who grow them. But the reforms were concerned with removing obstacles to the operation of market laws and grasped the nature of Egyptian agriculture according to the model of a market. This model has no place for the industry of domestic food manufacture and the crops and livestock that supported it, except a residual and insignificant one.

The result of reformers implementing the model of the market was to demonstrate its failure. Ending the compulsory government purchase of crops at low prices probably stimulated production. The yields of several major crops appeared to have increased significantly. But some of this increase may have been due to more accurate reporting and much of the rest to the continuing introduction of high yielding crop varieties, which have no necessary connection with market principles. (In the 1990s Egypt held the world record for yields of sugarcane, the one crop that the government still entirely controlled.) In general, the free-market reforms produced results opposite from those their proponents anticipated. Instead of moving toward high value export crops such as cotton and vegetables, farmers increased their production of staples such as wheat, maize, and rice. Markets did not work because of monopolization, hoarding, speculation, and the exposure of farmers to international price swings that everywhere in the world make free-market farming impossible. To deal with the instability their programs had caused, the reformers began to call for the introduction of futures markets, to enable farmers to sell their crops in advance at more stable prices. But futures markets seldom work for small farmers and tend simply to open up another field of financial speculation, shifting more of the income away from those who grow the food.[42] Better alternatives, such as farmer-run marketing cooperatives, which play a major role in Europe and the United States, were ignored by organizations like USAID and in some cases actively opposed.[43] Instead, the government was obliged to manage the crises by retaining or reintroducing acreage controls and floor prices. Even the reformers acknowledged, furthermore, that "the costs" of their policies, as they put it, had "become much more apparent." The costs they listed, with no hint of self-recrimination, included "growing unemployment, falling real wages, higher prices for basic goods and services, and widespread loss of economic security."[44]

Reformers claimed that these hardships were the necessary price for removing the barriers to agricultural growth. Once the growth began, the hardships would be overcome. Since removing the barriers exposed farmers to global price instability and local price fixing, however, it did not stimulate real growth. The World Bank had claimed that the old system of price controls was penalizing farmers and reducing agricultural GDP by 20 percent.[45] Yet in the seven years following the removal of controls in 1986, despite the reported increase in yields, agricultural GDP stagnated or even declined.[46] The reformers subsequently admitted that they did not know whether the old price controls had depressed output or what effect government interventions had on overall agricultural performance, an ignorance they had failed to mention when advocating the reforms.[47] Moreover, apparent success in the other major area of economic reform, currency stabilization (see chapter 9), encouraged large flows of foreign capital into Egypt, which the IMF claimed were causing the Egyptian pound to become overvalued in relation to the dollar, perhaps by as much as 30 percent.[48] If so, the decline of real agricultural income, as well as the obstacles to the further promotion of agricultural exports, was even greater.

Far from a temporary phenomenon, the costs of the reforms were to become a central part of the reformers' long-term plans for rural Egypt. Following the creation of a commercial market in crops, the next goal was a free market in land. The 1952 agrarian reform gave agricultural tenants and their heirs security against eviction and fixed the maximum rent at seven times the land tax. The U.S. government and international financial agencies argued that this arrangement was "creating disincentives to a more efficient use of land," although there was no evidence to support this view.[49] A law to abolish the 1952 reform was pushed through parliament in 1992 by the ruling National Democratic Party and the right-wing Wafd, the party of old landowning families (including the minister of agriculture).[50] The law raised the maximum rent from seven to twenty-two times the land tax for a five-year transition period, after which rents and tenancies were to be unregulated and all tenants could be evicted. Parliament enacted the law without any studies of its possible impact, nor even accurate figures about the number of tenants affected or the size of their landholdings.[51]

Popular opposition to the law was muted by a security regime that outlawed any form of unlicensed political activity—a regime that considerably tightened its grip during the period of free-market reforms—and at the same time by repeated suggestions from the government that the law would not seriously be implemented. Although it carried out the initial tripling of land rents, to twenty-two times the land tax, the government announced in October 1996 that this rent ceiling would be retained for an additional five-year period, until 2002.[52] By the end of 1996, however, farmers began to learn from changes at the local government cooperatives that the law would go ahead, and the protests began.[53] On December 31, 1996, tenant farmers from villages near Bani Suwaif, eighty miles south of Cairo, gathered on the main railway line and began stopping trains running to and from Cairo, then marched to the office of the provincial governor and demanded the abrogation of the law. The security forces arrested ten of the farmers.[54] The two opposition newspapers that reported this and similar events were later shut down.[55]

When the law was finally implemented in October 1997, the protests escalated, as did the violence of the state. The Land Center for Human Rights, set up to defend the claims of small farmers, reported that in 1997 and 1998 49 people were killed in disputes relating to the new law, 956 were injured, and 2,785 were arrested. In the first six months of 1999 another 17 lost their lives, 205 were injured, and 375 were arrested. Some of those arrested were also tortured.[56] Meanwhile, the government passed a new law to regulate nongovernment organizations such as the Land Center, banning their involvement in political activities.[57]

The impact of the tenancy law varied greatly from one village and district to the next, because tenancy arrangements depended on the history of estate formation, land distribution, and out-migration in a particular place.[58] Of the 905,000 tenant farmers affected, it was estimated that 432,000, or almost half, became landless (12,000 of these, or less than 1.5 percent of those affected, were given alternative land to farm by the government). The other half managed to continue farming, either because they owned other plots of land or because they renegotiated the tenancy.[59] These farmers experienced the change in the law less abruptly, as one more part of the pressure forcing them over several years into a harsher and more difficult life. "They put us in the mill," said Sayyid, a farmer in the village, "and turn it and turn it."

The impact of the law also varied with the factors and forces it interacted with, especially those of local family power. In some cases it was unenforceable in the village I studied. Rajab rented one of the four acres his family farmed and was able to prevent the owners from reclaiming it. Although the owners lived in a neighboring hamlet of the same village, they were the second-generation heirs of the original owner and had no idea of the exact location of the dispersed fragments to which they had title.[60] Even if they were to locate them, they would have no path to access them, as the land was now enclosed within the larger holdings of Rajab and his brothers. Nor were they powerful enough to find the political support they needed within the village to take back the land. On the other hand, a young widowed woman whose inherited landholding of less than an acre was rented out to a wealthy relative with more than fifty acres was able to reclaim the land. The latter at first refused but was persuaded when other relatives and the heads of the village intervened, arguing that the woman had no other means of support. In this case the ending of a tenancy contract created the opposite effect to that intended by the proponents of free-market reforms, removing land from a large commercial farm and returning it to a household-based woman farmer. Once again the logic of the free market produced different outcomes when displaced by other logics at work in the village.

The eviction of tenant farmers was not the only part of the reformers' longer-term plans. A conference in Cairo in March 1995 bringing together representatives of USAID, the Ministry of Agriculture, agribusiness consulting firms, and some of the U.S. and Egyptian academics they employed concluded that Egypt's agricultural future depended principally on increased use of technology to encourage "falling labor use," which in turn would release additional labor for industrial employment. This surplus labor, together with lower prices paid to farmers for producing food, would "help keep real urban wages low and industry more profitable."[61] The transitional costs of higher unemployment, falling real wages, and increased economic insecurity were now revealed as a long-term goal of the reforms.

Perhaps to hasten this process of pauperization, the conference repeated the demand of the U.S. government and the IMF for the early removal of the remaining subsidies on bread and flour, on the grounds that keeping staple food affordable resulted in "waste" and "excess consumption," proposing instead that a smaller amount of aid be given to the "ultrapoor 20 percent of the population."[62] This smaller subsidy would not have covered the proportion known, even before the impact of the reforms, to be suffering from serious malnutrition.[63] The decrease in the subsidy might have increased the proportion of those suffering from malnutrition, for there was no evidence that those who were eating subsidized bread were guilty of overconsumption. Even among the two-thirds of the population classified as nonpoor, food accounted on average for almost 50 percent of household expenditure, a large part of it consisting of bread and other carbohydrates. Surveys indicated that the average calorie intake of this better-off two-thirds remained below the minimum recommended allowance, even before most of the price increases and wage cuts of the 1990s.[64]

If the U.S. government was concerned with waste and excess consumption, it needed to look elsewhere. Its own estimates suggest that 5 percent of Egypt's population were affluent by U.S. standards and that the top 2 percent (more than one million people) were "exceptionally and often ostentatiously wealthy."[65] There was no evidence that this class purchased a significant quantity of subsidized bread (the bread reached only 75 percent of the urban population in 1984, after which it had declined in quality and availability).[66] The wealth and consumption of the affluent had increased with the U.S.-led reforms, widening the gap that separated them from the remaining 95 percent. In 1994 the United Nations' *Human Development Report* categorized Egypt as one of four countries "in danger of joining the world's list of failed states because of wide income gaps between sections of their population."[67]

Reading the proposals and reports of the proponents of free-market reforms for Egyptian agriculture, one is struck by the almost complete absence from their accounts of any of the detail or particularity of rural Egypt. One encounters no farmers or villages in their writing. Much more, too, is missing. Many of the most sweeping reform proposals were unsupported by adequate evidence. The demands to abolish price controls, crop quotas, food subsidies, and the protection of tenants were made with no reliable knowledge about the effects of these programs or the likely consequences of their removal. The result of removing them was a decline in rates of agricultural growth, a shift away from high value crops such as cotton, a large drop in Egypt's most valuable manufactured export, cotton textiles and clothes, and repeated crises of over- or underproduction of different crops. None of this, however, prevented the reformers from announcing the success of their plans. We should see the significance of these endless reports and announcements less as marking progress along the path of capitalist development, but more as constantly reiterating the language of market capitalism, thereby reproducing the impression that we know what capitalism is and that its unfolding determines our history.

The policy conferences, IMF documents, government programs, consulting reports, statistical information, newspaper announcements, and academic papers were part of the continuing project to format and reproduce the Egyptian economy. Once again, we should not mistake this economy for a freestanding object, but examine it as the relationship between expertise and the world to which it refers—a world that, on closer inspection, never has the simplicity, logic, or fixedness that the expertise of economics assumes.

How, then, can we understand rural Egypt and its relation to the market system (including its relation to this economic expertise)? There have so far been two alternatives, broadly speaking, neither without problems.[68] One points to a basic distinction in rural society between small peasant households, usually defined as those farming less than five acres, where production is oriented toward subsistence and the reproduction of the household, and capitalist farming integrated into national and international markets. The two kinds of farming are related, for the market-sector farms recruit wage laborers from among the landless and the smallest owners in the subsistence sector. The relationship allows the market sector to externalize the process of reproducing its labor force, since the costs are carried by the subsistence sector, which is dependent on jobs in the market sector for its survival.[69]

By taking seriously the subsistence household as a form of production and examining the methods of articulation between the household and capitalist sectors, the aim of this approach was to uncover the diversity of strategies with which rural populations try to resist or accommodate the penetration of capital, without reducing the phenomenon to the stubbornness of tradition or a mere delay in the process of proletarianization driven by the global expansion of capitalism.[70] Such an approach, it was hoped, would relocate the principal dynamic of change within rather than outside Middle Eastern societies and enable them to "recapture their own history"[71]

The problem with this way of thinking is that "their own history" must be a history outside capitalism yet, except in the writings of a Richard Critchfield, the outside of capitalism is not a place one can easily find.[72] The history of capitalism has to be written as the history of the West, as a history of others, so to recover a different history, the people of rural Egypt must see themselves outside the dynamic of capitalism. Here, it is hoped, they can locate a "dynamic" of their own. As we saw in the discussion of the *ʿizba* system in chapter 2, however, and as studies of the eighteenth century and earlier periods have shown, the history of rural Egypt has never been outside what is called the history of capitalism. At the end of the twentieth century, as this chapter has discussed, there was no self-contained "subsistence sector" in simple articulation with a sector external to itself called the market. There would be no coherent way to draw a line between the two. The difficulty in finding any analytic or descriptive method of separating the noncapitalist from the capitalist was what brought the theories of "the articulation of modes of production," as this problem became known, to a halt. A review essay concluded that the "almost infinitely multiplex and variable relations" that characterized so-called noncapitalist farming in the Third World made it difficult to explain "how a single mode of production can combine so large a number of variant 'forms.' " Its articulation with capitalist modes, the conclusion continued, involving links at several levels, heterogenous in form and content, "can mean little more than a (necessary) recognition of a level of interconnection, while presupposing almost nothing about its precise shape or character." In the end, all that could be offered was the hope that "what formulations like this lack in rigour, they more than make up for in vigour: they point unmistakably to the realities of our time, even if they do not do much as yet to unravel them."[73]

The second approach was to reject the idea that the household sector remained intact as it was incorporated into the wider capitalist system, or that its articulation with the capitalist sector could be thought of as an external relation.[74] It described household-based farmers either as small capitalists, stressing the variety of ways in which they dealt with the market and the entrepreneurial skill with which they turned meager resources into a basis for survival, or as petty commodity producers, meaning those who combined the role of capital and worker, and were thus capitalists who exploit themselves.[75] This way of thinking appeared to make better sense of the complexity of social relations and the central role of small farmers in what is called the market system. But in stressing the role of household farmers within capitalism it presented no real alternative to the story of the market. This means that what happened in rural Egypt was ultimately ascribed to the logic of capital. Other sorts of elements played only a secondary role and did not affect the development of capitalism itself.[76]

There is an alternative to both these approaches, as Gibson and Graham illustrate in the different context of the global finance industry.[77] It would start by questioning what is at stake in the assumption that there is some universal social form called capitalism, to which Egyptian farmers relate, and in relation to which they are to be explained. The various processes described as capitalist or market are not a self-contained system, imported intact into rural Egypt, whether in the nineteenth-century expansion of capitalism or in the late-twentieth-century free-market reforms. One of the proponents of the reforms in Egyptian agriculture argued that their introduction required "a seamless web" of simultaneous changes in the agricultural system ("seamless web" being the phrase introduced by the economist

Jeffrey Sachs to characterize shock therapy, the disastrous program he advocated for Russia and Eastern Europe).[78] The expansion of the market could not be seamless, however, for it had to be stitched together out of people and practices already involved in a multitude of agrarian and other social relations. The project of free-market capitalism not only encountered this range of existing practice, it depended upon it to proceed. In the village, as we saw, the major cash crop was sugarcane, whose profitability rested upon the use of unpaid, nonmarket labor for harvesting. The majority of cane growers, moreover, produced a cash crop not as market entrepreneurs but to support a larger system of self-provisioning. Self-provisioning itself was not incidental to the free-market project. The goal of capitalist expansion through lower wages required farm workers who avoided the market cost of food by growing and processing many of their own consumption needs directly. Following the reforms, crops intended mostly for the farm household accounted for more than two-thirds of the crop area. Even production intended for the market was often based on forms of organization that cannot easily be described as capitalist, structured neither by the price system of a market nor by the relationship between wage labor and capital—such as the compulsory labor of the military production sector, the oligopolies that controlled commercial animal raising, or the forms of patronage and kinship ties through which local merchants like the Qinawis or large-scale farmers like Salim managed their operations.

The picture of rural Egypt that emerges was not a system of small commodity producers incorporated into a larger capitalist economy. Nor, however, was there a separate noncapitalist sector in articulation with a market system. Rather, the so-called capitalist agriculture encouraged by the free-market reforms included and depended upon a far wider range of practices that do not fit with any common definition of the essential nature of capitalism. These apparently noncapitalist elements were so numerous and so central that they shaped the outcome of the reforms. The clearest example of this was that when the government relaxed its crop quotas and acreage controls there followed a boom not in market and export crops, but in staples and self-provisioning. When it relaxed its control of the marketing of farm products there followed not a free-market system but family-based cartels and price fixing on one side and the reintroduction of floor prices and acreage controls on the other. Advocates of the market attributed these setbacks and disruptions to the incomplete nature of the reforms, or the improper sequence, or unanticipated side effects. In other words, they ascribed the setbacks to the failure to introduce the market as a seamless web. Instead we should see them not as a coordinated resistance to the market by people making an alternative history, but as the displacements and reformulations that occur because of the dependence of so-called capitalist arrangements on such a multitude of seemingly noncapitalist logics. Given the dependence, these other logics no longer deserve the label of noncapitalist. But once we introduce them into the dynamic of capital, any attempt to attribute an essence to capitalism has to be abandoned.

The forms of displacement and reformulation I have described are not in any sense merely a characteristic of transitional arrangements, where supposed market principles are introduced into a nonmarket system. As my discussions of the role of subsidies in U.S. agriculture, of slavery in the origins of capitalism, and of the world sugar and grain markets indicate, these displacements are found everywhere. They are a characteristic of what is called advanced capitalism just as much as they are of situations labeled transitional. At the same time, the conclusion to be drawn is not that the situation in rural Egypt is therefore essentially no different from that of American farmers, or that the local reformulations might be celebrated as a coherent or organized challenge to the project of global capitalism. The project remains one that has immense concentrations of power and resources on its side. The conclusion, rather, is that we need to become much more attentive to the failures, diversions, and redirections of the project. The power of what we call capitalism rests increasingly on its ability to portray itself as a unique and universal form, on reproducing a view of history and of economics in which the market is the universal system, constituted and propelled forward by the power of its own interior logic. The displacements and reformulations of the capitalist project show its dependence on arrangements and forces that this logic needs to portray as noncapitalist. By revealing the absence of an interior logic, they require us to look elsewhere for its power.

9 Dreamland

During the second half of the twentieth century, economics established its claim to be the true political science. The idea of "the economy" provided a mode of seeing and a way of organizing the world that could diagnose a country's fundamental condition, frame the terms of its public debate, picture its collective growth or decline, and propose remedies for its improvement, all in terms of what seemed a legible series of measurements, goals, and comparisons. In the closing decade of the century, after the collapse of state socialism in the Soviet Union and Eastern Europe, the authority of economic science seemed stronger than ever.[1] Employing the language and authority of neoclassical economics, the programs of economic reform and structural adjustment advocated in Washington by the International Monetary Fund, the World Bank, and the United States government could judge the condition of a nation and its collective well-being by simply measuring its monetary and fiscal balances.

In Egypt, according to these ways of thinking, the 1990s was a decade of remarkable success that vindicated the principles of neoliberalism. After the government agreed to an IMF reform program, fiscal and monetary discipline brought the inflation rate below 5 percent and reduced the budget deficit from 15 percent of the country's gross domestic product (GDP) to less than 3 percent and for some years less than 1 percent, among the lowest levels in the world. The economy was said to be growing at more than 5 percent a year, and a revitalized private capitalism now accounted for two-thirds of domestic investment. The value of the Egyptian pound was pegged to the U.S. dollar, supported by hard currency reserves of more than $18 billion. These half a dozen financial figures, repeated countless times in government newspapers and television bulletins and in publications of the IMF, constituted the picture of the "remarkable turnaround in Egypt's macroeconomic fortunes" in the final years of the century.[2]

Yet if one looked beyond the official figures, even elsewhere in the same newspapers and television programs, other developments seemed to contradict this view. Accompanying the picture of monetary control and fiscal discipline was a contrasting image of uncontrolled expansion and limitless dreams. The most dramatic example was the country's rapidly expanding capital city. While government budgets were contracting, Cairo was exploding. "Dreamland," the TV commercials for the most ambitious of the new developments promised, "is the world's first electronic city." Buyers were invited to sign up now for luxury fiber optic–wired villas, as the shopping malls and theme park, golf course and polo grounds, rose out of the desert west of the Giza pyramids—but only minutes from central Cairo on the newly built ring road. Or one could take the ring road the other way, east of the Muqattam Hills, to the desert of "New Cairo," where speculators were marketing apartment blocks to expatriate workers saving for their futures in the Gulf. "Sign now for a future value beyond any dreams," prospective buyers were told, " . . . Before it is too late." Purchasers could start payments immediately (no deposit was required) at agencies in Jeddah and Dubai. "No factories, no pollution, no problems" was the advertisement's promise, accompanied by the developer's slogan, "The Egypt of My Desires."[3] The development tracts stretched out across the fields and deserts around Greater Cairo represented the largest real estate explosion Egypt had ever seen. Within the second half of the 1990s the area of its capital city seemed to have doubled—but a symptom of the way it happened was that there were no maps available that might confirm this.

The exuberance of the private developers was matched by the state. While speculative builders were doubling the size of Cairo, the government was proposing to duplicate the Nile River. In October 1996 President Mubarak announced the revival of plans from the 1950s to construct a parallel valley by pumping water out of the lake behind the Aswan High Dam in the south into a canal running northwards that would eventually irrigate two million acres of the Western Desert.[4] Unable to persuade the World Bank or commercial investors that the Toshka scheme, as it was known, was feasible, the government proceeded with building the pumping station and an initial seventy kilometers of the canal, broadcasting daily television pictures of Caterpillar earth movers toiling in the desert.[5] It allocated the first 100,000 acres of future farmland to a man described as the world's second-richest person, the Saudi financier Prince al-Walid bin Talal, whose Kingdom Agricultural Development Company appointed a

California agribusiness, Sun World, to develop and manage what would become the world's single largest farm, consuming by itself 1 percent of the waters of the Nile.[6]

Sun World specialized in growing grapes and other table fruits on irrigated lands and owned the global patents of more than fifty commercial varieties of fruit cultivar. The company was to invest no money of its own in the Toshka project, however, or even pay its own management expenses. In the excitement of the government's announcement that the project had found an American partner, the reason for this went unnoticed: Sun World had no money. The corporation was another failure of the U.S. farm industry and had recently gone bankrupt. A second struggling California agribusiness, Cadiz, had taken over Sun World, planning to pay off its debts by transforming it from a company producing crops into a marketing business that would sell its patents and trademarks, including its flagship brand, Superior Seedless™ grapes, around the world. Unable to make money growing and selling grapes, the company would sell the names of grapes instead. The company's global patents would guarantee it a future payment on every grape, peach, plum, and nectarine that Egyptian farmers laboring in the Western Desert might one day grow.[7] The government agreed to provide 20 percent of the farm's capital and granted it the twenty-year tax holiday enjoyed by large investors, but the government and Prince al-Walid were still looking for other private sector partners willing to put up money for the project.

In the meantime the state was subsidizing the urban property developers as well, selling public land cheaply and building the required expressways and Nile bridges in good time. The state was also involved directly, as a property developer. Down the road from Dreamland, adjacent to a U.S.-managed speculative development named Beverly Hills, the Radio and Television Union, a commercial arm of the Ministry of Information, was building a theme park and filmmaking facility called Media Production City, at thirty-five million square meters billed as the world's biggest media complex outside Hollywood.[8] And the largest builder of Cairo's new neighborhoods, far bigger than the builders of Dreamland or Beverly Hills, was the Ministry of Defense. Military contractors were throwing up thousands of acres of apartments on the city's eastern perimeter to create a new suburbia for the officer class.

If one's first reaction was amazement at the scale and speed of these developments, one soon began to wonder about the contradictions. The IMF and Ministry of the Economy spoke calmly of financial discipline and sustainable economic growth, but made no mention of the frenzied explosion of the capital city or the ecologically disastrous valley-making schemes in the desert.[9] The role of the state in subsidizing this speculative investment, and the networks linking speculators, bankers, and state officials, went unexamined. A further problem was that financial stabilization and structural adjustment were intended to generate an export boom, not a building boom. Egypt was to prosper by selling fruits and vegetables to Europe and the Gulf, not paving over its fields to build ring roads. But real estate had now replaced agriculture as the country's third-largest nonoil investment sector, after manufacturing and tourism.[10] Indeed it may have become the largest nonoil sector, since most tourism investment went into building hotels and vacation homes, another form of real estate.

The reforms were supposed to open Egypt to trade with the global market. In fact they had the opposite effect. The country's openness index, which measures the value of exports and imports of goods and services as a proportion of GDP, collapsed from 88 percent in 1985 to 47 percent in 1996–97. In the same period Egypt's share of world exports also dropped by more than half.[11] The value of nonoil exports actually shrank in 1995–96, then shrank again in 1996–97, leaving the country dependent on petroleum products for 52 percent of its export income. By the end of 1998 the situation was still worse, as the collapse of world petroleum prices forced Egypt briefly to halt its oil exports.[12] In 1998–99 the U.S. government quietly set about rebuilding the OPEC oil cartel, it was reported, holding secret negotiations with Iran, Saudi Arabia, and Venezuela in which it traded political concessions for promises to cut production. The negotiations were a success, doubling the price of oil again within six months.[13] But this unpublicized state management of world trade was too late to solve Egypt's new balance of payments crisis and the repeated shortages of foreign currency.

The most visible element in Egypt's picture of success, the stabilization of the value of its money, owed nothing to the power of the market. It came about because the government was now better able to insulate the local currency against speculative exchanges of international finance. In other words, the reforms depended not on freer trade and greater global integration but on reorganizing local protection against an international market in the buying and selling of money. The protection of the currency relied upon the often announced $18 billion of foreign reserves, a figure that alone came to symbolize the strength of the economy. The symbolism was so important that the government was unwilling actually to spend its reserves in defense of the currency. When exports fell even further and the trade balance worsened again in 1998–99, it resorted to a series of ingenious measures to impede the flow of imports and thus the exodus of hard currency, insulating the country further against the global market.[14]

How does one account for developments that seem so at odds with official representations? The conventional story was that by 1990 the Egyptian economy was in crisis, no longer able to support loss-making public industries, an overvalued currency, profligate government spending, an inflationary printing of money to cover the budget gap, and astronomical levels of foreign debt.[15] After fifteen years of foot dragging and partial reforms, including the agricultural price reforms discussed in chapter 8, in 1990–91 the government was forced to adopt an IMF stabilization plan that allowed the currency to collapse against the dollar, decreased the government budget, tightened the supply of money, and cut back subsidies to public sector enterprises, which the government reorganized into holding companies that were to privatize them or shut them down. These "prudent" fiscal policies were implemented more drastically than even the IMF had demanded, achieving a drop in the government deficit that the IMF called "virtually unparalleled in recent years."[16]

Some accounts were willing to admit that the story had more elements than this simple tale of a prodigal state starting a new life of prudence. They may have added, for example, that among the most profligate of the government's expenditures was the purchase of military equipment, much of it supplied and subsidized by the United States—as part of Washington's own system of subsidies to U.S. military industries. An impending default on these military debts, causing an automatic suspension of U.S. aid, helped trigger the collapse in 1990. (Egypt had begun to default as early as 1983, but as we know, for several years the U.S. government illegally diverted its own funds to pay off Egypt's military loans.)[17] Some accounts may also have acknowledged that the crisis was brought on not just by a spendthrift state but by wider disruptions beyond its control, in particular the decline after 1985 in the price of oil (the largest source of government revenue); the halting of secret U.S. purchases of Egyptian weapons for Washington's covert war against Afghanistan (1979–89); and the decrease in workers' remittances, arms exports to Iraq, and other foreign income caused by the 1990–91 Gulf conflict.[18] The Iraq crisis enabled the United States and other creditors in Europe and the Gulf to write off almost half Egypt's external debt, cutting it from U.S.$53 billion in 1988 to $28 billion. The savings on interest payments, amounting to $15.5 billion by 1996–97, accounted for all of the increase in currency reserves.[19] So the largest single contribution to Egypt's fiscal turnaround resulted from a political decision of the United States and its allies. It had nothing to do with neoliberalism.

Furthermore, an important part of government revenue in Egypt in the 1990s came not from taxing productive activities but from the rent derived from public resources. About one-third came from two state-owned enterprises, the Egyptian General Petroleum Corporation and the Suez Canal Authority. The revenues of these enterprises were earned in U.S. dollars, so the one-third devaluation of the Egyptian pound against the dollar increased their value by 50 percent. This increase contributed the bulk of the growth in government revenues in the stabilization period. Again, the fiscal magic was little connected with free-market principles. In this case it owed more to the extensive ownership of resources by the state.

Beyond all this there was another, still more complex story, one that exceeded the terms of official accounts and was pushed aside into footnotes. The crisis of 1990–91 was not just a problem of public enterprises losing money or a profligate government overspending. It was also a problem of the so-called private sector and the chaos brought on by deregulated international flows of speculative finance. The financial reforms that followed were not so much an elimination of state support, as the official version of events portrayed things, but more a change in who received it. The "free market" program in Egypt was better seen as a multilayered political readjustment of rents, subsidies, and the control of resources. In the following pages I retrieve this story from the footnotes. The second half of the chapter then considers what its burial there can tell us about the larger questions these events pose: How should we understand the relationship between the expertise of economics and the object we call the economy? What combination of understandings and silences, forces and desires, makes possible the economy? Why do these elements at the same time render the making of the economy incomplete?

First, it was not in fact the case that public sector enterprises were losing money. In 1989–90, on the eve of the reforms, 260 out of 314 nonfinancial state-owned enterprises were profitable and only 54 were suffering losses. While the latter lost E£300 million ($110 million), the profitable companies made after-tax profits of E£1.5 billion (about $550 million).[20] At the center of concern in 1990–91 was a crisis not of state-owned industry but of the financial sector, which brought the country's banking system close to collapse. Since 1974 the number of banks had increased from seven to ninety-eight, as commercial banks sprang up to finance the imports and investments of the oil-boom years. The four large state-owned banks made loans mostly to public sector enterprises. It was estimated that at least 30 percent of these loans were nonperforming.[21] But the state banks were also part owners of the private sector banks, enabling them to channel public funds toward a small group of wealthy and well-connected entrepreneurs.[22] These large private sector borrowers were also in trouble.

By 1989 26 percent of private and investment loans were in default, more than half of them belonging to just 3 percent of defaulters. Many of the big debtors were able to delay legal action, and others fled the country to avoid the courts.[23] The largest default came in July 1991, when the London-based Bank of Credit and Commerce International collapsed. (The biggest bank ever to collapse, BCCI had been the leading global finance house for the funding of secret wars, helping the CIA launder payments for U.S. wars in the 1980s against Nicaragua and Afghanistan.) Depositors in BCCI's Egyptian subsidiary were protected by an informal insurance scheme among Egyptian banks, which had to contribute 0.5 percent of their deposits and share the cost of a E£1 billion interest-free loan to make up the missing funds.[24]

These difficulties reflected the problems of a state in which public interests, as we will see, were increasingly entwined with the projects of a well-connected group of financiers and entrepreneurs, whose actions it was unable to discipline.[25] As with the 1997–99 global financial crisis, however, the problem of public resources overflowing into private networks cannot be separated from the difficulties caused by global speculation, especially currency trading.[26] Following the abandoning of international currency controls in 1980, pioneered by the United States and Canada, daily global foreign exchange turnover increased from $82.5 billion in 1980 to $270 billion in 1986 and $590 billion in 1989 (by 1995 it was to reach $1.23 trillion).[27] The growth of private and institutional speculation in national currencies overwhelmed the attempts of governments to manage their currencies according to local needs.

In Egypt global deregulation coincided with a sudden increase in private foreign currency transfers, as expatriate workers sent home earnings from the Gulf. More than one hundred unregulated money management firms were formed to transfer and invest such funds, five or six of them growing very large.[28] These Islamic investment companies (so called because they appealed to depositors by describing the dividend they paid as a profit share rather than an interest payment) invested successfully in currency speculation, later diversifying into local tourism, real estate, manufacturing, and commodity dealing, and paid returns that kept ahead of inflation. The public and private sector commercial banks, subject to high reserve requirements and low official interest rates (essential to the government financing of industry), could not compete and were increasingly starved of hard currency. The financial system was in crisis.

In 1988–89 the bankers finally persuaded the government to eliminate the investment companies. It passed a law that suspended their operations for up to a year, then closed down those it found insolvent (or in many cases made insolvent) and forced the remainder to reorganize as joint-stock companies and deposit their liquid assets in the banks. The measure protected the banks and their well-connected clients but provoked a general financial depression from which neither the banks nor the national currency could recover.[29]

In response to the financial crisis, the centerpiece of the 1990–91 reforms was an effort to rescue the country's banks. After allowing the currency to collapse and cutting public investment projects, the government transferred to the banks funds worth 5.5 percent of GDP, in the form of treasury bills.[30] To give an idea of the scale of this subsidy, in the United States during the same period the government paid for the rescue of the savings and loan industry, which had collapsed following financial deregulation, transferring a sum that amounted to about 3 percent of GDP over ten years. The Egyptian payment was almost twice as large in relation to GDP and occurred in a single year. Moreover, the government declared the banks' income from these funds to be tax free, a fiscal subsidy amounting to a further 10 percent of GDP by 1996–97. In 1998 the government attempted to end the subsidy by reintroducing the taxing of bank profits, but the bankers thwarted the implementation of the law.[31] The banks became highly profitable, enjoying rates of return on equity of 20 percent or more. All of these profits were accounted for by the income from the government rescue.[32]

A further support to the banking sector came when the government tightened the supply of money to raise interest rates, pushing them initially as high as 14 percent above international market levels. Nonmarket interest rates brought in a flood of speculative capital from abroad. This was quickly taken to indicate the success of neoliberal discipline and market orthodoxy. It was nothing of the sort. The money consisted of highly volatile investment funds chasing interest income whose attractiveness was due not to "market fundamentals" but state intervention. After two years interest rates were brought down and the miniboom passed.

In 1996–97 the government manufactured another miniboom by announcing an aggressive program of privatization. It began to sell shares in state-owned enterprises on the Cairo stock market, which it had reorganized to exclude small brokers and eliminate taxes on profits.[33] By June 1997 the government's income from the privatization sales amounted to E£5.2 billion ($1.5 billion). It used 40 percent of this income to provide further support to the banking sector by paying off bad debts. In May 1998 the IMF praised Egypt's "remarkable" privatization program, ranking it fourth in the world (after Hungary, Malaysia, and the Czech Republic) in terms of privatization income as a share of GDP.[34]

The sell-off fattened the banks and the government budget and fueled a short-lived stock market boom. But its outcome was not a switch from state-run enterprise to a reborn private sector. The conventional distinction between a private and a public sector, used by the government and the IMF, was too simple to capture the range of political and economic relations involved.[35] Many of the largest government-owned enterprises, such as Arab Contractors, the country's largest construction firm, and Eastern Tobacco, the cigarette-manufacturing monopoly, had their own "private sector" subsidiaries or joint ventures, typically run by members of the same family managing the public sector parent.[36] The state banks were part owners of private sector banks, as we saw, and of other nonstate enterprises. A large number of government ministers and other senior officials, together with their spouses, siblings, and offspring, were partners or principal investors in many of the largest so-called private sector ventures.[37]

In addition, the reorganization of state enterprises into corporate entities under the control of public holding companies further complicated the distinction between the public and private sectors. By June 30, 1999, the government had sold shares in 124 of its 314 nonfinancial public enterprises. However, it fully divested only a handful. The holding companies remained the largest shareholder in many, and the state managers continued to control others though employee shareholder associations.[38] The press was full of stories of phony privatizations, such as the December 1997 sale of al-Nasr Casting, which in fact had been sold to the public sector banks.[39] (A year later state officials forced the chairman of the stock exchange to resign after he tried to improve its surveillance of company finances and share trading.)[40] The state holding companies also set up new private sector subsidiaries, such as al-Ahram Cement, which was created by the state-owned cement companies and began to bid for shares in other cement companies the government was "privatizing."[41] And many government ministries, with the support of public sector banks, began to launch new profit-making ventures, typified by the vast Media Production City project of the Ministry of Information.

The IMF's confident report that Egypt ranked fourth in the world in privatization missed the complexity of these rearrangements and the multiple forms of ownership, interconnection, and power relationship involved. As David Stark argues in a study of Eastern Europe, by focusing on the enterprise as a unit and simply tallying the number and value of those moved from public to private ownership, orthodox accounts are unable to grasp the multiple methods of control, or the importance of the networks that combined them.[42] The blurred boundaries between "public" ownership and "private" had always offered ambiguities for state officials, enterprise managers, and other insiders to exploit to their own advantage. Structural adjustment offered opportunities for further combinations and new ambiguities. The economic reform was a complicated readjustment of the networks connecting and combining a variety of property assets, legal powers, information sources, and income flows.

The stock market boom lasted less than eighteen months, with the EFG index of large capitalization companies reaching a peak in September 1997 then losing one-third of its value over the following twelve months.[43] As the stock market slid the government halted the sell-offs, suspending most privatizations after the summer of 1998 and stalling on an IMF demand to begin privatizing the financial sector. Instead, to stem the collapse of the market, the government used its financial institutions to invest public funds. Between December 1997 and October 1998 the large state-owned banks and insurance companies and the state pension fund pumped at least E£2 billion ($600 million) into the market, suffering large losses.[44] In the process the state reacquired shares in most of the companies it had recently claimed to be privatizing—further complicating the simple story of private capital replacing public ownership. The market recovered briefly in the winter of 1998–99, when the financial crises in East Asia, Brazil, and Russia made Egypt appear, thanks to its state-subsidized banking system, one of the few safe havens for international speculative funds, but after February 1999 the decline resumed. By the following summer the market was so flat that a single stock, the country's newly privatized mobile phone monopoly, MobiNil, was regularly accounting for more than 50 percent of daily trading, and often up to 70 percent.[45]

Most of the remaining stock market activity, and privatization progress, was confined to just one economic sector, construction. The Toshka irrigation scheme and other large government projects, together with the state-subsidized real estate boom and tourism development, provided the only significant source of economic growth. Cement makers, manufacturers of steel reinforcing bars, and contracting companies all prospered, with the contractors' profit on government projects said to average 30 to 40 percent of income. The demand for cement increased so rapidly that the world's three largest cement makers, Holderbank of Switzerland, the French-based Lafarge group, and Cemex of Mexico, scrambled to buy up Egypt's government-owned cement plants.[46] The construction boom had turned the country into an importer of cement, so these foreign investments in local cement production should be classified as a return to the unfashionable policies of import-substitution industrialization. They had nothing to do with the growth of export-oriented industry that the economic reformers had promised.[47]

Real estate booms and stock market swings failed to address the problem of the country's low levels of domestic investment. Gross domestic investment dropped from 28 percent of GDP in 1980 to 19 percent in 1998, compared to an average of lower and middle income countries of 25 percent.[48] Between 1990 and 1997 investment grew at only 2.7 percent a year, compared to 7.2 percent for all middle income countries and 12.7 percent for those in East Asia.[49] In addition, by June 1996 the number of loss-making public enterprises had almost doubled since the start of the reforms, from fifty-four to one hundred, and accumulated losses had risen from E£2 billion to E£12 billion ($3.5 billion).[50] The government had redefined its finances to exclude public sector companies from the fiscal accounts, however, so this worsening situation was hidden from view.[51] The reformers could continue to claim that they were replacing government deficits with a balanced budget.

The reform program did not remove the state from the market or eliminate profligate public subsidies. Its main impact was to concentrate public funds into different hands, and many fewer. The state turned resources away from agriculture and industry and the underlying problems of training and employment. It now subsidized financiers instead of factories, cement kilns instead of bakeries, speculators instead of schools. Although the IMF showed no interest in examining the question, it was not hard to figure out who was benefiting from the new financial subsidies. The revitalized public-private commercial banks focused their tax-free lending on big loans to large operators. The minimum loan was typically over E£1 million and required large collateral and good connections.[52] So the subsidized funds were channeled into the hands of a relatively small number of ever more powerful and prosperous financiers and entrepreneurs.

At the top were about two dozen business groups, such as Bahgat, Seoudi, Mohamed Mahmoud, Mansour, Arabian International, Osman, and Orascom. These family-owned enterprise networks typically began as construction companies or import/export agents, which had prospered after 1974 when the government allowed large private entrepreneurs to reemerge following the years of import restrictions and state monopolies. Many depended on lucrative contracts to supply goods and services to the Egyptian military. Most expanded subsequently into tourism, real estate, food and beverages, and computer and internet services, and in some cases the manufacturing of construction materials or, where tariff protection made it profitable, the local assembling of consumer goods such as electronics or cars. Several shared in ownership of the private sector banks, which emerged in the same period. They enjoyed powerful monopolies or oligopolies, in particular as exclusive agents for the goods and services of Western-based transnationals. Nothing one reads in the documents of the IMF or USAID mentions the nature, history, or power of these groups, whose existence was hidden behind the bland formulations of "the private sector" and a revitalized "Egyptian economy."

The Seoudi Group, for example, had its origins in a local trading company set up in 1958 by Abdul Moniem Seoudi. In the mid-1970s, with the opening of the consumer economy, the company began to import foodstuffs, general merchandise, and Suzuki commercial vehicles, and used the new tax-free zones to manufacture and export acrylic yarns. The family was involved in establishing two of the new private sector banks, Al-Mohandes and Watany. In the 1980s they expanded into agribusiness, producing factory chickens and eggs with U.S.-subsidized feed grains and importing American pesticides, feed additives, and agricultural equipment. They also established their own construction company to build facilities for their expanding enterprises. By the 1990s they were assembling Suzuki vehicles and manufacturing car seats and radiators, were the sole importers of Nissan vehicles, and had become the exclusive agents for NCR computers.[53]

The Metwalli family took control of Arabian International Construction when the company was denationalized in 1987, and built it up as the local partner of transnational firms constructing power stations and other government projects. In the 1990s AIC acquired the local share of two of the largest government contracts, to pipe drinking water under the Suez Canal for the North Sinai Development Project and build the canal and pumping station for the Toshka scheme. The company's profits on such projects averaged 40 percent of turnover and enabled AIC to become the largest private construction company in Egypt. The income was channeled into eight other family-owned companies, all of them, it was claimed, becoming larger than AIC itself, the largest of them a real estate development company.[54]

The Mohamed Mahmoud Sons group traced its origins to 1895, when Mohamed Mahmoud inherited his father's shoe-making workshop, becoming a shoe retailer in the 1920s and by the 1950s the largest shoe manufacturer and exporter in the Middle East. Like other groups, they diversified in the mid-1970s into the wholesale import and distribution of consumer goods, and they became the country's largest manufacturer of corrugated cardboard boxes. In the 1980s they set up their own engineering and construction arm, and imported and later began to assemble aluminum windows and doors, household and office furniture, and Ukrainian-made tractors and irrigation pipes. By the 1990s the group's thirteen companies included the MM chain of luxury fashion stores, carrying lines such as Yves Saint Laurent, Church's, and Fratelli Rossetti; financial interests in the Egyptian Gulf Bank and the Pharaonic Insurance Company; the Datum internet service provider; the sole Egyptian agency for Jaguar Cars; and showrooms selling motor vehicles from Rolls Royce and Ferrari.[55]

The Mansour family were large cotton traders whose business was nationalized under President Nasser. In 1975, when private trading companies reemerged, Mansour began importing Chevrolet trucks from General Motors, and later Caterpillar earth-moving equipment and John Deere tractors. A decade later, as the local agents of General Motors, they began assembling Chevrolet and Isuzu commercial vehicles, and by 1993 they controlled 60 percent of the country's commercial vehicle market, including contracts with the Egyptian military. In the 1990s they acquired the licenses to distribute Marlboro cigarettes and other consumer products, half the Egyptian McDonald's franchises, and interests in tourism construction and internet technology.[56]

The Sawiris family worked abroad as contractors in Libya before Sadat's reopening of business to private entrepreneurs. They returned to make their money as local agents of Hewlett-Packard and AT&T, building U.S.-funded communications networks for the Egyptian military. The profits (30 to 50 percent of turnover was normal, the family claimed) funded an expansion into civilian communications, construction, and tourism. By the 1990s their holding company, Orascom, controlled a dozen subsidiaries that included Egypt's largest or second largest private construction, cement-making, and natural gas supply companies, the country's largest tourism developments (funded in part by the World Bank), a military technology import business with offices close to the Pentagon outside Washington, D.C., more than half the local market for Microsoft, Hewlett-Packard, and Lucent Technologies, 60 percent of the country's internet service provision, and mobile telephone businesses in collaboration with France Télécom controlling a majority of the Egyptian market and taking over local mobile operators in Jordan, Syria, Pakistan, and a dozen countries of sub-Saharan Africa.[57]

The Bahgat group, the biggest producer of televisions in the Middle East with a dominant position in the Egyptian market, graduated in the 1990s from assembling Korean sets to making Philips and own-name brands. It was linked to senior military officers and used military-owned factories to build its products. The group's forty companies (with just three thousand employees) were also involved in assembling electrical appliances and computers, importing medical equipment and irrigation systems, wholesale and retail marketing, tourism development, and computer software and internet service.[58] They were the builders of the internet-wired Dreamland. Dr. Ahmed Bahgat, the family head, was reputed to be a front man for unpublicized moneymaking by the presidential family, which may explain why the express roads out to Dreamland were built so rapidly.

Certain common features emerge from these descriptions. Most large business groups were nurtured on government contracts, both civilian and military. Many of these contracts involved projects promoted and supported by USAID. Besides receiving state funds, the business groups relied on close ties with private banks, which were often part of the same family networks. Most avoided the more public method of raising funds on the stock market. The exceptions were those groups that expanded faster than the banks or government could support. The Lakah family, for example, importers of timber and other construction materials since they arrived from Syria in the 1890s, claimed by 1999 to be the largest private business group in Egypt. Rami Lakah had diversified into importing medical equipment and setting up high-tech facilities for the government's new U.S.-supported "cost-recovery" hospitals for the affluent.[59] To fund further growth, in August 1999 Lakah had launched the stock market's largest ever share offer, and in November became the first Egyptian enterprise to borrow on the international bond market. (Disaster, as we will see, was not far ahead.) A final feature these groups shared was the relatively small numbers they employed. With the exception of one or two garment manufacturers, the largest business groups had workforces of only two or three thousand. Most employed considerably fewer.

By the 1990s these enterprises were increasingly concentrating on supplying goods and services affordable to only a small fraction of the population. A "Value Meal" at McDonald's cost more than the day's pay of most workers. A family outing to Dreampark, the entertainment complex under construction at Dreamland, would consume a fortnight's average wages. A pair of children's shoes at MM's fashion stores might exceed the monthly pay of a schoolteacher. The Ahram Beverages Company, which produced soft drinks, bottled water, and beer, calculated its potential market (including expatriates and tourists) at just five to six million, in a country of more than sixty million.[60] This narrow market was the same part of the population that could afford, or could just imagine affording, the country's 1.3 million private cars—which is why local manufacturers concentrated on assembling Mercedes, BMWs, Jeep Cherokees, and other luxury models.[61] A company selling upmarket flower bouquets under the U.S. franchise Candy Boutique did its own market research and arrived at a narrower and perhaps more accurate assessment of the affluent: "Egypt has a population of 60 million, but only 20,000 can afford what we are selling."[62] Beyond this small group of state-subsidized super-rich, modest affluence probably extended to no more than 5 percent of the population.[63]

What of the other 95 percent? Real wages in the public industrial sector dropped by 8 percent from 1990–91 to 1995–96. Other public sector wages remained steady, it was claimed, but could be held up only because the salaries remained below a living wage.[64] A schoolteacher took home less than $2 a day. One small sign of the times was the reappearance of soup kitchens in Cairo, offering free food to the poor. A more telling sign was that an article in the national press interpreted their appearance not as a mark of how harsh conditions had become but as a welcome return to the kind of private benevolence among the wealthy not seen since the days of the monarchy.[65]

Household expenditure surveys showed a sharp decline in real per capita consumption between 1990–91 and 1995–96. The proportion of people below the poverty line increased in this period from about 40 percent (urban and rural) to 45 percent in urban areas and over 50 percent in rural. There was no reliable guide to the changing share of consumption by the very wealthy, because the surveys failed to record most of their spending. If household expenditure surveys for 1991–92 are extrapolated to the national level, the figures show the population as a whole spent E£51 billion. Yet national accounts gave the total expenditure as E£100 billion. In other words, half the country's consumer spending was missing from the surveys (although this did not deter the World Bank and other agencies from referring to such figures as reasonable indicators of income distribution).[66] As in India, where a similar disparity was discovered following a decade of economic restructuring, the household surveys probably missed the sharply rising consumption by the very rich, who "downplay their extravagance when the survey people come calling" (or simply have the servants deal with them).[67] An examination of the kind of expenditures missing from the Egyptian survey and the relative proportion of incomes that different groups spent on food supported the view that the figures underrepresented the concentration of wealth among the rich. Even when categorized quite broadly as those spending more than E£14,000 (about $4,000) a year, wealthy households in Egypt represented only 1.6 million people. One study estimated that this group, less than 3 percent of the population, accounted for half of all consumer spending.[68]

The difficulty of knowing how much of the country's wealth was becoming concentrated in the hands of the rich was a small part of a larger problem. The politics of economic reform was based upon a fabrication. It depended on the idea that the economy existed as a space that could be surveyed and mapped, much as the Nile valley had been surveyed by Colonel Lyons a century before. It imagined the economy as a territory whose boundaries could be drawn and whose separate elements could be located, transcribed, enumerated, and reorganized. In 1941, when Simon Kuznets of the National Bureau of Economic Research in Cambridge, Massachusetts, first systematized a method for estimating the total size of a nation's income, he had warned that "a national total facilitates the ascription of independent significance to that vague entity called the national economy."[69] Although many economists since Kuznets might have agreed with his warning, the method of their work enabled this vague entity, the economy, to acquire its independence.[70] The numbers representing national income and output, consumption and savings, employment and productivity, deficits and debt, whatever their degree of reliability, were taken to refer to processes that in principle formed a finite and mappable object.

Some of the problems with this fabrication are well known. The most frequently mentioned is the impossibility of measuring what is called the informal or parallel sector of the economy. In Egypt the household- or neighborhood-based production and distribution of small-scale goods and services, unregistered with the state and operating on the margins of its systems of revenue and regulation, represents a large but unknown proportion of the country's productive life.[71] These activities were traditionally excluded from calculations of GDP and other representations of the economy, although increasing efforts were made to include some estimate. To give one idea of their scale, in 1996 about three-quarters of the population of Greater Cairo was living in informal housing, covering two-thirds of the land area and accounting for 85 percent of its dwelling units.[72] Those living in informal housing were not necessarily employed in informal livelihoods, but the figures indicate the extent to which one sector, the construction and possession of urban housing, was conducted outside the regulation of the state. Estimates of the overall size of informal economic activities ranged from 20 to 35 percent of GDP, but these were guesses and implied a straightforward division between formal and informal that, as we saw with agriculture in the previous chapter, was too simple to capture the interconnections involved.[73] The economic reforms were aimed chiefly at formal economic activities. As Mahmoud Abdel-Fadil points out, however, policies aimed at the formal sector may have had an opposite impact on the parallel sector, while transformations in the latter, such as those I discussed in agriculture, had a profound effect on the former.

Not all activities of the parallel sector were small-scale and local. Some played a large role in the country's international trade and finance, as the example of the hemp industry illustrates. In the 1980s Egypt imported large quantities of processed hemp—cannabis resin— from the Beqaʿa valley in central Lebanon, where civil war had stimulated export-oriented production. The value of Egypt's clandestine imports was estimated at two to four billion U.S. dollars. Even the lower of these figures exceeded all Egypt's income from nonpetroleum exports.[74] After the end of the civil war in 1990, Syria gradually eliminated Lebanese production.[75] This coincided with currency devaluation in Egypt, which raised import prices, and with declining personal incomes and a tough government campaign against drug importers—conviction for drug dealing now carried the death penalty. As Lebanese hashish became scarce and unaffordable, consumers responded by developing a taste for smoking *bango,* locally grown, milder, unprocessed cannabis (few regions in the world can produce hemp rich enough in resins to process into hashish).[76] Hemp production rapidly became a minor village industry, especially in southern Egypt and Sinai, facilitated by the ending of government crop controls.[77] Thus another import-substitution industry had sprung up, eliminating one of the country's largest demands for hard currency. None of this was captured in official representations of the Egyptian economy—although the IMF puzzled over an unexplained and unusually rapid decline in the circulation of dollars.[78]

Discussions of the problem of measuring informal and clandestine activities usually imply a contrast with the formal sector, which in comparison is assumed to be fixed and known. Yet with the formal sector too it is difficult to ascribe an "independent significance" to the economy. There can be legal activities whose extent and value is never made public, such as the extensive production, trade, and consumption organized by the Egyptian armed forces. As the U.S. government put it, military spending in Egypt was "not transparent," so none of this activity was accurately represented in national accounts or in the government budget. In 1989 government spending on the armed forces was estimated at E£4.7 billion, or about

20 percent of government outlays, a figure that excluded foreign military assistance from the United States ($1.3 billion) and Saudi Arabia, income from Egyptian arms exports, and possibly the army's civilian agriculture and manufacturing projects.[79] So one-fifth of government spending and perhaps 10 percent of GDP was unmeasured and unreported. In fact the entire government budget was misleading, for in the 1990s Toshka and other giant investment projects were financed without being accounted for in the official figures. The government reported a spending deficit of just 1.3 percent of GDP for 1998–99, but a year later quietly revised this figure to reflect "off-budget spending," which more than tripled the deficit to 4.3 percent of GDP.[80]

The problems of informal, clandestine, and unreported economic activities are so great that these alone would provide sufficient reason to question the idea that the economy is an object that can be mapped and measured. But these issues are not the real problem. The idea of the economy presents a larger difficulty. Even the most visible and regulated acts of economic exchange have effects that escape observation or measurement. In any economic transaction the parties involved attempt to calculate, as best they can, what they will gain from the exchange and what it will cost them. The transaction will also affect others, however, either positively or negatively. These further costs and gains will not enter into the calculation, because those affected are not parties to the transaction. Since the size of the economy is measured as the aggregate of all individual transactions, the additional effects are excluded from the representation of the national economy. Economists call the excluded elements "externalities," and often give the example of pollution: the owners of a cement factory contract with a customer to supply so many tons of cement, and do not include in the price the cost of the air pollution the factory creates, because those living nearby who are harmed by the bad air are not parties to the exchange. In the language of neoclassical economics, externalities are an example of "market failure," situations where the price mechanism that governs exchanges fails to reflect the true costs involved, and therefore is unable to act as an efficient regulator of social action.[81]

By using examples such as pollution, and by labeling them as externalities or failures, the method and language of economics treat these uncounted costs as something residual. They represent an imperfection in the market, a lapse in its mechanisms, a secondary rather than essential aspect of its operation. The example of pollution inadvertently points to much larger externalities, however, such as the destructive impact of a general level of economic activity on the ecological balance. These represent not individual market failures but an inability of the principle of the market to account for complex effects whose value cannot be monetarized. But in addition to these wider issues, there is a more general problem with treating externalities as something exceptional. Since no transaction takes place in a vacuum, all acts of exchange produce externalities. Every purchase of an object or service involves all the costs that went into it that were excluded, or not properly recognized or compensated.

It is not surprising that an economic actor should want to acquire something without paying all the associated costs—without accounting for all the ways its production and consumption might affect others. On the contrary, exchange would be impossible if people were made to account for every cost. A market economy requires conventions and powers that enable the completion of an exchange without satisfying such a standard. So when the calculation of the economy excludes not only much that is informal or clandestine, but also the "external" aspects that occur within what is considered formal and regulated, the exclusion is not exceptional or secondary in significance. As Callon points out, a lot of work and expense goes into achieving these acts of exclusion.[82] Without them, in fact, the market would cease to function. For example, to sell the cement a factory produces the management of the factory must prove they own the product. They must deny the claims of others who may demand some share, such as the kiln workers who produced the cement but may not have been fully compensated for the value contributed by their labor, or those who supplied the machinery or the raw materials, as well as those who demand compensation for the damage pollution has done to their health and other outsiders. By proving ownership the managers exercise a form of exclusion, the power to deny the claims of others.

In chapter 2 I examined the genealogy of one kind of ownership claim in Egypt, the private ownership of land. I traced the process by which a person called the "landowner" came to monopolize the rights to the produce of the land and exclude the entitlements that cultivators, the indigent, the ruling household in Cairo, and other claimants had previously enjoyed. Organizing these exclusions was a complex political project, requiring a variety of forms of violence, supervision, policing, military occupation, legal argument, imprisonment, and economic theory. As that example showed, property is not a simple arrangement, nor a static one. In the twentieth century the cultivators managed to reestablish some of their claims, as did the government. Toward the end of the century, as we saw in chapter 8, reasserting the prerogatives of private ownership required new rounds of violence, policing, and economic argument.

Thus the simple idea of "externality" rests upon the operation of complex and mobile forms of law, international convention, government, corporate power, and economics. These multiple arrangements make possible the economy. Property rights, tax rules, contract and criminal law, administrative regulation, and policing all contribute to fixing the difference between the formal and the informal, between the act of exchange and its externalities, between those with rights and those without, between measurable values and the unmeasurable. In economic theory many of these forms of regulation and enforcement are called institutions. A distinction is sometimes made between formal institutions, such as laws and administrative rules, and informal institutions, such as codes of conduct, implicit understandings, and norms of social action. Institutional economics understands these rules and norms as constraints that organize and set limits to human action.[83] Like the concept of externality, the term "constraint" characterizes these arrangements once again as secondary, as something outside the economic process itself. The economic act is by definition the expression of an individual choice, the fulfillment of a desire, just as the economy is the sum total of these economic choices and their fulfillment. The desire is the starting point of the economic, while institutions are understood as arrangements that limit the desire, restrict the ways in which needs can be satisfied, prevent others from disrupting their satisfaction, and reduce delinquency or misunderstanding. Constraint is the opposite of desire, an element of incompatibility, and can combine with it only as something external and subordinate. Yet these secondary, external, residual arrangements at the same time are something prior. The rules, norms, and unwritten understandings must exist before the act of exchange, otherwise they could not regulate it.[84] They are also ubiquitous, dwelling surreptitiously within every economic act. So although economics must portray them as external, secondary, and residual, they are also the condition of possibility of the economic.

The constraints, understandings, and powers that frame the economic act, and the economy as a whole, and thus make the economy possible, at the same time render it incomplete. They occur as that strange phenomenon, the constitutive outside.[85] They are an interior-exterior, something both marginal and central, simultaneously the condition of possibility of the economy and the condition of its impossibility. Callon describes what he calls the "dual nature" of these constraints or frames.[86] Their purpose is to exclude, to keep out of the picture all those claims, costs, interruptions, and misunderstandings that would make the act of exchange, and thus the economy itself, impossible to complete. To achieve this "enframing," the rules, procedures, institutions, and methods of enforcement are thought to have a special status.[87] Just as a frame seems distinct from the picture it enframes, and a rule is supposedly an abstraction in relation to the concrete actions it governs, the institutions that enframe the economy are imagined to have a different, and extraeconomic, nature. They are the arena of economic actions, as distinct from the actions themselves. In practice, however, this distinction is not a stable one. Each piece of the frame, each rule, procedure, understanding, constraint, enforcement, and sanction, involves potential exchanges of its own. To apply a rule, for example, one must negotiate its limits and exceptions, since no rule contains its own interpretation. These negotiations become part of the act of exchange they are supposed to regulate. To act according to an implicit understanding, or an accepted norm, one must engage over time in a series of exchanges, economic and noneconomic, out of which the norm or understanding emerges. To enforce a regulation involves all the expense and interactions of adjudication, resort to force, and monitoring. At every one of these points the "frame" opens up and reveals its dual nature. Instead of acting as a limit, containing the economic, it becomes a series of exchanges and connections that involve the act of exchange in a potentially limitless series of further interactions.[88] Thus the problem of fixing the economy is not a residual one of accounting for informal and clandestine activities, or turning externalities into internal costs. The problem is that the frame or border of the economy is not a line on a map, but a horizon that at every point opens up into other territories.

There are three issues to elaborate before we return to the question of the relationship between economics and the economy. First, the rules of the market are by no means the only kind of frame for economic transactions. Despite the importance given to laws of property and the principles of the price mechanism, it would be difficult to establish that the market is even the most significant arena of exchange. Many other forms of social practice structure the way transactions occur, often with the purpose of preventing them from leaking across into the market. One institution that has always offered alternative rules and powers to those of property and contract is the household or family. We have seen how in Egypt, as in many parts of the world, the new large-scale economic activities that flourished with free-market reforms operated through networks of family-held businesses. Here the main economic institution was not the market or even the business enterprise, but a web of personal ties drawing together a series of businesses, often establishing connections within and across state institutions, the banking sector, the armed forces, or the local agencies of transnational corporations. These networks operate through relations of kinship or marriage and put to work all the powers of loyalty, affection, discipline, and compulsion on which such relations depend.

These powers, like so many other noncapitalist forces operating at the center of so-called capitalism, need constant attention. They are never entirely controlled by those who use them and can easily take their own course. Trouble can follow, for example, when the forces of affection or ties of matrimony break down. The rupture can cause mundane economic difficulties, or can lead to major crises. In 1995 the entire Egyptian banking and political system was shaken by the rupturing of one family network. The Ayuti family controlled, among other interests, one of Egypt's large private sector financial houses, Nile Bank. ʿIsa al-Ayuti, the eighty-one-year-old chairman of the bank, had become estranged from his daughter ʿAliya al-Ayuti, the bank's managing director, following her marriage to Mahmud ʿAzzam, a large contractor and a member of parliament. In December 1995 the father accused his daughter of making unsecured loans to her new husband, providing his construction company with almost E£80 million. A government investigation of the fraud later widened to include thirty-two bankers and entrepreneurs involved in E£1 billion in fraudulent deals, including a former minister of tourism, Tawfiq ʿAbdu Ismaʿil, who was chairman of Dakhiliya Bank and also an MP, and two other members of parliament.[89] This was one of a number of fraud cases in this period arising from the breakdown of family networks. What such incidents reveal is not that all family networks involve fraud. Rather, the sensational cases publicized in the media indicate the quieter, everyday work that must be done to maintain family networks, and the costs that can follow from their collapse. Once again, the borders of the economic do not occur as a simple constraint or frame, but open up into further territories, draw upon further forces, and channel other powers and desires.

Another well-known example of a large-scale nonmarket economic network is the transnational corporation—an institution whose history and power must be discussed in relation to a parallel mechanism for limiting the operation of the market, the nation-state. Of course we know from Marx that any capitalist enterprise is a means of employing nonmarket arrangements to produce goods or services for the market. While the owners of the enterprise sell its products on the market, those who are employed to produce the products are typically subject to multiple forms of discipline, surveillance, compulsion, and, in many cases, the threat or use of violence. The fact that the employment relation takes the outward form of a contract only thinly disguises the "dull compulsion of economic relations," as Marx described it in volume one of *Capital,* that gives most employees—especially those outside the more privileged economic enclaves of the West—little room to bargain over the terms of their labor.[90] The large corporation, however, develops nonmarket arrangements to a much further extent. It establishes extensive hierarchies and controls based on supervision, surveillance, rules, sanctions, and the manufacture of a corporate culture. It separates the management of economic processes from the old powers of ownership. And it organizes multiple transactions within the corporation itself, producing, distributing, and consuming goods and services among its various divisions and subsidiaries. Indeed the closely governed, nonmarket movement of goods and services within corporate hierarchies represents as much as one-third of international trade.[91]

By the time he drafted volume three of *Capital,* Marx was aware that the modern corporation represented a break with the principles of capitalism he had outlined in volume one. He described the joint-stock company as "the abolition of the capitalist mode of production within the capitalist mode of production itself."[92] For Marx this contradiction illustrated the crisis-ridden nature of capitalism and its tendency toward internal conflict and eventual collapse. But it could equally be taken to illuminate the continuous force of noncapitalist elements within the core of what is called capitalism. To describe the joint-stock corporation as the relatively recent outcome of the internal development of capitalism implies that market capitalism came into being first and the large corporation arrived afterward, setting limits to the market and contradicting its logic. Given the power that global corporations had reestablished by the end of the twentieth century, it is important to recall that, if anything, the history of the market and the corporation happened the other way around. The major institutions for organizing large-scale global trade in the seventeenth and eighteenth centuries were not markets but monopolistic colonizing corporations, such as the Dutch and English East India companies and the joint-stock companies that were given monopolies for the colonization of North America.[93] Neoclassical economists like to trace the origins of their field to the formulation of the market principle in the classical work of Adam Smith. But Smith wrote *The Wealth of Nations* as an attack on the power of these colonizing corporations and formulated the idea of individual exchange in "the market" as the program for an alternative. He devoted long sections of the book to discussing the world's first successful campaign against the corporate monopolies, the revolt of Britain's American colonies, and to examining the simultaneous crisis in the largest such monopoly, the

East India Company. Writings such as *The Wealth of Nations* helped to construct the idea of the "self-regulating market" as a novel alternative to corporate power, and this and subsequent writings in political economy began to formulate the market's rules and principles. But the idea of "the market" was not the only response to the crisis of the colonizing corporation. In 1776, the year *The Wealth of Nations* appeared, two alternative methods of governing the wealth of nations were devised. The American colonists articulated an antimarket principle of economic organization, the nation-state; and the East India Company proposed a new system of colonial government, the Plan of Settlement, recasting arbitrary corporate power as a colonial "rule of property."[94] Within fifty years, moreover, the United States and Britain began to resort once more to the joint-stock corporation as an institution with which to organize nonmarket transactions. As I mentioned in chapter 3, the unusual legal powers of incorporation were no longer restricted to ostensibly public projects, such as colonization, but were made available for any large economic purpose. At the same time, further projects of colonization were undertaken by Americans and Europeans using the new powers of the state itself. So the framing of the market once again was limited by the larger and more significant framings of the corporation and the colonial monopoly.

The point of this historical detour is the following. By the twentieth century the colonizing corporation had been replaced by directly ruled colonies on the one hand and modern joint-stock companies on the other, the largest of which developed into transnational corporations far larger than most postcolonial states. By mid-century the system of colonies was giving way in most places to one of nation-states. Like the colony, the nation provided a nonmarket method for organizing economic exchange, especially for preventing free markets in labor and money. Since the science of economics had concentrated its efforts on framing the rules of the market, parallel fields of expertise emerged to help coordinate the forms of knowledge needed for the nonmarket institutions: for the corporation, law, accounting, and business studies; for the nation, statistical organizations and the field of macroeconomics, which as we have seen developed around the concept of "the economy" in the middle decades of the century. In addition immigration laws, national banks or reserve systems, complex taxation and tariff systems, and extensive state planning and investment all helped to fabricate the twentieth-century nation/economy, as, like the family network, an alternative to the market. The practices that attempt to frame the economy are not only those that regulate the act of market exchange. They include other forms of social network, powers of desire, technologies of control, and modes of government. Each of these, like the regulations of the market, constitutes both a limit and a horizon, opening the economic to other forces and logics.

The second general point concerns the question of violence. The market, the family, the economy, and the nation can all be understood as institutions, based on the operation of rules and conventions. The notion of "framing" used to describe the working of such institutions is often derived from the work of Erving Goffman, who made particular use of metaphors from the theater.[95] This choice of language and metaphor can give the impression of an essentially benign process, in which rules and roles operate by convention, and coercion has only a residual or reserve function. This reflects a tradition that sees rules and violence, law and coercion, as opposites. One is based upon reason, on the application of principles "unquestionably true in every country."[96] The other is an element of irrationality and disorder. However, as I argued in the case of property in chapter 2, the opposing of law to violence is misleading. The opposition is itself an effect of the methods of enframing that enable an abstract code or structure of rules to appear separate from the practices in which they are brought into being and reproduced. The act of enframing is a work of force as much as reason, and the two should not be seen as opposites but examined together.

In the Egyptian economic reforms, the reports of the IMF and other bodies describing the plan and progress of reform had nothing to say on the question of the kinds of force and coercion that were required. Yet if one follows closely the way in which economic expertise carried out its free-market experiment, it becomes clear that this scientific experiment could only have been conducted by force. Alternative claims, costs, visions, and agendas had to be kept out of the picture, using various combinations of persuasion, argument, threat, and violence. Those pursuing alternative political agendas in Egypt had very little space for maneuver before the economic reforms, although the judiciary, the press, opposition political parties, religious groups, universities, human rights organizations, and professional associations all offered limited arenas in which people could criticize the authorities and challenge aspects of the state's political program. The economic reforms were facilitated by a continuous narrowing of these limited opportunities for dissent. The new repressions included a parliament more than one hundred of whose members the courts declared fraudulently elected, but that announced itself to be above the law in such matters; and in which the handful of opposition deputies were increasingly deprived of opportunities to question the government.[97] It included removing the right of villagers to select their own heads, of religious communities to choose their own preachers, and of university faculties to elect their deans.[98] It included a regime that admitted no right to organize political opposition or hold political meetings, and allowed the few legal opposition parties no right to public activities. It included a steady remilitarization of power, especially as control shifted away from ministries, many of which were now run by technocrats, to provincial governors, most of whom were still appointed from the high ranks of the military. It included the systematic use of torture against those detained in police stations and the offices of the State Security Intelligence, including electric shocks, beatings, suspension by the wrists or ankles, and threats of death or sexual abuse of the detainee or a female relative.[99] It included prisons holding tens of thousands of political prisoners, detained without court orders or judicial process, under emergency powers in place for twenty years, in conditions described as cruel, inhuman, or degrading.[100] It included the silencing of professional associations, with the engineers' and lawyers' associations placed under judicial sequestration in 1996, and the doctors', pharmacists', teachers', and scientists' associations prevented from holding elections.[101] And it included the repeated intimidation of human rights workers and opposition journalists by closures, court cases, and imprisonment.[102] In 1999 the regime consolidated these new restrictions by passing a law on civic associations that dissolved all the country's licensed nongovernmental organizations and required them to apply for permission to re-form under new and more restrictive regulations, including a ban on any activity the state considered political. Meanwhile, the United States and other Western governments refused every appeal to speak out in public on these issues. Washington quietly dropped the "Democracy Initiative" it had introduced in the early 1990s, when political transformations in Eastern Europe seemed to threaten the system of autocracy it had helped sustain in the Middle East, and declared no serious concerns in Egypt beyond the endurance of the regime and its neoliberal reforms.[103]

It is not uncommon, among the proponents as well as critics of the reforms, to admit that structural adjustment and the opening of markets may be accompanied by political repression. However, the tendency is to see one as the consequence as the other, and in that way make the violence something secondary. From a perspective that favors the market, the repression is an unforeseen, unfortunate, intermittent, and probably temporary side effect of the shocks that accompany the expansion of the global market. From a more critical perspective, that of the Marxist tradition, violence is a common instrument of capitalist development, in particular the penetration of capitalist relations into new territories. It is often required to speed up the development of capitalism "like a hot-house," as Marx himself put it, in regions where changes in the relations of production have lagged behind the global history of capital.[104] For this reason, however, violence must be considered "a common contingency" rather than something "*logically* necessary."[105] It aids the logic of capital, but, as an element of randomness and unpredictability, or as a means of simply forcing the pace of history, it must be contingent or external to the logic of history itself.

I would argue against either approach to the question of violence. In both cases the violence becomes something residual, either the unexpected side effect of the development of capitalism or merely the contingent instrument of its logic. The secondary or reserve nature of violence is required if one is to present history in terms of the unfolding of a larger logic. By homogenizing contemporary politics into ineluctable and universal logics of capitalist globalization, we attribute to reform programs, to the market, to capital, or to globalization a coherence, energy, and rationality that they could never otherwise claim. To counteract this tendency we need to put together accounts of contemporary politics, as I have tried to do here, that bring to light the incoherences, reversals, and reformulations that accompany the apparent logics of globalization. The continuous political struggles under way in places such as Egypt are not the consequences of a more global logic, but an active political process whose significance is repeatedly marginalized and overlooked in reproducing the simple narratives of globalization, whether for or against.

The third point also relates to this question of other logics, and represents another feature and difficulty of enframing. As Callon stresses, the interactions that must be contained within the economy are not merely those among human agents. An economy is assembled out of a variety of agencies and forces, some human and some nonhuman. The powers that combine to make an economy include those of machines, humans, corporations, money, electrical and other forms of energy, technology, and chemical and biological processes, among others. In chapter 1, for example, I examined in a critical period of Egyptian politics the multiple interactions of human agency with the technology of war, the virulence of epidemic disease, the unexpected properties of DDT, the dual use of artificial nitrates, and the hydropower of the river Nile. In economic science, a fundamental distinction is made between the agency of humans and the role of all the other elements of an economy, which by contrast are considered essentially passive. The latter are treated as inputs (raw materials or machinery, for example), and are represented in terms of their cost to the human agents. This conventional view of things aids certain kinds of economic calculation, but is an incomplete and unsatisfactory account of how economic relations occur.

In practice the nonhuman elements are never so passive. Those with money to invest can find themselves driven by the reproductive yet unstable power of capital. Those developing a technology can be quite surprised by its outcome. Those putting physical, chemical, or biological processes to work, whether in a cement kiln, a pumping station, a mobile phone network, or a field of sugarcane, enter into a partnership with processes whose fate they do not completely command. There will always be what Latour calls "the slight surprise of action," the tendency of the human agent to be "slightly *overtaken* by the action."[106] The nonhuman agencies enter into human partnership not just as passive elements to be costed and arranged, but as dynamic and mobile forces with their own powers and logics. Economic practice always comes into being in combination with these noneconomic elements, which it cannot fully contain or account for.

Even the element that economics takes as the origin and essence of the economic process, individual human utility or desire, is neither an absolute origin nor a simple, human essence. On the one hand, desires must constantly be manufactured, generated within the nonhuman machinery of consumption industries or even the psychological and biochemical mechanisms of addiction. On the other, while the concept of utility in economics is the foundation that makes possible a rational, calculable world, the utility itself stands for desire, an incalculable and irrational force that can overtake and disrupt the most carefully calculated actions. An element of irrationality, of something not quite human, inhabits the rational, human core of the economic.

To sum up, the attempt to enframe the economy occurs alongside other forms of structuring and network making, including those of the household or family, large corporations, and nation-states, all in interaction with one another. Enframing is a work of violence as well as theory. And the forces and overflows it must contain are not limited to those of human agency, whose rationality itself contains forms of the irrational and nonhuman. With these points in mind, we can return to the question of relationship between economics and the economy. We are in a better position to understand the role of economics and what seem the silences and limitations of the IMF and other official agencies in Egypt.

Economic expertise is forced largely to overlook the forms of leakage, network, energy, control, violence, and irrationality I have been discussing. It cannot take them seriously, for that is not its task. The role of economics is to help make possible the economy by articulating the rules, understandings, and equivalences out of which the economic is made. This has been its impossible project. Economics is part of the enframing that attempts to make what is internal to the economy distinct from what is external, and thus make calculation and exchange possible. It is therefore obliged to treat all these other processes as something secondary, minor, or exceptional. The self-deception is essential, for otherwise it would have to follow these links, powers, and leakages, and admit that there could be no economy.

Economics must start from the assumption that the act of exchange, and the aggregation of all acts of exchange in the economy, occur essentially as forms of closure or equilibrium. The exchange or the economy must be self-contained, and thus in principle measurable and manageable. It is well known that economics begins from this abstraction, from a model, and considers what actually occurs as secondary, as an approximation to this model or a deviation from it. But this is not just a methodological preference, expressing a desire for a certain form of scientific rigor. It reflects the fact that the complex social world of the science must be simplified in the same way, and that economics is hard at work in this project of simplification. The existence of an economy depends upon these methods in practice: methods of designating certain costs as external, certain claims as secondary.

Likewise, making the economy depends upon instituting a fundamental separation between human action and the world in which this action occurs. If economics attributes agency only to human actors and treats all other forces as a passive world of nature, this corresponds to an entire politics of the twentieth century. The construction of the first great barrage at Aswan in southern Egypt at the start of the century, the centerpiece of Britain's colonial project, established on the ground forms of calculation, engineering, control, and profit that simplified the world into nature on one side and economy on the other. On the one hand were the natural resources of the Nile, agricultural lands, irrigation systems, and hydropower, on the other the human agency that could calculate, transform, manage, and make wealth from these material elements. Again, if economics treats economic relations as essentially rational and consensual, and reduces coercion and violence to residual questions of enforcement and sanction, this corresponds to the discipline's role in the larger project of embedding the exercise of coercion in the forces of nature and the laws of markets—in subsuming them under logics of history, capital, or exchange.

At the start of this discussion I called the economy a fabrication, but that term should not be misunderstood. It does not mean that the economy is merely a work of imagination, or that the problem with the economy is that it is not real. Such criticisms slide back into the language of real versus imaginary, original versus copy, an object world versus its representation. These distinctions are complicit in the project of making the economy and cannot be used to understand it. As we saw in the first three chapters, the politics of the late-nineteenth and twentieth centuries attempted to organize a world whose complexities were resolved into the simple dualities of real and representation, objects and ideas, nature and techno-science, land and the abstraction of law, the country and the map. The social sciences emerged in the same period to confirm and reproduce this binary world. The role of economics was to produce the economy, not as a work of imagination but as a practical project. The economy is an artifactual body—a fabrication, yes, but as solid as other fabricated objects, and as incomplete.

Thus economic discourse works very hard to help format and reproduce the exclusions that make the economy possible. This is why there are no particular farmers or villages in economic discourse on Egypt. It is the reason why the Sawiris family and Ahmed Bahgat, the Seoudi group and the Metwallis, are never encountered in the writings of the IMF. It is why nowhere in the reports of USAID can one discover the role of government ministers, senior officials, and their families in the rent circuits of the so-called private sector. It is why the extensive importing, manufacturing, and consumption of goods by the Egyptian armed forces are left opaque in official statistics. Examining any one of these issues leads away from a closed economy, away from the map, away from what is transparent and calculable, into farming, households, family, state, and power. The closure unravels.

The project of economic reform in Egypt was a work of theory and violence. Making the market economy required a series of framings, which attempted to fix and to exclude. Less than a decade after the project began, it had come apart. The confident success story told by the IMF and the government media was no longer possible to sustain.

The Cairo stock market had collapsed, losing almost 50 percent of its value during the year 2000. By the end of that year prices were lower than when the government first revived the exchange in 1995.[107] The real estate boom had gone bust. Ahmed Bahgat, the builder of Dreamland, suffered a heart attack in July 2000 while on a trip to Washington, where he was part of an official delegation making an unsuccessful effort to encourage investments from large U.S. corporations. When news reached Cairo that he was in the hospital in Bethesda, Maryland, undergoing surgery to the aorta, shares in his company collapsed. Dreamland was effectively bankrupt. Beverly Hills and most of the other, smaller developments also came to a halt as speculators discovered they had overbuilt, and luxury property prices dropped by more than half.[108] Public sector entrepreneurs were in the same trouble. The debts of the Radio and Television Union, the commercial arm of the Ministry of Information creating the media complex next door to Beverly Hills, reached E£3.8 billion, and the Ministry of Finance had to bail it out.[109] The Arab Contractors Company, the family-run, state-owned construction corporation building Media Production City and many other large projects, was facing financial crisis.[110] There was panic in the banks, which had overextended credit for real estate projects. The chairman of the National Bank of Egypt, the bank with the largest investments in failed speculations, was removed.[111]

As a recession set in and the government began to fall far behind on domestic payments, other businesses whose prosperity came from contracts with the state began to fail. Rami Lakah, the thirty-nine-year-old entrepreneur who had developed the country's largest business group by building fee-paying government hospitals for the affluent, hailed in 1999 as the first Egyptian enterprise to borrow on the international bond market, within a year had fled the country. He returned only after the government and the banks agreed to reschedule his debts, which were reported to have reached E£1.5 billion.[112] "Cost recovery" in health care had acquired a new meaning. As the government tried to slow the flow of funds the supply of dollars dried up, affecting importers, including manufacturers, who needed supplies from abroad. Toward the end of 2000 the government was forced to give up the attempt to peg the currency to the dollar, and the Egyptian pound lost 20 percent of its value. Almost the only economic activity that seemed to thrive was the use of mobile telephones. The country's million or so subscribers used four times as many minutes per month per subscriber as the worldwide average. The E£5.6 billion they spent talking on their telephones in 2000 exceeded the country's revenue that year from exports.[113]

Some blamed the money spent on mobile phone conversations for the country's recession. Others blamed it on the off-budget spending by the state. The government had pushed ahead with what it called its "Pharaonic" development projects, concentrating its resources on the most ambitious of them, the Toshka irrigation scheme. Convinced, like the United States Agency for International Development, that Egypt's fundamental problems were defined by the limits of natural resources—not enough land, too many people—it pursued President Mubarak's dream of creating a second river Nile in the desert. Toshka was a very twentieth-century idea. The century that opened with the construction of the first Aswan Dam ended with an even bigger project, not just to store up all the waters of the world's longest river, but to divert them to build another.

Dreamland was an amusement park in the desert, a mirage under construction, a place of desire promised in television commercials and newspaper advertisements long before it was finished. Perhaps it would remain forever a mirage, an unfulfilled desire. It was one of many dreamlands. Toshka was the object of a ruler's desire, as he passed his seventieth birthday, to build something by which his rule would be remembered, a fairy tale to be fulfilled with the help of a billionaire prince and the bankrupt owner of Superior Seedless™ grapes. These dreamlands are the places of desire that global capitalism cannot contain.

Capitalism, as I proposed in chapter 1, has no singular logic, no essence. It survives parasitically, like the *Plasmodium falciparum,* taking up residence in human bodies and minds, or in sugarcane or private property, drawing its energies from the chemistry of others, its force from other fields, its momentum from others' desires. The projects of economic reform in Egypt had to excite the desires that fueled the building of Dreamland and Toshka, yet capitalism could not discipline those desires. Such desires, such forces, such other logics, are presented as something exterior to capitalism. They appear as a noncapitalist excess that derails capitalism from its course. Yet this outside, these excesses, are at the same time vital to capitalism. They are a source of its energies, the condition of its success, the possibility of its power to reproduce. They are a heterogeneity that makes possible the logic of capital, and thus ensures both its powers and its failures.

Notes

CHAPTER 1. CAN THE MOSQUITO SPEAK?

1. Jill Edwards, ed., *Al-Alamein Revisited: The Battle of Al-Alamein and Its Historical Implications* (Cairo: American University in Cairo Press, 2000), 41. Al-Alamein may have been less a decisive turning point than an indicator of changes in the relative strengths of the two sides determined by factors outside the immediate battlefield. Ibid., 55–98

2. Al-Alamein was the testing ground for the new methods of large-scale mine warfare, which were often unpredictable, especially since the mines did not remain under the control of those who laid them. Each side at various times incorporated the other's minefields in its own defenses. U.S. Department of State, Bureau of Political-Military Affairs, "Hidden Killers: The Global Landmine Crisis," Jan. 27, 1995. On the number of mines see http://www.icbl.org/resources/mideast4 and *Middle East Times,* Aug. 20, 1999; on their impact on the local community see Lila Abu-Lughod, *Writing Women's Worlds: Bedouin Stories* (Berkeley: University of California Press, 1993), 56–65.

3. Malaria specialists recognize four forms of malaria, caused by four species of protozoans in the genus *Plasmodium:* the often lethal *Plasmodium gambiae* and the less dangerous *P. vivax, P. malariae,* and *P. ovale.* The plasmodium parasite is transmitted to humans by about 60 out of the 380 recognized species of anopheline mosquito.

4. I have taken the history of the epidemic mostly from the informative account in Nancy E. Gallagher, *Egypt's Other Wars: Epidemics and the Politics of Public Health* (Syracuse, N.Y.: Syracuse University Press, 1990), 20–95. My interest in the question of malaria was widened after reading the study of malaria and Zionist politics in Palestine by Sandra Sufian, "Healing the Land and the Nation: Malaria and the Zionist Project in Mandatory Palestine, 1920–1947," Ph.D. diss., New York University, 1999.

5. I have changed the names of people from the village.

6. The first Aswan dam was built in 1898–1902, strengthened and raised in height in 1907–12, and raised again in 1929–33. Willcocks and Craig, *Egyptian Irrigation*, 2 vols., 3rd ed. (London: E. & F. N. Spon, 1913), 2:718–58.

7. Doreen Warriner, *Land and Poverty in the Middle East* (Westport, Conn.: Hyperion Press, 1948), 30–31.

8. Charles Issawi, *Egypt in Revolution: An Economic Analysis* (Oxford: Oxford University Press, 1963), 35.

9. Egypt was Germany's largest export market for synthetic nitrates. Robert Vitalis, *When Capitalists Collide: Business Conflict and the End of Empire in Egypt* (Berkeley: University of California Press, 1995), 88–89.

10. Measures introduced before the war had limited landowners to growing cotton on a maximum of 50 percent of their land. During the war the government lowered the limit to between 16 and 22 percent, according to the region, and banned cotton cultivation altogether in parts of Upper Egypt. The decline in crop yields was also attributed in part to the disruption of rotation cycles. Jean Anhouri, "Les Répercussions de la guerre sur l'agriculture égyptienne," *L'Egypte Contemporaine* 38, nos. 238–39 (Mar.–Apr. 1947): 233–51, at 241, 251.

11. Average sugarcane yields per acre dropped by 30 percent between 1935–39 and 1942–45, yet despite the drop in yields total production at the end of the war was higher than in the preceding period, reflecting the increased acreage devoted to sugar (Anhouri, "Les Répercussions de la guerre," 241). Cotton is a summer crop and allows the cultivation of grain, pulses, or fodder on the same land in the winter, whereas cane occupies the ground year-round and cannot be combined with grain production.

12. Gallagher, *Egypt's Other Wars*, 83.

13. Ibid., 33.

14. On the impact of large dams see World Commission on Dams, *Dams and Development: A New Framework for Decision Making* (2000), available at http://www.damsreport.org.

15. Mike Samuels and Hal Zina Bennett, *Well Body, Well Earth* (San Francisco: Sierra Club, 1985).

16. It was estimated to cause one to two million deaths a year, and to be a contributing factor in perhaps another million. See http://www.who.int/ctd/html/malaria.html.

17. William H. McNeill, *Plagues and Peoples* (Garden City, N.Y.: Anchor Press / Doubleday, 1976), 279–80. The loss of Java spurred the development of synthetic alternatives to quinine.

18. The pyrethrum spray was invented and tested as an insecticide by a German scientist, G. Giemsa, in 1910–13, but was ignored in the treatment of malaria epidemics until the South African epidemic of 1929–35. Gordon Harrison, *Mosquitoes, Malaria and Man: A History of the Hostilities Since 1880* (New York: E. P. Dutton, 1978), 209–11.

19. Emil Ludwig, *The Nile: The Mighty Story of Egypt's Fabulous River—6,000 Years of Thrilling History*, trans. Mary H. Lindsay (New York: Viking

Press, 1937), 265. Schistosomiasis was already prevalent in Lower Egypt, brought there by the earlier development of perennial irrigation. The Aswan Dam brought the disease to Upper Egypt, where infection rates reached 80 percent or more. From the 1920s, health authorities began mass injection campaigns against schistosomiasis. The needles they used, although disinfected with procedures then considered sufficient, spread hepatitis C, a viral infection that can lead to liver failure. By the 1990s up to 20 percent of population tested positive for the chronic illness. The *Lancet,* Mar. 11, 2000.

20. Gallagher, *Egypt's Other Wars,* 18. The acknowledgment was not made seriously, for the report added that although the survivors would be healthier, half the population would die of hunger. The main purpose of the dams, however, was to support industrial crops (cotton and sugarcane) rather than food production, so it was not the rural population who would have suffered from a return to basin irrigation and the growing of more wheat, beans, and chickpeas.

21. Ibid., 24.

22. Ibid., 33.

23. Luis Camargo, "Re: Sugar cane juice during malaria treatment," message posted May 20, 1997, on the Malaria Discussion List, http://www.wehi.edu.au/MalDB-www/discuss/ listserv.html. The pharmacological properties of sugarcane in relation to blood flow were investigated in Cuba, where the pharmaceutical industry developed a drug from sugarcane, policosanal (PPG), to combat arteriosclerosis.

24. Gallagher, *Egypt's Other Wars,* 25, 38.

25. McNeill, *Plagues and Peoples,* 280–82.

26. On Soper's Brazil campaign see R.M. Packard and P. Gadelha, "A Land Filled with Mosquitoes." *Parassitologia* 36 (1994), 197–213.

27. Gallagher, *Egypt's Other Wars,* 27.

28. Lord Killearn (Sir Miles Lampson), *Diaries,* Private Papers Collection, Middle East Centre, St. Antony's College, Oxford, entry dated Jan. 14, 1944.

29. Harrison, *Mosquitoes, Malaria and Man,* 220–22; Gallagher, *Egypt's Other Wars,* 28–31, 77–95.

30. Bruno Latour, *We Have Never Been Modern* (Cambridge, Mass.: Harvard University Press, 1993), 1.

31. Europe, as Dipesh Chakrabarty says, is "the sovereign, theoretical subject of all histories." "Postcoloniality and the Artifice of History: Who Speaks for 'Indian' Pasts?" *Representations* 37, no. 1 (1992): 1–26, at 1–3. See also Dipesh Chakrabarty, "The Two Histories of Capital," in *Provincializing Europe: Postcolonial Thought and Historical Difference* (Princeton, N.J.: Princeton University Press, 2000), 47–71; Gyan Prakash, "Can the 'Subaltern' Ride? A Reply to O'Hanlon and Washbrook," *Comparative Studies in Society and History* 34, no. 1 (1992): 168–84; and Gayatri Chakravorty Spivak, "Can the Subaltern Speak?" in *Marxism and the Interpretation of Culture,* ed. C. Nelson and L. Grossberg (Basingstoke: Macmillan Education, 1988), 271–313, reprinted in *Colonial Discourse and Post-Colonial Theory,* ed. Patrick Williams and Laura Chrisman (New York: Columbia University Press, 1994), 66–111.

32. Emile Durkheim, *The Rules of Sociological Method* (New York: Free Press, 1938), xlvi. On the question of nonhuman agency and knowing the protagonists in advance see Bruno Latour, *The Pasteurization of France* (Cambridge, Mass.: Harvard University Press, 1988); and Donna Haraway, *Modest-Witness@SecondMillennium.FemaleMan© Meets OncoMouse™: Feminism and Technoscience* (New York: Routledge, 1997).

33. Karl Marx, *Capital: A Critique of Political Economy*, vol. 1, *The Process of Capitalist Production* (New York: Modern Library, 1906), 170.

34. Jacques Derrida, *Specters of Marx: The State of the Debt, the Work of Mourning, and the New International* (New York: Routledge, 1994), 170.

35. My account of ʿAbbud is drawn largely from Vitalis's fine revisionist study of Egyptian business and politics in this period, based upon the case of ʿAbbud. The government took control of ʿAbbud's business empire in a series of nationalizations between 1955 and 1963. It seized the remainder of the Armant estate in October 1961, when it sequestered the property of 168 "reactionary capitalists." ʿAbbud died in London in December 1963 (Vitalis, *When Capitalists Collide*, 210–14). I visited the estate in 1997, by which time the last sequestration had been reversed and some of the property returned.

36. In Iraq, ʿAbbud worked with Sir William Willcocks on the construction of the Euphrates Dam in 1913. Eric Davis, *Challenging Colonialism: Bank Misr and Egyptian Industrialization, 1920–1941* (Princeton, N.J.: Princeton University Press, 1983), 152–53.

37. On the business politics of the 1940s see also Eric Davis, *Challenging Colonialism*, and Robert L. Tignor, *The State, Private Enterprise, and Economic Change in Egypt, 1918–1952* (Princeton, N.J.: Princeton University Press, 1984), and *Egyptian Textiles and British Capital, 1930–1956* (Cairo: American University in Cairo Press, 1989). Studies of the broader class politics include ʿAbd al-ʿAzim Ramadan, *Siraʿ al-tabaqat fi misr (1837–1952)* (Beirut: al-Muʾassasa al-ʿArabiyya li-ʾl-Dirasat wa-ʾl-Nashr, 1978) (who gives the size of the Armant estate, purchased from "Count Fortunas," on p. 75) and *Tatawwur al-haraka al-wataniyya fi misr: min sanat 1937 ila sanat 1948* (Cairo: al-Hayʾa al-Misriyya al-ʿAmma li-ʾl-Kitab, 1998); ʿAsim al-Disuqi, *Kibar mullak al-aradi al-ziraʿiyya wa dawruhum fi al-mujtamaʿ al-misri* (Cairo: Dar al-Thaqafa al-Jadida, 1976); and Magda Baraka, *The Egyptian Upper Class Between Revolutions, 1919–1952* (Reading, Eng.: Ithaca Press, 1998).

38. The seventy-meter-tall Immobilia Building, completed in January 1940, contained 38 shops, 82 offices, and 218 apartments. Mercedes Volait, *L'Architecture moderne en Egypte et la revue Al-ʿImara, 1939–1958*, Dossiers du CEDEJ 1987, no. 4 (Cairo: Centre d'Etudes et de Documentation Economique, Juridique et Sociale, 1988), 62–63; Arthur Goldschmidt Jr., *Biographical Dictionary of Modern Egypt* (Boulder, Colo.: Lynne Rienner, 2000), 4.

39. Gallagher, *Egypt's Other Wars*, 20, 89, 188.

40. Makram ʿUbayd, the dismissed minister and until his dismissal the number two man in the party, was an old nemesis of ʿAbbud. Two months later he was expelled from the party. His replacement as finance minister, Amin

ʿUthman, was a close friend of ʿAbbud. Vitalis, *When Capitalists Collide,* 120–24; Yunan Labib Rizq, *al-Wafd wa-ʾl-kitab al-aswad* (Cairo: Muʾassasat al-Dirasat al-Siyasiyya wa-ʾl-Istratijiya, 1978), 17–122; Muhammad Husayn Haykal, *Mudhakkirati fi al-siyasa al-misriyya,* 3 vols. (Cairo: Dar al-Maʿarif, 1977–78), vol. 2, *Min 29 yuliya 1938 ila 26 yuliya 1952: ʿAhd Faruq,* 193–245.

41. Lord Killearn (Sir Miles Lampson), *Diaries,* Private Papers Collection, Middle East Centre, St. Antony's College, Oxford, entry dated Feb. 19–Mar. 30, 1943; Vitalis, *When Capitalists Collide,* 122.

42. Vitalis, *When Capitalists Collide,* 121.

43. Ibid., 126.

44. Ibid., 119–28; Ramadan, *Siraʿ al-tabaqat fi misr,* 108–10.

45. Robert L. Tignor, "Nationalism, Economic Planning, and Development Projects in Interwar Egypt," *International Journal of African Historical Studies* 10, no. 2 (1977): 185–208, examines the struggles over the control of irrigation and hydroelectric schemes in interwar Egypt.

46. There is an important anthropological literature that opens up the concept of commodity to examine its involvement in wider circulations outside those defined by economics. See Arjun Appadurai, "Introduction: Commodities and the Politics of Value," in *The Cultural Life of Things,* ed. Arjun Appadurai (Cambridge: Cambridge University Press, 1986), and Nicholas Thomas, *Entangled Objects: Exchange, Material Culture, and Colonialism in the Pacific* (Cambridge, Mass.: Harvard University Press, 1991).

47. A classic statement of this argument is in Clifford Geertz, "Thick Description," in *The Interpretation of Cultures: Selected Essays* (New York: Basic Books, 1973).

48. Willcocks and Craig, *Egyptian Irrigation,* 2:677–78. Willcocks extended this argument in Sir William Willcocks, *Irrigation of Mesopotamia* (London: E. & F. N. Spon, 1917), where he compared the advantages of the system of basin irrigation to the new methods of barrages and storage reservoirs.

49. Emil Ludwig, *Der Nil: Lebenslauf Eines Stromes* (Amsterdam: Querido Verlag, 1935–36), English translation, *The Nile: The Mighty Story of Egypt's Fabulous River—6,000 Years of Thrilling History,* trans. Mary H. Lindsay (New York: Viking Press, 1937), 7.

50. Willcocks and Craig, *Egyptian Irrigation,* 2:744–45.

51. On studying science as it happens in action rather than its outcome, see Latour, *Pasteurization of France* and *Pandora's Hope: Essays on the Reality of Science Studies* (Cambridge, Mass.: Harvard University Press, 1999). Rather than Latour's term "factish" (*Pandora's Hope,* 274), I prefer "artifactual," borrowed from Derrida, *Specters of Marx,* 170. Latour's brief dismissal of Derrida's work in *We Have Never Been Modern* is disappointing. On the nature/culture distinction see Jacques Derrida, *Of Grammatology,* trans. Gayatri Chakravorty Spivak (Baltimore, Md.: Johns Hopkins University Press, 1976), 46–48.

52. Willcocks and Craig, *Egyptian Irrigation,* 2:718–58. The quotation is from 738.

53. Robert Mabro, *The Egyptian Economy, 1952–1972* (Oxford: Clarendon Press, 1974), 86.

54. Ibid., 89. On the increasing difficulty in calculating the impact of dams, see World Commission on Dams, *Dams and Development.*

55. On the colonial production of science, see Gyan Prakash, *Another Reason: Science and the Imagination of Modern India* (Princeton, N.J.: Princeton University Press, 1999).

56. R. B. Buckley, *Irrigation Pocket-Book* (London: Spon, 1913), quoted in Willcocks and Craig, *Egyptian Irrigation,* 152–53.

57. Arundhati Roy discusses the power of dams to take away local knowledge in "The Greater Common Good," in *The Cost of Living,* available at http://www.narmada.org.

58. A. B. De Guerville, *New Egypt* (London: William Heinemann, 1905), 224–27.

59. Tignor, "Nationalism, Economic Planning, and Development Projects." See also John Waterbury, *Hydropolitics of the Nile Valley* (Syracuse, N.Y.: Syracuse University Press, 1979).

60. Approaching seventy, Willcocks was spared imprisonment and allowed to return to Bengal, where he had been born and raised and had studied engineering, to work as a government advisor on irrigation. Goldschmidt, *Biographical Dictionary,* 225.

61. Hussein Kamel Selim, *Twenty Years of Agricultural Development in Egypt* (Cairo: Ministry of Finance, Egypt, 1940), 66–67. The author was vice-dean, Faculty of Commerce, Fu'ad I University.

62. *Al-Ahram,* Dec. 1, 1942, cited in Gallagher, *Egypt's Other Wars,* 26.

63. Mirrit Butrus Ghali, *Siyasat al-ghad: barnamij siyasi wa-iqtisadi wa-ijtima'i* (Cairo: Matba'at al-Risala, 1938), 145, English translation *The Policy of Tomorrow,* trans. Ismail R. el-Faruqi (Washington, D.C.: American Council of Learned Societies, 1953), 102. There is no discussion of land reform in a series of books published in the late 1930s addressing the problems of rural Egypt, such as Henry Habib Ayrout, *Moeurs et coutumes des fellahs* (Paris: Payot, 1938), published in Arabic as *al-Fallahun,* trans. Muhammad Ghallab (Cairo: Matba'at al-Kawthar, 1943); 'A'isha 'Abd al-Rahman (pseudonym Bint al-Shati'), *al-Rif al-misri* (Cairo: Maktabat al-Wafd, 1936); Hafiz 'Afifi, *'Ala hamish al-siyasa: ba'd masa'ilna al-qawmiyya* (Cairo: Dar al-Kutub al-Misriyya, 1938). See also Gabriel Baer, *Landownership in Modern Egypt, 1800–1950* (Oxford: Oxford University Press, 1962), 201–22, and chapter 4, below.

64. Warriner, *Land and Poverty in the Middle East,* 49.

65. Gallagher, *Egypt's Other Wars,* 40–55.

66. Ihsan 'Abd al-Qaddus, *Ruz al-Yusuf,* Mar. 2, 1944, discussed in Gallagher, *Egypt's Other Wars,* 49–50.

67. Baer, *Landownership in Modern Egypt,* 210–15. The 1944 draft law was amended by the Social Affairs Committee of the Senate (the upper house of

the legislature) to raise the proposed ceiling to one hundred acres, the limit advocated in Mirrit Butrus Ghali's influential blueprint for land reform *al-Islah al-zira'i* (Cairo: Jama'at al-Nahda al-Qawmiyya, 1945). He argued that existing estates larger than one hundred acres would be broken up by inheritance within two or three generations. The term acre in this chapter refers to an Egyptian acre, or feddan.

68. 'Asim al-Disuqi, *Kibar mullak al-aradi al-zira'iyya*, 306–12. Outside parliament, the socialist left saw these land reform proposals as simply an effort by the bourgeoisie to limit the monopolization of land, which was forcing up prices, and therefore wages, and reducing the consumption of consumer goods. Nevertheless, it was argued, the proposals had the useful effect of revealing to the people that private property was not something sacred. Ahmad Sadiq Sa'd, writing in *al-Fajr al-jadid*, July 16, 1945, and Aug. 16, 1945, discussed in Rif'at al-Sa'id, *al-Sihafa al-yasariyya fi misr, 1925–1948* (Cairo: Maktabat Madbuli, 1977), 130–31.

69. Some 575 families received land in March 1948, 597 in February 1951, and 240 in May 1951. United States National Archives, Record Group 59, Department of State, Central Files, Egypt 1950–54, 874.16/2–1951, U.S. Embassy Cairo to State, Feb. 19, 1951, Presentation of Land to Peasants, and 874.16/5–1851, U.S. Embassy Cairo to State, May 18, 1951, Distribution of Land at Kafr Saad. Microform (University Publications of America, 1985), hereafter referred to as USRG 59.

70. Vitalis, *When Capitalists Collide*, 179–80. On the perfume venture, a plant at Kesma, see USRG 59, 1950–54, 874.395/10–352, U.S. Embassy Cairo to State, Oct. 3, 1952. On the paper factory, see USRG 59, 1950–54, 874.392/4–2252, Department of State, Memorandum of a conversation, Construction of paper products plant in Egypt; and USRG 59, 1950–54, 874.392/8–454, Aug. 4, 1954. The paper plant was to be built at Naj' Hamadi in collaboration with W. R. Grace & Co. using a new procedure developed by a Grace subsidiary in Peru to make kraft paper and newsprint from sugarcane bagasse, the refuse from crushed sugarcane. Grace had previously found another use for the bagasse, using it to dilute the ammonium nitrate in the manufacture of explosives.

71. USRG 59, 1950–54, 874.3972/11–851, Caffery to State, Nov. 8, 1951, enclosing memorandum of meeting between Randall S. Williams, First Secretary, and Clark Davis of Suez Fertilizer Works, Nov. 6, 1951. On the postwar politics of development see Arturo Escobar, *Encountering Development: The Making and Unmaking of the Third World* (Princeton, N.J.: Princeton University Press, 1995); James Ferguson, *The Anti-Politics Machine: "Development," Depoliticization, and Bureaucratic Power in Lesotho* (Cambridge: Cambridge University Press, 1990); Akhil Gupta, *Postcolonial Developments: Agriculture in the Making of Modern India* (Durham, N.C.: Duke University Press, 1998); and three collections of essays: Jonathan Crush, ed., *Power of Development* (London: Routledge, 1995), Frederick Cooper and Randall Packard, eds., *Interna-*

tional Development and the Social Sciences: Essays on the History and Politics of Knowledge (Berkeley: University of California Press, 1997), and Wolfgang Sachs, ed., *The Development Dictionary: A Guide to Knowledge and Power* (London: Zed Press, 1992).

72. USRG 59, 1950–54, 874.3971/1–951, Letter from Mohamed Salmawy, President, Salmawy Co., to Egyptian Desk, Department of State; USRG 59, 1950–54, 874.00-TA/8–2552, American Embassy Cairo to Department of State, Program and Budget, TCA-Egypt, for Fiscal Years 1953 and 1954, 3; USRG 59, 1950–54, 874.00-TA/9–652, American Embassy Cairo to Department of State, Priority of Project Needs for FY 1953.

73. USRG 59, 1950–54, 874.00-TA/11–2351, American Embassy Cairo to Technical Cooperation Administration, Cairo, A Plan for Technical Assistance for Egypt. Budgets for FY 1952 and FY 1953, 3–4.

74. USRG 59, 1950–54, 874.00-TA/10–852, American Embassy Cairo to Department of State, The Point IV Program in Egypt.

75. USRG 59, 1950–54, 874.00-TA/5–1253, American Embassy Cairo to Department of State, Report of Point IV Activities from April 1 through April 30, 1953, 5–6, 18; USRG 59, 1950–54, 874.00-TA/7–2053, American Embassy Cairo to Department of State, Current Difficulties in Egypt of Arthur D. Little, Inc.

76. USRG 59, 1950–54, 874.3972/11–851, Caffery to State, Nov. 8, 1951, enclosing memorandum of meeting between Randall S. Williams, First Secretary, and Clark Davis of Suez Fertilizer Works, Nov. 6, 1951. ʿAbbud had already traveled to Washington to seek a rescheduling of his U.S. loan repayments for the fertilizer plant, blaming his financial difficulties on the 1949 devaluation of the Egyptian pound. USRG 59, 1950–54, 874.39/1–1950, Department of State, Washington, memorandum of meeting with Abboud Pasha and General Porter of Chemical Construction Company, Jan. 19, 1950.

77. James Scott, *Seeing Like a State: How Certain Schemes to Improve the Human Condition Have Failed* (New Haven, Conn.: Yale University Press, 1998), examines many of the same kinds of techno-politics that I explore in this and subsequent chapters. While I admire many of Scott's arguments, my own analysis differs from his in important ways. In particular, whereas Scott is concerned with the way modern states have misused the powers of science, and distinguishes this misuse from proper science, I am concerned with the kinds of social and political practice that produce simultaneously the powers of science and the powers of modern states.

78. Ramadan, *Siraʿ al-tabaqat fi misr*, 213; Salib Sami, *Dhikriyyat Salib Basha Sami, 1891–1952*, ed. Sami Abu al-Nur (Cairo: Maktabat Madbuli, 1999).

79. My account of the events of 1952 is based largely on Joel Gordon, *Nasser's Blessed Movement: Egypt's Free Officers and the July Revolution* (Oxford: Oxford University Press, 1992), 14–57. ʿAbd al-ʿAzim Ramadan also says that the army officers had not considered the question of land reform before seizing power: *ʿAbd al-Nasir wa-azmat maris* (Cairo: Ruz al-Yusuf, 1976), 14–18.

80. The 1952 agrarian reform law laid down that "no person may own more than 200 acres of land," but allowed owners to keep another 100 acres by giving up to 50 acres to each of two children. Land over the 300-acre limit was to be requisitioned by the government over five years and sold to small farmers in holdings of two to five acres. The price of the land, to be paid over thirty years, was fixed at seventy times the land tax, which represented less than half its market value. The five-year implementation period gave owners time to evade the law through private sales or transfers to other relatives. Doreen Warriner, *Land Reform and Development in the Middle East: A Study of Egypt, Syria, and Iraq*, 2nd ed. (London: Oxford University Press, 1962), 31–35. See also chapters 5 and 7 below.

81. Vitalis, *When Capitalists Collide*, 172–214.

82. The plant was uneconomical because the U.S. government, afraid that American scientists and engineers would not be able to handle the high-pressure and high-temperature Haber-Bosch nitrogen-fixing technology recently developed in Germany, contracted with the American Cyanamid Corporation to build the fertilizer plant at Muscle Shoals using the cyanamid process, which consumed much greater amounts of electricity.

83. Thomas P. Hughes, *Networks of Power: Electrification in Western Society, 1880–1930* (Baltimore, Md.: Johns Hopkins University Press, 1983), 286–87, 293–95. See also Preston J. Hubbard, *Origins of the TVA: The Muscle Shoals Controversy, 1920–1932* (New York: Norton, 1961).

84. Feliks Bochenski and William Diamond, "TVA's in the Middle East," *Middle East Journal* 4, no. 1 (1950): 52–82, at 55.

85. At least 113,000 people were displaced by the High Dam, five to eight meters of coastline were lost every year, and degradation of the land and salination continued. By 1989 the irrigated area was no greater than before the dam. *World Rivers Review*, Feb. 2000, 5, available at http://www.irn.org. The blueprint for Nile development published by the Ministry of Public Works in 1920 had argued that 200,000 acres of coastal lakes in the delta should not be brought under cultivation because their yield in fish was more valuable. Government of Egypt, Ministry of Public Works, *Nile Control* (Cairo, 1920), cited Tignor, "Nationalism, Economic Planning, and Development Projects," 191. See also Tom Little, *High Dam at Aswan* (New York: John Day, 1965).

86. Marx, *Capital*, 1:198. Marx makes it clear in passages that follow that this is only a preliminary account of human intentionality. He goes on to explore how the mechanized world of modernity removes consciousness from individuals and makes it appear to them as an intelligence residing in the machinery of modern technology. For a discussion, see Moishe Postone, *Time, Labor, and Social Domination* (Cambridge: Cambridge University Press, 1993).

87. Timothy Mitchell, *Colonising Egypt* (Berkeley: University of California Press, 1991), and "The Stage of Modernity," in *Questions of Modernity*, ed. Timothy Mitchell (Minneapolis: University of Minnesota Press, 2000), 1–34.

88. In 1918 J. R. Geigy S.A. joined with Switzerland's two other chemical companies, Ciba and Sandoz, to form the Interessengemeinschaft Basel (Basel

Syndicate) to compete with I. G. Farben. In 1929–39 the two cartels joined with British and French chemical firms to form the Quadrapartite Cartel, which lasted until World War II.

89. Professor G. Fischer, "Presentation Speech, Nobel Prize in Physiology or Medicine, 1948," available at http://www.nobel.se/laureates/medicine-1948-press.html.

90. Harrison, *Mosquitoes, Malaria and Man*, 218–27.

91. Gallagher, *Egypt's Other Wars*, 198 n. 64.

92. See Fischer, "Presentation Speech."

93. Fischer, "Presentation Speech." A description of the Peet-Grady chamber, named after its inventors, is available at http://www.clorox.com/science/labs/insect_lab.html.

94. For the analysis of science in these terms, see Bruno Latour, *The Pasteurization of France*.

95. Harrison, *Mosquitoes, Malaria and Man*, 219, 222, 223.

96. Ibid., 218–27.

97. Ibid.

98. Titus Bradley, "Malaria: History and Distribution," available at http://www.micro.msb.le.ac.uk/224/Bradley/history.html.

99. The year 2007 was chosen because it was the date that Mexico, one of the world's largest remaining DDT producers, had set to stop manufacturing and using the pesticide.

100. World Wildlife Fund Canada and World Wildlife Fund U.S., *Resolving the DDT Dilemma: Protecting Biodiversity and Human Health* (Toronto and Washington, D.C.: WWF Canada and WWF U.S., 1998). In the 1990s, international healthcare agencies began to seriously promote alternatives to DDT for the management of mosquitoes. Interestingly, the methods employed—cloths baited with human odor and insecticide, bed nets impregnated with synthetic pyrethrum, and locally based, community-participant projects in place of centralized, military-style campaigns—tried to take advantage of the fact that the mosquito is a social insect, dependent upon human communities.

101. USRG 59, 1950–54, 874.3972/10–651, Cairo to State, Aug. 28, 1951, Chemical Fertilizers—Egypt.

102. In 1954 Imperial Chemical Industries (Egypt) Ltd., a subsidiary of the British chemical giant ICI, and Salmawy & Co., the local agent for the Gresselli Chemicals division of E. I. du Pont de Nemours & Co., were importing DDT concentrate and other chemicals to produce about seven thousand metric tons a year of DDT-based cotton dust and other pesticides. Salmawy, whose offices were in ʿAbbud's Immobilia building in Cairo, also imported the helicopters. USRG 59, 1950–54, 874.3971/1–951, Letter from Mohamed Salmawy, President, Salmawy Co., to Egyptian Desk, Dept of State; USRG 59, 1950–54, 874.397/11–1754, Nestor Lardicos, Commercial Assistant, U.S. Embassy Cairo to State, Nov. 17, 1954, Survey of Pest Control Products, Egypt.

103. Vitalis, *When Capitalists Collide*, 178.

104. USRG 59, 1950–54, 874.3971/5–2851, Myles Standish III, 3rd Secretary, U.S. Embassy Cairo to State, Construction of DDT Plant; USRG 59, 1950–54, 874.395/10–352, U.S. Embassy Cairo to State, Oct. 3, 1952; USRG 59, 1950–54, 874.397/6–1351, U.S. Embassy Cairo to State, June 13, 1951.

105. In 1954 it was reported that the plant was under construction and scheduled to begin production in 1956. The WHO provided four technicians and UNICEF provided $250,000 to purchase machinery. USRG 59, 1950–54, 874.397/11–1754, Nestor Lardicos, Commercial Assistant, U.S. Embassy Cairo to State, Nov. 17, 1954, Survey of Pest Control Products, Egypt; USRG 59, 1950–54, 874.3971/8–1152, Jefferson Caffery, Ambassador, U.S. Embassy Cairo to State, Agreement between WHO and UNICEF and the GOE to build DDT plant.

106. USRG 59, 1950–54, 874.397/11–1754, Nestor Lardicos, Commercial Assistant, U.S. Embassy Cairo to State, Nov. 17, 1954, Survey of Pest Control Products, Egypt.

CHAPTER 2. PRINCIPLES TRUE IN EVERY COUNTRY

1. The more senior officials received estates of one thousand acres or more, but most were given amounts between one and two hundred acres. Amin Sami, *Taqwim al-nil wa-asma' man tawallaw amr misr wa-muddat hukmihim 'alayha wa-mulahazat ta'rikhiyya 'an ahwal al-khilafa al-'amma wa-shu'un misr al-khassa*, vol. 3., in 3 parts, *1264–1289 (1848–1872)* (Cairo: Matba'at Dar al-Kutub, 1936), 3:490–93, 496–97, 499–500, 502–5, 513–16, 518–21, 529–39, 542, 561.

2. Sir Philip Francis, *Original Minutes of the Governor-general and Council of Fort William on the Settlement and Collection of the Revenues of Bengal* (London, 1782), 152, quoted in Ranajit Guha, *A Rule of Property for Bengal: An Essay on the Idea of Permanent Settlement*, 2nd ed. (New Delhi: Orient Longman, 1981), 95.

3. The classic statement of this view is H. L. A. Hart, *The Concept of Law* (Oxford: Oxford University Press, 1961). For a recent critique see Peter Fitzpatrick, *Modernism and the Grounds of Law* (Cambridge: Cambridge University Press, 2001), 70–107.

4. Robert Tignor, *Modernization and British Colonial Rule in Egypt, 1882–1914* (Princeton, N.J.: Princeton University Press, 1966), 106–10.

5. Yacoub Artin, *La Propriété foncière en Egypte*, printed under the Auspices of the Ministry of Finance (Cairo: Institut Egyptien, 1883). Artin notes that it was Sir Auckland Colvin, the English controller at the Ministry of Finance in Cairo, who proposed that the ministry fund the publication of his study. The following year an Italian study of Ottoman property law by Domenico Gatteschi, published in Alexandria in 1869, was translated into English by Edward Van Dyck and published under the title *Real Property, Mortgage, and Wakf According to Ottoman Law* (London: Wyman and Sons, 1884).

6. Artin drew especially on Noma Denis Fustel de Coulanges, *La Cité antique*, 9th ed. (Paris: Hachette, 1881). He turned to this work after failing to de-

rive any conclusive view of Islamic property rights from Islamic legal sources (*La Propriété foncière*, 68–82). Kenneth Cuno, *The Pasha's Peasants: Land, Society and Economy in Lower Egypt, 1740–1858* (Cambridge: Cambridge University Press, 1992), 204–5, traces the French view to the work of the orientalist Silvestre de Sacy, and discusses the sources in Islamic law from which de Sacy derived his analysis.

7. Fustel de Coulanges published *La Cité antique* in 1864 at the height of the controversy over French land seizures, ignited by the criticisms of Ismayl Urbain, a creole from French Guiana who traveled with the Saint-Simonians to Egypt in the 1830s, became an interpreter and advisor to the French in Algeria, and then published a pamphlet (under the pseudonym Georges Voisin) attacking the land seizures, *L'Algérie pour les Algériens* (Paris: Michel Lévy Frères, 1861). See John David Ragan, "A Fascination for the Exotic: Suzanne Volquin, Ismayl Urbain, Jehan D'Ivray, and the Saint-Simonians—French Travelers in Egypt on the Margins" (Ph.D. diss., New York University, 2000), chap. 7.

8. Gabriel Baer, *A History of Landownership in Modern Egypt, 1800–1950* (Oxford: Oxford University Press, 1962).

9. Yacoub Artin Pasha, *Artin Bey: Ministère des Affaires Etrangères et du Commerce sous le règne de Môhémet-Aly Pacha 1800–1859* (Cairo: Imprimerie Nationale, 1896).

10. On this rupturing, see Jacques Derrida, "The Force of Law," *Cardozo Law Review* 11 (1990). Samera Esmair explores the implications of Derrida's work in an insightful essay on colonial law, "Colonies of Legalities," unpublished paper, May 2000, to which I am indebted. On the question of the contradictions in European liberal theory made apparent by colonialism, see Uday Mehta, *Liberalism and Empire: A Study in Nineteenth-Century British Liberal Thought* (Chicago: University of Chicago Press, 1999).

11. Cuno, *The Pasha's Peasants.* For a re-examination of the scholarly discussions before the nineteenth century, see Baber Johansen, *The Islamic Law on Land Tax and Rent: The Peasant Loss of Property Rights as Interpreted in the Hanafite Legal Literature of the Mamluk and Ottoman Periods* (London: Croom Helm, 1988).

12. Huri Islamoglu-Inan, *State and Peasant in the Ottoman Empire: Agrarian Power Relations and Regional Economic Development in Ottoman Anatolia during the Sixteenth Century* (Leiden: E. J. Brill, 1994), chaps. 1 and 3; and "Property as a Contested Domain: A Re-Evaluation of the Ottoman Land Code of 1858," unpublished paper, 1999. Baber Johansen shows that the development of large estates in the classical period was legitimated by Hanafite jurists by means of a complex legal fiction, whereby tenants were considered to be engaged, hour by hour, in a continuous "purchase" of the land's produce. The fiction was necessary, Johansen explains, because the yield of the land was held to be a relation (in Abdellah Hammoudi's terms) rather than a substance. In the Ottoman period, jurists attempted to reestablish the legitimacy of these estates with another complex fiction, by which the estates were imagined to have been obtained through original purchase from the ruler—the only source, in Ot-

toman doctrine, of legitimate revenue claims. Johansen, *Islamic Law on Land Tax;* Abdellah Hammoudi, "Substance and Relation: Water Rights and Water Distribution in the Dra Valley," in *Property, Social Structure and Law in the Modern Middle East,* ed. Ann Elizabeth Mayer (Albany: State University of New York Press, 1985), 27–57.

13. Khedival order of 1 Rabi al-thani 1280h (Sept. 15, 1863), in Sami, *Taqwim al-nil,* 3:513. Sharqiyya is a province in the eastern Nile Delta. Dates based on the Islamic calendar (derived from the year of the Hijra) are indicated with the suffix "h."

14. John Bowring, "Report on Egypt and Candia," in Great Britain, House of Commons, *Sessional Papers* 1840, vol. xxi, 1– 227, cited in E. R. J. Owen, *Cotton and the Egyptian Economy, 1820–1914: A Study in Trade and Development* (Oxford: Oxford University Press, 1969), 328. Bowring advocated a market system in place of monopolies, for by the time he wrote the failures of the coercion were clear.

15. See Timothy Mitchell, *Colonising Egypt* (Berkeley: University of California Press, 1991), 34, 40–43.

16. Khaled Fahmy, *All the Pasha's Men: Mehmed Ali, His Army and the Making of Modern Egypt* (Cambridge: Cambridge University Press, 1997), 107.

17. The right to the income of a village or group of villages was called an *ʿuhda,* a term referring to the "responsibility" imposed on the recipient.

18. ʿAbbas Hilmi ruled 1848–54. The situation was exacerbated particularly when Said Pasha (ruled 1854–63) increased the land tax. Baer, *History of Landownership,* 30, 32.

19. Cuno, *The Pasha's Peasants.*

20. Artin, *La Propriété foncière,* 280–81; Cuno, *The Pasha's Peasants,* 192–93.

21. Sami, *Taqwim al-nil,* 3:451. Law of 15 Jumada al-akhira 1279h (Dec. 7, 1862).

22. In the eighteenth century, for example, the Hawwara were the effective rulers of the Nile valley from Jirja south to Aswan, while other groups controlled large areas of the Delta. ʿAbd al-Rahim ʿAbd al-Rahim ʿAbd al-Rahim, *al-Rif al-misri fi al-qarn al-thamin ʿashar,* 2nd ed. (Cairo: Maktabat Madbuli, 1986), 169–78; the reference to "emirates" (*imarat*) is on 173.

23. Gabriel Baer, "The Settlement of the Beduins," in *Studies in the Social History of Modern Egypt* (Chicago: University of Chicago Press, 1969), 3–16.

24. While recognizing the Arab claims to the land, the regime repeatedly (and thus unsuccessfully) ordered them not to employ fellahin to cultivate it. Sami, *Taqwim al-nil,* 3:41; Baer, "Settlement of the Beduins," 5.

25. Jean Lozach and Georges Hug, *L'Habitat rural en Egypte* (Cairo: Société Royale de Géographie d'Egypte, 1930), 157.

26. Sami, *Taqwim al-nil,* 3:522.

27. David S. Landes, *Bankers and Pashas: International Finance and Economic Imperialism in Egypt,* 2nd ed. (Cambridge, Mass.: Harvard University Press, 1979), 129.

28. Sami, *Taqwim al-nil,* 3:452. Other measures taken at the start of the new regime to reduce the problem of the abandoning of land included revoking the 1861 land tax increase and ordering that the forced labor on irrigation works for reclaimed land no longer go unpaid, but be remunerated at the established wage. Ibid., 3:450–51.

29. The heads of tribal sections were to receive between 50 and 150 acres, depending on the size and importance of their household. Khedival order of 28 Jumada al-ula 1280h (Nov. 10, 1863), in Sami, *Taqwim al-nil,* 3:522–27.

30. Khedival order of 28 Jumada al-ula 1280h (Nov. 10, 1863), in Sami, *Taqwim al-nil,* 3:522–27.

31. This is not a question of writing a "history from below." It is not a matter of introducing into the history of the law the lives of ordinary people and their resistance to the law-state. Such stories, however valuable, have a tendency to reproduce the divisions we need to question.

32. The canal was completed in 1873. Sir William Willcocks and J. I. Craig, *Egyptian Irrigation,* 3rd ed., 2 vols. (London: E. & F. N. Spon, 1913), 1:434–41.

33. Khedival order of 17 Jumada al-ula 1281h (Oct. 18, 1864), in Sami, *Taqwim al-nil,* 3:572.

34. Sami, *Taqwim al-nil,* 3:503.

35. Khedival order of 17 Jumada al-ula 1281h (Oct. 18, 1864), in Sami, *Taqwim al-nil,* 3:299, 572.

36. Sami, *Taqwim al-nil,* 3:598.

37. Ibid.; and Lucie Duff-Gordon, *Letters from Egypt,* revised ed. (London: R. Brimley Johnson, 1902), 208–12.

38. Duff-Gordon, *Letters,* 208–9.

39. The four villages were al-Rayaniyya, al-ʿAqqal, Shaykh Jabir, and al-Nazra.

40. This account of the 1865 revolt is based on ʿAli Mubarak, *al-Khitat al-tawfiqiyya li-misr al-qahira wa-muduniha wa-biladiha al-qadima wa-ʾl-shahira* (Cairo: al-Matbaʿa al-Kubra al-Amiriyya, 1886–88), 11:82, 14:53, 94–5; Duff-Gordon, *Letters,* 215–35; Sami, *Taqwim al-nil,* 3:605; Juan R. Cole, *Colonialism and Revolution in the Middle East: Social and Cultural Origins of Egypt's ʿUrabi Movement* (Princeton, N.J.: Princeton University Press, 1993), 196; and Gabriel Baer, "Submissiveness and Revolt of the Fellah," in *Studies in the Social History of Modern Egypt* (Chicago: University of Chicago Press, 1969), 99. After completing this chapter I came across the insightful study of the uprising in Martina Rieker, "The Saʿid and the City: Subaltern Spaces in the Making of Modern Egyptian History" (Ph.D. diss., Temple University, 1997), 67–135.

41. The committees were called *majlis al-asʿar* and *majalis al-tijara.* Khedival order of 10 Shaʿban 1281h (Jan. 8, 1865), in Sami, *Taqwim al-nil,* 3:592; Duff-Gordon, *Letters,* 218.

42. Cole, *Colonialism and Revolution,* 196.

43. Duff-Gordon, *Letters,* 217. The ulema are the local legal-religious leadership.

44. Khedival orders of 14 and 15 Shawwal 1281h (Mar. 12 and 13, 1865), in Sami, *Taqwim al-nil*, 3:601–2.

45. Baer, *History of Landownership*, 30.

46. Khedival order of 1 Jumada al-ula 1282h (Sept. 22, 1865), cited in H. G. Lyons, *The Cadastral Survey of Egypt 1892–1907* (Cairo: Ministry of Finance, Survey Dept., 1908), 62–63; Artin, *Propriété foncière*, 281.

47. Sami, *Taqwim al-nil*, 3:622.

48. Ibid., 3:536, 597, 625.

49. Ibid., 3:615.

50. Laverne Kuhnke, *Lives at Risk: Public Health in Nineteenth-Century Egypt* (Berkeley: University of California Press, 1989), 65–68.

51. I have estimated the cholera deaths from the mortality tables in Charles Edmond, *L'Egypte à l'Exposition Universelle de 1867* (Paris: Dentu, 1867), 280–83. The number of recorded deaths increased from a yearly average of 110,000 in the period 1272h-1279h (1855–56 to 1862–63) to 174,270 in 1282h (May 1865–May 1866). For the last year, the figures are broken down by province and by month on p. 283, which shows the severity of the epidemic in the south. The figure of 60,000 is corroborated by other sources, cited in Kuhnke, *Lives at Risk*, 66, 198.

52. Duff-Gordon, *Letters from Egypt*, 270; Kuhnke, *Lives at Risk*, 49, 66.

53. Landes, *Bankers and Pashas*, 241–42, 269.

54. Ibid., 147–49. The figure for the number of cattle that died of the murrain varies according to estimates of the total number of cattle in the country at that time.

55. See the mortality tables in Edmond, *L'Egypte à l'Exposition Universelle*, 280–83.

56. Artin, *Propriété foncière*, 128–31; Cuno, *The Pasha's Peasants*, 158.

57. F. Robert Hunter, *Egypt Under the Khedives, 1805–1879: From Household Government to Modern Bureaucracy* (Pittsburgh, Penn.: University of Pittsburgh Press, 1984).

58. The government abolished the *muqabala* in 1880 and returned taxes to their 1871 levels. Artin, *Propriété foncière*, 152–54. Henry Villiers Stuart, *Egypt after the War, Being the Narrative of a Tour of Inspection* (London: John Murray, 1883).

59. Cole, *Colonialism and Revolution*, 61.

60. In February 1864, for example, Isma'il issued an order to the Railway Authority that wherever conscript troops were employed away from their villages the authority was "to build them huts at the sites of the stations at which they are working to accommodate them at night with their families." Order of 23 Sha'ban 1280h (Feb. 2, 1864), in Sami, *Taqwim al-nil*, 3:127.

61. See Mitchell, *Colonising Egypt*, 44; on Arthur D. Little, see chapter 1.

62. Hekekyan, "Journals 1851–54" (British Library Add Ms. 37452, vol. 4), folio 355 recto and verso. I am grateful to Kenneth Cuno for bringing this material to my attention.

63. Lozach and Hug, *L'Habitat rural,* 156–59. The word *ʿizba* originally referred to the temporary straw huts built by cultivators to provide seasonal shelter in the fields for those working at a distance from the village. In the early 1860s official documents refer to *ʿizba*s in terms suggesting that they were already found quite widely—and that their isolation on the new estates represented a particular problem of security. Departing for Istanbul just after assuming power in January 1863, Ismaʿil sent orders by telegraph to all his provincial officials instructing them to look after the well-being and security of the inhabitants of all towns and villages, "and especially the inhabitants of the *ʿizba*s isolated from them." Sami, *Taqwim al-nil,* 3:463.

64. Reem Saad Mikhail, "Peasant Perceptions of Recent Egyptian History" (D. Phil. thesis, University of Oxford, 1994), 62.

65. Lozach and Hug, *L'Habitat rural,* 159.

66. Joseph F. Nahas, *Situation économique et sociale du fellah égyptien* (Paris: Arthur Rousseau, 1901), 141.

67. Jean Lozach, *Le Delta du Nil: Etude de géographie humaine* (Cairo: Société Royale de Géographie d'Egypte, 1935), 205.

68. This critique of law was elaborated in the United States in the 1920s and 1930s by the legal realist school. Morris R. Cohen, "Property and Sovereignty," *Cornell Law Quarterly* 13, no. 1 (1927), 8–30 and Elizabeth Mensch, "A History of Mainstream Legal Thought," in *The Politics of Law,* ed. David Kairys (New York: Pantheon, 1990), 13–37. My discussion of the exceptional forms of colonial sovereignty is indebted to Esmain, "Colonies of Legalities."

69. Baer, *History of Landownership,* 20.

70. Rifaʿa Rafiʿ al-Tahtawi, *al-Aʿmal al-kamila,* ed. Muhammad al-ʿImara (Beirut: Al-Muʾassasa al-ʿArabiyya li-ʾl-Dirasat wa-ʾl-Nashr, 1973–78), vol. 1, *al-Tamaddun wa-ʾl-hadara wa-ʾl-ʿumran,* 316; quoted in Cole, *Colonialism and Revolution,* 57.

71. Alan Richards, *Egypt's Agricultural Development 1800–1980: Technical and Social Change* (Boulder, Colo.: Westview Press, 1982), 58–69. On the mobile workforces see James Toth, *Rural Labor Movements in Egypt and Their Impact on the State, 1961–1992* (Gainesville: University Press of Florida, 1999), 25–98.

72. Roger Owen, "The Development of Agricultural Production in Nineteenth-Century Egypt: Capitalism of What Type?" in *The Islamic Middle East 700–1900: Studies in Economic and Social History,* ed. A. L. Udovitch (Princeton, N.J.: Darwin Press, 1981), 521–46, at 523, 543.

73. Egyptian Government Press, *Index to Place Names* (Cairo: Egyptian Government Press, 1932), cited in Henry Habib Ayrout, *Fellahs* (Cairo: Editions Horus, 1942), 111, n. 1. Of 14,166 place names in Egypt, 7,800 carried the prefix *ʿizba.* This was less than the total number of estates, as many *ʿizba*s did not have the status of separate villages or hamlets.

74. Some estates were created informally by powerful local households through the purchase of village land. Since they were not granted by the ruling family, such properties would continue to be counted as village land in the tax

registers (Owen, "Development of Agricultural Production," 147–48). But even property acquired by the ruling family and its officials might continue to be registered as village land. For example, on January 12, 1864, Isma'il transferred to his son Ibrahim Pasha two thousand acres he controlled in the Delta villages of Kafr al-Batikh, Kafr Sulayman al-Bahri, and Suwalim, together with "all their stores, equipment and supplies." The order he issued to the administrator of his estates indicates that more than three-quarters of the land was classified as village (*athariyya*) land and less than one-quarter as estate (*'ushr*) land. Khedival order of 2 Sha'ban 1280h (Jan. 12, 1864), in Sami, *Taqwim al-nil,* 3:533.

75. In many cases the seizure of village land was constructed as a "sale," in which the cultivator exchanged his land for an equivalent plot elsewhere. In practice the cultivator was never given the alternative plot, or was allocated land in a different part of the country, or found the new plot already cultivated by others. 'Ali Barakat, *Tatawwur al-milkiyya al-zira'iyya fi misr wa-atharuhu 'ala al-haraka al-siyasiyya* (Cairo: Dar al-Thaqafa al-Jadida, 1977), 287–91.

76. Barakat, *Tatawwur al-milkiyya al-zira'iyya,* 297. Most estates were created from village land that was not registered as tax-paying, categorized either as untaxed (*ib'adiyya*), abandoned (*matruka*), or additional to the area surveyed (*ziyadat al-misaha*). However, none of these taxation categories necessarily implied that the land was uncultivated.

77. Villiers Stuart, *Egypt after the War,* 34–35.

78. Sami, *Taqwim al-nil,* 3:623; Nahas, *Fellah Egyptien,* 134–43. For analyses of the *'izba* system see Ra'uf 'Abbas Hamid, *Al-nizam al-ijtima'i fi misr fi zill al-milkiyyat al-zira'iyya al-kabira* (Cairo: Dar al-Fikr al-Hadith, 1973), 174–89; Owen, "Development of Agricultural Production," 524–25; and Richards, *Egypt's Agricultural Development,* 62–64.

79. The courts also administered legal relations between foreigners of different nationalities. On the history of the Mixed Courts see Jasper Yeates Brinton, *The Mixed Courts of Egypt,* 2nd ed. (New Haven, Conn.: Yale University Press, 1968), and the discussion in Esmair, "Colonies of Legalities."

80. Jacques Berque, *Egypt: Imperialism and Revolution,* trans. Jean Stewart (New York: Praeger, 1971), 130.

81. Villiers Stuart, *Egypt after the War,* 157.

82. The Earl of Cromer, *Modern Egypt,* 2 vols. (New York: Macmillan, 1908), 2:707.

83. On the broader social origins of the 'Urabi movement, as it is known, named after its leader Ahmad 'Urabi, see Cole, *Colonialism and Revolution in the Middle East.*

84. Five separate European bodies controlled Egyptian finances after 1876: the Public Debt Commission controlled the revenue from provincial government taxes, the local customs duties (*octrois*) of Cairo and Alexandria, the foreign customs of Egyptian ports other than Alexandria, and the salt and tobacco taxes, among others; the Railway and Port Commission controlled the revenues of the Egyptian railways and the port of Alexandria; the Khedive's es-

tates (the Da'ira Saniya, or Sanieh), mostly sugarcane plantations in the south, were managed by the Da'ira Sanieh Administration; and from 1878 other Khedival estates, transferred to the state and renamed state domain, were administered by the Dominial Commission. Each of these bodies took the entire revenue under their control to service a different group of bank loans. Revenue from any other source went to the Egyptian government, but even so remained under foreign supervision: two controllers, one French and one English, directed all government revenue and expenditure. For an account of these arrangements see Herbert Feis, *Europe: The World's Banker, 1870–1914: An Account of European Foreign Investment and the Connection of World Finance with Diplomacy Before the War* (New Haven, Conn.: Yale University Press, 1930, reprint ed. Clifton, N.J.: Augustus M. Kelley, 1974), 382–97.

85. Cuno, *The Pasha's Peasants;* Owen, "Development of Agricultural Production."

86. On the question of the state, see Timothy Mitchell, "Society, Economy, and the State Effect," in *State/Culture: State-Formation After the Cultural Turn,* ed. George Steinmetz (Ithaca, N.Y.: Cornell University Press, 1999), 76–97.

87. Barakat, *Tatawwur al-milkiyya al-zira'iyya,* 283–366; Hunter, *Egypt Under the Khedives,* 69.

88. They could acquire only government land sold by public auction. Khedival order of 24 Jumada al-ula 1281h (Oct. 25, 1864), in Sami, *Taqwim al-nil,* 3:576.

89. Holders of an *'uhda,* that is, were forbidden to purchase *atyan kharajiyya.* Sami, *Taqwim al-nil,* 3:629.

90. Hunter, *Egypt Under the Khedives,* 68–69.

91. Sami, *Taqwim al-Nil,* 3:520.

92. Baer, *History of Landownership,* 41.

93. Under Isma'il's predecessors some of the family's lands had been taken over and managed by the provincial governors. On coming to office Isma'il issued orders to separate these areas from the provincial administration and divided them into estates for his dependents. Khedival order of 13 Shawwal 1279h (Apr. 2, 1863), in Sami, *Taqwim al-nil,* 3:469.

94. Hunter, *Egypt Under the Khedives,* 65.

95. Ibid., 66.

96. The domains were known collectively as *al-da'ira al-'amma* or *al-saniyya* (the general or viceregal domain). Isma'il's own estates were called *al-da'ira al-khassa.* Khedival order of 26 Dhu al-Hijja, 1281h (May 22, 1865), in Sami, *Taqwim al-nil,* 3:615.

97. Mitchell, *Colonising Egypt.*

98. Henri Lefebvre, *The Production of Space,* trans. Donald Nicholson-Smith (Oxford: Blackwell, 1991), 26, 46–53. For a further discussion of the question of space, see my essay "The Stage of Modernity," in *Questions of Modernity,* ed. Timothy Mitchell (Minneapolis: University of Minnesota Press, 2000).

CHAPTER 3. THE CHARACTER OF CALCULABILITY

1. Georg Simmel, "Die Grossstadt und das Geistesleben," in *Die Grossstadt,* Vorträge und Aufsätz zur Städteausstellung, ed. K. Bücher et al., Gehe-Stiftung zu Dresden, Winter 1902–3, *Jahrbuch der Gehe-Stiftung zu Dresden,* vol. 9 (Dresden: von Zahn & Jaensch, 1903). English translation, "The Metropolis and Mental Life," trans. Edward A. Shils, in *Second-Year Course in the Study of Contemporary Society (Social Science II): Syllabus and Selected Readings,* 5th edition, ed. Harry D. Gideonse et al. (Chicago: University of Chicago Press, 1936), 221–38, quotations from 194.

2. Simmel, "The Metropolis and Mental Life," trans. Shils, 196.

3. Ibid.

4. The translation, by Hans Gerth and C. Wright Mills, was appended to an English version of Simmel's *Soziologie.* Georg Simmel, *Soziologie, Untersuchungen über die Formen der Vergesellschaftung,* ed. Otthein Rammstedt, *Gesamtausgabe,* vol. 2 (Frankfurt: Suhrkamp, 1992, 1st ed. 1908). English translation, Kurt H. Wolff, *The Sociology of Georg Simmel* (New York: Free Press, 1950), including "The Metropolis and Mental Life," trans. H. H. Gerth with C. Wright Mills, 409–24.

5. Robert Palgrave, *Palgrave's Dictionary of Political Economy,* 2nd ed. (London: Macmillan, 1925–26), 6:678.

6. Simmel, "The Metropolis and Mental Life," trans. Gerth and Mills, 411.

7. See Timothy Mitchell, "Fixing the Economy," *Cultural Studies* 12, no. 1 (1998): 82–101, and "Society, Economy, and the State Effect," in *State/Culture: State Formation after the Cultural Turn,* ed. George Steinmetz (Ithaca, N.Y.: Cornell University Press, 1999), 76–97.

8. Simmel, "The Metropolis and Mental Life," trans. Gerth and Mills, 411, 412.

9. In *Economy and Society,* Weber defined the term "economy" as "autocephalous economic action," meaning action "concerned with the satisfaction of a desire for 'utilities.' " Parsons altered this definition in his translation to "an autocephalous *system* of economic action." Adding the word "system" made it seem that Weber was talking about the new conception of the economy as a self-contained structure or totality. Max Weber, *Wirtschaft und Gesellschaft: Grundriss der Verstehenden Soziologie,* 2 vols. in 1 (Tübingen: Mohr 1972), 31; and *The Theory of Economic and Social Organization,* ed. Talcott Parsons, trans. A. M. Henderson and Talcott Parsons (New York: Oxford University Press, 1947), 158, emphasis added. See Timothy Mitchell, "Origins and Limits of the Modern Idea of the Economy," Advanced Study Center, University of Michigan, *Working Papers Series* no. 12, Nov. 1995.

10. Karl Polanyi, *The Great Transformation: The Political and Economic Origins of Our Time* (Boston: Beacon Press, 1944); Keith Tribe, *Land, Labour, and Economic Discourse* (London: Routledge & Kegan Paul, 1978); Michel Foucault, "Governmentality," in Graham Burchell, Colin Gordon, and Peter Miller, eds., *The Foucault Effect: Studies in Governmentality* (Hemel Hempstead,

Herts: Harvester Wheatsheaf, 1991), 87–104; Susan Buck-Morss, "Envisioning Capital: Political Economy on Display," *Critical Inquiry* 21, no. 2 (1995): 434–67; Louis Dumont, *From Mandeville to Marx: The Genesis and Triumph of Economic Ideology* (Chicago: University of Chicago Press, 1977).

11. For an illuminating essay on List and his influence outside Europe, see Manu Goswami, "From *Swadeshi* to *Swaraj:* Nation, Economy, Territory in Colonial South Asia, 1870–1907," *Comparative Studies in Society and History* 40, no. 4 (1998): 609–36. I would qualify Goswami's argument by noting that List is using the word "economy" in the sense of government, or the proper management of wealth, not in its twentieth-century sense. Thus "national economy," which List uses interchangeably with "people's economy" and in contrast to "finance economy" (and without the definite article), is not an object or sphere to be managed but the process of governing a territory and its resources in the interests of its people, the nation. Friedrich List, *Das nationale System der politischen Oekonomie* (Stuttgart: Cotta, 1841), English translation, *National System of Political Economy,* trans. Sampson S. Lloyd (London: Longmans, Green, 1885; reprint ed. Fairfield, N.J.: A. M. Kelley, 1977).

12. See Mitchell, "Fixing the Economy."

13. In 1910, the second issue of *L'Egypte Contemporaine* published a review of Georges Blanchard, *Cours d'Economie politique,* a law school textbook that portrayed economics as a part of law, a discipline that was becoming more "realist" through the study of economic and social questions. *L'Egypte Contemporaine,* no. 2 (Mar. 1910), 360–62.

14. On the national character of Keynesian theory, see Hugo Radice, "The National Economy: A Keynesian Myth?" *Capital and Class,* no. 22 (Spring 1984): 111–40.

15. John Maynard Keynes, *Indian Currency and Finance* (London: Macmillan, 1913).

16. The Egyptian University opened on December 21, 1908, occupying a rented mansion that had belonged to a Greek cigarette magnate, Nestor Gianaclis. The mansion later housed the American University in Cairo. See Donald M. Reid, *Cairo University and the Making of a Modern Egypt* (Cambridge: Cambridge University Press, 1990), 31.

17. *L'Egypte Contemporaine,* no. 1 (Jan. 1910), 2.

18. Germain Martin, "Rapport sur l'organisation des travaux de la Société," *L'Egypte Contemporaine,* no. 1 (Jan. 1910), 17–33, at 19.

19. David Ricardo, "An Essay on the Influence of a Low Price of Corn on the Profits of Stock" [1815], in *The Works and Correspondence of David Ricardo,* ed. Piero Sraffa, vol. 4, *Pamphlets and Papers, 1815–1823,* published for the Royal Economic Society (Cambridge: Cambridge University Press, 1951), 9–41; *On the Principles of Political Economy, and Taxation* (London: John Murray, 1817).

20. H. G. Lyons, *The Cadastral Survey of Egypt 1892–1907* (Cairo: Ministry of Finance, Survey Dept., 1908).

21. Jacques Fresco, "Histoire et organisation de la statistique officielle en Egypte," *L'Egypte Contemporaine* 31, nos. 191–92 (1940), 339–91. Two impor-

tant essays on the history of the census, and statistical work in general, in Egypt are François Ireton, "Eléments pour une sociologie de la production statistique en Egypte," *Peuples méditerranéens,* nos. 54–55 (Jan./June 1991): 53–92, and Roger Owen, "The Population Census of 1917 and its Relationship to Egypt's Three Nineteenth-Century Statistical Regimes," *Journal of Historical Sociology* 9, no. 4 (1996): 457–72.

22. The smallest plot "commonly met with," according to the director of the survey, was about 4 *sahm,* or just under 30 square meters (1 acre, or *feddan,* is divided into 24 *qirats,* and the *qirat* is in turn divided into 24 *sahm,* so 4 *sahm* is 1/144 of an acre). Lyons, *Cadastral Survey,* 349.

23. Ibid., 365–66.

24. For an excellent discussion of the problems of the land survey in Britain, see Alain Pottage, "The Measure of Land," *The Modern Law Review* 57, no. 3 (1994): 361–84. Two important studies of British colonial mapping are: J. H. Andrews, *A Paper Landscape: The Ordnance Survey in Nineteenth-Century Ireland* (Oxford: Clarendon Press, 1975), and Mathew Edney, *Mapping an Empire: The Geographical Construction of British India, 1765–1843* (Chicago: University of Chicago Press, 1997).

25. Stanford J. Shaw, *The Financial and Administrative Organization and Development of Ottoman Egypt, 1517–1798* (Princeton, N.J.: Princeton University Press, 1962), 16–19; Anne Godlewska, "Napoleon's Geographers (1797–1815): Imperialists and Soldiers of Modernity," in *Geography and Empire,* ed. Anne Godlewska and Neil Smith (Oxford: Blackwell, 1994), 31–53.

26. Charles Edmond, *L'Egypte à l'Exposition Universelle de 1867* (Paris: Dentu, 1867), 227–31, 334–35.

27. The published maps portrayed the provinces of Qalyubiyya, Minufiyya, and Gharbiyya at 1:100,000 and the other Delta provinces at 1:200,000. Lyons, *Cadastral Survey,* 69–74.

28. Lyons, *Cadastral Survey,* 77–101. On the cholera epidemic see Sa'id Isma'il 'Ali, *Al-Mujtama' al-misri fi 'ahd al-ihtilal al-biritani* (Cairo: Anglo-Egyptian Bookshop, 1972), 217.

29. Theodolites were introduced in 1885, but there was no systematic use of triangulation until the 1898–1907 survey. Lyons, *Cadastral Survey,* 193.

30. E. H. H., Review of *The Cadastral Survey of Egypt, The Geographical Journal* 34, no. 5 (1909): 564–65.

31. Lyons, *Cadastral Survey,* 179.

32. Ibid., 179–80.

33. Ibid., 180.

34. E. H. H., Review of *The Cadastral Survey of Egypt,* 564–65.

35. I have borrowed the phrase from J. H. Andrews, *A Paper Landscape.*

36. Lyons, *Cadastral Survey,* 347–53.

37. Ibid., 77.

38. Ibid.

39. Ibid., 345.

40. Lyons, a British army engineer, first came to attention in 1895 when he was given the task of surveying and underpinning the Temple of Philae, which the building of the Aswan Dam left partially submerged. He later directed the Archaeological Survey of Nubia, which mapped the sites to be submerged by the subsequent raising of the dam. "Colonel Sir Henry Lyons, F.R.S.," *Empire Survey Review,* no. 55 (Jan. 1945): 38–40. On the dam, see chapter 1, above.

41. On the significance of these acts of removal or separation, see Timothy Mitchell, *Colonising Egypt* (Berkeley: University of California Press, 1991), chap. 1, and Bruno Latour, "Circulating Reference," in *Pandora's Hope: Essays on the Reality of Science Studies* (Cambridge, Mass.: Harvard University Press, 1999), 24–79.

42. Originally extending to 426,000 acres, by 1913 the state domains were reduced to 149,000 acres. Gouvernement d'Egypte, Ministère des Finances, Département de la Statistique Générale, *L'Annuaire Statistique 1914* (Cairo: Imprimerie Nationale, 1915), 34.

43. It is worth adding here that, as privately owned villages, the hamlets on the new estates were usually run as part of the business enterprise of the estate. There was typically a supervisor (*nazir*), accountant (*katib*), and labor supplier (*khuli*) running a meticulous system of management based on bookkeeping (Malak D. Rouchdy, "Change and Continuity in the Village of Batra: Family Strategies," in *Directions of Change in Rural Egypt,* ed. Nicholas S. Hopkins and Kirsten Westergaard [Cairo: American University in Cairo Press, 1998], 237–55, at 245.) So besides fixing and mapping the countryside, the new system of private estates organized rural life as a system of "income" and "expenditures" and represented it in this way in its books. The much larger khedival estates were managed by the European bankers to whom they were mortgaged using similar methods. Thus in much of the countryside the daily life of the village was run according to principles of annual accounting and management that were soon to provide a new way of organizing the political process of the country as a whole.

44. E. R. J. Owen, *Cotton and the Egyptian Economy, 1820–1914: A Study in Trade and Development* (Oxford: Oxford University Press, 1969), 217–19.

45. Ricardo, "An Essay on the Influence of a Low Price of Corn" and *On the Principles of Political Economy, and Taxation.*

46. The figures cover grain, meat, dairy produce, and wool. Leland Hamilton Jenks, *The Migration of British Capital to 1875* (London: Alfred A. Knopf, 1927), 329.

47. W. Stanley Jevons, *The Theory of Political Economy* (London: Macmillan, 1871); Karl Menger, *Grundsätze der Volkswirthschaftslehre* (Vienna: W. Braumüller, 1871), English translation *Principles of Economics,* trans. and ed. James Dingwall and Bert F. Hoselitz (New York: New York University Press, 1976); Leon Walras, *Eléments d'économie politique pure, ou, Théorie de la richesse sociale,* 1 vol. in 2 (Lausanne: L. Corbaz, 1874–77).

48. Jacques Lumbroso, "Le coton: son influence sur la prospérité générale de l'Egypte," *L'Egypte Contemporaine,* no. 2 (Mar. 1910), 257–76, at 257.

49. Gouvernement d'Egypte, Ministère des Finances, Département de la Statistique Générale, *L'Annuaire Statistique 1912* (Cairo: Imprimerie Nationale, 1913), 526–27.

50. The Companies Acts of 1855 and 1862 eliminated the need for an act of Parliament to establish limited liability companies in Britain. Jonathan Barron Baskin and Paul J. Miranti Jr., *A History of Corporate Finance* (Cambridge: Cambridge University Press, 1997), 127–45.

51. Simmel, "The Metropolis and the Mental Life," trans. Gerth and Mills, 421–22.

52. See Mitchell, *Colonising Egypt.*

53. Georges Vaucher, "La Livre égyptienne, de sa création par Mohamed Aly à ses récentes modifications," *L'Egypte Contemporaine* 41, no. 256 (Jan. 1950), 115–46, at 126–8; Keynes, *Indian Currency and Finance*, 50.

54. Vaucher, "La Livre égyptienne," 128–30. E£ is the abbreviation for the Egyptian pound.

55. Gouvernement d'Egypte, *L'Annuaire Statistique 1914*, xxxvi.

56. Gouvernement d'Egypte, Ministère des Finances, Département de la Statistique Générale, *L'Annuaire Statistique 1915* (Cairo: Imprimerie Nationale, 1916), xxxi.

57. *L'Egypte Contemporaine*, no. 2 (Mar. 1910), 683.

58. See Mitchell, *Colonising Egypt.*

59. E. de Regny, *Statistique de l'Egypte d'après des documents officiels* (Alexandria, 1870–72). See Fresco, "La Statistique officielle en Egypte," 346.

60. *L'Egypte Contemporaine* 35, no. 218/19 (1944), 365.

61. In 1941 the National Institute of Economic and Social Research in London set up an inquiry into techniques of national income accounting, or social accounting as it was briefly called before the invention of the term "gross national product," in colonial territories. Phyllis Deane organized the study and published an interim report in 1948, *The Measurement of Colonial National Incomes*, National Institute of Economic and Social Research Occasional Paper XII (Cambridge University Press, 1948), and a final study five years later, *Colonial Social Accounting*, National Institute of Economic and Social Research, Economic and Social Studies No. 11 (Cambridge University Press, 1953; reprint ed., Hamden, Conn.: Archon Books, 1973).

62. Mahmoud Anise, *A Study of the National Income of Egypt*, monograph, published as *L'Egypte Contemporaine*, no. 261/262 (Cairo: Société Fouad 1er d'Économie Politique, de Statistique et de Législation, 1950), 736. Anise drew on the work of Phyllis Deane (see previous note), as well as James Meade and Richard Strue, *National Income and Expenditure*, 2d ed. (Cambridge: Bowes and Bowes, 1948).

63. Government of Egypt, Ministry of Finance, *Statistical Yearbook of Egypt for 1909* (Cairo: National Printing Office, 1910). After appearing in English the first year, the yearbook switched to French in 1910 and changed its title to *Annuaire Statistique.* From 1911 it appeared in French and Arabic.

64. Government of Egypt, Ministry of Finance, Survey Department, *A Report on the Work of the Survey Department in 1909* (Cairo: Ministry of Finance, 1909).

65. I. G. Lévi, "La réforme de la statistique officielle égyptienne," *L'Egypte Contemporaine* 15, no. 80 (1924), 412–42, at 423, cited in Ireton, "La production statistique en Egypte," 78.

66. *L'Egypte Contemporaine,* no. 1 (Jan. 1910), 2.

67. Ibid., no. 3 (July 1910), 682–83.

68. Arjun Appadurai argues that the production of official statistics in colonial India on a scale that defeated any unified bureaucratic program was "part of the illusion of bureaucratic control and a key to the colonial imaginary in which countable abstractions, of people and resources at every imaginable level and for every conceivable purpose, created the sense of a controllable indigenous reality." Arjun Appadurai, "Number in the Colonial Imagination," in *Modernity at Large: Cultural Dimensions of Globalization* (Minneapolis: University of Minnesota Press, 1997), 114–35.

69. Roger Owen makes this point in discussing the 1917 population census, whose publication was used to present statistical work as an essential part of modern government. "Population Census of 1917," 460. See also Owen, *Cotton and the Egyptian Economy,* 326–51, on British economic thinking on Egypt in the period before World War I.

70. Lumbroso, "Le coton," 257; Giuseppe Randone, "Preface," *Statistical Yearbook of Egypt for 1909* (Cairo: National Printing Office, 1910), vi; *L'Egypte Contemporaine,* no. 1 (Jan. 1910), 2.

71. Gouvernement d'Egypte, *L'Annuaire Statistique 1914,* 1.

72. *L'Egypte Contemporaine,* no. 1 (Jan. 1910), 20.

73. "Middle East Financial Conference Resolutions," *L'Egypte Contemporaine* 35, no. 218/19 (1944), 363–71, 363; "Résolutions de la Conférence Financière du Moyen-Orient," idem, 345–52, 345; and "Qirarat al-mu'tamar al-mali li-'l-sharq al-awsat," idem, 353–61, 354.

74. A. N. Cumberbatch, *Economic and Commercial Conditions in Egypt,* Overseas Economic Surveys, published for Commercial Relations and Exports Department of the Board of Trade (London: Her Majesty's Stationery Office, 1952), 2.

75. *Al-ahram al-iqtisadi,* Sept. 1952.

76. Lyons, *Cadastral Survey,* 370.

77. Ibid., 370.

78. Ibid., 355.

79. Ibid., 368.

80. Ibid., 199, 219.

81. Anise, *National Income of Egypt,* 736.

82. Ibid., 753–55.

83. Owen, *Cotton and the Egyptian Economy.*

84. E. M. Dowson and J. I. Craig, *Collection of Statistics of the Area Planted in Cotton in 1909* (Cairo: Survey Department, 1910).

85. The department was upgraded to a separate ministry two years later. Owen, *Cotton and the Egyptian Economy*, 346.

86. Simmel presented a fuller version of this argument in *Philosophie des geldes* (Leipzig: Duncker & Humbolt, 1900), English translation, *The Philosophy of Money* (London: Routledge and Kegan Paul, 1978).

87. Viviana A. Zelizer, *The Social Meaning of Money: Pin Money, Paychecks, Poor Relief and Other Currencies* (Princeton, N.J.: Princeton University Press, 1997).

88. Yacoub Artin, "Essai sur les causes du renchérissement de la vie matérielle au Caire dans le courant de xixe siècle (1800 à 1907)," *Mémoires présentés à l'Institut égyptien*, vol. 5 (1908), 58–140.

89. Fresco, "La Statistique officielle en Egypte," 388.

90. Luigi Bodio (1840–1910) became the head of the new Italian state's Direzione de Statistica in 1872 and later head of the International Statistical Institute. Silvana Patriarca, *Numbers and Nationhood* (Cambridge: Cambridge University Press, 1996), 233.

91. Edouard Papasian, "Les opérations du change, au point de vue de sa balance actuelle en Egypte," *L'Egypte Contemporaine*, no. 1 (Jan. 1910), 47–54.

92. A. L. Bowley, "The Definition of National Income," *Economic Journal* 32, no. 125 (1922), 1–11, at 3.

93. "L'Augmentation des revenus de l'état: possibilités et moyen d'y parvenir," *L'Egypte Contemporaine*, no. 68 (Dec. 1922), 596–617; Lévi also drew on the article by Bowley, and on A. C. Pigou's *Wealth and Welfare* (London: Macmillan, 1912).

94. James Baxter, "Notes on the Estimate of the National Income of Egypt for 1921–1922," *L'Egypte Contemporaine* 73 (May 1923), 405–27.

95. Germain Martin went on to a career in French politics and served as minister of finance or the budget in several prewar French governments. He was the brother of Louis Martin, director of the Institut Pasteur. *New York Times*, Oct. 7, 1943, quoted in Kristin Koptiuch, *A Poetics of Political Economy in Egypt* (Minneapolis: University of Minnesota Press, 1999), 84.

96. I. G. Lévi, "Le Recensement de la population de l'Egypte de 1917," *L'Egypte Contemporaine* 67 (Nov. 1922), 471–506, at 475–76, 481–83.

97. Ibid., 478–81.

98. Anise, *National Income of Egypt*, 663.

99. See here Talal Asad's discussion of statistics as a "strong language," in "Ethnographic Representation, Statistics and Modern Power," *Social Research* 61, no. 1 (1994): 55–88, at 78.

100. Lyons, *Cadastral Survey*, 296.

101. Ibid., 302.

102. Ibid., 303.

103. See in this respect the work of Michel Callon, ed., *The Laws of the Markets* (Oxford: Blackwell, 1998).

104. Germain Martin and I. G. Lévi, "Le Marché égyptien et l'utilité de la publication des mercuriales," *L'Egypte Contemporaine,* no. 3 (July 1910), 441–89, at 441.

105. Karl Polanyi, *The Great Transformation: The Political and Economic Origins of Our Time* (Boston: Beacon Press, 1944).

106. On the question of enframing, see Mitchell, *Colonising Egypt,* chap. 2, and the discussion in Michel Callon, "Introduction: The Embeddedness of Economic Markets in Economics," and "An Essay on Framing and Overflowing: Economic Externalities Revisited By Sociology," in *The Laws of the Markets,* 1–57, 244–69.

107. "Colonel Sir Henry Lyons, F.R.S.," *Empire Survey Review,* no. 55 (Jan. 1945): 38–40.

108. Sir Ernest Dowson and V. L. O. Sheppard, "Evolution of the Land Records," *Empire Survey Review,* no. 60 (1956): 202. Sheppard had worked with Dowson on the Egyptian survey, and they served together as members of a commission of inquiry in 1917–21 to propose measures to establish a uniform system of land registration, following the failure of the cadastral map to provide the accuracy that would enable it to serve as an authoritative register. *Empire Survey Review,* no. 56 (1945): 43. I am grateful to Munir Fakhr al-Din for bringing these articles to my attention.

CHAPTER 4. INVENTION AND REINVENTION OF THE PEASANT

1. George Foster, foreword to Richard Critchfield, *Shahhat: An Egyptian* (Syracuse, N.Y.: Syracuse University Press, 1978), ix, emphasis added.

2. Vivian Gornick, "Metaphor for Egypt," *New York Times Book Review,* Jan. 14, 1979, 12.

3. Pierre Gourou, *Les paysans du delta tonkinois: Etude de géographie humaine* (Paris: Mouton, 1936), 577; English translation, *The Peasants of the Tonkin Delta: A Study of Human Geography,* 1 vol. in 2 (New Haven, Conn.: Human Relations Area Files, 1955), 664.

4. Popular political movements in provincial Egypt, in particular the Muslim Brotherhood, were galvanized by the Palestine revolt. Their organizing and agitation in provincial towns and villages, as well as the main cities, culminated in mass demonstrations in the summer of 1938, which the authorities violently suppressed. Israel Gershoni, "The Muslim Brothers and the Arab Revolt in Palestine, 1936–39," *Middle Eastern Studies* 22, no. 3 (1986): 367–97.

5. Henry Habib Ayrout, *Moeurs et coutumes des fellahs,* Collection d'études, de documents et de témoignages pour servir a l'histoire de notre temps (Paris: Payot, 1938; reprint ed. New York: AMS Press, 1978), i, 12. In the United States in the same period, Robert Redfield's *Tepoztlán: A Mexican Village: A Study of Folk Life* (Chicago: University of Chicago Press, 1930) marked a shift in interest among anthropologists from "primitive" to "folk," or later "peasant," societies. The shift was in part a reaction to the 1919–20 Mexican revo-

lution, which had its origins in the resistance of Indian villages to the colonization of their land by Mexican sugar estates.

6. See James C. Scott, *The Moral Economy of the Peasant: Rebellion and Subsistence in Southeast Asia* (New Haven, Conn.: Yale University Press, 1976); Samuel Popkin, *The Rational Peasant: The Political Economy of Rural Society in Vietnam* (Berkeley: University of California Press, 1979).

7. The major editions of Ayrout's work are: Henry Habib Ayrout, *Moeurs et coutumes des fellahs* (Paris: Payot, 1938; reprinted New York: AMS Press, 1978); 2nd revised ed., entitled *Fellahs* (Cairo: Editions Horus, 1942); Arabic ed., *al-Fallahun,* trans. Muhammad Ghallab (Cairo: Matbaʿat al-Kawthar, 1943, 8th Arabic ed. 1968); English ed., *The Fellaheen,* trans. Hilary Wayment (Cairo: R. Schindler, 1945); Russian ed., *Fellakhi Yigipta* (Moscow: n.p., 1954); U.S. ed., *The Egyptian Peasant,* trans. John Alden Williams (Boston: Beacon Press, 1963). I have quoted mainly from the Wayment translation of 1945, as this is the version used by Critchfield. Further references to *The Fellaheen* are cited parenthetically in the text.

8. Bowles was removed from the State Department in November 1961 and made special representative of the president for African, Asian and Latin American affairs. He visited Cairo and met with President Nasser in February 1962. William J. Burns, *Economic Aid and American Policy Towards Egypt, 1955–81* (Albany: State University of New York Press, 1985), 131, 249.

9. Ayrout, *Egyptian Peasant,* xvi.

10. Ibid., v–vi.

11. Richard Critchfield, *Villages* (Garden City, N.Y.: Anchor Press / Doubleday, 1981, reprint ed. 1983), 64.

12. Richard Critchfield, *The Long Charade: Political Subversion in the Vietnam War* (New York: Harcourt, Brace & World, 1968), 208.

13. Critchfield, *Villages,* 66, emphasis added. The bulk of the short chapter on Vietnam in this book is repeated from *The Long Charade,* but quotations from the British military advisors in the first book are repeated in the second without quotation marks as Critchfield's own views.

14. Mohamed Heikel, *Autumn of Fury: The Assassination of Sadat* (New York: Random House, 1983), 8–10.

15. See John Waterbury, *The Egypt of Nasser and Sadat: The Political Economy of Two Regimes* (Princeton, N.J.: Princeton University Press, 1983), 261.

16. Robert Fernea, Review of Richard Critchfield, *Shahhat: An Egyptian, Middle East Journal* 33, no. 4 (1979): 506–7.

17. Critchfield, *Shahhat,* xiii–xiv. Further references to *Shahhat* are cited parenthetically in the text.

18. Fred H. Lawson, "Rural Revolt and Provincial Society in Egypt, 1820–1824," *International Journal of Middle East Studies* 13, no. 2 (1981): 131–53, at 146.

19. J. A. St. John, *Egypt and Nubia, Their Scenery and Their People* (London: Chapman and Hall, 1845), 378–86; Lawson, "Rural Revolt."

20. Critchfield seems to be well aware of the effects of this kind of imagery. One of his earlier studies of peasants is an account of a group of Arabic-speaking pastoral nomads in southwestern Iran, written during the regime of the Shah and told through the life of an individual named Yaʿqub, which Critchfield spells as Jacob. In his preface to the book's second edition, published by Indiana University Press in 1988, he explains that "I spelled Jacob the Biblical way to underscore its old testament quality"—for in those days "nobody mentioned Ayatollah Khomeini . . . and Islam, though a total way of life for Bedouins, seemed relatively benign." *The Golden Bowl Be Broken: Peasant Life in Four Cultures,* 2nd ed. (Bloomington: University of Indiana Press, 1988), ix.

21. Cf. Timothy Mitchell, *Colonising Egypt* (Berkeley: University of California Press, 1991), 21–32.

22. This is Critchfield's only acknowledgment of his debt to Ayrout, from whom the passage is lifted almost verbatim: "Under foreign domination for years and centuries at a time, by Persians, Greeks, Romans, Byzantines, Arabs, Turks, French and English," wrote Ayrout, " . . . the fellaheen have changed their masters, their religion, their language and their crops, but not their manner of life." Ayrout, *The Fellaheen,* 19.

23. Critchfield spells the name of the village as Berat.

24. Ayrout, *The Egyptian Peasant,* 13. The museum was opened in 1938, the same year Ayrout's book appeared and as part of the same new ethnographic interest in the peasantry.

25. See Mitchell, *Colonising Egypt,* 122–25.

26. Gustave Le Bon, *Les lois psychologiques de l'évolution des peuples* (Paris: Felix Alcan, 1898), English translation, *The Psychology of Peoples* (New York: Macmillan, 1898), 4–5, 13, 199–200.

27. Gardner Lindzey and Elliot Aronson, eds., *Handbook of Social Psychology,* 2nd ed. (Reading, Mass.: Addison-Wesley, 1968), 1:41.

28. Gustave Le Bon, *Psychologie des foules* (Paris: Felix Alcan, 1895), English translation, *The Crowd: A Study of the Popular Mind* (New York: Macmillan, 1896), 36.

29. Ayrout, *Moeurs et coutumes,* 132.

30. The father, Habib Ayrout, was a Paris-educated engineer-architect who participated in the planning and construction of the model suburb of Heliopolis. Fr. Ayrout's two brothers, Charles and Max, were also architects practicing in Cairo. Yvette Senn-Ayrout, personal communication, Mar. 23, 1993.

31. The peasant, Ayrout explained, "being of a childlike disposition, cannot be presented a model house without being taught, in a kindly way, the 'directions' which go with it. . . . This pedagogy is more important than the material realization" (*Egyptian Peasant,* 130). For a discussion of this relationship between effects of structure, individuality, and pedagogy in colonial practice, see Mitchell, *Colonising Egypt,* 44–48, 92–94. On the model villages see also chapters 2 and 6.

32. Ayrout, *Egyptian Peasant,* 19–20, 151.

33. There was also an active debate on these issues in the press. In *al-Ahram* on Feb. 17, 18, and 19, 1937, for example, Bint al-Shatiʾ (the pseudonym of

ʿA'isha ʿAbd al-Rahman), the author of *al-Rif al-misri* (Rural Egypt) (Cairo: Maktabat al-Wafd, 1936), described the evils of the cotton processing industry, explaining how twenty-five thousand children aged eight to fifteen were employed that year loading and unloading the ginning machines in cotton ginning and pressing factories, working amid stifling dust from 5 A.M. to 9 P.M. each day without a break (Ayrout, *The Fellaheen,* 63). The various Cairo editions of Ayrout also continued the debate. The French edition of 1943 had a preface by Fu'ad Abaza Pasha. The English-language edition published in Cairo in 1945 had a foreword by Muhammad Taher Pasha, a prominent landowner and businessman who was a member of the royal family and a member of parliament. Tahir praised Ayrout's "objectivity," and warned that at this "turning-point of its history" the country needed "a complete and intimate collaboration among all classes" based on "a particularly sympathetic understanding . . . of their peasantry by the upper class and landowners" (Ayrout, *The Fellaheen,* 5). On Tahir, see Eric Davis, *Challenging Colonialism: Bank Misr and Egyptian Industrialization, 1920–1941* (Princeton, N.J.: Princeton University Press, 1983), 141.

34. When Mirrit Butrus Ghali stopped opposing land reform and published a proposal in 1945 to halt the accumulation of land by large estates (to affect only future land purchases, not existing or inherited holdings), he argued for a limit of one hundred acres rather than fifty on the grounds that the lower limit would "restrict the initiative of the rural middle class, those rural notables who, in our opinion, have the vital task of infusing life into rural society." Quoted in Gabriel Baer, *A History of Landownership in Modern Egypt, 1800–1950* (Oxford: Oxford University Press, 1962), 212.

35. The quotations in this and the following paragraph come from the back cover of the paperback edition of the book, except where noted otherwise.

36. Ibrahim ʿAmir, *al-Ard wa-'l-fallah: al-mas'ala al-ziraʿiyya fi misr* (Cairo: Matbaʿat al-Dar al-Misriyya, 1958). Jacques Berque, "Sur la structure de quelques villages égyptiens," *Annales: Economie, Société, Civilisations* 10, no. 2 (1955): 199–215; and *Histoire sociale d'un village égyptien au xx*ème *siècle* (Paris: Mouton, 1957). Berque was the first writer to describe analytically the social transformations brought by irrigation work, industrial crops, and private ownership in the nineteenth century, relying largely on information from ʿAli Mubarak, *Al-khitat al-tawfiqiya li-misr al-qahira wa-muduniha wa-biladiha al-qadima wa-'l-shahira* (Cairo: al-Matbaʿa al-Kubra al-Amiriyya, 1886–88).

37. Ayrout's claim, echoing Le Bon, that the Egyptian village "is not a community in the social sense, not an organism, but a mass" was the main evidence used by Gabriel Baer, an Israeli scholar who for a generation became a leading authority on the modern history of rural Egypt, to argue that by the nineteenth century the Egyptian village no longer existed as a corporate community. "The Dissolution of the Egyptian Village Community," in *Studies in the Social History of Modern Egypt* (Chicago: University of Chicago Press, 1969), 17–29. Cf. Haim Gerber, *The Social Origins of the Modern Middle East* (Boulder, Colo.: Lynne Rienner, 1987), 145.

38. Morroe Berger, *The Arab World Today* (Garden City, N.Y.: Doubleday, 1962), 154–55, 158, 171.

39. Ayrout, *al-Fallahun* (1968), 7.

40. Ayrout, *The Egyptian Peasant,* 18; cf. Gabriel Baer, "Submissiveness and the Revolt of the Fellah," in *Studies in the Social History of Modern Egypt* (Chicago: University of Chicago Press, 1969), 93–108, at 102.

41. This is one of numerous passages where Ayrout repeats things from earlier European sources. Lord Kitchener, British agent and consul general in Egypt from 1911 to 1914, who no doubt read many of the same sources, reported to the Foreign Office in 1912 that in rural Egypt, "Human life appears to be of little account and the most trifling incidents result in homicide. . . . Such crimes aris[e] from sudden quarrels, family feuds or revenge." Public Record Office, London, PRO/FO/30/57/9, Kitchener to Grey, 1912, quoted in Martina Rieker, "The Sa'id and the City: Subaltern Spaces in the Making of Modern Egyptian History" (Ph.D. diss., Temple University, 1997), 168.

42. When the villagers have had enough of all the violence, there remains the possibility of *kayf,* "a word of profound significance" according to Ayrout. He says it denotes "a kind of wakeful passivity which means doing nothing, saying nothing, thinking nothing" (136). Critchfield explains that "in Egypt there is a mental state called *kaif,* when a man does nothing, says nothing, and thinks nothing. It is a kind of wakeful passivity" (183).

43. See Edward Said, *Orientalism* (New York: Pantheon, 1978), 160–64; Mitchell, *Colonising Egypt,* 26–27.

44. Boutros Wadieh, personal communication.

45. M. Yaşar Işcan, Review of Critchfield, *Shahhat: An Egyptian, American Anthropologist* 82, no. 4 (1980): 961; Sam Beck, Review of Critchfield, *Shahhat: An Egyptian, Journal of American Folklore* 93, no. 370 (1980): 487–88; John G. Kennedy, Review of Critchfield, *Shahhat: An Egyptian, American Ethnologist* 7, no. 1 (1980): 220–21.

46. Critchfield, *Villages,* vii.

47. The book was first published in 1973. The press's catalogue recommended the book for use in university courses and included an endorsement from *The Annals of the American Academy of Political Science.*

48. Winifred S. Blackman, *The Fellahin of Upper Egypt: Their Religious, Social and Industrial Life Today with Special Reference to Survivals from Ancient Times* (London: G. G. Harrap, 1927).

49. Yvette Senn-Ayrout, personal communication, Mar. 19, 1993; Janette De Bono-Ayrout, personal communication, June 1993; "Biography du P. Ayrout," *Le Messager* (Alexandria), Apr. 9, 1989.

50. *Newsletter of the American Research Center in Egypt* (Cairo), no. 142, summer 1988.

51. "Biography du P. Ayrout."

52. See Richard Critchfield, "A Response to 'The Invention and Reinvention of the Egyptian Peasant,' " and Timothy Mitchell, "A Reply to Richard Critchfield," *International Journal of Middle Eastern Studies* 23, no. 2 (1991):

277–80, from where I have drawn material in this and the following paragraph.

53. A photograph taken in the 1870s shows the site of Shahhat's hamlet, Kom Lolah, to consist entirely of fields, with no houses yet built. A photo taken circa 1930 shows at most one or two houses. See Deborah Bull, *Up the Nile: A Photographic Excursion, Egypt 1839–98* (New York: C. N. Potter, 1979), 88; James Henry Breasted, *The Oriental Institute of the University of Chicago,* The University of Chicago Survey, vol. 12 (Chicago: University of Chicago Press, 1933), fig. 97.

54. Wilbour (1833–96), an American businessman, studied archaeology under Maspero, the French head of the Egyptian antiquities service, in Paris and Berlin, and spent the last twenty years of his life in Egypt and France. Khalifa, who farmed ten acres of land, was his host and general agent in the area, and supplied him with donkeys to get around and other needs. Charles Edwin Wilbour, *Travels in Egypt (December 1880 to May 1891): Letters of Charles Edwin Wilbour,* ed. Jean Capart (New York: Brooklyn Museum, 1936), 58. I am grateful to Caroline Simpson for this reference.

55. Richard Critchfield, *The Villagers. Changed Values, Altered Lives: The Closing of the Urban-Rural Gap* (New York: Anchor Books / Doubleday, 1994).

56. See "An Interview with James Critchfield," in *The Survival of Saddam,* at http://www.pbs.org/wgbh/pages/frontline/shows/saddam/interviews /critchfield.html.

57. Thomas Powers, "Strategic Intelligence: Part One, An Isolated Man," the *Atlantic Monthly,* Apr. 1979. See also the hearings and report of the Senate Select Committee to Study Governmental Operations with Respect to Intelligence Activities (the Church Committee), 1976. James Akins, an attaché at the U.S. Embassy in Baghdad at the time, recalled U.S. support for the Baʿth as follows: "The Baʿath Party had come to control. We were very happy. They got rid of a lot of communists. A lot of them were executed, or shot. This was a great development." In "The Survival of Saddam: An Interview with James Akins," PBS/Frontline, at http://www.pbs.org/wgbh/pages/frontline/shows/saddam /interviews/akins.html.

58. Powers, "Strategic Intelligence."

59. Melinda Liu, "When Heaven Shed Blood," *Newsweek,* international edition, Apr. 19, 1999. The CIA operation was launched in March 1959, following the Dalai Lama's flight from Tibet.

60. Ibid.

61. In November 1973, when details began to emerge about the extent of the CIA's involvement in U.S. politics, the initial revelations concerned the CIA's use of American journalists. The first newspaper singled out for employing members of the CIA was the *Washington Star.* See Daniel Brandt, "Journalism and the CIA: The Mighty Wurlitzer," *NameBase NewsLine,* no. 17, Apr.–June 1997, at http://www.pir.org/news17.html; Carl Bernstein, "The CIA and the Media," *Rolling Stone,* Oct. 20, 1977, 65–67; and the series of articles

in the *New York Times:* John M. Crewdson and Joseph B. Treaster, "The CIA's 3-Decade Effort to Mold the World's Views," *New York Times,* Dec. 25, 1977, 1, 12; Terrence Smith, "CIA Contacts With Reporters," *New York Times,* Dec. 25, 1977, 13; Crewdson and Treaster, "Worldwide Propaganda Network Built by the CIA," *New York Times,* Dec. 26, 1977, 1, 37; Crewdson and Treaster, "CIA Established Many Links to Journalists in U.S. and Abroad," *New York Times,* Dec. 27, 1977, 1, 40–41.

62. The executive secretary of the Alicia Patterson Fund was Richard H. Nolte, a former Rhodes Scholar in Arabic Studies who, with no previous diplomatic experience, had been appointed U.S. Ambassador to Egypt in April 1967 in the midst of the crisis leading to the Six Day War (he was forced to abandon the post a month later, after Egypt and the U.S. broke diplomatic ties). Nolte had previously been a Middle East Associate of the American Universities Field Staff.

63. In November 2000 in a case brought by the Chagos Islanders, the High Court in London declared that their deportation had been illegal and ordered the British government to allow them to return home and pay them compensation. When the facts of the deportation first emerged, the U.S. and British governments had fabricated a story that the islanders were merely migrant workers from Mauritius with no indigenous rights. The United States continued to oppose their right of return. Ewan MacAskill, "Evicted Islanders to Go Home," the *Guardian,* Nov. 4, 2000, 1, 3. For details of the secret history see *Hansard* 208 (May 18–June 5, 1992), Oral Questions and Debates, June 4, 1992, columns 1010–12, at http://www.parliament.the-stationery-office.co.uk/pa/cm/cmhansrd.htm; and Ewan MacAskill and Rob Evans, "Thirty Years of Lies, Deceit and Trickery that Robbed a People of their Island Home," *Guardian,* Nov. 4, 2000, 3.

64. The other villages Critchfield wrote about were in the Philippines, South Korea, India, and Mexico. After receiving his MacArthur prize, however, he abandoned the Third World peasant and turned to studies of life in the rural United States and in Britain. He conducted his last study in a village on the Polish borderlands with Russia, just as the Soviet Union began its collapse.

65. *Al-Ahram al-iqtisadi,* Oct. 4, 1982. The series of articles was published in *al-Ahram al-iqtisadi* in October and November 1982. Several important criticisms were made in these and other articles, drawing attention to the way Egyptian scholars and scientific centers had been co-opted into consultancy work or joint research projects under American auspices, in which the goals, methods, and assumptions of the analysis were determined by the agenda of American development policy, and pointing out how the bulk of the fees and the credit for such joint research were earned by the Americans, even in the frequent cases in which most of the research was done by Egyptians and the foreigner did little more than correct the English of the final draft. However, some authors also called for the Egyptian state to become more directly involved in the control and direction of research, for CAPMAS (the Central Agency for Public Mobilization and Statistics) to reassert its power to license all research projects in the country, and even for the prosecutor general and the

state security services to enforce more strictly a 1960 law providing six-month prison sentences for those disclosing state information on national planning, food consumption, and trade (*al-Ahram al-iqtisadi,* Nov. 8, 1982).

66. "Hukumat zill amrikiyya bi-ʾl-qahira," *al-Ahram al-Iqtisadi,* Oct. 11, 1982, 11–14.

67. The Egyptian state security forces arrested Saʿd Eddin Ibrahim on July 1, 2000, and charged him with spreading "false reports" about Egypt and "tarnishing Egypt's image abroad." The case was tried before a state security court, whose verdicts could only be appealed through the Court of Cassation and then only on procedural grounds and not on the substance of the case. Ibrahim had been organizing an attempt to monitor the legality of the Egyptian parliamentary elections of November 2000. *Middle East Times,* Jan. 26, 2001, at http://www.metimes.com/2K1/issue2001–4, and May 18, 2001, at http://www.metimes.com/2K1/issue2001–21.

68. Frances Stonor Saunders, *The Cultural Cold War: The CIA and the World of Arts and Letters* (New York: New Press, 1999), originally published as *Who Paid the Piper: The CIA and the Cultural Cold War* (London: Granta Books, 1999).

69. Saunders, *The Cultural Cold War,* 334.

70. Alan M. Wald, *The New York Intellectuals: The Rise and Decline of the Anti-Stalinist Left from the 1930s to the 1980s* (Chapel Hill: University of North Carolina Press, 1987), 311–21.

71. Personal communication from Ibrahim Abu-Lughod, Aug. 3, 2000. Berger had attempted to recruit Abu-Lughod to edit the magazine. Berger did not reveal the source of the funds, but the amount of money on offer and the stipulation concerning the Soviet Union made Abu-Lughod immediately suspicious. When the facts about their involvement with the CIA emerged in the late 1960s, many of the American intellectuals who received funds from the CIA claimed that they had not realized who was paying them. Saunders, *The Cultural Cold War,* effectively refutes the claim.

CHAPTER 5. NOBODY LISTENS TO A POOR MAN

1. Two important studies of rural rebellion in Egypt are Nathan Brown, *Peasant Politics in Modern Egypt: The Struggle Against the State* (New Haven, Conn.: Yale University Press, 1990), and Reinhard Schulze, *Die Rebellion der ägyptischen Fallahin 1919* (Berlin: Baalbek Verlag, 1981). The study of rural rebellion was revived by postcolonial theory in the 1980s and 1990s following the influence of the work of Ranajit Guha, *Elementary Aspects of Peasant Insurgency in Colonial India* (Delhi: Oxford University Press, 1983) and the Subaltern Studies School. See *Selected Subaltern Studies,* ed. Ranajit Guha and Gayatri Chakravorty Spivak (New York: Oxford University Press, 1988), and *A Subaltern Studies Reader, 1986–1995,* ed. Ranajit Guha (Minneapolis: University of Minnesota Press, 1997). In the United States, from a different perspective, the work of James Scott, *Weapons of the Weak: Every-*

day Forms of Peasant Resistance (New Haven, Conn.: Yale University Press, 1985), was also influential. For a critical discussion of the latter see Timothy Mitchell, "Everyday Metaphors of Power," *Theory and Society* 19, no. 5 (1990): 545–77.

2. Michael T. Taussig, "Culture of Terror—Space of Death: Roger Casement's Putumayo Report and the Explanation of Torture," *Comparative Studies in Society and History* 26, no. 3 (1984): 467–97.

3. Hamied Ansari, *Egypt: The Stalled Society* (Albany: State University of New York Press, 1986).

4. The deliberations of the committee and further examples of the reports can be found in Muhammad Rashad, *Sirri jiddan: min milaffat al-lajna al-ʿulya li-tasfiyat al-iqtaʿ* (Top Secret: From the Dossiers of the Higher Committee for the Liquidation of Feudalism) (Cairo: Dar al-Taʿawun, 1977), 209–352.

5. Ansari, *Egypt: The Stalled Society*, Appendix D, 257–58.

6. Ibid., 258–59. For a discussion of what these reports tell us about the language of powerlessness among the poor, see Timothy Mitchell, "The Ear of Authority," *MERIP Middle East Report*, no. 147 (1987): 32–35, from which the preceding two paragraphs are drawn.

7. Ansari, *Egypt: The Stalled Society*, 258.

8. Rashad, *Sirri jiddan*, 311–13.

9. Ibid., 314–15.

10. Samir Radwan, *Agrarian Reform and Rural Poverty: Egypt, 1952–1975* (Geneva: International Labour Organization, 1977), 23. This estimate is corroborated by Radwan and Lee's detailed survey in 1977 of one thousand households in eighteen Egyptian villages. They found that only 36 percent of households owned land, and that even including those households with tenancy agreements the proportion with access to land was less than 50 percent. It is unclear what proportion of the remaining households were landless by choice, having access to other sources of income. But even if one counts as "landless" only the landless households living below the poverty line, as measured in the same survey, the total is still somewhere between 40 and 50 percent of rural households. Samir Radwan and Eddy Lee, *Agrarian Change in Egypt: An Anatomy of Rural Poverty* (London: Croom Helm, 1986), 48–49, 60–66.

11. Radwan, *Agrarian Reform and Rural Poverty*, 19. After 1965 the degree of inequality among landholders decreased, according to official figures, not through land reform but through subdivision: by 1978, the area of land registered in holdings of less than one acre had grown by about 10 percent, with the area in holdings of 10 or more acres decreasing by a similar amount. But the latter category still accounted for 20 percent of the total land area, controlled by just 2.3 percent of landholders. Mohaya A. Zaytoun, "Income Distribution in Egyptian Agriculture and its Main Determinants," in *The Political Economy of Income Distribution in Egypt*, ed. Gouda Abdel-Khalek and Robert Tignor (New York: Holmes and Meier, 1982), 268–306, at 277.

12. It should also be noted that the official figures exclude land an owner legally rents out, which is recorded under the name of the tenant. Nicholas

Hopkins, *Agrarian Transformation in Egypt* (Boulder, Colo.: Westview Press, 1987), 61. This may tend to reduce the size of large landownerships in the statistics.

13. Nicholas Hopkins, "The Social Impact of Mechanization," in *Migration, Mechanization, and Agricultural Labor Markets in Egypt*, ed. Alan Richards and Philip L. Martin (Boulder, Colo.: Westview Press, 1983), 181–97. Besides these two farms, Hopkins estimates that another five or six farmers in the village of Musha, near Asyut, were operating more than one hundred acres, and perhaps another dozen were operating more than fifty acres. Thus about twenty landowners, in a village of 2,500 households, controlled somewhere between a third and a half of the village's five thousand acres.

14. Simon Commander, *The State and Agricultural Development in Egypt Since 1973*, published for the Overseas Development Institute (London: Ithaca Press, 1987), 53–55.

15. Richard Adams, *Development and Social Change in Rural Egypt* (Syracuse, N.Y.: Syracuse University Press, 1986), 89. An extreme case of land reform evasion was the village of al-Barnugi, in Buhaira in the Egyptian Delta, where the Nawwar family was discovered in 1963 to still control twenty thousand acres. Iliya Harik, *The Political Mobilization of Peasants: A Study of an Egyptian Community* (Bloomington: Indiana University Press, 1974), 6.

16. Ansari, *Egypt: The Stalled Society*, 257.

17. Ibid., 259, translation modified.

18. Taussig, "Culture of Terror," 469.

19. Ansari, *Egypt: The Stalled Society*, 259.

20. Iliya Harik with Susan Randolph, *Distribution of Land, Employment and Income in Rural Egypt* (Ithaca, N.Y.: Rural Development Committee, Center for International Studies, Cornell University, 1979), 9–10; Iliya Harik, "Continuity and Change in Local Development Policies in Egypt: From Nasser to Sadat," *International Journal of Middle East Studies* 16, no. 1 (1984): 46–47.

21. This interpretation of the Higher Committee was made at the time by Lutfi al-Khuli and other intellectual critics of the regime. See Leonard Binder, *In a Moment of Enthusiasm: Political Power and the Second Stratum in Egypt* (Chicago: University of Chicago Press, 1978), 343, and Raymond Baker, *Egypt's Uncertain Revolution Under Nasser and Sadat* (Cambridge, Mass.: Harvard University Press, 1978), 108–13. It is corroborated by the minutes of the committee's meetings, reproduced in Rashad, *Sirri jiddan*.

22. ʿAbd al-Basit ʿAbd al-Muʿti, *al-Siraʿ al-tabaqi fi al-qarya al-misriyya* (Cairo: Dar al-Thaqafa al-Jadida, 1977).

23. Ansari, *Egypt: The Stalled Society*, xiii; Binder, *In a Moment of Enthusiasm*.

24. Studies of rural society in the Nasser period by Egyptian scholars, such as Mahmoud Abdel-Fadil, *Development, Income Distribution and Social Change in Rural Egypt, 1952–70: A Study in the Political Economy of Agrarian Transition* (Cambridge: Cambridge University Press, 1975), and Radwan, *Agrarian Reform and Rural Poverty*, offer a detailed analysis of agrarian re-

form and its effect on landownership, income, consumption, and prices. But they suffer from having to rely on aggregate quantitative data taken from official sources, whose problems were mentioned earlier. Nor do they examine the actual workings of political power in the countryside.

25. Harik, *Political Mobilization*, 52.

26. Ibid., 27.

27. Ibid., 73, 75.

28. Adams, *Development and Social Change;* Hopkins, *Agrarian Transformation in Egypt.*

29. See Mona Abaza, *The Changing Image of Women in Rural Egypt*, Cairo Papers in Social Science 10, monograph 4 (Cairo: American University in Cairo Press, 1987); Richard H. Adams, "The Effect of Remittances on Household Behavior and Rural Development in Upper Egypt," *Newsletter of the American Research Center in Egypt* (Fall 1987): 139; Commander, *The State and Agricultural Development in Egypt Since 1973;* Elizabeth Taylor, "Egyptian Migration and Peasant Wives," *MERIP Reports*, no. 124 (1984): 3–10.

30. For some of the broader theoretical issues in the study of agrarian politics in Egypt and the Middle East, see the exchange between Kathy Glavanis and Pandeli Glavanis, "The Sociology of Agrarian Relations in the Middle East: The Persistence of Household Production," *Current Sociology* 31, no. 2 (1983): 1–106, and David Seddon, "Commentary on Agrarian Relations in the Middle East: A New Paradigm for Analysis?" *Current Sociology* 34, no. 2 (1986): 151–72. I discuss these debates in Timothy Mitchell, "Fixing the Economy," *Cultural Studies* 12, no. 1 (1998): 82–101, and in chapter 8 below. James Toth, *Rural Labor Movements in Egypt and Their Impact on the State, 1961–1992* (Gainesville: University Press of Florida, 1999), a detailed study of the role of the rural poor in Egyptian politics, is an important addition to the theoretical debates on agrarian political economy.

31. James B. Mayfield, *Rural Politics in Nasser's Egypt: A Quest for Legitimacy* (Austin: University of Texas Press, 1971), 61–63.

32. Morroe Berger, *The Arab World Today* (Garden City, N.Y.: Doubleday, 1962), 160, cited in Mayfield, *Rural Politics*, 70.

33. Mayfield, *Rural Politics*, 71.

34. Ibid., 67–72.

35. Ibid., 72–73.

36. Ibid., 69–71.

37. Ibid.

38. Ibid., 5.

39. Gabriel Baer, "Submissiveness and Revolt of the Fellah," *Studies in the Social History of Modern Egypt* (Chicago: University of Chicago Press, 1969), 93–108, offered a critique of one of these traits, the submissiveness of the peasant, but attributed its popularity simply to the superficiality of travelers' observations. On the colonial origins and uses of these kinds of racial stereotypes in another part of the world, see Hussein Syed Alatas, *The Myth of the Lazy Native: A Study of the Image of the Malays, Filipinos, and Javanese from the*

16th to the 20th Century and its Function in the Ideology of Colonial Capitalism (London: Frank Cass, 1977). For an analysis of their more recent uses in the Egyptian case, see chapter 4.

40. These remarks may suggest an approach similar to that of Scott, *Weapons of the Weak*. Scott, however, examines the behavior of the poor to find signs of an otherwise unnoticed spirit of peasant resistance, an approach I find problematic (see Mitchell, "Everyday Metaphors of Power"). I am suggesting that one can examine the same practices for signs of otherwise unnoticed forms of domination. For the latter argument, see Lila Abu-Lughod, "The Romance of Resistance," *American Ethnologist* 17, no. 1 (1990): 41–55.

41. Harik, *Political Mobilization*, 8.

42. Ibid., 260–70.

43. Harik remained, however, one of the most optimistic writers on Egyptian rural development. A decade later he reiterated the conclusions established by his influential book, describing rural Egypt as a place without exploitation, middlemen, large landowners, or class conflict. Iliya Harik, "Continuity and Change in Local Development Policies in Egypt: From Nasser to Sadat," *International Journal of Middle East Studies* 16, no. 1 (1984): 43–66. For a useful but neglected critique of some of the problems of the political development literature, see Irene Gendzier, *Managing Political Change: Social Scientists and the Third World* (Boulder, Colo.: Westview Press, 1985). More recent critiques are mentioned in chapter 1, above.

44. Harik, "Continuity and Change in Local Development Policies," 263.

45. There was a parallel problem in studies of urban Egypt, where the workplace was neglected as a site for the construction of political relations on the ground that workers are not an active political force. The neglect has now been repaired by a number of studies, especially Joel Beinin and Zachary Lockman, *Workers on the Nile: Nationalism, Communism, Islam and the Egyptian Working Class, 1882–1954* (Princeton, N.J.: Princeton University Press, 1987); Marsha Pripstein Posusney, *Labor and the State in Egypt : Workers, Unions, and Economic Restructuring* (New York: Columbia University Press, 1997); and Samer Shehata, "Plastic Sandals, Tea, and Time: Shop Floor Politics and Culture in Egypt" (Ph.D. diss., Princeton University, 2000).

46. The state did this by lowering the price it paid for staple and export crops that predominantly small farmers were forced to grow, while subsidizing the cost of seeds, pesticides, fertilizer, and credit, the bulk of which went to large farmers. On agricultural pricing in Egypt prior to the reforms of the late 1980s and 1990s, see William Cuddihy, "Agricultural Price Management in Egypt," *World Bank Staff Working Paper* no. 388 (Washington, D.C.: The World Bank, 1980), and for a broader analysis, Yahya Sadowski, *Political Vegetables? Businessman and Bureaucrat in the Development of Egyptian Agriculture* (Washington, D.C.: Brookings Institution, 1991).

47. Adams, *Development and Social Change*, 138.

48. Mahmoud Hussein, *Class Conflict in Egypt: 1945–1970* (New York: Monthly Review Press, 1973), 231–32.

49. The alleged discovery of evidence that a secret "organization" of the Muslim Brotherhood was plotting to overthrow the regime, evidence the Ministry of the Interior refused to believe, had enabled the military to intervene instead, ordering the widespread arrests and thus extending its own domestic influence as well as its control over the apparatus of government. It was this same internal struggle for control of the regime that resurfaced the following year in the formation of the Higher Committee for the Liquidation of Feudalism. See Ahmad Hamrush, *Qissat thawrat 23 yuliyu,* vol. 2, *Mujtamaʿ Jamal ʿAbd al-Nasir* (Cairo: Maktabat Madbuli, 1975), 240–61.

50. Ansari, *Egypt: The Stalled Society,* Appendix C, 251–54.

51. John Waterbury reported an alternative version of the Kamshish story that was later put in circulation, according to which Salah Husain was murdered at the behest of his wife, who hoped to marry into the large landowning family. John Waterbury, *The Egypt of Nasser and Sadat: The Political Economy of Two Regimes* (Princeton, N.J.: Princeton University Press, 1983), 340. Although Waterbury appeared to lend credence to the story, it was clearly a fabrication, illustrating how political grievances can be delegitimized by transforming them into personal slurs against the victim, the slur depending on the old tactic of impugning the morals of a woman. There is sufficient evidence in the documents collected in Muhammad Rashad, *Sirri jiddan,* and in the appendix to Ansari, *Egypt: The Stalled Society,* to corroborate Ansari's version of the story. I discussed these events with Salah Husain's widow, Shahinda Maqlad, in May 1993.

52. Harik, *Political Mobilization,* 217.

53. Ibid., 111, 126.

54. Ibid., 138.

55. According to Harik's figures, only 44 percent of the village's adult males cultivate their own land, leaving 56 percent who make their living by other means. It is not clear what proportion of the latter have adequate incomes from other sources and what proportion form the "landless" poor to whom I am referring. Harik, *Political Mobilization,* 290, table 2. My figure of 40 percent is obtained from the table by adding together 100 percent of "agricultural laborers" with 70 percent of "craftsmen and tradesmen" and 70 percent of "native employees" (70 percent being my estimate of the proportion of these two groups earning less than the poverty level of E£12 per month [see note 57, below], based on the income figures given on p. 47), totaling 539, or 40 percent of the adult male population of 1,350. This figure may underestimate the proportion of families living in poverty, for two reasons: the survey excludes women, even those heading a household—Radwan and Lee's survey of 18 villages found that 8.5 percent of rural households were female-headed and that such households ranked among the poorest (*Agrarian Change in Egypt,* 64, table 4.10)—and it excludes those who own or rent land, but in amounts too small to keep them out of poverty.

56. Harik, *Political Mobilization,* 47.

57. Calculated from the poverty table in Adams, *Development and Social Change,* 14, adjusted for 1967 using the cost of living index given on p. 138,

table 6.2. The average family size, taken from population censuses, is calculated by Adams at 4.37 "adult equivalent units" (AEUs), where it is estimated that, on average, 1.0 person equals 0.830 AEUs.

58. Small shopkeepers and the more senior government employees appear to have a similar level of income, but the resources they control may give them a distinct social position. Harik, *Political Mobilization,* 47.

59. Ibid., 43.

60. Ibid., 47.

61. John P. Powelson and Richard Stock, *The Peasant Betrayed: Agriculture and Land Reform in the Third World* (Boston: Oelgeschlager, Gunn & Hain, in association with the Lincoln Institute of Land Policy, 1987), 84, 189.

62. Samir Amin (pseudonym Hasan Riad), *L'Egypte nassérienne* (Paris: Editions de Minuit, 1964).

63. Harik, *Political Mobilization,* 115.

64. The actual income of the Kuras would have been much higher. Apart from the possibility that they controlled a larger area of land than recorded in the official registers or in answers to questionnaires, they appear to have been involved in several other ventures including livestock trading, and Muhammad Kura earned an income from his position in a government cotton firm in Tanta.

65. Harik, *Political Mobilization,* 253.

66. The system of debt bondage among migrant agricultural laborers is illustrated in Sawsan el-Messiri, "*Tarahil* Laborers in Egypt," in *Migration, Mechanization and Agricultural Labor Markets in Egypt,* ed. Alan Richards and Philip L. Martin (Boulder, Colo.: Westview Press, 1983), 88–92, with the case of a laborer who keeps his family alive with loans from a labor contractor and is obliged in return to spend most of the year in labor camps elsewhere in Egypt. Adams offers another illustration, an agricultural laborer who frequently has to borrow money to buy basic needs like food or clothing and must then work for his creditor "a week or more without pay in order to discharge his loans." Adams, *Development and Social Change,* 136.

67. Harik, *Political Mobilization,* 252–54. On the wider history of this attempt by the state to organize migrant labor and eliminate the labor contractors, see Toth, *Rural Labor Movements,* 133–63.

68. Harik, *Political Mobilization,* 255–56.

69. Although in anthropology and cultural studies the problems of the scholar's relation to those being studied has been extensively explored for a generation, these debates have by-passed the discipline of political science, which still attempts to model itself on the procedures of techno-scientific enquiry. For an example see Gary King, Robert O. Keohane, and Sidney Verba, *Designing Social Inquiry: Scientific Inference in Qualitative Research* (Princeton, N.J.: Princeton University Press, 1994). For a classic discussion of these issues in anthropology, see James Clifford, "On Ethnographic Authority," *Representations* 1, no. 2 (1983): 118–46.

70. Harik, *Political Mobilization,* 92.
71. Ibid., 244.
72. Ibid., 248.
73. Ibid., 249.
74. Ibid., 243, 245.
75. Ibid., 247.
76. Ibid., 30.
77. Ibid., 27.
78. For a conventional critique of behavioralism that seems to reproduce its dualisms in more sophisticated terms, see for example Charles Taylor, "Interpretation and the Sciences of Man," *The Review of Metaphysics* 25, no. 1 (1971): 3–51. On the use of questionnaires, see Robert Chambers, *Rural Development: Putting the Last First* (London: Longman, 1983), 49–58.
79. Harik, *Political Mobilization,* 227.
80. Pierre Bourdieu, *Outline of a Theory of Practice* (Cambridge: Cambridge University Press, 1977), 191. There is a brief discussion of how a culture of deference helps maintain social inequality in an Upper Egyptian village in Hopkins, *Agrarian Transformation in Egypt,* 175–76, 187–88.
81. Harik, *Political Mobilization,* 192–93.

CHAPTER 6. HERITAGE AND VIOLENCE

1. Influential contributions to the debate on nationalism and the invention of the past include those of Eric Hobsbawm and Terence Ranger, eds., *The Invention of Tradition* (Cambridge: Cambridge University Press, 1983); Ernest Gellner, *Nations and Nationalism* (Oxford: Oxford University Press, 1983); Benedict Anderson, *Imagined Communities: Reflections on the Origins and Spread of Nationalism,* 2nd ed. (London: Verso, 1991); and Partha Chatterjee, *Nationalist Thought and the Colonial World: A Derivative Discourse?* (Minneapolis: University of Minnesota Press, 1993), and *The Nation and its Fragments: Colonial and Postcolonial Histories* (Princeton, N.J.: Princeton University Press, 1993).
2. Anderson, *Imagined Communities.*
3. Ernest Renan, *Qu'est-ce qu'une nation? What is a nation?* Introduction by Charles Taylor, English translation by Wanda Romer Taylor (Toronto: Tapir Press, 1996).
4. For a further discussion of the questions about space raised by Anderson's work, see Timothy Mitchell, "The Stage of Modernity," in Timothy Mitchell, ed., *Questions of Modernity* (Minneapolis: University of Minnesota Press, 2000), 1–34.
5. Henry Dodwell, *The Founder of Modern Egypt: A Study of Muhammad ʿAli* (Cambridge: Cambridge University Press, 1931). A former curator of the Madras Record Office, Dodwell wrote numerous studies of British India and was an editor of *The Cambridge History of India* and *The Cambridge History of the British Empire.*

6. Khaled Fahmy, *All the Pasha's Men: Mehmed Ali, His Army and the Making of Modern Egypt* (Cambridge: Cambridge University Press, 1997).

7. Sudipta Kaviraj makes this argument with respect to India in "The Imaginary Institution of India," *Subaltern Studies VII,* ed. Partha Chatterjee and Gyanendra Pandey (New Delhi: Oxford University Press, 1992), 1–39.

8. The Ottoman Province of Sham, usually translated as Syria, would appear to be an exception to this. But in nineteenth-century Ottoman and Arabic sources, al-Sham is a name for the city of Damascus, and by extension the countryside around it (Khaled Fahmy, personal communication).

9. In Arabic, *al-diyar al-misriyya* and *bilad misr.* The most important nineteenth-century scholarly work on the country, ʿAli Pasha Mubarak's geographical encyclopedia published in 1886–88, illustrates how the relationship between city and region was understood. The book was entitled "The Description of Cairo [misr al-qahira] and its Towns and Villages." *Al-Khitat al-tawfiqiyya li-misr al-qahira wa-muduniha wa-biladiha al-qadima wa-ʾl-shahira* (Cairo: al-Matbaʿa al-Kubra al-Amiriyya, 1886–88).

10. See Gerard Coudougnan, *Nos ancêtres les Pharaons: L'Historie pharaonique et copte dans les manuels scolaires égyptiens,* Dossiers du CEDEJ 1998, no. 1 (Cairo: Centre d'Etudes et de Documentation Economique, Juridique et Sociale, 1988).

11. Such treasure hunting had provided the main incentive for Western archaeology, and its major means of support. Its ending led to a sharp reduction in Western archaeological excavations in Egypt. They did not expand again until the late 1950s, when funds from UNESCO and other nonprofit sources became available, in response to the imminent destruction of ancient sites caused by the building of the High Dam at Aswan.

12. Mercedes Volait, *L'Architecture moderne en Egypte et la Revue Al-ʿImara, 1939–59,* Dossiers du CEDEJ 1987, no. 4 (Cairo: Centre d'Etudes et de Documentation Economique, Juridique et Sociale, 1988).

13. Nicholas B. Dirks, "History as a Sign of the Modern," *Public Culture* 2, no. 1 (1990): 25–32.

14. On Egyptian nationalism in this period, see the two books by Israel Gershoni and James P. Jankowski, *Egypt, Islam and the Arabs: The Search for Egyptian Nationhood* (Oxford: Oxford University Press, 1986), and *Redefining the Egyptian Nation, 1930–1945* (Cambridge: Cambridge University Press, 1995). For criticisms of this work see my review of the latter book, *American Political Science Review* 90, no. 2 (1996): 451–52, and the review essay by Charles D. Smith, "Imagined Identities, Imagined Nationalisms: Print Culture and Egyptian Nationalism in the Light of Recent Scholarship," *International Journal of Middle East Studies* 29, no. 4 (1997): 607–22. For further discussion of the intellectual debates of this period see, among others, Charles D. Smith, *Islam and the Search for Social Order in Modern Egypt: A Biography of Muhammad Husayn Haykal* (Albany: State University of New York Press, 1983); and Joel Beinin and Zachary Lockman, *Workers on the Nile: Nationalism, Communism, Islam, and the Egyptian*

Working Class, 1882–1954 (Princeton, N.J.: Princeton University Press, 1987).

15. Homi K. Bhabha, "DissemiNation: Time, Narrative, and the Margins of the Modern Nation," in *The Location of Culture* (London: Routledge, 1994), 139–70, at 145.

16. For an example, see Gershoni and Jankowski, *Redefining the Egyptian Nation.*

17. There is now a large literature dealing with Fathy's life and accomplishments. For an overview and guide to further works, see James Steele, *An Architecture for the People: The Complete Works of Hassan Fathy* (London: Thames and Hudson, 1997).

18. Kees van der Spek, "Dead Mountain vs. Living Community: The Theban Necropolis as Cultural Landscape," paper presented at the UNESCO Third International Forum, "University and Heritage," Deakin University, Melbourne and Geelong, Australia, Oct. 4–9, 1998.

19. Hassan Fathy, *Gurna: A Tale of Two Villages* (Cairo: Ministry of Culture, 1969); reprinted as *Architecture for the Poor: An Experiment in Rural Egypt* (Chicago: University of Chicago Press, 1973), 43, 51, 40.

20. Fathy was educated in British schools in Cairo. In 1956, with the collapse of the European presence in Egypt following the failed British, French, and Israeli invasion that year, he chose to leave Egypt himself and spent the next five years based in Athens. Thus he abandoned Egypt at the moment of triumph of an alternative vision of national heritage, that of Arab nationalism. *Architecture for the Poor* was translated into Arabic only in the 1980s. See Steele, *An Architecture for the People,* 96, 109. On the problems of Fathy's cosmopolitanism see Nezar AlSayyad, "From Vernacularism to Globalism: The Temporal Reality of Traditional Settlements," *Traditional Dwellings and Settlements Review* 7, no. 1 (1995): 13–24. Fathy's cosmopolitanism, however, may have been central to his achievement. Perhaps it gave him a certain distance from the narrower materialism and less generous paternalism of the landowning class from which he came, and opened him to the influence of other inventions of the modern vernacular, such as French colonial architecture in Morocco. For example, the Habous neighborhood built in the late 1930s in Casablanca, and copied some years later in Rabat, was widely discussed in this period as a reaction against the modernist movement and Le Corbusier (Muhammed Hamdouni Alami, personal communication, Feb. 10, 1999).

21. Luxor City Council, "El Gurna Region Resident Relocation Study and New El Tarif Village Planning through Community Participation: Terms of Reference," mimeo, Luxor, Egypt, Oct. 1992. The funds for the planning process were given to the U.S. consulting firm Chemonics, under a USAID Local Development II grant. Interview with a Chemonics consultant, Cairo, May 1993.

22. *Al-Ahram Weekly,* Feb. 12–18, 1998.

23. Ibid., May 7–13, 1998; *Middle East Times,* Nov. 22, 1998.

24. Mariz Tadros, "A House on the Hill," *Al-Ahram Weekly,* Apr. 1–8, 1998.

25. Fathy, *Architecture for the Poor,* 60.

26. For the history of the malaria and cholera epidemics, see chapter 1, above, and Nancy Gallagher, *Egypt's Other Wars: Epidemics and the Politics of Public Health* (Syracuse, N.Y.: Syracuse University Press, 1990). Toward the end of his book, Hassan Fathy correctly distinguishes the two epidemics. *Architecture for the Poor,* 166.

27. Gallagher, *Egypt's Other Wars,* 32–35.

28. Ibid., 60–66.

29. On the role of Egyptian sociologists in promoting rural reform, see Alain Roussillon, "Project colonial et traditions scientifique: aux origines de la sociologie égyptienne," mimeo.

30. Volait, *L'Architecture moderne en Egypte,* 78.

31. Henry Habib Ayrout, *Moeurs et coutumes des fellahs* (Paris: Payot, 1938; reprint ed. New York: AMS Press, 1978); 2nd revised ed., entitled *Fellahs* (Cairo: Editions Horus, 1942); Arabic ed., *al-Fellahin,* trans. Muhammad Ghallab (Cairo: Matbaʿat al-Kawthar, 1943); English ed., *The Fellaheen,* trans. Hilary Wayment (Cairo: R. Schindler, 1945). On Ayrout's work, see chapter 4, above.

32. Volait, *L'Architecture moderne en Egypte,* 76–77.

33. Fathy, *Architecture for the Poor,* 63–64.

34. Ibid., 113, 127, 134.

35. See chapter 2, above, and Timothy Mitchell, *Colonising Egypt* (Berkeley: University of California Press, 1991).

36. Fathy, *Architecture for the Poor,* 39.

37. Ibid., 17.

38. Ibid., 1; Steele, *An Architecture for the People,* 96.

39. Fathy, *Architecture for the Poor,* 5. For a chronology of Fathy's designs see Steele, *An Architecture for the People,* 188–201.

40. Nathan Brown, *Peasant Politics in Modern Egypt: The Struggle Against the State* (New Haven, Conn.: Yale University Press 1990), 114–15, 133, citing *al-Muqattam,* Jan. 24 and 28, 1908, and Kitchener to Grey, Apr. 27, 1913, in United Kingdom Foreign Office Records, Public Record Office, London, FO 371/20291, file 1638.

41. Fathy, *Architecture for the Poor,* 51.

42. See chapter 1.

43. Fathy, *Architecture for the Poor,* 3–4.

44. Steele, *An Architecture for the People,* 24.

45. Fathy, *Architecture for the Poor,* 6–7.

46. It is also instructive that Fathy either failed to notice or chose not to mention an earlier introduction of domed, mud-brick architecture, the work of the English architect and archaeologist Somers Clarke. Clarke's work before World War I included at least three domed railway stations, at Idfu, Silsila, and Kom Ombo, the three stops Fathy passed on the train before reaching Aswan. See Caroline Simpson, "Nubia, Somers Clarke, and Hassan Fathy," *Bulletin of the Association for the Study of Travel in Egypt and the Near East,* no. 9 (Apr. 2000).

47. The local method consisted of building a parallel series of mud-brick arches, set about an arm's length apart. The gaps between them were filled with a thick mud plaster mixed with a large amount of straw, laid up by hand working in circular fashion (*tuuf*) from the edges towards the center, as though making an inverted clay bowl. (Indeed, *tuuf* was typically a woman's skill, used for making large bowls and the domed roofs of bread ovens and grain silos.) The resulting vault was quite shallow, but strong enough to allow another floor to be built above—another advantage over Fathy's more highly arched method, which, like the dome, did not easily allow the later addition of an upper floor. Nessim Henry Henein, *Mārī Girgis: Village de Haute-Egypte* (Cairo: Institut français d'archéologie orientale du Caire, 1988), 40–41, 49; Boutros Wadieh, personal communication, Jan. 2001.

48. The pollen from the male tree is harvested by hand and distributed among the females.

49. Lori Pottinger, "The Environmental Impact of Large Dams," International Rivers Network, available at http://www.irn.org/basics/impacts.shtml.

50. See Anne M. Jennings, *The Nubians of West Aswan: Village Women in the Midst of Change* (Boulder, Colo.: Lynne Rienner, 1995), 35–36. There may have been some settlement prior to the Aswan Dam, but most families moved to Gharb Aswan in 1903, when the dam was built, or in 1933, when it was raised and further areas of Nubia were flooded. I am grateful to Elizabeth Smith for this reference.

51. *Al-Ahram Weekly*, May 7–13, 1993.

52. U.S. National Archives, Record Group 286, Department of State, Central Files, Egypt 1950–54, Box 33, folder 1031, Mar. 23, 1953. I am grateful to Robert Vitalis for a copy of this record.

53. World Bank, "Staff Appraisal Report: Arab Republic of Egypt Tourism Project," mimeo, Washington, D.C., Apr. 26, 1979, 19–22. The contractors building new tourist roads initially agreed to employ some of the villagers. But as one of the villagers who did this work later told me, when they discovered that for twelve hours a day of heavy labor they were to be paid only E£5 (about $1.50 at that time) they refused to work, and the contractors brought in cheaper labor from other, more destitute villages. The major local construction contract, building a new river embankment at Luxor, which might also have employed local workers, was awarded (following perhaps the World Bank's new free-market principles) to a military workforce from China.

54. Government of Egypt, Ministry of Tourism, Tourism Development Authority, Information Management Department, "1992 Tourism Data Bulletin," Jan. 1993. Tourist arrivals dropped from 3.21 million in 1992 to 2.51 million in 1993, recovering to 2.87 million in 1995, 3.53 million in 1996, and 3.66 million in 1997, before dropping again to 3.22 million in 1998. In 1999 the total jumped to an estimated 4.49 million arrivals. Economist Intelligence Unit, *Egypt: Country Profile 1997/98* (London: Economist Intelligence Unit, 1997), 68; World Tourism Organization, *World Tourism Highlights 2000*, available at http://www.world-tourism.org.

55. Happy and other names of locals used in this chapter are pseudonyms.

56. Government of Egypt, Ministry of Tourism, "Taba Touristic Development Company," mimeo, Cairo, 1991, 54–55.

57. Business International, "Egypt: Profile of a Market in Transition," Geneva, 1989, 75.

58. See Tilman G. Freitag, "Enclave Tourism Development: For Whom the Benefits Roll?" *Annals of Tourism Research* 21, no. 3 (1994): 538–54.

59. After working for the IMF in North Yemen, in 1974 Fu'ad Sultan set up one of the first new private sector banks, the Egyptian-Iranian Investment Bank, and was one of the earliest Egyptian voices advocating the IMF program of economic restructuring. Following his spell as minister of tourism, he enjoyed substantial private holdings in tourism through his company Al-Ahli for Investment and Tourism. John Waterbury, *The Egypt of Nasser and Sadat: The Political Economy of Two Regimes* (Princeton, N.J.: Princeton University Press, 1983), 138; *Middle East Times*, June 23, 2000, at http://www.me-times.com.

60. The management companies typically took 15 to 20 percent of profit. Coopers and Lybrand Deloitte, "Egyptian Hotels Privatisation Study: Interim Report," mimeo, Cairo, June 19, 1991.

61. John Urry, *The Tourist Gaze: Leisure and Travel in Contemporary Societies* (London: Sage, 1990), 64. Attempts to measure the exact proportion of tourist expenditure that remains in the host country are inconclusive, in part because circumstances differ so much from one economy to the next. See E. Philip English, *The Great Escape? An Examination of North-South Tourism* (Ottawa: North-South Institute, 1986), 17–45. The measurements are also inconclusive because the very nature of the industry, organized around the consumption of experience, as I discuss below, makes conventional economic measurement impossible.

62. In Britain, for example, by 2000 just four companies controlled more than 80 percent of the overseas tour industry, each with its own retail chain, tour operator, and airline. The largest two, Thomson Travel group and Thomas Cook, were themselves taken over by the German tourism, shipping, and industrial conglomerate Preussag. Preussag was set up in the 1920s as a Prussian state-owned mining company, and used slave or forced labor during the National Socialist period. See http://www.preussag.com, and http://www.cmht.com/ajc-companies.htm.

63. Arthur D. Little, *Study on Visitor Management and Associated Investments on the West Bank of the Nile at Luxor*, Apr. 1982, VII-9, emphasis added.

64. Luxor City Council, "El Gurna Region Resident Relocation Study," 21.

65. Siona Jenkins, "Lifting Roots and Moving Home," *Al-Wakaleh* (Cairo), Mar. 1997, 36–37.

66. See Lila Abu-Lughod, "Television and the Virtues of Education: Upper Egyptian Encounters with State Culture," in *Directions of Change in Rural Egypt*, ed. Nicholas Hopkins and Kirsten Westergaard (Cairo: American University in Cairo Press, 1998), 147–65.

67. Shyam Bhatia, "Villagers Cursed by Tombs of the Pharaohs," *The Observer*, Jan. 7, 1996, 13.

68. Lynn Meskell, ed., *Archaeology Under Fire: Nationalism, Politics and Heritage in the Eastern Mediterranean and the Middle East* (London: Routledge, 1998) offers a collection of essays on the political and cultural context of the practice of archaeology in the Middle East.

69. Mahmoud Kassem, "Ill Gotten Gains," *Business Monthly,* Apr. 2000, available at http://www.amcham.org.eg/HTML/news.publication/Business-Monthly. Neil Brodie of Cambridge University's Illicit Antiquities Research Center pointed out that Sotheby's, Christie's, and other auction houses refused to reveal the provenance of antiquities they auctioned (ibid.). A Cairo-based archaeologist informed me that the antiquities he saw offered for sale in Gurna had been engraved with identifiable excavation register numbers, indicating that they came from government storehouses, not undiscovered tombs hidden among the houses of Gurna.

70. See http://www.unesco.org/culture/laws/1970/html_eng/page3.shtml. In the case of Britain, successive governments claimed for thirty years that legal obstacles relating to British property law prevented ratification of the treaty. In November 2000, after an advisory panel showed this argument to be specious, the government said it would consider signing the convention. "UK Concession Over Art Treasures," the *Guardian,* Dec. 19, 2000, 9.

71. United Nations Educational, Scientific and Cultural Organization, "30th Anniversary of UNESCO Convention on the Means of Prohibiting and Preventing the Illicit Import, Export and Transfer of Ownership of Cultural Property," available at http://www.unesco.org/opi/eng/unescopress/2000/00–116e.shtml.

72. In the early 1990s, for example, scholars on the Cultural Property Advisory Commission in the United States tried to persuade the Egyptian government to ask the United States to ban the importation of artifacts illegally exported from Egypt, but no ban was introduced.

73. See van der Spek, "Dead Mountain vs. Living Community."

74. Ibid.

75. Ibid.

76. Arthur D. Little, *Study on Visitor Management,* VIII-2; Government of Egypt, "1992 Tourism Data Bulletin."

77. Petition from the people of Gurna, in Arabic, signed "Ahali al-Qurna, 'anhum 'Abd al-Sallam Ahmad Suli, al-Qurna, Naj' al-Hurubat, al-Uqsur," mimeo, in the author's possession, Nov. 1996.

CHAPTER 7. THE OBJECT OF DEVELOPMENT

1. Khalid Ikram, *Egypt: Economic Management in a Period of Transition,* Report of a Mission Sent to the Arab Republic of Egypt by the World Bank (Baltimore: Johns Hopkins University Press, for the World Bank, 1980), 3.

2. Pamela R. Johnson et al., *Egypt: The Egyptian American Rural Improvement Service, a Point Four Project, 1952–63,* AID Project Impact Evaluation, no. 43 (Washington, D.C.: Agency for International Development, 1983), 1.

3. Ikram, *Egypt: Economic Management in a Period of Transition,* 3.

4. Susan George, "Conscience 'planétaire' et 'trop nombreux' pauvres," *Le Monde Diplomatique*, no. 434, May 1990: 18.

5. World Bank, *Trends in Developing Economies 1989* (Washington, D.C.: World Bank, 1989), 129.

6. Food and Agriculture Organization of the United Nations (FAO), *The State of Food and Agriculture* (Rome: Food and Agriculture Organization, 1989), Annex, table 12b.

7. FAO, *Inter-Country Comparisons of Agricultural Production Aggregates*, FAO Economic and Social Development Paper 61 (Rome: Food and Agriculture Organization, 1986), table 5.7, 36.

8. FAO, *Yearbook 1987: Production*, vol. 41 (Rome: Food and Agriculture Organization, 1988), table 1.

9. FAO, *Inter-Country Comparisons*, table 5.6, 34.

10. George, "Conscience 'planétaire,' " 18.

11. World Bank, *World Development Report 1989* (Washington, D.C.: World Bank, 1989), table 5.

12. United States Department of Agriculture (USDA), *Egypt: Major Constraints to Increasing Agricultural Productivity*, Foreign Economic Report no. 120 (Washington, D.C.: Department of Agriculture, 1976), 48. Despite the seriousness with which they viewed the population problem, development agencies devoted relatively few resources to it. USAID, which claimed to account for about 75 percent of all foreign assistance for family planning in Egypt, devoted only 1 percent of its total economic assistance to population programs from 1975 to 1989. United States Agency for International Development, Cairo, *Status Report: United States Economic Assistance to Egypt* (Cairo: USAID, 1989), 105–8. In 1991, USAID was forced to suspend a program to distribute 50 million condoms in Egypt, after discovering that pharmacies were supplying the condoms to dealers who resold them as toy balloons. *Washington Post*, Dec. 14 1991, A1.

13. World Bank, *World Development Report 1993* (New York: Oxford University Press, 1993), table 15.

14. World Bank, *Egypt: Alleviating Poverty* (Washington, D.C.: World Bank, 1991), tables 2, 26.

15. FAO, *Yearbook 1992: Production*, vol. 46 (Rome: Food and Agriculture Organization, 1992), table 9.

16. World Bank, *World Development Report 1990* (New York: Oxford University Press, 1990), table 28.

17. FAO, *Yearbook 1988: Production*, vol. 42 (Rome: Food and Agriculture Organization, 1989), table 107.

18. Population Council, "Egypt 1988: Results from the Demographic and Health Survey," *Studies in Family Planning* 21, no. 6 (1990): 351.

19. Central Agency for Public Mobilization and Statistics and UNICEF, *The State of Egyptian Children* (Cairo: CAPMAS, 1988).

20. A. S. Nockrashy, Osman Galal, and Jay Davenport, *More and Better Food: An Egyptian Demonstration Project* (Washington, D.C.: National Research Council, 1987), 30–32.

21. World Bank, *Egypt: Alleviating Poverty,* 23.

22. Jean-Jacques Dethier, *Trade, Exchange Rate, and Agricultural Pricing Policies in Egypt,* vol. 1, *The Country Study* (Washington, D.C.: World Bank, 1989), 20.

23. Saad Eddin Ibrahim, *Social Mobility and Income Distribution,* mimeo, Egyptian Income Distribution Research Project, no. 4, 1979, table 2.

24. Alan Richards and John Waterbury, *A Political Economy of the Middle East* (Boulder, Colo.: Westview Press, 1990), 282.

25. Alan Richards and Raymond Baker, *Political Economy Review of Egypt,* prepared for USAID's Governance and Democracy Program (Washington, D.C.: Management Systems International, 1992), 21, 42. On the increased poverty and inequality that followed the structural adjustment program, see chapters 8 and 9.

26. USDA, *Egypt: Major Constraints to Increasing Agricultural Productivity,* 23.

27. Harold Alderman and Joachim von Braun, *The Effects of the Egyptian Food Ration and Subsidy System on Income Distribution and Consumption,* Research Report no. 45 (Washington, D.C.: International Food Policy Research Institute, 1984), table 12.

28. Jean-Jacques Dethier, *Trade, Exchange Rate, and Agricultural Pricing Policies in Egypt,* vol. 1, *The Country Study,* 19.

29. FAO, *Yearbook 1987: Production,* vol. 41.

30. Eating protein in the form of animal products cost the Egyptian consumer in real terms (discounting subsidies) about ten times the price of eating it in the form of legumes (broad beans, lentils). See Ibrahim Soliman and Shahla Shapouri, *The Impact of Wheat Price Policy Change on Nutritional Status in Egypt,* U.S. Department of Agriculture, International Economics Division. Economic Research Service, Staff Report no. AGES831129, 1984, table 13, 21.

31. These figures cover wheat, maize, barley, and sorghum but exclude rice. Rice production remained at about the same level from the mid-1960s to late 1980s. Per capita consumption was maintained by reducing exports. USAID, *Agricultural Data Base* (Cairo: USAID, 1989), 221.

32. These figures may severely underestimate the proportion of grain fed to animals. The figures for wheat consumption are based on the estimate that animals consumed 18 percent of domestic production, and that this proportion had not increased since 1966 despite the large rise in fodder prices and the relative decrease in the price of imported flour. The actual proportion is difficult to estimate because almost all domestic wheat was consumed within the village. Some sources suggest that 80 percent of domestic wheat was used as fodder (Economist Intelligence Unit, *Egypt: Country Report,* no. 4, 1989 [London: Economist Intelligence Unit, 1989], 13). If so, then per capita food consumption of grains dropped by 10 percent between 1966 and 1988, and nonfood usage increased by 357 percent to more than 9 million tons—surpassing the 7.45 million tons fed to humans.

33. Calculated from USAID, *Agricultural Data Base,* 209.

34. USAID, *Common Misconceptions about USAID in Egypt / Mafahim khati'a ʿan barnamij al-musaʿidat al-amrikiyya li-misr,* pamphlet (Cairo: USAID Public Affairs Office, 1989).

35. Economist Intelligence Unit, *Egypt: Country Profile 1993/94* (London: Economist Intelligence Unit, 1993), 46; World Bank, *World Development Report 1991* (New York: Oxford University Press, for the World Bank, 1991), tables 23 and 24.

36. Economist Intelligence Unit, *Egypt: Country Profile 1993/94,* 45–46.

37. Georg Stauth, "Capitalist Farming and Small Peasant Households in Egypt," in *The Rural Middle East: Peasant Lives and Modes of Production,* ed. Kathy Glavanis and Pandeli Glavanis (Ramallah: Bir Zeit University, and London: Zed Press, 1989), 122.

38. As in previous chapters, unless specified otherwise the term "acre" here refers to an Egyptian acre or *feddan,* equal to 1.038 British or U.S. acres or 0.420 hectares.

39. USAID, *Agricultural Data Base.*

40. Ikram, *Egypt: Economic Management in a Period of Transition,* 175.

41. See Dethier, *Trade, Exchange Rate, and Agricultural Pricing,* 246–65.

42. Simon Commander, *The State and Agricultural Development in Egypt Since 1973* (London: Ithaca Press, 1987), table 4–13, 80.

43. Allen C. Kelley, Atef M. Khalifa, and M. Nabil el-Khorazaty, *Population and Development in Rural Egypt* (Durham, N.C.: Duke University Press, 1982), 9.

44. M. El-Rafie, W. A. Hassouna, N. Hirschhorn, S. Loza, P. Miller, A. Nagaty, S. Nasser, and S. Riyad, "Effect of Diarrhoeal Disease Control on Infant and Child Mortality in Egypt," *Lancet,* vol. 335 (Feb. 10, 1990): 334–38; Population Council, "Egypt 1988."

45. USDA, *Egypt: Major Constraints to Increasing Agricultural Productivity,* 172.

46. Thierry Ruf, *Histoire contemporaine de l'agriculture égyptienne: Essai de synthèse* (Bondy, France: Editions de l'Orstom, 1988), 236.

47. Ibid., 214, 220, 236.

48. Mohaya A. Zaytoun, "Income Distribution in Egyptian Agriculture and Its Main Determinants," in *The Political Economy of Income Distribution in Egypt,* ed. Gouda Abdel-Khalek and Robert Tignor (New York: Holmes and Meier, 1982), 277.

49. Robert Springborg, "Rolling Back Egypt's Agrarian Reform," *Middle East Report,* no. 166 (Sept.–Oct. 1990), 29.

50. Ibid.

51. International Finance Corporation, "Report and Recommendation of the President to the Board of Directors on a Proposed Investment in Delta Sugar Company S.A.E., Arab Republic of Egypt" (Washington, D.C.: International Finance Corporation, 1983).

52. The Japanese land reform, imposed by the United States after World War II to break the power of large landowners, set the landholding ceiling at

one hectare (2.38 Egyptian acres, or *feddans*). The 1949 Land Reform Act in South Korea, introduced in response to the 1944 land reform in North Korea, redistributed land above the limit of 3 *chongbo* (1 *chongbo* = 0.992 hectare), or 7.08 Egyptian acres. In Taiwan, the 1953 Land to the Tiller program placed the limit at 3 *chia* (1 *chia* = 0.958 hectare), corresponding to 6.84 Egyptian acres. John P. Powelson and Richard Stock, *The Peasant Betrayed: Agriculture and Land Reform in the Third World* (Boston: Oelgeschlager, Gunn & Hain, in association with the Lincoln Institute of Land Policy, 1987), 179, 189; "Contemporary Thinking on Land Reform," paper prepared by J. Riddell and the staff of the Land Tenure Service, Rural Development Division, FAO, posted Mar. 24, 2000, available at http://www.fao.org/sd/ltdirect/ltan0037.htm.

53. Eddy Lee, "Egalitarian Peasant Farming and Rural Development: The Case of South Korea," *World Development* 7, nos. 4/5 (1979): 510; Springborg, "Rolling Back Egypt's Agrarian Reform," 29.

54. Springborg, "Rolling Back Egypt's Agrarian Reform," 29.

55. Dethier, *Trade, Exchange Rate, and Agricultural Pricing*, 5.

56. The success of the East Asian land reforms depended on several factors beside the elimination of large farms, including the development of local village government and agricultural cooperatives, support for rural industry, and the protection of agricultural prices against subsidized U.S. imports. When the Uruguay Round free trade agreements forced the removal of price supports, the Republic of Korea launched the New Agricultural Policy (1994–2004), whose ten-year funding equaled the entire annual budget of the state. The funds supported the development of specialized farms and early retirement for less productive farmers. However, the removal of the three-hectare limit on landholdings immediately encouraged land speculation, which undermined the other aspects of the reform. Hyunseok Oh, "La réforme de la politique agricole en République de Corée, ses défis et ses problèmes: la nouvelle orientation du développement rural face à la libéralisation," *Land Reform* 2000/1, 108–17, available at http://www.fao.org/sd/ltdirect/landrf.htm.

57. Calculated from Springborg, "Rolling Back Egypt's Agrarian Reform," table 1, 29.

58. See Gershon Feder, "The Relation Between Farm Size and Farm Productivity," *Journal of Development Economics* 18, nos. 2–3 (1985): 297–313; Hans Binswanger, Klaus Deininger, and Gershon Feder, "Power, Distortions, Revolt and Reform in Agricultural Land Relations," in *Handbook of Development Economics*, vol. 3b, ed. J. Behrman and T. N. Srinivasan (Amsterdam: Elsevier, 1995), 2659–72. For evidence from Egypt, see Nicholas S. Hopkins, "Small Farmer Households and Agricultural Sustainability in Egypt," in *Sustainable Agriculture in Egypt*, ed. Mohamed A. Faris and Mahmood Hasan Khan (Boulder, Colo.: Lynne Rienner, 1993), 185–95; and M. Z. Moussa and T. T. Jones, "Efficiency and Farm Size in Egypt: A Unit Output Price Profit Function Approach," *Applied Economics* 23, no. A1 (1991): 21–29. Graham Dyer's study of data from eighteen Egyptian villages confirms the greater productivity of small farmers, except in the case of one sugarcane-producing village. His evidence,

and my own research in the same region, indicates that large cane farmers achieved higher yields by monopolizing the supply of inputs, especially fertilizer. Unfortunately, Dyer draws the strange conclusion that this represents a more "developed" form of agriculture, so the greater productivity of small farmers elsewhere is likely to disappear. He adds that this would be a good thing, since small farmers can achieve higher yields only by "extreme levels" of self-exploitation—a claim for which there is no evidence. *Class, State, and Agricultural Productivity in Egypt: A Study of the Inverse Relationship Between Farm Size and Land Productivity* (London: Frank Cass, 1997), 146.

59. Yu-Shan Wu, *Comparative Economic Transformations: Mainland China, Hungary, the Soviet Union, and Taiwan* (Stanford, Calif.: Stanford University Press, 1994).

60. See Peter Gran, "Modern Trends in Egyptian Historiography: A Review Article," *International Journal of Middle East Studies* 9, no. 3 (1978): 370.

61. Ruf, *Histoire contemporaine de l'agriculture égyptienne,* 214; USAID, *Agricultural Data Base,* 224.

62. Calculated from data on crop yields for Egypt available at http://apps.fao.org.

63. See Gustav Ranis, "Rural Linkages and Choice of Technology," in *The Other Policy: The Influence of Policies on Technology Choice and Small Enterprise Development,* ed. Frances Stewart, Henk Thomas, and Tom de Wilde (London: Intermediate Technology Publications, 1990), 43–57, at 48–49.

64. For example, using the open pan sulphitation method to process sugarcane employed three to five times as many workers per unit of output, compared to the vacuum pan method used in large factories, and cost 15 to 30 percent less. Frances Stewart and Gustav Ranis, "Macro-Policies for Appropriate Technology: A Synthesis of Findings," in *The Other Policy: The Influence of Policies on Technology Choice and Small Enterprise Development,* ed. Frances Stewart, Henk Thomas, and Tom de Wilde (London: Intermediate Technology Publications, 1990), 2–42, at 6.

65. Taiwan's successful industrialization program in the second half of the twentieth century did not begin with export-oriented industry. The country first focused on improving agricultural and nonagricultural rural livelihoods. In the 1960s, a large proportion of industrial employment was in rural industry, initially based on agricultural processing (starting with rice and sugar, then moving to vegetables such as mushrooms and asparagus). Ranis, "Rural Linkages," 45.

66. "Contemporary Thinking on Land Reform," paper prepared by J. Riddell and the staff of the Land Tenure Service, Rural Development Division, FAO, posted Mar. 24, 2000, available at http://www.fao.org/sd/ltdirect/ltan0037.htm.

67. Roy Prosterman, an American land reform specialist, proposed in 1987 that USAID help fund a program to transfer ownership from Egyptian landlords, who functioned as little more than tax collectors, to the tenants who farmed the land and were in a position to improve it. USAID refused to fund or even endorse the proposal. Yahya Sadowski, *Political Vegetables? Businessman*

and Bureaucrat in the Development of Egyptian Agriculture (Washington, D.C.: Brookings Institution, 1991), 297. See also Robert Springborg, "State-Society Relations in Egypt: The Debate over Owner-Tenant Relations," *Middle East Journal* 45, no. 2 (1991): 231–49; and Raymond A. Hinnebusch, "Class, State, and the Reversal of Egypt's Agrarian Reform," *Middle East Report*, no. 184 (Sept.–Oct. 1993): 20–23; and chapters 8 and 9 below.

68. Ikram, *Egypt: Economic Management in a Period of Transition*, 5.

69. Johnson et al., *Egypt: The Egyptian American Rural Improvement Service*, 1.

70. USDA, *Egypt: Major Constraints to Increasing Agricultural Productivity*, 1.

71. Iliya Harik, "Decentralization and Development in Rural Egypt: A Description and Assessment," mimeo, prepared for USAID, Egypt, 1977, 1.

72. USDA, *Egypt: Major Constraints to Increasing Agricultural Productivity*, 25.

73. Ikram, *Egypt: Economic Management in a Period of Transition*, 5.

74. USAID, *Status Report: United States Economic Assistance to Egypt*, 60.

75. Louis Berger International Inc., *Agricultural Mechanization Project: Final Report* (East Orange, New Jersey: Louis Berger International Inc., 1985), 2.1.

76. Theodore Schultz, *Transforming Traditional Agriculture* (New Haven, Conn.: Yale University Press, 1964), 23, 29.

77. Louis Berger International Inc., *Agricultural Mechanization Project*, 2.1.

78. Polly Hill, *Development Economics on Trial: The Anthropological Case for a Prosecution* (Cambridge: Cambridge University Press, 1986), 25–26. Schultz emphasized the rationality of peasant agriculture in order to criticize the idea that low productivity was due to the fatalism of peasants and their ignorance of markets. Nevertheless, the absence of any concept of inequality made his work the foundation for the view, still prevailing, that technology is a panacea for the problems of rural poverty.

79. Sol Tax, *Penny Capitalism* (Chicago: University of Chicago Press, 1953); W. D. Hopper, "The Economic Organization of a Village in North Central India" (Ph.D. diss., Cornell University, 1957).

80. Cited in Hill, *Development Economics on Trial*, 25–26.

81. Ibid., 26.

82. Ibid.

83. Commander, *The State and Agricultural Development in Egypt Since 1973*, 233.

84. ERA 2000 Inc., "Further Mechanization of Egyptian Agriculture," mimeo, New York, 1979.

85. Hans Binswager, "Agricultural Mechanization: A Comparative Historical Analysis," *World Bank Research Observer* 1, no. 1 (1986): 27–56, at 30–32.

86. Alan Richards, "Egypt's Agriculture in Trouble," *MERIP Reports*, no. 84 (1980), 11.

87. Winrock International, *Policy Guidelines for Agricultural Mechanization in Egypt*, mimeo, Cairo, 1986, 41.

88. Commander, *The State and Agricultural Development in Egypt Since 1973*, 162–66; James Toth, *Rural Labor Movements in Egypt and Their Impact on the State, 1961–1992* (Gainesville: University Press of Florida, 1999), 164–88.

89. Dethier, *Trade, Exchange Rate, and Agricultural Pricing*, 220.

90. J. Allen Singleton, "The Training of Local Development Fund Officials and the Decentralization Process in Egypt" (paper presented at the Conference on Organizational Policy and Development, University of Louisville, Louisville, Kentucky, 1983), 1.

91. Ibid., 2.

92. Ikram, *Egypt: Economic Management in a Period of Transition.*

93. USAID, *Status Report*, 37.

94. Harik, "Decentralization and Development," 22.

95. Ibid., 24.

96. Ibid., 24, 26.

97. Ibid., 24.

98. United States Agency for International Development, *Congressional Presentation, FY 1990, Annex II: Asia and the Near East* (Washington, D.C.: USAID, 1989), 83.

99. United States Agency for International Development, *Annual Budget Submission, FY 1990: Egypt* (Washington, D.C.: USAID, 1988), 76–78.

100. USAID, *Status Report*, 111.

101. World Bank, *World Development Report 1989*, table 10.

102. See also Timothy Mitchell, *Colonising Egypt* (Berkeley: University of California Press, 1991).

103. The argument in this paragraph draws on George, "Conscience 'planétaire.' "

104. Calculated from World Bank, *World Development Report 1989*, table 14.

105. Ibid., tables 14 and 16. These figures are intended to indicate the scale of the problem rather than the details of an export-led program. Such a program would attempt to spread the growth over many years (a 12 percent annual growth in exports would achieve the forty-fold increase after about a third of a century). But assuming that the trade of the industrialized and newly industrialized countries also continued to grow, there would be no guarantee with such a program that Egypt would improve its share of world trade or its trade balance.

106. Lee, "Egalitarian Peasant Farming," shows the importance to Korean development of the egalitarian land reforms of 1949–57 and of continuing efforts after that to limit the reversion to inequality.

107. Harriet Friedmann, "The Political Economy of Food: A Global Crisis," *New Left Review*, no. 197 (1993): 50.

108. Paul Streeten, "A Cool Look at Outward-Looking Strategies for Development," *The World Economy* 5, no. 2 (1982): 166–67.

109. Irma Adelman, "Beyond Export-Led Growth," *World Development* 12, no. 9 (1984): 937–49.

110. Partha Chatterjee, *The Nation and its Fragments: Colonial and Postcolonial Histories* (Princeton, N.J.: Princeton University Press, 1993), 207.

111. Harik, "Decentralization and Development," 24.

112. Robert Springborg, *Mubarak's Egypt: Fragmentation of the Political Order* (Boulder, Colo.: Westview Press, 1989), 280.

113. Cf. Zaki Laïdi, *Enquête sur la Banque Mondiale* (Paris: Fayard, 1989).

114. International Finance Corporation, "Report and Recommendation of the President to the Board of Directors," 1983.

115. James Wessel with Mort Hantman, *Trading the Future: Farm Exports and the Concentration of Economic Power in Our Food System* (San Francisco: Institute for Food and Development Policy, 1983), 91–93.

116. See U.S. Congress Senate Committee on Foreign Relations, Subcommittee on Multinational Corporations, *Hearings on International Grain Companies* (Washington, D.C.: 94th Congress, June 1976); and U.S. Congress House Committee on Small Businesses, *Export Grain Sales* (Washington, D.C.: 96th Congress, June 1979); cited in Wessel, *Trading the Future.*

117. In the decade 1980–89 alone, the number of farms in the United States declined by 11 percent. Unlike the attrition pattern of previous decades, which was concentrated in small farms, the collapse in the 1980s spread to medium-sized operations. In the 1990s the collapse continued. USDA, *Agricultural Outlook* (Oct. 1989), 20; Nicholas D. Kristof, "As Life for Family Farmers Worsens, The Toughest Wither," *New York Times,* Apr. 2, 2000, 1:1, 1:18.

118. Wessel, *Trading the Future.*

119. The FY (fiscal year) 1991 Department of Agriculture budget for food assistance included $17.3 billion for food stamps, $3.5 billion for school lunches, $2.3 billion for the special program for women, infants, and children, and smaller amounts for food for the elderly, summer camps, Puerto Rico, and Indian reservations. USDA, "Domestic Food Assistance Reached Record Levels," *Food Review* 15, no. 2 (July–Sept. 1992), 22.

120. As Harriet Friedmann shows, the combination of price supports for farmers, import quotas, and export subsidies was replicated after World War II by the European Community. This postwar international "food regime" generated chronic surpluses and was dependent on forcing open Third World markets by the dumping of food aid and the conversion of these countries to meat consumption. Friedmann, "The Political Economy of Food."

121. Kristof, "As Life for Family Farmers Worsens, The Toughest Wither," 1:18.

122. The only exception that did not require a purchase was PL 480 Title II aid, which provided free milk and grain products estimated to be worth $179 million (about 5 percent of PL 480 aid and 1 percent of total U.S. economic aid to Egypt) to voluntary child-feeding programs. The program was canceled after FY 1989.

123. The major hard-currency purchase was the PL 480 Title I food program, amounting to $2.87 billion between 1975 and 1989. PL 480 Title III (canceled after FY 1983) provided an additional $72 million of food, primarily

wheat, purchased in Egyptian pounds. The Commodity Import Program (CIP) provided $3.660 billion worth of imports purchased in Egyptian pounds and about $700 million in U.S. dollars. Agricultural commodities and equipment represented one-third of CIP purchases (USAID, *Status Report*, 1–8, figure 3).

124. By mid-1988 Egypt owed $11.7 billion to the United States, of which $5.7 billion was for military purchases, mostly from the late 1970s and early 1980s. Unlike the easy credit terms given for food and other U.S. imports, these debts were contracted at high fixed interest rates of 12 to 14 percent, and in some cases 18 percent. By the late 1980s interest payments on the military debt to the United States reached $600 million annually. Economist Intelligence Unit, *Egypt: Country Report*, no. 4, 1989, 56.

125. U.S. Congress House Committee on Foreign Affairs, Subcommittee on Europe and the Middle East, *Foreign Assistance Legislation for Fiscal Year 1985 (Part 3): Economic and Military Aid Programs in Europe and the Middle East* (Washington, D.C.: 98th Congress, second session, Feb.–Mar. 1984), 508.

126. U.S. Congress House Committee on Foreign Affairs, Subcommittee on Europe and the Middle East, *Hearings on Agency for International Development Policy on the Use of Cash Transfer: The Case of Egypt* (Washington, D.C.: 100th Congress, second session, Dec. 10, 1987), 78. The cable leaked to the *Washington Post* (Feb. 3, 1984) recorded a conversation in Cairo in which the visiting head of USAID asked a high Egyptian official "if the $103 million [cash transfer] would be sufficient to enable the GOE [Government of Egypt] to meet its FMS [Foreign Military Sales] debt servicing obligations through the elections." USAID officials admitted in Congress that such military use of USAID funds was a violation of the 1978 Security Assistance Act, explained away the cable by saying that Egyptian officials often referred to FMS debt when they meant nonmilitary debt (ignoring the fact that it was the head of USAID, not the Egyptian, who specified FMS debt, and that only an FMS default would trigger adverse political consequences before the elections), and promised that this illegal use of funds would not occur. But despite repeated Congressional requests, USAID produced no accounting of how the Cash Transfers were actually spent. See U.S. Congress, *Foreign Assistance Legislation for Fiscal Year 1985*, 119–22, 149–52; U.S. Congress, *Foreign Assistance Legislation for Fiscal Years 1986–87*, 175–78.

127. U.S. Congress, *Hearings on Agency for International Development Policy on the Use of Cash Transfer*, 25.

128. *New York Times*, Sept. 20, 1990, A8; Economist Intelligence Unit, *Egypt: Country Profile 1993/94*, 46.

129. USAID, *Status Report*.

130. United States Agency for International Development, Washington, *Annual Budget Submission, FY 1990: Egypt* (Washington, D.C.: USAID, 1988), main volume, 21.

131. The USAID budget for FY 1990 stated that the first priority for these local currency funds was to support the local-currency operating expenses of the Cairo mission (representing about half its total operating expenses of $12

million), and the second priority was "to ensure that all the LE [Egyptian pound] funds required for implementation of dollar-funded projects are met." United States Agency for International Development, Washington, *Annual Budget Submission, FY 1990: Egypt,* main volume, 21.

132. See Dina Galal, *al-Ma'una al-amrikiyya li-man: misr am amrika?* (Cairo: al-Ahram, 1988), 'Adil Husayn, *Nahw fikr 'arabi jadid: al-nasiriyya wa-l-tanmiya wa-l-dimuqratiyya* (Cairo: Dar al-Mustaqbal al-'Arabi, 1985), and the defensive pamphlet USAID published in Arabic in response, "Common Misconceptions about USAID in Egypt."

133. *Al-Ahram al-iqtisadi,* July 9, 1990, 96.

134. USAID, *Status Report,* 8.

135. Springborg, *Mubarak's Egypt,* 258–59.

136. This larger purpose of U.S. assistance funds is made quite clear in government publications intended for U.S. corporations. See, for example, U.S. Department of Commerce International Trade Administration, *Foreign Economic Trends and their Implication for the U.S.* (Washington, D.C.: U.S. Department of Commerce, 1989), 15–16.

137. Economist Intelligence Unit, *Egypt: Country Report,* no. 4, 1989, 53; USAID, *Annual Budget Submission, FY 1990: Egypt,* main volume, 293.

138. Springborg, *Mubarak's Egypt,* 111. On the Egyptian military see also the essays collected in Ahmad 'Abd Allah, ed., *al-Jaysh wa-'l-dimuqratiyya fi misr* (Cairo: Dar Sina, 1990).

139. Library of Congress, Federal Research Division, *Egypt: A Country Study,* Country Studies / Area Handbook series, sponsored by the Department of the Army (Washington, D.C.: Library of Congress, 1991), 404; Springborg, *Mubarak's Egypt,* 110.

140. Springborg, *Mubarak's Egypt,* 113.

141. According to U.S. prosecutors, Lockheed agreed in 1988 to pay a commission of $600,000 per plane to a consulting company owned by the M.P., Layla Takla, and her husband. The Pentagon discovered evidence of the fee agreement in 1989, and Lockheed executives told the Pentagon it would not be paid, but in 1990 the company agreed to pay a $1 million "termination fee" to Takla in lieu of the sale commission. Lockheed pleaded guilty in a case brought under the Foreign Corrupt Practices Act of 1977 and was fined $24.8 million, twice its profit from the sale. "$24.8 Million Penalty Paid by Lockheed," *New York Times,* Jan. 28, 1995, A35.

142. Library of Congress, Federal Research Division, *Egypt: A Country Study,* 397.

143. Springborg, *Mubarak's Egypt,* 107.

CHAPTER 8. THE MARKET'S PLACE

1. The discussion that follows here draws on the work of Ernesto Laclau, *New Reflections on the Revolution of Our Time* (London: Verso, 1990), and the insightful essay by Julie Graham and Katherine Gibson, published under the

pseudonym J. K. Gibson-Graham, "Identity and Economic Plurality: Rethinking Capitalism and 'Capitalist Hegemony,' " *Environment and Planning D: Society and Space* 13, no. 3 (1995): 275–82. Gibson-Graham extend their argument in *The End of Capitalism (As We Knew It): A Feminist Critique of Political Economy* (Cambridge, Mass.: Blackwell, 1996). See also Dipesh Chakrabarty's important essay, "The Two Histories of Capitalism," in *Provincializing Europe: Postcolonial Thought and Historical Difference* (Princeton, N.J.: Princeton University Press, 2000), 47–71.

2. "Homoficence" was the term introduced by Aidan Foster Carter in his discussion of the work of Pierre-Philippe Rey, *Colonialisme, néo-colonialisme, et transition au capitalisme* (Paris: Maspero, 1971). The concept of the homoficence of capitalism, Foster Carter suggested, would make it possible "to preserve the coherence of Marxism." The phrasing is revealing. It used to be hoped that Marxism would help reveal the incoherence of capitalism. Instead, capitalism was to be rendered homificent, to preserve the coherence of a certain kind of Marxism. "The Modes of Production Controversy," *New Left Review,* no. 107 (Jan.–Feb. 1978): 47–77.

3. On the critique of essentialized notions of the economy see Timothy Mitchell, "Origins and Limits of the Modern Idea of the Economy," Advanced Study Center, University of Michigan, *Working Papers Series,* no. 12, Nov. 1995. For an anti-essentialist theory of the social, see Ernesto Laclau and Chantalle Mouffe, *Hegemony and Socialist Strategy: Towards a Radical Democratic Politics* (London: Verso, 1985). On contesting the discourse of capitalist modernity in accounts of the Third World see, among others, Timothy Mitchell, *Colonising Egypt* (Berkeley: University of California Press, 1991); Homi K. Bhabha, *The Location of Culture* (London: Routledge, 1994); Gyan Prakash, "Writing Post-Orientalist Histories of the Third World: Perspectives from Indian Historiography," *Comparative Studies in Society and History* 32, no. 2 (1990): 383–408, and "Can the 'Subaltern' Ride? A Reply to O'Hanlon and Washbrook," *Comparative Studies in Society and History* 34, no. 1 (Jan. 1992): 168–84; Talal Asad, "Introduction," *Genealogies of Religion: Discipline and Reasons of Power in Christianity and Islam* (Baltimore, Md.: Johns Hopkins University Press, 1993), 1–24; Dipesh Chakrabarty, *Provincializing Europe;* and Gayatri Chakravorty Spivak, "Can the Subaltern Speak?" in *Marxism and the Interpretation of Culture,* ed. C. Nelson and L. Grossberg (Basingstoke: Macmillan Education, 1988), 271–313, reprinted in *Colonial Discourse and Post-Colonial Theory,* ed. Patrick Williams and Laura Chrisman (New York: Columbia University Press, 1994), 66–111.

4. See Mitchell, "Origins and Limits of the Modern Idea of the Economy."

5. Soheir Mehanna, Nicholas S. Hopkins, and Bahgat Abdelmaksoud, *Farmers and Merchants: Background to Structural Adjustment in Egypt,* Cairo Papers in Social Science 17, Monograph 2 (Cairo: American University in Cairo Press, 1994); Nicholas S. Hopkins, *Agrarian Transformation in Egypt* (Boulder, Colo.: Westview Press, 1987), and "Small Farmer Households and Agricultural Sustainability in Egypt," in *Sustainable Agriculture in Egypt,* ed. Mohamed A.

Faris and Mahmood Hasan Khan (Boulder, Colo.: Lynne Rienner, 1993), 185–95. On the history of rural markets, see Barbara K. Larson, "The Rural Marketing System in Egypt over the Last Three Hundred Years," *Comparative Studies in Society and History* 27, no. 3 (1985): 494–530.

6. I elaborate this argument in my essay "The Stage of Modernity," in *Questions of Modernity,* ed. Timothy Mitchell (Minneapolis: University of Minnesota Press, 2000), on which the present paragraph draws. In political economy, Michael J. Piore and Charles F. Sabel, *The Second Industrial Divide: Possibilities for Prosperity* (New York: Basic Books, 1984), popularized the idea of alternative paths of capitalist development within the industrialized West. These alternatives, however, are understood within a historicist framework. They occur as different branches on the same tree of historical development, rather than as differences internal to every instance of capitalism and thus marks of a radical indeterminacy within.

7. For a more extensive analysis of the impact of structural adjustment programs, see Ray Bush, *Economic Crisis and the Politics of Reform in Egypt* (Boulder, Colo.: Westview Press, 1999).

8. David Ricardo, "An Essay on the Influence of a Low Price of Corn on the Profits of Stock" [1815], in *The Works and Correspondence of David Ricardo,* ed. Piero Sraffa, vol. 4, *Pamphlets and Papers, 1815–1823,* published for the Royal Economic Society (Cambridge: Cambridge University Press, 1951), 9–41.

9. Harriet Friedman, "World Market, State, and Family Farm: Social Bases of Household Production in the Era of Wage Labor," *Comparative Studies in Society and History* 20, no. 4 (1978): 545–86, at 545–46.

10. Yahya Sadowski, *Political Vegetables? Businessman and Bureaucrat in the Development of Egyptian Agriculture* (Washington, D.C.: Brookings Institution, 1991), 156.

11. See, for example, "Kabir khubara' al-iqtisadiyyin bi-sanduq al-naqd al-dawli," *al-Ahram,* Jan. 25, 1997, 21; Douglas Jehl, "Egypt Adding Corn to Bread: An Explosive Mix?" *New York Times,* Nov. 27, 1996, A4.

12. See Harold Alderman and Joachim von Braun, *Egypt's Food Subsidy and Rationing System: A Description* (Washington, D.C.: International Food Policy Research Institute, 1982).

13. Hassan Khedr, Rollo Ehrich, and Lehman B. Fletcher, "Nature, Rationale, and Accomplishments of the Agricultural Policy Reforms, 1987–1994," in *Egypt's Agriculture in a Reform Era,* ed. Lehman B. Fletcher (Ames: Iowa State University Press, 1996), 51–83, at 63.

14. There is no space in this chapter to give a full account of the political economy of the village, or to discuss the ways tourism affects it. Briefly, scores of households derive some income from tourism or the related industry of archaeology, typically by employment as government workers or guards at the archaeological sites, as seasonal workers on archaeological excavations, or as unskilled employees of the hotels in Luxor and the Nile cruise ships based there. This low-paid work provides a supplement to farm income, rarely an alternative. Only a handful of households have made large profits from tourism,

by finding the capital to invest in building a budget-class hotel or providing tourist transportation. The effects of tourism employment are, first, that fewer men have had to migrate elsewhere to find work (although many have migrated, either to Cairo, the tourist towns of the Red Sea coast, or the Gulf states); second, many households are vulnerable to the repeated contraction of the tourist industry in periods of political instability or violence; and third, the village does not specialize in labor-intensive farming, such as large-scale vegetable production (villages to the south, between Armant and Esna, supply the large demand for vegetables for the Luxor tourist trade), or in other nonfarm industries such as weaving, furniture making, brick making, or pottery found in neighboring villages. See Timothy Mitchell, "Worlds Apart: An Egyptian Village and the International Tourism Industry," *Middle East Report,* no. 196 (Sept.–Oct. 1995): 8–11, 23.

15. The 1986 census recorded the village's population as 10,850, consisting of 2,385 dwelling units and 1,914 families. Central Agency for Public Mobilization and Statistics, *Census of Egypt 1986, Qina Governorate* (Cairo, n.d.), 96.

16. I have changed the names and certain descriptions of people in the village. As in previous chapters, the term "acre" here refers to an Egyptian acre, or *feddan,* equal to 0.42 hectares or 1.038 British or U.S. acres. It is divided into 24 qirats, each qirat being 175 square meters.

17. The methods are described in Food and Agriculture Organization of the United Nations, *National Methods of Collecting Agricultural Statistics,* Supplement no. 18, *Egypt, Mexico, Puerto Rico* (Rome: FAO, 1983), 1–3.

18. Cotton is an interesting example. The area planted with cotton is said to have dropped by 17 percent in the early years of the reforms, from 1.05 million acres in 1986 to 880,000 acres in 1993. Yet total production remained virtually unchanged, dropping from 6.9 million qantars (hundredweight) to 6.88 million. The official figures conclude that the decline in acreage was exactly balanced by a dramatic and largely unexplained increase in yield, from 6.54 to 7.78 qantars per acre. An alternative explanation would be that the ending of quotas and compulsory procurement prices for wheat and other food crops removed the need to misreport the area planted with cotton, and that its actual area, yield, and production remained constant.

19. There are other examples of this move toward self-provisioning elsewhere in the world following the promotion of free-market agriculture. An interesting case is that of cotton farmers in Andra Pradesh in southern India, who switched to growing chickpeas. The switch ended their battles with pests and markets and their need for extensive fertilizer suppliers and labor. Chickpeas, which are nitrogen-fixing, restored the fertility of the soil and ended protein malnourishment in local diets. International Crop Research Institute for the Semi-Arid Tropics, "A Silent Pulse Revolution," *Food From Thought,* available at http://www.icrisat.org/text/pubs/fft/gpub2.html.

20. In the case of cotton, the area planted began (or continued) to decline sharply following the removal of acreage controls in 1992 and 1993, dropping from 850,000 acres in 1990 to 720,000 in 1994 and 710,000 in 1995. The Min-

istry of Supply had to raise procurement prices as much as 30 percent above world market prices to maintain supplies to the textile industry. (Khedr, Ehrich, and Fletcher, "The Agricultural Policy Reforms," 63, 67). Marketing was partially deregulated in 1994, but the government retained a floor price. (There were reports that a single merchant, Mahmud Wahba, monopolized the commercial market that year.) In 1996 import restrictions were lifted and merchants refused to buy domestic cotton at the floor price of E£500 per qantar. The government spent E£1 billion purchasing the surplus crop. In January 1997 the Finance Ministry, supported by merchants and private sector firms, called for the floor price to be abolished, but the Ministries of Agriculture and Supply insisted successfully that the market could not be deregulated and price supports had to be retained. The government retained the E£500 floor price and announced that cotton acreage would be extended to one million acres ("al-Hukuma tahammalat 522 malyun ginaih li-'l-mawsim al-qutn 96/97," *al-Ahram al-iqtisadi,* Feb. 24, 1997, 40; Jamal Imbabi, "Tusa'id al-khilafat baina al-zira'a wa-'l-maliyya wa-'l-rayy hawla tahdid misahat al-ruz wa-'l-qutn," *al-Sha'b,* Jan. 31, 1997, 8; "Zira'at milyun faddan qutnan fi al-mawsim al-qadim," *al-Ahram,* Feb. 7, 1997, 1). As international cotton prices continued to fall, the higher Egyptian floor price caused exports of cotton textiles and clothes to decline sharply. Exports in 1996 were 21 percent lower than 1995 (*Business Today Egypt,* Mar. 1997, 12).

21. See Saad Nassar, Fenton Sands, Mohamed A. Omran, and Ronald Krenz, "Crop Production Responses to the Agricultural Policy Reforms," in Fletcher, ed., *Egypt's Agriculture in a Reform Era,* 84–111, table 5.1, 92. Unlike wheat, rice became less profitable during the reform period (Khedr, Ehrich, and Fletcher , "The Agricultural Policy Reforms," 69). This evidence supports the argument that farmers were shifting to staples to avoid the market rather than in response to market signals.

22. The government limited the rice area to 900,000 acres in 1996, but farmers planted 1.2 million acres (Imbabi, "Tusa'id al-khilafat," 8). Production that year reached 4.5 million tons, but exports dropped from a previous high of 800,000 tons to only 200,000 ("Ma'rakat al-ruzz ma zalat mustamirra," *Akhbar al-yawm,* Nov. 23, 1996, 22). The Minister of Public Works and Water Supplies wanted to limit the use of irrigation water for rice in part because he was the proponent of ambitious land reclamation schemes that would require vast new supplies of water. Shortly before his death in November 1996 he won the president's support for a plan to create a "New Delta," the Toshka project in southern Egypt (see chapter 9). An important benefit of rice cultivation was that the large amount of water used in its irrigation prevented the ingress of salt water in the coastal regions of the northern Delta. Nadir Nur al-Din Muhammad, "Hiwarat al-zira'iyyin hawl al-miyah wa-'l-aruzz wa-'l-qasab," *al-Ahram,* Mar. 11, 2001, 12.

23. Crop areas for 1990–93 (percent of total) were: berseem 21.7, maize 19.6, wheat 18.0, rice 10.9, cotton 8.8, vegetables 6.2, others 14.8. Nassar et al., "Crop Production Responses to the Agricultural Policy Reforms," 91. The four

largest crops, accounting for 70.2 percent of the crop area, were produced mostly for household use. A survey in 1989–91 of 665 farmers in three different parts of the country found that about 70 percent of those growing wheat, almost 80 percent of those growing maize, and nearly half of those growing berseem used the crop entirely for their own consumption. Most of the rest sold only a part of the crop, and often to other households within the village, almost entirely so in the case of berseem. Mehanna et al., *Farmers and Merchants,* 68–77.

24. The symbol "E£" indicates the Egyptian pound. One U.S. dollar was equivalent to E£2.75 in 1989–90 and about E£3.40 during remainder of the 1990s.

25. On the mechanization of Egyptian agriculture see chapter 7.

26. A survey in 1989–91 found the costs of marketing to be an important concern among farmers. Mehanna et al., *Farmers and Merchants,* 133.

27. Sidney W. Mintz, *Sweetness and Power: The Place of Sugar in Modern History* (New York: Viking Penguin, 1985), 46–61.

28. In 1983 the sugar protection policies of the industrialized countries caused Third World producers to lose $7.4 billion in revenue, cutting their real income by $2.1 billion and increasing price instability by 25 percent. The World Bank, *World Development Report 1986* (Washington, D.C.: World Bank, 1986); World Commission on Environment and Development, *Our Common Future* (Oxford: Oxford University Press, 1987), 82.

29. Brazil accounted for 28 percent of the increase in production from 1993/94 to 1999/2000. Its dominant role in the market was due to lower production costs, but also to its alcohol sector providing an alternative outlet for cane. United States Department of Agriculture, Foreign Agricultural Service, "Sugar: World Markets and Trade," Circular, Nov. 1999, at http://www.fas.usda.gov/htp2/sugar/1999/november/toc.html; *Economist,* Nov. 27, 1999, 108.

30. The Center for Responsive Politics cites the sugar industry as a leading example of how pressure groups use money to influence voting in Congress. In 1996 the industry paid an average of $13,000 to the sixty-one senators who voted to preserve sugar subsidies, compared to an average of $1,500 to those who voted against. *Cashing In: A Guide to Money, Votes, and Public Policy in the 104th Congress* (Washington, D.C.: Center for Responsive Politics, Jan. 1997). The price of U.S. sugar also included the cost of the embargo on Cuban sugar, another part of the protection system.

31. Friedmann, "World Market, State, and Family Farm," 582–86.

32. The figure of $29,000 is from the Organization for Economic Cooperation and Development, cited Kevin Watkins, "Fast Route to Poverty," *Guardian Weekly,* Feb. 16, 1997, 29. Egypt's 1994 per capita GNP was estimated at $720 (World Bank, *World Development Report 1996* [New York: Oxford University Press, 1996], table 1, 188). In 1991, annual agricultural producer subsidies were estimated at $83 billion in the European Union, $34 billion in the United States, and $30 billion in Japan. These subsidies represented 30 percent of farmers' incomes in the United States, 49 percent in the EU, and 66 percent in

Japan (*Economist,* Dec. 12, 1992). Despite these subsidies, U.S. farmers required extensive nonfarm income to survive. In 1992, income from nonfarm sources represented on average 41 percent of farm operator households' income. United States Department of Agriculture, *Agriculture Fact Book 1994* (Washington, D.C.: USDA, 1994), 33.

33. In 1993 the U.S. food stamp program served 27 million people and cost $27 billion (fiscal year 1994). Another $8 billion was spent on other subsidized food programs, including the school lunch and the Women, Infants and Children programs. Ibid., 76–79.

34. The ardeb is a dry measure, equal to 198 liters. One ardeb of wheat weighs 150 kilograms.

35. I am grateful to Reem Saad for the information about the events in Aswan governorate.

36. Six months later a similar crisis occurred with the 1996 rice harvest. Despite a bumper crop, the government mills were unable to obtain supplies to run at even 20 percent of capacity. The cooperative authorities claimed that speculators were buying the crop with bank loans and storing it in granaries belonging to the banks, in the expectation that new acreage controls by the Ministry of Irrigation would force prices up the following year. Other officials blamed the shortage on the existence of forty thousand village-based mills and hulling machines, most of them unlicensed and some of them milling rice for sale to others rather than the farmer's personal consumption, which was banned by the government. General Fakri Dhikr, director of the Investigations Department of the Ministry of Supply, announced that 115 village mills had been closed for these reasons. A plan to ban the transport of rice between governorates, as with wheat, was abandoned. Since only eight governorates produced rice the ban would have left the other twenty with no supplies ("Maʿrakat al-ruzz ma zalat mustamirra," *Akhbar al-yawm,* Nov. 23, 1996, 22).

37. In January 1997 the Minister of Supply acknowledged the existence of this cartel and promised government legislation against monopolies to give it "a harsh rap on the knuckles." "Basic Commodities Abundant in Ramadan," *Egyptian Gazette,* Jan. 10, 1997, 10.

38. On the history of this trade, see Terence Walz, *Trade Between Egypt and Bilad as-Sudan, 1700–1820* (Cairo: Institut Français d'Archéologie Orientale du Caire, 1978).

39. A. John De Boer, Forrest E. Walters, and M. A. Sherafeldin, "Impacts of the Policy Reforms on Livestock and Feed Production, Consumption and Trade," in Fletcher, ed., *Egypt's Agriculture in a Reform Era,* 112–48, at 119–20, 126, 129–31. The ban on importing frozen poultry was reimposed, protecting the cartel.

40. Following the reforms a local butcher reported that he now slaughtered and sold only one calf a week, when before the reforms he had slaughtered four or five. Their price had more than doubled in five years.

41. The government controlled the supply of fertilizer through the Principal Bank for Development and Agricultural Credit. When its monopoly ended

in 1994, local producers began to export much of their supply. Bush, *Economic Crisis and the Politics of Reform in Egypt,* 69; Mohamed Abd al-Aal, "Farmers and Cooperatives in the Era of Structural Adjustment," in *Directions of Change in Rural Egypt,* ed. Nicholas S. Hopkins and Kirsten Westergaard (Cairo: American University in Cairo Press, 1998), 279–302.

42. Futures markets stabilize prices but tend to leave quantities unstable. As a result, incomes may be less stable than if prices were unstabilized and allowed to adjust to changes in quantity. David M. Newberry, "Futures Markets, Hedging, and Speculation," in *The New Palgrave Dictionary of Money and Finance,* ed. David M. Newberry, Murray Milgate, and John Eatwell, vol. 2 (New York: Stockton Press, 1992), 202–10.

43. In 1986 E. Lee Fuller, an American expert in agricultural marketing, proposed helping to break the marketing oligopolies in Egypt by introducing a variety of nonmarket organizations common in Europe and the United States, including cooperatives. Some Egyptian officials were receptive to the proposal, but USAID blocked it, as their free-market program ruled out any support for building cooperative institutions. Sadowski, *Political Vegetables,* 181.

44. Lehman B. Fletcher, "Introduction and Overview," in Fletcher, ed., *Egypt's Agriculture in a Reform Era,* 3–8, at 4.

45. Jean-Jacques Dethier, *Trade, Exchange and Agricultural Pricing Policies in Egypt,* World Bank Comparative Studies (Washington, D.C.: World Bank, 1989).

46. The index of the real value of agricultural output (1980 = 100) was calculated at 145 in 1986, 158 in 1987, 144 in 1992, and 154 in 1993. Abdel-Moneim Rady, Mohamed A. Omran, and Fenton B. Sands, "Impacts of the Policy Reforms on Agricultural Income, Employment and Rural Poverty," in Fletcher, ed., *Egypt's Agriculture in a Reform Era,* 149–64; table 7.1, 153.

47. Khedr, Ehrich, and Fletcher, "The Agricultural Policy Reforms," 61.

48. "Tadaffuq ru'us amwal ajnabiyya kathira li-misr qad yamthul quwa daghita ʿala taghyir siʿr al-sarf wa bi-ʾl-tali yuʿaqqid min al-wadʿ al-iqtisadi," *al-Ahram,* Jan. 25, 1997, 21, quoting the views of Dr. Arvind Subramanian, Permanent Representative of the IMF in Egypt. See also Fletcher, "Introduction and Overview," 5.

49. Ngozi Okonjo-Iweala [Chief of Agricultural Operations, World Bank] and Youssed Fuleihan, "Structural Adjustment and Egyptian Agriculture: Some Preliminary Indication of the Impact of Economic Reforms," in *Sustainable Agriculture in Egypt,* ed. Mohamed A. Faris and Mahmood Hasan Khan (Boulder, Colo.: Lynne Rienner, 1993), 127–39, at 134. If tenants hold land in perpetuity and can pass it to their heirs, they have no reason to treat it any differently than those who own the land. Nor is there any evidence that they do. Arguably, removing this security is more likely to discourage tenants from improving the land or maintaining its quality. If so, it was not the 1952 law but the act of repealing it that was "creating disincentives."

50. When the government allowed opposition parties to form in the late 1970s, one of the first members of the Wafd, successor of the pre-1952 party of

the same name, was Yusuf Wali, the future minister of agriculture responsible for the free-market reforms. He belonged to one of the largest landowning families of Fayyum. His connection with the Wafd was seldom mentioned, as all ministers were officially members of the ruling party.

51. Law 96 of 1992, amending law 178 of 1952, known as the First Agrarian Reform Law. See Reem Saad, "State, Landlord, Parliament and Peasant: The Story of the 1992 Tenancy Law in Egypt," in *Agriculture in Egypt from Pharaonic to Modern Times*, ed. Alan Bowman and Eugene Rogin, Proceedings of the British Academy, no. 96 (Oxford: Oxford University Press, 1999), 387–404; and Robert Springborg, "State-Society Relations in Egypt: the Debate over Owner-Tenant Relations," *Middle East Journal* 45, no. 2 (1991): 231–49.

52. *Al-Ahram*, ca. Oct. 12, 1996. As the opposition parties began to demand in parliament and the press that the government postpone implementing the law or take measures to reduce its impact, however, the government was forced to insist that the reform would proceed, promising only that they would give priority to evicted tenants in allocating ownership of newly reclaimed land. "Fi majlis al-shaʿb," *al-Ahram*, Feb. 25, 1997, 13; "Amanat al-fallahin tutalib bi-taʾjil tanfidh qanun al-malik wa-ʾl-mustaʾjir," *al-Shaʿb*, Feb. 25, 1997, 1.

53. Agricultural cooperatives had begun collecting information in preparation for the evictions. Mujahid al-ʿArusi, "Badʾ ijraʾat tard al-mustaʾjirin min al-ard," *al-Shaʿb*, Feb. 25, 1997, 1.

54. "Muzahirat Bani Suwayf," *al-Dustur*, Jan. 22, 1997, 5.

55. *Al-Dustur* was shut down in February 1998 and its editor and two other journalists were fined and sentenced to two years hard labor for libeling the Ministry of Agriculture. The Socialist Labour Party and its newspaper, *al-Shaʿb*, were shut down in May 2000. *Middle East Times*, May 20, 2000.

56. The center was able to list only those incidents reported to it or mentioned in the national media. The Land Center for Human Rights, "Report on Farmers' Conditions in Egypt's Rural Areas During 1998," mimeo, Land and Farmer Series, no. 3 (Cairo: Land Center for Human Rights, Mar. 1999); "Violence in Egypt's Countryside Claimed Life of 18 Persons, Injured 97, 135 Detained in Six Months," mimeo, Land and Farmer Series, no. 4 (Cairo: Land Center for Human Rights, Sept. 1999).

57. The state already controlled the licensing of all nongovernment organizations. The new law dissolved existing organizations and required them to register under more stringent conditions, including state control over their sources of funds and appointments to their governing boards. In June 2000 the Constitutional Court invalidated the law on technical grounds, but the government announced that an amended law would be reissued. *Middle East Times*, June 9, 2000.

58. Mohamed Abdel Aal and Reem Saad carried out a study of the impact of the new law in six villages in Upper Egypt: "Social and Economic Impact of the New Egyptian Land Reform Law Legislation on Rural Economy," mimeo (Cairo: American University in Cairo, Social Research Center, 1999). See also

Reem Saad, "Agriculture and Politics in Contemporary Egypt: The 1997 Tenancy Crisis," in *Discourses in Contemporary Egypt: Political and Social Issues*, ed. Enid Hill, Cairo Papers in Social Science 22, monograph 4 (Cairo: American University in Cairo Press, 1999), 22–35.

59. Figures from the Land Center for Human Rights, quoted in "Egypt 2000," Financial Times Survey, available at http://specials.ft.com/ln/ftsurveys/country/scdcf6.htm.

60. Property transactions used to be registered with the district court in Luxor, with a record kept in the Finance Ministry archives (Dar al-Mahfuzat) in Cairo. But this practice largely ended after the 1940s, making property claims harder to establish. Rajab's land was first rented in 1944, perhaps as a consequence of the malaria epidemic in Upper Egypt that year that had killed so many of the village (see chapter 1).

61. Lehman B. Fletcher, "Egypt's Agricultural Future," in Fletcher, ed., *Egypt's Agriculture in a Reform Era*, 331–41, at 333–34.

62. Khedr, Ehrich, and Fletcher, "Agricultural Policy Reforms," 75.

63. A 1991 survey found that stunting (low height for age) affected 23 percent of urban children under five years of age and 34 percent of rural. In rural Upper Egypt the rate reached almost 40 percent. Rady, Omran, and Sands, "Impacts of the Policy Reforms," 159. Following the reforms, a doctor in the village reported to me a marked increase in the incidence of stunting.

64. Based on the 1990/91 Income, Expenditure and Consumption Survey (Cairo: Central Agency for Public Mobilization and Statistics, 1993), Abla Abdel-Latif and Heba El-Laithy estimate that the nonpoor (defined as those with household incomes above a poverty line of E£3,994 in urban areas and E£3,399 in rural areas, representing the annual cost of basic food and nonfood needs) had an average daily per capita calorie intake of 2,488 in urban areas and 2,468 in rural areas. "Protecting Food Security for the Poor in a Liberalizing Economy," in Fletcher, ed., *Egypt's Agriculture in a Reform Era*, 294–327, at 299–301. The Food and Agriculture Organization recommended a minimum level of 2,540 calories. Rady, Omran, and Sands, "Impacts of the Policy Reforms," 159.

65. U.S. Embassy report, quoted in Economist Intelligence Unit, *Egypt: Country Profile 1996/97* (London: Economist Intelligence Unit, 1996), 22.

66. Harold Alderman and Joachim von Braun, *The Effects of the Egyptian Food Ration and Subsidy System on Income Distribution and Consumption*, Research Report no. 45 (Washington, D.C.: International Food Policy Research Institute, 1984).

67. United Nations Development Program, *Human Development Report 1994*, quoted in Economist Intelligence Unit, *Egypt: Country Profile 1996/97*, 22–23.

68. There was a long debate on peasant farming and its relation to the expansion of capitalism. Its origins lay in discussions of the Russian peasantry, but it was taken up again in the 1970s and 1980s in writing on Latin America, Africa, South Asia, and the Middle East. For an early review see Foster Carter,

"The Modes of Production Controversy." For the debate in Middle Eastern studies, see Timothy Mitchell, "Fixing the Economy," *Cultural Studies* 12, no. 1 (1998): 82–101, on which the current paragraph draws.

69. Georg Stauth, *Die Fellachen im Nildelta: Zur Struktur des Konflikts zwischen subsistenz- und warenproduktion in Ländlichen Ägypten* (Wiesbaden: Franz Steiner, 1983); and "Capitalist Farming and Small Peasant Households in Egypt," in *The Rural Middle East: Peasant Lives and Modes of Production,* ed. Kathy Glavanis and Pandeli Glavanis (London: Zed Press, 1990), 122–41.

70. Kathy and Pandeli Glavanis drew on the work of Stauth, as well as the earlier contribution of Islamoglu and Keyder and the broader debate on the articulation of modes of production, to propose a new approach to the study of agrarian society in the Middle East, one that takes seriously the phenomenon of peasant agriculture and attempts to explain its persistence. Kathy Glavanis and Pandeli Glavanis, "The Sociology of Agrarian Relations in the Middle East: The Persistence of Household Production," *Current Sociology* 31, no. 2 (1983): 1–106; Glavanis and Glavanis, *The Rural Middle East;* Huri Islamoglu-Inan and Çağlar Keyder, "Agenda for Ottoman History," *Review* 1, no. 1 (1977): 31–55. Islamoglu revised her views in Huri Islamoglu-Inan, *State and Peasant in the Ottoman Empire: Agrarian Power Relations and Regional Economic Development in Ottoman Anatolia during the Sixteenth Century* (Leiden: E. J. Brill, 1994).

71. Glavanis and Glavanis, "The Sociology of Agrarian Relations in the Middle East," 36.

72. On Critchfield, see chapter 4.

73. Foster Carter, "The Modes of Production Controversy," 75–77.

74. David Seddon makes these criticisms, drawing on the work of Bernstein, and argues that trying to help peasants recapture their own history represents an illusory and reactionary form of peasant populism. David Seddon, "Commentary on Agrarian Relations in the Middle East: A 'New Paradigm' for Analysis?" *Current Sociology* 34, no. 2 (1986): 151–72; Henry Bernstein, "Concepts for the Analysis of Contemporary Peasantries," in *The Political Economy of Rural Development: Peasants, International Capital, and the State,* ed. Rosemary Galli (Albany: State University of New York Press, 1981), 3–24.

75. The view of household farmers in Egypt as small capitalists is best articulated in the work of Nicholas Hopkins, *Agrarian Transformation in Egypt,* and "Small Farmer Households and Agricultural Sustainability in Egypt." On household farmers as petty commodity producers see Henry Bernstein, "Agrarian Classes in Capitalist Development," in *Capitalism and Development,* ed. Leslie Sklair (London: Routledge, 1994), 40–71, and P. Gibbon and M. Neocosmos, "Some Problems in the Political Economy of 'African Socialism,'" in *Contradictions of Accumulation in Africa: Studies in Economy and State,* ed. Henry Bernstein and B. K. Campbell (Beverly Hills, Calif.: Sage, 1985).

76. There is no place here to consider the attempts to theorize household-based economic activity abstractly, within the tradition of neoclassical econom-

ics. Both the "new household economics" of Gary Becker and others and more recent work treating households as "institutions" based upon "implicit contracts" have been effectively critiqued elsewhere. See Naila Kabeer, "Benevolent Dictators, Maternal Altruists, and Patriarchal Contracts: Gender and Household Economics," in *Reversed Realities: Gender Hierarchies in Development Thought* (London: Verso, 1994), 95–135.

77. Gibson-Graham, "Identity and Economic Plurality."

78. Fletcher, "Introduction and Overview," 3; Jeffrey Sachs, "What is to be Done?" *Economist*, June 13, 1990, 25.

CHAPTER 9. DREAMLAND

1. "State socialism" is an inadequate term for describing the multiple logics of the Soviet system, just as "capitalism" is for other systems. See the discussions in Simon Clarke, ed., *What about the Workers? Workers and the Transition to Capitalism in Russia* (London: Verso, 1993), and David Stark, "Recombinant Property in East European Capitalism," in *The Laws of the Markets*, ed. Michel Callon, *Sociological Review* monograph series (Oxford: Blackwell, 1998), 116–46.

2. International Monetary Fund (IMF), Middle Eastern Department, "The Egyptian Stabilization Experience: An Analytical Retrospective," prepared by Arvind Subramanian, *Working Papers of the International Monetary Fund*, WP/97/105, Sept. 1997.

3. *Al-Ahram*, Jan. 1, 1999, 40.

4. *Al-Wafd*, Jan. 12, 1999, 1, 3.

5. The Toshka scheme, named after the depression fifty kilometers north of Abu Simbel through which the Nile waters were to be pumped, was budgeted to cost $86.5 billion over twenty years (1997–2017). United States, Department of State, *FY 2001 Country Commercial Guide: Egypt*, July 2000, available at http://www.state.gov/www/about_state/business/com_guides/2001.

6. Economist Intelligence Unit (EIU), *Country Report: Egypt*, 3rd quarter 1999, 25. Prince al-Walid bin Talal bin ʿAbd al-ʿAziz Al Saʿud's assets included ownership of 5 percent or more of Citigroup, Saks Fifth Avenue, TWA, Apple Computer, News Corporation, Disneyland, and Daewoo. He was also the principal investor in "New Cairo," in partnership with the Talʿat Mustafa Group. See *Middle East Times*, Egypt edition, Jan. 19, 2001, available at http://www.metimes.com, and http://www.medea.be/en/index327.htm.

7. See the Cadiz quarterly report to the U.S. Securities and Exchange Commission at http://www.sec.gov/Archives/edgar/data/727273/0000727273–99–000018.txt, and http://www.sun-world.com. The parent company, Cadiz, was reorganizing itself along similar lines, moving away from agribusiness to earn rents from the groundwater storage basins beneath its agricultural properties in California. In Egypt Cadiz agreed to a separate joint venture with Prince al-Walid to pursue a groundwater project in Sharq al-ʿUwainat (East Oweinat), to the west of Toshka, where the government planned to irrigate 200,000 acres

from deep wells. A third "Pharaonic" development project, as these schemes were called, extensive land reclamation in northern Sinai, was facing difficulties, including criticisms for the serious damage it threatened to the ecology of Sinai and the northern Nile Delta. See http://www.nile-river.org.

8. Beverly Hills was a 10.4 million-square-meter luxury housing development managed by a U.S.-Swiss joint venture, Turner-Steiner International S.A., and owned by Sixth of October Development and Investment Company, a venture formed by a group of Egypt's largest entrepreneurs. *Business Monthly,* Dec. 1998, available at http://www.amcham.org.eg/HTML/news.publication/BusinessMonthly. On Media Production City see www.toure-gypt.net/mpc.htm.

9. Toshka was to divert 10 percent of Egypt's share of the Nile River into the desert. This was likely to have a serious impact on the ecology of the existing river valley, which already suffered from soil salinity, coastal erosion, and declining water quality. See http://www.nile-river.org.

10. Economist Intelligence Unit (EIU), *Country Report: Egypt,* 3rd quarter 1998, 10.

11. IMF, "Egyptian Stabilization," 59.

12. EIU, *Country Profile: Egypt, 1998–99,* table 28, 54.

13. Peter R. Odell, "Oil Price Fears Have No Strong Base," *Financial Times,* Sept. 9, 1999, 12. The success was so great that less than a year later the United States was back negotiating oil prices with OPEC member governments again—to try to reduce them. Judith Miller, "Kuwait Is Said to Be Opposed to U.S. Effort to Cut Oil Prices," *New York Times,* Feb. 24, 2000, C4.

14. The import restrictions included much tighter limits on credit, abolishing duty-free imports, and introducing new and onerous customs inspections requirements. Economist Intelligence Unit (EIU), *Country Report: Egypt,* 1st quarter 1999, 33; *Middle East Times,* Aug. 27, 1999.

15. IMF, "Egyptian Stabilization," 5.

16. Ibid., 4.

17. For details of this illegal diversion of funds see chapter 7.

18. Iraq was the major destination for Egyptian arms exports, which were valued at $1 billion in 1982 and $500 million in 1983–84. Library of Congress, Federal Research Division, *Egypt: A Country Study* (Washington, D.C.: Library of Congress, 1991), 408.

19. IMF, "Egyptian Stabilization," 47.

20. Howard Handy and Staff Team, *Egypt: Beyond Stabilization, Towards a Dynamic Market Economy,* IMF Occasional Paper, no. 163 (Washington, D.C.: IMF, 1998), table 21, 50. E£ is the symbol for the Egyptian pound. For this chapter, the number of Egyptian pounds to the U.S. dollar is calculated at the average rate of 2.74 for 1989–90, 3.34 for 1991–92 to 1993–94, and 3.39 for 1994–95 to 1997–98 (based on Handy et al., *Egypt: Beyond Stabilization,* table 1, 2). It is not clear whether the figures on the profitability of state-owned enterprises take full account of the cost of state subsidies and protections (just as they do not take account of the social benefit of the employment they pro-

vided). Clearly what triggered the crisis, however, was not the long-term problems of management and reinvestment in state enterprise, but the impending collapse of the banking sector.

21. Mahmoud Mohieldin, "Causes, Measures, and Impact of State Intervention in the Financial Sector: The Egyptian Example," *Working Papers of the Economic Research Forum for the Arab Countries, Iran and Turkey,* no. 9507 (Cairo, 1995), 20.

22. Robert Springborg, *Mubarak's Egypt: Fragmentation of the Political Order* (Boulder, Colo.: Westview Press, 1989), 83–85.

23. Mohieldin, "State Intervention," 20–21.

24. Ibid., 17. On BCCI and the CIA, see United States Congress, Senate Committee on Foreign Relations, *The BCCI Affair: A Report to the Committee on Foreign Relations, United States Senate, by Senator John Kerry and Senator Hank Brown* (Washington, D.C.: United States Government Printing Office, 1992).

25. On similar problems faced by the Indian state in the same period, and the importance of discipline, see Prabhat Patnaik and C. P. Chandrasekhar, "India: *Dirigisme,* Structural Adjustment, and the Radical Alternative," in *Globalization and Progressive Economic Policy,* ed. Dean Baker, Gerald Epstein, and Robert Pollin (Cambridge: Cambridge University Press, 1998), 67–91.

26. The term "crony capitalism" came into vogue with the IMF during the global financial crisis. I prefer the term "indiscipline," for it points to the continuous difficulty in subjecting economic exchanges, within and outside the state, to law and regulation.

27. David Felix, "Asia and the Crisis of Financial Globalization," in Baker et al., *Globalization and Progressive Economic Policy,* table 1, 172.

28. The following is based on Yahya Sadowski, *Political Vegetables?: Businessman and Bureaucrat in the Development of Egyptian Agriculture* (Washington, D.C. Brookings Institution, 1991).

29. An UNCTAD report on the 1998–99 global financial crisis confirmed that the best predictor of economic crises in countries of the south was not state-led development but the deregulation of finances. United Nations Conference on Trade and Development, *Trade and Development Report 1998* (New York: UNCTAD, 1999).

30. IMF, "Egyptian Stabilization," 31.

31. Ibid., 35; Economist Intelligence Unit, *Country Report: Egypt,* 3rd quarter 1998, 19–20. Other benefits were transferred to the banks in 1991, including a reduction in reserve requirements (a source of fiscal income) from 25 percent to 15 percent. Mohieldin, "State Intervention," 13.

32. Handy, *Egypt: Beyond Stabilization,* 62; IMF, "The Egyptian Stabilization Experience," 34.

33. Handy, *Egypt: Beyond Stabilization,* 59.

34. Ibid., 52.

35. Stark, "Recombinant Property in East European Capitalism," makes the same point in regard to Hungary, both before and after the collapse of "socialism."

36. On the Arab Contractors see Sadowski, *Political Vegetables*, 105–26; on Eastern Tobacco, see Sophia Anninos, "Creating the Market: An Examination of Privatization Policies in Kazakhstan and Egypt," Ph.D. diss., New York University, 2000.

37. Aida Seif El Dawla, "Egypt: The Eternal Pyramid," report of the New Woman Research Center, available at http://www.socwatch.org.uy/1998/english/reports/egypt.htm.

38. The government liquidated twenty-seven companies. Of the ninety-seven other companies in which the government sold shares, it retained a majority of the shares in eighteen, remained the largest single shareholder in a further twenty-five, retained significant share holdings in another twelve, and transferred twenty-eight more to "employee shareholder associations," which in practice allowed continued control by the same managers. Fourteen companies were said to have been sold directly to large "anchor investors." EIU, *Country Report: Egypt*, 3rd quarter 1998, 19; EIU, *Country Report: Egypt*, 3rd quarter 1999, 20.

39. Marat Terterov, "Is SOE Asset-swapping Privatization?" *Middle East Times*, Aug. 9, 1998.

40. *Financial Times*, Jan. 15, 1999, 36.

41. Sherine Abd Al-Razek, "Market in Overdrive," *Al-Ahram Weekly*, Feb. 17–23, 2000, available at http://www.ahram.org.eg/weekly.

42. Stark, "Recombinant Property in East European Capitalism," 128–29.

43. EIU, *Country Report: Egypt*, 3rd quarter 1998, 21. *Business Today Egypt*, Nov. 1988, 29. The EFG index is available at http://www.efg-hermes.com/docs/market/home.

44. Rafy Kourian, "Throwing Good Money after a Bad Market," *Middle East Times*, Oct. 25, 1998.

45. Following the "privatization" of MobiNil—sold to the Orascom Group (see below) in consortium with the state-owned France Télécom—the government licensed a second mobile phone operator, Click GSM, to placate the powerful Alkan group, which had lost out in the bidding for MobiNil. See EIU, *Egypt: Country Report*, 3rd quarter 1999, 29–30.

46. The scramble also reflected a global reorganization of the cement industry. A decade earlier there had been no global cement makers. But declining growth in their home markets led these three companies to expand around the world, following the path of financial crises—and hence cheap acquisitions—first into Latin America, then into East Asia, and by the late 1990s into the Middle East and Africa, regions where expanding populations promised long-term growth (cement production is driven by demographics). In 1997 Holderbank, the world's largest cement maker with operations in sixty countries, including subsidiaries in Morocco and Lebanon, purchased 25 percent of the Egyptian Cement Company and began to build three new kilns near Suez. In July 1999 Lafarge S.A., the world's largest building products group and second largest cement maker, also operating in sixty countries, purchased 76 percent of Beni Suef Cement, and was set to increase its share to 95 percent. It arranged to then sell half its holding of Beni Suef Cement to the Greek cement

company Titan, which already owned two cement-importing facilities in Egypt jointly with the local 4M Group, Egypt's largest importer of construction materials. In November 1999 the government sold 90 percent of Assiut Cement to Cemex of Mexico, the largest cement producer in the Americas, and sold 74 percent of Alexandria Portland Cement to Blue Circle Industries, the largest British cement producer with operations in Europe and Africa. See EIU, *Egypt: Country Report,* 3rd quarter 1999, 20–21; *Business Monthly,* Jan. 2000, 18; http://www.cemex.com; http://www.titan.gr/en/news; http://www.4mgroup.com.eg; http://www.holderbank.com; and http://www.lafarge.fr.

47. Another large industrialization project of the 1990s, described as a leading example of the new private sector–funded, export-oriented investment (and the first big Egyptian-Israeli industrial venture), turned out to be relying on state funds and to be oriented, once again, to the domestic market. The Middle East Oil Refinery (Midor), a project to build a $1.5 billion oil refinery announced in 1996 by the Swiss-based Masaka company, owned by an Egyptian financier, Hussein Salem, and the Israeli Merhav Group, owned by Yosef Maiman, failed to attract private investment. So the Egyptian government increased its funding to 60 percent, the two private financiers reduced their shares to 20 percent each, and the Egyptian-Swiss partner passed on all except 2 percent of this share to other, mostly state-owned Egyptian finance houses (16 percent to NBE Finance of the Cayman Islands, an off-shore subsidiary of the National Bank of Egypt, and 2 percent to the local joint sector Suez Canal Bank). Instead of refining petroleum products for export, the government announced, most of the production would be for the domestic market. EIU, *Egypt: Country Report,* 3rd quarter 1999, 27.

48. World Bank, *World Development Report 1999/2000,* table 13, 254–55.

49. World Bank, *World Development Report 1998/99,* table 11, 210–11.

50. Handy, *Egypt: Beyond Stabilization,* table 21, 50.

51. IMF, "Egyptian Stabilization," 12.

52. *Cairo Times,* Dec. 10, 1998, 12.

53. See http://www.seoudi.com.

54. See "Arabian International Construction," at http://www.winne.com/Egypt.

55. See http://www.mmsons.com.

56. Nadine El Sherif, "Face of Business: Mohamed Mansour," *Business Today Egypt,* Feb. 2001, 42–43.

57. Fariba Khorasanizadeh, "Sector Survey: Telecommunications," *Business Today Egypt,* Feb. 2001, 51–61; "Egypt Supplement," *Forbes Magazine,* May 31, 1998, available at http://www.winne.com/Egypt.

58. See http://www.eief.org/bahgat.html, and Clement M. Henry and Robert Springborg, *Globalization and the Policies of Development in the Middle East* (Cambridge: Cambridge University Press, 2000), 154.

59. See http://www.lakahgroup.com. On "cost recovery" in medical care, see chapter 8.

60. *Business Today Egypt,* Nov. 1998, 19.

61. In 1999 Egyptians purchased 68,609 new cars, 23,193 of them locally assembled and 45,416 imported. A significant proportion of these was sold for use as taxis rather than for private use. Dow Jones Newswires, Dec. 17, 2000, quoted in *Cairo Times,* Jan. 4–11, 2001.

62. Rehab El-Bakry, "Sweet Dreams," *Business Today Egypt,* Feb. 2001, 41.

63. Osman M. Osman, "Development and Poverty-Reduction Strategies in Egypt," *Working Papers of the Economic Research Forum for the Arab Countries, Iran and Turkey,* no. 9813 (Cairo, 1998), 7–8.

64. IMF, "Egyptian Stabilization," 50.

65. *Al-Ahram,* Jan. 1, 1999, Supplement, 3.

66. Ulrich Bartsch, "Interpreting Household Budget Surveys: Estimates for Poverty and Income Distribution in Egypt," *Working Papers of the Economic Research Forum for the Arab Countries, Iran and Turkey,* no. 9714 (Cairo, 1997), 17–19.

67. "Indian Poverty and the Numbers Game," *Economist,* Apr. 29, 2000, 37–38. The discrepancy between national accounts and household surveys in India is also discussed in World Bank, *Global Economic Prospects and the Developing Countries: 2000* (Washington, D.C.: World Bank, 1999), 31.

68. Bartsch, "Interpreting Household Budget Surveys," 17–19.

69. Simon Kuznets, *National Income and Its Composition, 1919–1939,* vol. 1 (New York: National Bureau of Economic Research, 1941), xxvi.

70. Leading economists frequently acknowledge the difficulty of measuring the economy. Asking why "economists have not been very successful in explaining what has happened to the economy during the last two decades," Zvi Griliches, in his 1994 address as president of the American Economic Association (AEA), argued that whereas in the 1950s about half the overall economy was measurable, by 1990 the proportion had fallen to below one-third ("Productivity, R&D, and the Data Constraint," *American Economic Review* 14, no. 1 [1994]: 1–23, at 13). In an earlier AEA presidential address, Robert Eisner said that measures of the main macroeconomic variables—income, output, employment, prices, productivity, consumption, savings, investment, capital formation, wealth, debt, and deficits—were so unreliable that he and his fellow economists "have literally not known what we are talking about." "Divergences of Measurement and Theory and Some Implications for Economic Policy," *American Economic Review* 79, no. 1 (1989): 1–13, at 2.

71. Mahmoud Abdel-Fadil, "Informal Sector Employment in Egypt," in *Urban Research Strategies for Egypt,* ed. R. Lobbon, Cairo Papers in Social Science 6, Monograph 2 (Cairo: American University in Cairo Press, 1983), 16–40.

72. The study defined informal dwellings as housing built since 1950 on land that was not formally subdivided or planned and not following regulatory regimes for construction. The total also included an estimate of those living in formal areas as squatters or other conditions of informality. Egyptian Center for Economic Studies and Institute for Liberty and Democracy, "Situational Analysis of Urban Real Estate in Egypt: Report," mimeo, Cairo, Oct. 2000.

73. Sadowski, *Political Vegetables,* 233.

74. Ibid., 221, citing Midhat Hasanayn, "al-Iqtisad al-sirri fi misr," *al-Ahram al-iqtisadi,* Dec. 15, 1985, 16. Nonpetroleum exports were worth $1.7 billion in 1988. Library of Congress, Federal Research Division, *Egypt: A Country Study,* 442.

75. See United Nations Office for Drug Control and Crime Prevention, Regional Office for the Middle East and North Africa, at http://www.undcp.org/egypt/country_profile_lebanon.html.

76. Yomna Kamel, "A Better Life with Bango," *Middle East Times,* July 18, 1999. On methods of hemp production see *Encyclopædia Britannica,* s.v. "Hemp," available at http://www.britannica.com. *Bango* is more commonly known in the West as marijuana.

77. Sinai production was also facilitated by the 1979 Camp David agreement between Israel and Egypt, the terms of which allowed no Egyptian military forces in the eastern part of Sinai after Israel returned the territory to Egypt. The government was prevented from using helicopters, for example, to search for hemp fields. The Egyptian Interior Ministry's Anti-Narcotic General Administration (established in 1929 and said to be the oldest drug control agency in the world) reported rapidly increasing seizures of cannabis herb (*bango*) in the later 1990s, reaching approximately 31 metric tons in 1998. Yet prices remained steady, according to the Cairo regional office of the U.N. Office for Drug Control, indicating increased cultivation rather than improved law enforcement. See http://www.undcp.org/egypt/country_profile_egypt.

78. IMF, "The Egyptian Stabilization Experience," 22.

79. International Institute for Strategic Studies, *The Military Balance 1989–90,* cited in Library of Congress, Federal Research Division, *Egypt: A Country Study,* 22–23, 399.

80. U.S. Department of State, *2001 Country Commercial Guide: Egypt,* 7–8.

81. My discussion of externalities and framing draws on Michel Callon, "An Essay on Framing and Overflowing: Economic Externalities Revisited by Sociology," in *The Laws of the Markets,* ed. Michel Callon, the *Sociological Review* monograph series (Oxford: Blackwell, 1998), 244–69.

82. Ibid.

83. For example, Douglas North, *Institutions, Institutional Change and Economic Performance* (Cambridge: Cambridge University Press, 1990).

84. The priority of the rule is reflected, and suppressed, in the forgotten history of economics. In eighteenth- and nineteenth-century Europe, before the rise of professional economics, the intellectual field that helped develop the regulations and understandings that formatted and made possible modern forms of property, exchange, and profit was the field of law. As I mentioned in chapter 3, in France and other parts of Europe the profession of economics developed as a branch of the study of law.

85. On the "constitutive outside," see the work of Jacques Derrida, for example, the essays in *Margins of Philosophy* (Chicago: University of Chicago Press, 1982), and "Structure, Sign and Play in the Discourse of the Human Sciences," in *Writing and Difference,* trans. Alan Bass (Chicago: University of Chicago

Press, 1978), 278–93. I draw on this work in *Colonising Egypt* (Berkeley: University of California Press, 1991). See also the discussion in Ernesto Laclau, *New Reflections on the Revolution of Our Time* (London: Verso, 1990).

86. Callon, "An Essay on Framing and Overflowing," 254.

87. See my discussion of "enframing" in Mitchell, *Colonising Egypt*, and of the state as an effect of enframing in Mitchell, "Society, Economy, and the State Effect," in *State/Culture: State-Formation After the Cultural Turn*, ed. George Steinmetz (Ithaca, N.Y.: Cornell University Press, 1999), 76–97.

88. Here is a simple example: Before a foreign food product can be imported and enter the market in Egypt, the food itself must go through some complex exchanges. At Egyptian customs it is inspected to ensure it complies with packaging and labeling regulations (language and placement of labels, production and expiration dates, ingredients, name of manufacturer and importer), local shelf-life standards (less than half the life must have expired by completion of customs inspection), and international and local product specifications. Samples of the product must be inspected in government laboratories to ensure compliance with Ministry of Health regulations on fitness for human consumption, contagious diseases, and prohibited coloring, additives, and preservatives, and international regulations on pesticide residues. See United States Department of Agriculture, Foreign Agricultural Service, "Egypt: Food and Agricultural Import Regulations and Standards, Country Report 2000," Global Agriculture Information Network, Report No. EG0023, July 30, 2000.

89. In July 2000 thirty-one defendants were found guilty (the thirty-second had died). Three had fled the country and received sentences of fifteen years hard labor, fourteen received ten years hard labor, and the rest sentences of one to five years. Six months later the sentences were annulled and a retrial was ordered because the investigation had violated banking secrecy laws. Tariq Hassan-Gordon, "Case of 31 Businessmen to Be Retried," *Middle East Times*, Jan. 19, 2001.

90. Karl Marx, *Capital: A Critique of Political Economy*, vol. 1 (New York: Modern Library, 1906), 809.

91. Sarah Anderson and John Cavanagh, with Thea Lee, *Field Guide to the Global Economy* (New York: New Press, 2000), 29.

92. Karl Marx, *Capital*, vol. 3 (London: Penguin, 1981), 569.

93. Fernand Braudel's studies of the rise of capitalism formulate a distinction between markets, which tended to be places of local, small-scale exchange and difficult profits, and the large-scale monopolies out of which what came to be called capitalism emerged. *Afterthoughts on Material Civilization and Capitalism*, trans. Patricia Ranum (Baltimore, Md.: Johns Hopkins University Press, 1977), 52, 111.

94. Adam Smith, *An Inquiry into the Wealth and Nature of the Wealth of Nations*, ed. R. H. Campbell and A. S. Skinner, the Glasgow edition of the works and correspondence of Adam Smith, vol. 2 (Oxford: Clarendon Press, 1976). See also Ranajit Guha, *A Rule of Property for Bengal: An Essay on the Idea of Permanent Settlement* (Durham, N.C.: Duke University Press, 1996).

95. Erving Goffman, *Frame Analysis: An Essay on the Organization of Experience* (New York: Harper & Row, 1974).

96. See chapter 2. The phrase is from Sir Philip Francis, quoted in Guha, *A Rule of Property for Bengal,* 95.

97. Gamal Essam El-Din, "MPs Rage over Erosion of Parliamentary Power," *al-Ahram Weekly,* Jan. 7–13, 1999, 3.

98. A 1993 law replaced the election of village heads and deans of university faculties with appointment by the government.

99. In May 1999 the United Nations Committee Against Torture recommended effective steps be taken against the use of torture in Egypt. Amnesty International, *Annual Report 2000: Egypt,* available at http://www.amnesty.org/web/ar2000web.nsf/countries.

100. Colonel Mohammed Ghanem, "The Tragedy of Administrative Detention," *Middle East Times,* June 3, 1999. The article was censored from the printed edition but is available at http://metimes.com/issue99–24/opin/detention.htm. The author was previously the chairman of administration of legal research at the Ministry of Interior and a professor of criminal law at the Egyptian Police Academy. On prison conditions, see Amnesty International, *Annual Report 2000: Egypt.*

101. The government repressed the professional associations after board elections were won by members of the Muslim Brothers, a nonlegal political organization opposed to the regime. Fareed Ezz-Edine, "Egypt: An Emerging 'Market' of Double Repression," Press Information Note no. 10, Middle East Research and Information Project, Nov. 18, 1999, available at http://www.merip.org.

102. Amnesty International, "Egypt: Muzzling Civil Society," Sept. 19, 2000.

103. For a discussion of the U.S. democracy initiative, see Timothy Mitchell, "The 'Wrong Success': America's Fear of Democracy in the Middle East," in Arabic, in Timothy Mitchell, *al-Dimuqratiyya wa-'l-dawla fi al-ʿalam al-ʿarabi* (Damascus: Dar ʿIybal, 1996).

104. Marx, *Capital,* 1:326.

105. Aidan Foster Carter, "The Modes of Production Controversy," *New Left Review,* no. 107 (Jan.–Feb. 1978): 47–77, at 61–62, emphasis in original. For a reading of Marx that explores his understanding of violence in these terms, see Timothy Mitchell, "The Stage of Modernity," in *Questions of Modernity,* ed. Timothy Mitchell (Minneapolis: University of Minnesota Press, 2000), 1–34.

106. Bruno Latour, *Pandora's Hope: Essays on the Reality of Science Studies* (Cambridge, Mass.: Harvard University Press, 1999), 281, emphasis in original.

107. See Dahlia Reda, "La région dans la tourmente politique," *Al-Ahram Hebdo,* Jan. 10–16, 2001, 11, and http://www.efg-hermes.com/docs/market/home.

108. An industry source reported that "larger developments such as Dreamland (Bahgat Group) and Beverly Hills (SODIC)" were effectively bankrupt.

Hadia Mostafa, "Something to Build On," *Business Today Egypt*, Feb. 2001, 22–27, at 25.

109. The Ministry of Finance agreed to pay E£1.5 billion of the debts of the Radio and Television Union (RTU) to the National Investment Bank over six years, in exchange for equity in the RTU, and the bank agreed to convert a further E£1 billion of debt into RTU equity. *Al-Ahram Hebdo*, Jan. 10–16, 2001, 12.

110. The government put four bankers on the board of Arab Contractors to increase its control of the company. *Business Monthly*, Mar. 2001.

111. The British Embassy quarterly economic report reported that banks had overextended credit to construction and other nonproductive projects, leading to a large-scale default. Ibid., 23.

112. Lakah, who had French as well as Egyptian citizenship, had gone to Paris for a month, but threatened to sue anyone who claimed he had fled to avoid paying his debts. "Banks Put Squeeze on Businessmen," *Business Monthly*, Nov. 2000; *Wall Street Journal*, Nov. 30, 1999.

113. The two mobile phone operators claimed a total of 1.35 million subscribers, but many users subscribed to both services, since one or the other network was frequently unavailable due to excess demand. *Business Today Egypt*, Feb. 2001, 12, 20; EIU, *Egypt: Country Report*, 3rd quarter 1999, 29–30.

Select Bibliography

ʿAbbas Hamid, Raʾuf. *Al-nizam al-ijtimaʿi fi misr fi zill al-milkiyyat al-ziraʿiyya al-kabira.* Cairo: Dar al-Fikr al-Hadith, 1973.

ʿAbd Allah, Ahmad, ed. *Al-jaysh wa-ʾl-dimuqratiyya fi misr.* Cairo: Dar Sina, 1990.

ʿAbd al-Muʿti, ʿAbd al-Basit. *Al-siraʿ al-tabaqi fi al-qarya al-misriyya.* Cairo: Dar al-Thaqafa al-Jadida, 1977.

ʿAbd al-Rahim, ʿAbd al-Rahim ʿAbd al-Rahim. *Al-rif al-misri fi al-qarn al-thamin ʿashar.* 2d ed. Cairo: Maktabat Madbuli, 1986.

ʿAbd al-Rahman, ʿAʾisha [Bint al-Shatiʾ, pseud.]. *Al-rif al-misri.* Cairo: Maktabat al-Wafd, 1936.

Abdel-Fadil, Mahmoud. *Development, Income Distribution and Social Change in Rural Egypt, 1952–70: A Study in the Political Economy of Agrarian Transition.* Cambridge: Cambridge University Press, 1975.

Abu-Lughod, Lila. "The Romance of Resistance." *American Ethnologist* 17, no. 1 (1990): 41–55.

———. *Writing Women's Worlds: Bedouin Stories.* Berkeley: University of California Press, 1993.

———. "Television and the Virtues of Education: Upper Egyptian Encounters with State Culture." In *Directions of Change in Rural Egypt.* Edited by Nicholas Hopkins and Kirsten Westergaard, 147–65. Cairo: American University in Cairo Press, 1998.

Adams, Richard H. *Development and Social Change in Rural Egypt.* Syracuse, N.Y.: Syracuse University Press, 1986.

Adelman, Irma. "Beyond Export-Led Growth." *World Development* 12, no. 9 (1984): 937–49.

ʿAfifi, Hafiz. *ʿAla hamish al-siyasa: baʿd masaʾilna al-qawmiyya.* Cairo: Dar al-Kutub al-Misriyya, 1938.

Alderman, Harold, and Joachim von Braun. *Egypt's Food Subsidy and Rationing System: A Description.* Washington, D.C.: International Food Policy Research Institute, 1982.

———. *The Effects of the Egyptian Food Ration and Subsidy System on Income Distribution and Consumption.* Research Report no. 45. Washington, D.C.: International Food Policy Research Institute, 1984.

ʿAli, Saʿid Ismaʿil. *Al-mujtamaʿ al-misri fi ʿahd al-ihtilal al-biritani.* Cairo: Anglo-Egyptian Bookshop, 1972.

Amin, Samir [Hasan Riad, pseud.]. *L'Egypte nassérienne.* Paris: Editions de Minuit, 1964.

ʿAmir, Ibrahim. *Al-ard wa-'l-fallah: al-mas'ala al-ziraʿiyya fi misr.* Cairo: Matbaʿat al-Dar al-Misriyya, 1958.

Anderson, Benedict. *Imagined Communities: Reflections on the Origins and Spread of Nationalism.* 2d ed. London: Verso, 1991.

Anderson, Sarah, John Cavanagh, and Thea Lee. *Field Guide to the Global Economy.* New York: New Press, 2000.

Andrews, J. H. *A Paper Landscape: The Ordnance Survey in Nineteenth-Century Ireland.* Oxford: Clarendon Press, 1975.

Anhouri, Jean. "Les Répercussions de la guerre sur l'agriculture égyptienne." *L'Egypte Contemporaine* 38, nos. 238–39 (Mar.–Apr. 1947): 233–51.

Anise, Mahmoud. *A Study of the National Income of Egypt.* Monograph, published as *L'Egypte Contemporaine,* nos. 261–62. Cairo: Société Fouad 1er d'Economie Politique, de Statistique et de Législation, 1950.

Ansari, Hamied. *Egypt: The Stalled Society.* Albany: State University of New York Press, 1986.

Appadurai, Arjun. ed. *The Cultural Life of Things.* Cambridge: Cambridge University Press, 1986.

———, "Number in the Colonial Imagination." In *Modernity at Large: Cultural Dimensions of Globalization,* 114–35. Minneapolis: University of Minnesota Press, 1997.

Artin, Yacoub. *La Propriété foncière en Egypte.* Printed under the Auspices of the Ministry of Finance. Cairo: Institut Egyptien, 1883.

———. *Artin Bey: Ministère des Affaires Etrangères et du Commerce sous le règne de Môhémet-Aly Pacha 1800–1859.* Cairo: Imprimerie Nationale, 1896.

———. "Essai sur les causes du renchérissement de la vie matérielle au Caire dans le courant de xixe siècle (1800 à 1907)." *Mémoires présentés á l'Institut Egyptien* 5 (1908): 58–140.

Asad, Talal. *Genealogies of Religion: Discipline and Reasons of Power in Christianity and Islam.* Baltimore, Md.: Johns Hopkins University Press, 1993.

———. "Ethnographic Representation, Statistics and Modern Power." *Social Research* 61, no. 1 (1994): 55–88.

Ayrout, Henry Habib. *The Egyptian Peasant,* translated by John Alden Williams. Boston: Beacon Press, 1963.

———. *Moeurs et coutumes des fellahs.* Paris: Payot, 1938. English translation: *The Fellaheen,* translated by Hilary Wayment. Westport, Ct.: Hyperion Press, 1981.

Baer, Gabriel. *A History of Landownership in Modern Egypt, 1800–1950.* Oxford: Oxford University Press, 1962.

———. *Studies in the Social History of Modern Egypt.* Chicago: University of Chicago Press, 1969.

Baker, Raymond. *Egypt's Uncertain Revolution under Nasser and Sadat.* Cambridge, Mass.: Harvard University Press, 1978.

Baraka, Magda. *The Egyptian Upper Class Between Revolutions, 1919–1952.* St. Antony Middle East Monographs. Reading, Eng.: Ithaca Press, 1998.

Barakat, ʿAli. *Tatawwur al-milkiyya al-ziraʿiyya fi misr wa-atharuhu ʿala al-haraka al-siyasiyya.* Cairo: Dar al-Thaqafa al-Jadida, 1977.

Bartsch, Ulrich. "Interpreting Household Budget Surveys: Estimates for Poverty and Income Distribution in Egypt." *Working Papers of the Economic Research Forum for the Arab Countries, Iran and Turkey,* no. 9714. Cairo, 1997.

Baskin, Jonathan Barron, and Paul J. Miranti Jr. *A History of Corporate Finance.* Cambridge: Cambridge University Press, 1997.

Beinin, Joel, and Zachary Lockman. *Workers on the Nile: Nationalism, Communism, Islam and the Egyptian Working Class, 1882–1954.* Princeton, N.J.: Princeton University Press, 1987.

Berger, Morroe. *The Arab World Today.* Garden City, N.Y.: Doubleday, 1962.

Bernstein, Henry. "Concepts for the Analysis of Contemporary Peasantries." In *The Political Economy of Rural Development: Peasants, International Capital, and the State.* Edited by Rosemary Galli, 3–24. Albany: State University of New York Press, 1981.

———. "Agrarian Classes in Capitalist Development." In *Capitalism and Development.* Edited by Leslie Sklair, 40–71. London: Routledge, 1994.

Berque, Jacques. "Sur la structure de quelques villages égyptiens." *Annales: Economie, Société, Civilisations* 10, no. 2 (1955): 199–215.

———. *Histoire sociale d'un village égyptian au xxème siècle.* Paris: Mouton, 1957.

———. *Egypt: Imperialism and Revolution.* Translated by Jean Stewart. New York: Praeger, 1971.

Bhabha, Homi K. *The Location of Culture.* London: Routledge, 1994.

Binder, Leonard. *In a Moment of Enthusiasm: Political Power and the Second Stratum in Egypt.* Chicago: University of Chicago Press, 1978.

Binswanger, Hans. "Agricultural Mechanization: A Comparative Historical Analysis." *World Bank Research Observer* 1, no. 1 (1986): 27–56.

Binswanger, Hans, Klaus Deininger, and Gershon Feder. "Power, Distortions, Revolt and Reform in Agricultural Land Relations." In *Handbook of Development Economics,* vol. 3b. Edited by J. Behrman and T. N. Srinivasan, 2659–72. Amsterdam: Elsevier, 1995.

Blackman, Winifred S. *The Fellahin of Upper Egypt: Their Religious, Social and Industrial Life Today with Special Reference to Survivals from Ancient Times.* London: G. G. Harrap, 1927.

Bochenski, Feliks, and William Diamond. "TVA's in the Middle East." *Middle East Journal* 4, no. 1 (1950): 52–82.

Bourdieu, Pierre. *Outline of a Theory of Practice.* Cambridge: Cambridge University Press, 1977.

Braudel, Fernand. *Afterthoughts on Material Civilization and Capitalism.* Translated by Patricia Ranum. Baltimore, Md.: Johns Hopkins University Press, 1977.

Brinton, Jasper Yeates. *The Mixed Courts of Egypt.* 2d ed. New Haven, Conn.: Yale University Press, 1968.

Brown, Nathan. *Peasant Politics in Modern Egypt: The Struggle Against the State.* New Haven, Conn.: Yale University Press, 1990.

Buck-Morss, Susan. "Envisioning Capital: Political Economy on Display." *Critical Inquiry* 21, no. 2 (1995): 434–67.

Burns, William J. *Economic Aid and American Policy Towards Egypt, 1955–81.* Albany: State University of New York Press, 1985.

Bush, Ray. *Economic Crisis and the Politics of Reform in Egypt.* Boulder, Colo.: Westview Press, 1999.

Callon, Michel, ed. *The Laws of the Markets. Sociological Review* monograph series. Oxford: Blackwell, 1998.

Central Agency for Public Mobilization and Statistics and UNICEF. *The State of Egyptian Children.* Cairo: CAPMAS, 1988.

Chakrabarty, Dipesh. "Postcoloniality and the Artifice of History: Who Speaks for 'Indian' Pasts?" *Representations* 37, no. 1 (1992): 1–26. Reprinted in abridged form in Dipesh Chakrabarty, *Provincializing Europe: Postcolonial Thought and Historical Difference,* 27–46.

———. *Provincializing Europe: Postcolonial Thought and Historical Difference.* Princeton, N.J.: Princeton University Press, 2000.

Chambers, Robert. *Rural Development: Putting the Last First.* London: Longman, 1983.

Chatterjee, Partha. *Nationalist Thought and the Colonial World: A Derivative Discourse?* Minneapolis: University of Minnesota Press, 1993.

———. *The Nation and its Fragments: Colonial and Postcolonial Histories.* Princeton, N.J.: Princeton University Press, 1993.

Clarke, Simon, ed. *What About the Workers? Workers and the Transition to Capitalism in Russia.* London: Verso, 1993.

Clifford, James. "On Ethnographic Authority." *Representations* 1, no. 2 (1983): 118–46.

Cohen, Morris R. "Property and Sovereignty." *Cornell Law Quarterly* 13, no. 1 (1927): 8–30.

Cole, Juan R. *Colonialism and Revolution in the Middle East: Social and Cultural Origins of Egypt's ʿUrabi Movement.* Princeton, N.J.: Princeton University Press, 1993.

Commander, Simon. *The State and Agricultural Development in Egypt Since 1973.* Published for the Overseas Development Institute. London: Ithaca Press, 1987.

Cooper, Frederick, and Randall Packard, eds. *International Development and the Social Sciences: Essays on the History and Politics of Knowledge.* Berkeley: University of California Press, 1997.

Coudougnan, Gerard. *Nos ancêtres les Pharaons: L'Historie pharaonique et copte dans les manuels scolaires égyptiens.* Dossiers du CEDEJ 1998, no. 1. Cairo: Centre d'Etudes et de Documentation Economique, Juridique et Sociale, 1988.

Critchfield, Richard. *The Long Charade: Political Subversion in the Vietnam War.* New York: Harcourt, Brace & World, 1968.

———. *Shahhat: An Egyptian.* Syracuse, N.Y.: Syracuse University Press, 1978.

———. *Villages.* Garden City, N.Y.: Anchor Press / Doubleday, 1981; reprint ed. 1983.

———. *The Golden Bowl Be Broken: Peasant Life in Four Cultures,* 2d ed. Bloomington: University of Indiana Press, 1988.

———. *The Villagers. Changed Values, Altered Lives: The Closing of the Urban-Rural Gap.* New York: Anchor Books / Doubleday, 1994.

Cromer, Earl of. *Modern Egypt.* 2 vols. New York: Macmillan, 1908.

Crush, Jonathan, ed. *Power of Development.* London: Routledge, 1995.

Cuddihy, William. "Agricultural Price Management in Egypt." *World Bank Staff Working Paper* no. 388. Washington, D.C.: The World Bank, 1980.

Cumberbatch, A. N. *Economic and Commercial Conditions in Egypt.* Overseas Economic Surveys, published for Commercial Relations and Exports Department of the Board of Trade. London: Her Majesty's Stationery Office, 1952.

Cuno, Kenneth. *The Pasha's Peasants: Land, Society and Economy in Lower Egypt, 1740–1858.* Cambridge: Cambridge University Press, 1992.

Davis, Eric. *Challenging Colonialism: Bank Misr and Egyptian Industrialization, 1920–1941.* Princeton, N.J.: Princeton University Press, 1983.

Deane, Phyllis. *The Measurement of Colonial National Incomes.* National Institute of Economic and Social Research Occasional Paper XII. Cambridge: Cambridge University Press, 1948.

———. *Colonial Social Accounting.* National Institute of Economic and Social Research, Economic and Social Studies No. 11. Cambridge: Cambridge University Press, 1953. Reprint ed., Hamden, Conn.: Archon Books, 1973.

De Guerville, A. B. *New Egypt.* London: William Heinemann, 1905.

De Regny, E. *Statistique de l'Egypte d'après des documents officiels.* Alexandria: n.p., 1870–72.

Derrida, Jacques. *Of Grammatology.* Translated by Gayatri Chakravorty Spivak. Baltimore, Md.: Johns Hopkins University Press, 1976.

———. *Writing and Difference.* Translated by Alan Bass. Chicago: University of Chicago Press, 1978.

———. *Margins of Philosophy.* Translated by Alan Bass. Chicago: University of Chicago Press, 1982.

———. "The Force of Law." *Cardozo Law Review* 11 (1990).

———. *Specters of Marx: The State of the Debt, the Work of Mourning, and the New International.* New York: Routledge, 1994.

Dethier, Jean-Jacques. *Trade, Exchange Rate, and Agricultural Pricing Policies in Egypt.* Washington, D.C.: World Bank, 1989.

Dirks, Nicholas B. "History as a Sign of the Modern." *Public Culture* 2, no. 1 (1990): 25–32.

Disuqi, ʿAsim al-. *Kibar mullak al-aradi al-ziraʿiyya wa dawruhum fi al-mujtamaʿ al-misri.* Cairo: Dar al-Thaqafa al-Jadida, 1976.

Dowson, E. M., and J. I. Craig. *Collection of Statistics of the Area Planted in Cotton in 1909.* Cairo: Survey Department, 1910.

Dowson, Sir Ernest, and V. L. O. Sheppard. "Evolution of the Land Records." *Empire Survey Review* 60 (1956): 202.

Duff-Gordon, Lucie. *Letters from Egypt.* Revised ed. London: R. Brimley Johnson, 1902.

Dumont, Louis. *From Mandeville to Marx: The Genesis and Triumph of Economic Ideology.* Chicago: University of Chicago Press, 1977.

Durkheim, Emile. *The Rules of Sociological Method.* New York: Free Press, 1938.

Dyer, Graham. *Class, State, and Agricultural Productivity in Egypt: A Study of the Inverse Relationship between Farm Size and Land Productivity.* London: Frank Cass, 1997.

Edmond, Charles. *L'Egypte a l'Exposition Universelle de 1867.* Paris: Dentu, 1867.

Edney, Mathew. *Mapping an Empire: The Geographical Construction of British India, 1765–1843.* Chicago: University of Chicago Press, 1997.

Edwards, Jill, ed. *Al-Alamein Revisited: The Battle of Al-Alamein and Its Historical Implications.* Cairo: American University in Cairo Press, 2000.

Eisner, Robert. "Divergences of Measurement and Theory and Some Implications for Economic Policy." *American Economic Review* 79, no. 1 (1989): 1–13.

El-Rafie, M., W. A. Hassouna, N. Hirschhorn, S. Loza, P. Miller, A. Nagaty, S. Nasser, and S. Riyad. "Effect of Diarrhoeal Disease Control on Infant and Child Mortality in Egypt." *Lancet* 335 (Feb. 10, 1990): 334–38.

English, E. Philip. *The Great Escape? An Examination of North-South Tourism.* Ottawa: North-South Institute, 1986.

Escobar, Arturo. *Encountering Development: The Making and Unmaking of the Third World.* Princeton, N.J.: Princeton University Press, 1995.

Fahmy, Khaled. *All the Pasha's Men: Mehmed Ali, His Army and the Making of Modern Egypt.* Cambridge: Cambridge University Press, 1997.

Fathy, Hassan. *Gurna: A Tale of Two Villages.* Cairo: Ministry of Culture, 1969. Reprinted as *Architecture for the Poor: An Experiment in Rural Egypt.* Chicago: University of Chicago Press, 1973.

Feder, Gershon. "The Relation Between Farm Size and Farm Productivity." *Journal of Development Economics* 18, nos. 2–3 (1985): 297–313.

Feis, Herbert. *Europe: The World's Banker, 1870–1914: An Account of European Foreign Investment and the Connection of World Finance with Diplomacy Before the War.* New Haven, Conn.: Yale University Press, 1930. Reprint ed. Clifton, N.J.: Augustus M. Kelley, 1974.

Ferguson, James. *The Anti-Politics Machine: "Development," Depoliticization, and Bureaucratic Power in Lesotho.* Cambridge: Cambridge University Press, 1990.

Fitzpatrick, Peter. *Modernism and the Grounds of Law.* Cambridge: Cambridge University Press, 2001.

Fletcher, Lehman B., ed. *Egypt's Agriculture in a Reform Era.* Ames: Iowa State University Press, 1996.

Food and Agriculture Organization of the United Nations. *National Methods of Collecting Agricultural Statistics.* Supplement no. 18, *Egypt, Mexico, Puerto Rico.* Rome: FAO, 1983.

Foster Carter, Aidan. "The Modes of Production Controversy." *New Left Review,* no. 107 (Jan.–Feb. 1978): 47–77.

Foucault, Michel. "Governmentality." In *The Foucault Effect: Studies in Governmentality.* Edited by Graham Burchell, Colin Gordon, and Peter Miller, 87–104. Hemel Hempstead, Herts: Harvester Wheatsheaf, 1991.

Fresco, Jacques. "Histoire et organisation de la statistique officielle en Egypte." *L'Egypte Contemporaine* 31, nos. 191–92 (1940): 339–91.

Friedmann, Harriet. "World Market, State, and Family Farm: Social Bases of Household Production in the Era of Wage Labor." *Comparative Studies in Society and History* 20, no. 4 (1978): 545–86.

———. "The Political Economy of Food: A Global Crisis." *New Left Review,* no. 197 (1993): 29–57.

Fustel de Coulanges, Noma Denis. *La Cité antique.* 9th ed. Paris: Hachette, 1881.

Galal, Dina. *Al-maʿuna al-amrikiyya li-man: Misr am amrika?* Cairo: al-Ahram, 1988.

Gallagher, Nancy. *Egypt's Other Wars: Epidemics and the Politics of Public Health.* Syracuse, N.Y.: Syracuse University Press, 1990.

Geertz, Clifford. *The Interpretation of Cultures: Selected Essays.* New York: Basic Books, 1973.

Gendzier, Irene. *Managing Political Change: Social Scientists and the Third World.* Boulder, Colo.: Westview Press, 1985.

Gerber, Haim. *The Social Origins of the Modern Middle East.* Boulder, Colo.: Lynne Rienner, 1987.

Gershoni, Israel, and James P. Jankowski. *Egypt, Islam and the Arabs: The Search for Egyptian Nationhood.* Oxford: Oxford University Press, 1986.

———. *Redefining the Egyptian Nation, 1930–1945.* Cambridge: Cambridge University Press, 1995.

Ghali, Mirrit Butrus. *Siyasat al-ghad: barnamij siyasi wa-iqtisadi wa-ijtimaʿi.* Cairo: Matbaʿat al-Risala, 1938. English translation, *The Policy of Tomorrow,* translated by Ismail R. el-Faruqi. Washington, D.C.: American Council of Learned Societies, 1953.

———. *Al-islah al-ziraʿi.* Cairo: Jamaʿat al-Nahda al-Qawmiyya, 1945.

Gibbon, P., and M. Neocosmos. "Some Problems in the Political Economy of 'African Socialism.' " In *Contradictions of Accumulation in Africa: Studies in Economy and State.* Edited by Henry Bernstein and B. K. Campbell. Beverly Hills, Calif.: Sage, 1985.

Gibson, Katherine, and Julie Graham [J. K. Gibson-Graham, pseud.]. "Identity and Economic Plurality: Rethinking Capitalism and 'Capitalist Hegemony.' " *Environment and Planning D: Society and Space* 13, no. 3 (1995): 275–82.

———. *The End of Capitalism (As We Knew It): A Feminist Critique of Political Economy.* Cambridge, Mass.: Blackwell, 1996.

Glavanis, Kathy, and Pandeli Glavanis. "The Sociology of Agrarian Relations in the Middle East: The Persistence of Household Production." *Current Sociology* 31, no. 2 (1983): 1–106.

———. *The Rural Middle East: Peasant Lives and Modes of Production.* London: Zed Press, 1989.

Godlewska, Anne. "Napoleon's Geographers (1797–1815): Imperialists and Soldiers of Modernity." In *Geography and Empire.* Edited by Anne Godlewska and Neil Smith. Oxford: Blackwell, 1994.

Goffman, Erving. *Frame Analysis: An Essay on the Organization of Experience.* New York: Harper & Row, 1974.

Goldschmidt Jr., Arthur. *Biographical Dictionary of Modern Egypt.* Boulder, Colo.: Lynne Rienner, 2000.

Gordon, Joel. *Nasser's Blessed Movement: Egypt's Free Officers and the July Revolution.* Oxford: Oxford University Press, 1992.

Government of Egypt, Central Agency for Public Mobilization and Statistics. *Census of Egypt 1986.* Cairo: n.p., n.d.

Government of Egypt, Ministry of Finance, Survey Department. *A Report on the Work of the Survey Department in 1909.* Cairo: Ministry of Finance, 1909.

Gran, Peter. "Modern Trends in Egyptian Historiography: A Review Article." *International Journal of Middle East Studies* 9, no. 3 (1978): 367–71.

Griliches, Zvi. "Productivity, R&D, and the Data Constraint." *American Economic Review* 14, no. 1 (1994): 1–23.

Guha, Ranajit. *Elementary Aspects of Peasant Insurgency in Colonial India.* New Delhi: Oxford University Press, 1983.

———. *A Rule of Property for Bengal: An Essay on the Idea of Permanent Settlement.* Durham, N.C.: Duke University Press, 1996.

Guha, Ranajit, ed. *A Subaltern Studies Reader, 1986–1995.* Minneapolis: University of Minnesota Press, 1997.

Guha, Ranajit, and Gayatri Chakravorty Spivak, eds. *Selected Subaltern Studies.* New York: Oxford University Press, 1988.

Gupta, Akhil. *Postcolonial Developments: Agriculture in the Making of Modern India.* Durham, N.C.: Duke University Press, 1998.

Hammoudi, Abdellah. "Substance and Relation: Water Rights and Water Distribution in the Dra Valley." In *Property, Social Structure and Law in the Modern Middle East.* Edited by Ann Elizabeth Mayer. Albany: State University of New York Press, 1985.

Hamrush, Ahmad. *Qissat thawrat 23 yulyu.* Vol. 2, *Mujtamaʿ Jamal ʿAbd al-Nasir.* Cairo: Maktabat Madbuli, 1975.

Handy, Howard, and Staff Team. *Egypt: Beyond Stabilization, Towards a Dynamic Market Economy.* IMF Occasional Paper, no. 163. Washington, D.C.: IMF, 1998.

Haraway, Donna. *ModestWitness@SecondMillennium.FemaleMan© Meets OncoMouse™: Feminism and Technoscience.* New York: Routledge, 1997.

Harik, Iliya. *The Political Mobilization of Peasants: A Study of an Egyptian Community.* Bloomington: Indiana University Press, 1974.

———. "Continuity and Change in Local Development Policies in Egypt: From Nasser to Sadat." *International Journal of Middle East Studies* 16, no. 1 (1984): 43–66.

Harik, Iliya, and Susan Randolph. *Distribution of Land, Employment and Income in Rural Egypt.* Ithaca, N.Y.: Rural Development Committee, Center for International Studies, Cornell University, 1979.

Harrison, Gordon. *Mosquitoes, Malaria and Man: A History of the Hostilities Since 1880.* New York: E. P. Dutton, 1978.

Hart, H. L. A. *The Concept of Law.* Oxford: Oxford University Press, 1961.

Haykal, Muhammad Husayn. *Mudhakkirati fi al-siyasa al-misriyya.* 3 vols. Cairo: Dar al-Maʿarif, 1977–78.

Heikel, Mohamed. *Autumn of Fury: The Assassination of Sadat.* New York: Random House, 1983.

Hekekyan. "Journals 1851–54." British Library Add Ms. 37452. London.

Henein, Nessim Henry. *Mārī Girgis: Village de Haute-Egypte.* Cairo: Institut Français d'Archéologie Orientale du Caire, 1988.

Henry, Clement M., and Robert Springborg. *Globalization and the Politics of Development in the Middle East.* Cambridge: Cambridge University Press, 2001.

Hill, Polly. *Development Economics on Trial: The Anthropological Case for a Prosecution.* Cambridge: Cambridge University Press, 1986.

Hinnebusch, Raymond A. "Class, State, and the Reversal of Egypt's Agrarian Reform." *Middle East Report,* no. 184 (Sept.–Oct. 1993): 20–23.

Hopkins, Nicholas S. "The Social Impact of Mechanization." *In Migration, Mechanization, and Agricultural Labor Markets in Egypt.* Edited by Alan Richards and Philip L. Martin, 181–97. Boulder, Colo.: Westview Press, 1983.

———. *Agrarian Transformation in Egypt.* Boulder, Colo.: Westview Press, 1987.

———. "Small Farmer Households and Agricultural Sustainability in Egypt." In *Sustainable Agriculture in Egypt.* Edited by Mohamed A. Faris and Mahmood Hasan Khan, 185–95. Boulder, Colo.: Lynne Rienner, 1993.

Hopkins, Nicholas S., Soheir R. Mehanna, and Bahgat Abdelmaksoud. *The State of Agricultural Mechanization in Egypt.* Cairo: Ministry of Agriculture, 1982.

Hopkins, Nicholas S, and Kirsten Westergaard, eds. *Directions of Change in Rural Egypt.* Cairo: American University in Cairo Press, 1998.

Hubbard, Preston J. *Origins of the TVA: The Muscle Shoals Controversy, 1920–1932.* New York: Norton, 1961.

Hughes, Thomas P. *Networks of Power: Electrification in Western Society, 1880–1930*. Baltimore, Md.: Johns Hopkins University Press, 1983.

Hunter, F. Robert. *Egypt Under the Khedives, 1805–1879: From Household Government to Modern Bureaucracy*. Pittsburgh, Penn.: University of Pittsburgh Press, 1984.

Husayn, ʿAdil. *Nahw fikr ʿarabi jadid: al-nasiriyya wa-l-tanmiya wa-l-dimuqratiya*. Cairo: Dar al-Mustaqbal al-ʿArabi, 1985.

Hussein, Mahmoud. *Class Conflict in Egypt: 1945–1970*. New York: Monthly Review Press, 1973.

Ikram, Khalid. *Egypt: Economic Management in a Period of Transition*. Report of a Mission Sent to the Arab Republic of Egypt by the World Bank. Published for the World Bank. Baltimore, Md.: Johns Hopkins University Press, 1980.

International Monetary Fund, Middle Eastern Department. "The Egyptian Stabilization Experience: An Analytical Retrospective." Prepared by Arvind Subramanian. *Working Papers of the International Monetary Fund*, WP/97/105, September 1997.

Ireton, François. "Eléments pour une sociologie de la production statistique en Egypte." *Peuples méditerranéens*, nos. 54–55 (Jan.–June 1991): 53–92.

Islamoglu-Inan, Huri. *State and Peasant in the Ottoman Empire: Agrarian Power Relations and Regional Economic Development in Ottoman Anatolia during the Sixteenth Century*. Leiden: E. J. Brill, 1994.

Islamoglu-Inan, Huri, and Çağlar Keyder. "Agenda for Ottoman History." *Review* 1, no. 1 (1977): 31–55.

Issawi, Charles. *Egypt in Revolution: An Economic Analysis*. Oxford: Oxford University Press, 1963.

Jenks, Leland Hamilton. *The Migration of British Capital to 1875*. London: Alfred A. Knopf, 1927.

Jennings, Anne M. *The Nubians of West Aswan: Village Women in the Midst of Change*. Boulder, Colo.: Lynne Rienner, 1995.

Jevons, W. Stanley. *The Theory of Political Economy*. London: Macmillan, 1871.

Johansen, Baber. *The Islamic Law on Land Tax and Rent: The Peasant Loss of Property Rights as Interpreted in the Hanafite Legal Literature of the Mamluk and Ottoman Periods*. London: Croom Helm, 1988.

Johnson, Pamela R., et al. *Egypt: The Egyptian American Rural Improvement Service, a Point Four Project, 1952–63*. AID Project Impact Evaluation, no. 43. Washington, D.C.: Agency for International Development, 1983.

Kabeer, Naila. *Reversed Realities: Gender Hierarchies in Development Thought*. London: Verso, 1994.

Kairys, David, ed. *The Politics of Law: A Progressive Critique*. 2d ed. New York: Pantheon, 1990.

Kamel Selim, Hussein. *Twenty Years of Agricultural Development in Egypt*. Cairo: Ministry of Finance, Egypt, 1940.

Kaviraj, Sudipta. "The Imaginary Institution of India." In *Subaltern Studies VII.* Edited by Partha Chatterjee and Gyanendra Pandey, 1–39. New Delhi: Oxford University Press, 1992.

Kelley, Allen C., Atef M. Khalifa, and M. Nabil el-Khorazaty. *Population and Development in Rural Egypt.* Durham, N.C.: Duke University Press, 1982.

Keynes, John Maynard. *Indian Currency and Finance.* London: Macmillan, 1913.

Killearn, Baron of [Sir Miles Lampson]. *Diaries.* Private Papers Collection, Middle East Centre, St. Antony College, Oxford.

Koptiuch, Kristin. *A Poetics of Political Economy in Egypt.* Minneapolis: University of Minnesota Press, 1999.

Kuhnke, Laverne. *Lives at Risk: Public Health in Nineteenth-Century Egypt.* Berkeley: University of California Press, 1989.

Kuznets, Simon. *National Income and Its Composition, 1919–1939.* New York: National Bureau of Economic Research, 1941.

Laclau, Ernesto. *New Reflections on the Revolution of Our Time.* London: Verso, 1990.

Laclau, Ernesto, and Chantalle Mouffe. *Hegemony and Socialist Strategy: Towards a Radical Democratic Politics.* London: Verso, 1985.

Laïdi, Zaki. *Enquête sur la Banque Mondiale.* Paris: Fayard, 1989.

Landes, David S. *Bankers and Pashas: International Finance and Economic Imperialism in Egypt.* 2d ed. Cambridge, Mass.: Harvard University Press, 1979.

Larson, Barbara K. "The Rural Marketing System in Egypt over the Last Three Hundred Years." *Comparative Studies in Society and History* 27, no. 3 (1985): 494–530.

Latour, Bruno. *The Pasteurization of France.* Cambridge, Mass.: Harvard University Press, 1988.

———. *We Have Never Been Modern.* Cambridge, Mass.: Harvard University Press, 1993.

———. *Pandora's Hope: Essays on the Reality of Science Studies.* Cambridge, Mass.: Harvard University Press, 1999.

Lawson, Fred H. "Rural Revolt and Provincial Society in Egypt, 1820–1824." *International Journal of Middle East Studies* 13, no. 2 (1981): 131–53.

Le Bon, Gustave. *Psychologie des foules.* Paris: Felix Alcan, 1895. English translation, *The Crowd: A Study of the Popular Mind.* New York: Macmillan, 1896.

———. *Les lois psychologiques de l'évolution des peuples.* Paris: Felix Alcan, 1898. English translation, *The Psychology of Peoples.* New York: Macmillan, 1898.

Lee, Eddy. "Egalitarian Peasant Farming and Rural Development: The Case of South Korea." *World Development* 7, nos. 4/5 (1979): 510.

Lefebvre, Henri. *The Production of Space.* Translated by Donald Nicholson-Smith. Oxford: Blackwell, 1991.

Lévi, I. G. "Le recensement de la population de l'Egypte de 1917." *L'Egypte Contemporaine* no. 67 (Nov. 1922): 471–506.

———. "La réforme de la statistique officielle égyptienne." *L'Egypte Contemporaine* 15, no. 80 (1924): 412–42.

———. "L'augementation des revenus de l'état: possibilités et moyen d'y parvenir." *L'Egypte Contemporaine* no. 68 (Dec. 1992): 596–617.

Library of Congress, Federal Research Division. *Egypt: A Country Study.* Country Studies / Area Handbook series. Washington, D.C.: Library of Congress, 1991.

List, Friedrich. *Das nationale System der politischen Oekonomie.* Stuttgart: Cotta, 1841. English translation, *National System of Political Economy,* translated by Sampson S. Lloyd. London: Longmans, Green, 1885. Reprint ed. Fairfield, N.J.: A. M. Kelley, 1977.

Little, Tom. *High Dam at Aswan.* New York: John Day, 1965.

Lozach, Jean. *Le Delta du Nil: Etude de géographie humaine.* Cairo: Société Royale de Géographie d'Egypte, 1935.

Lozach, Jean, and Georges Hug. *L'Habitat rural en Egypte.* Cairo: Société Royale de Géographie d'Egypte, 1930.

Ludwig, Emil. *Der Nil: Lebenslauf Eines Stromes.* Amsterdam: Querido Verlag, 1935–36. English translation, *The Nile: The Mighty Story of Egypt Fabulous River—6,000 Years of Thrilling History,* translated by Mary H. Lindsay. New York: Viking Press, 1937.

Lyons, H. G. *The Cadastral Survey of Egypt 1892–1907.* Cairo: Ministry of Finance, Survey Department, 1908.

Mabro, Robert. *The Egyptian Economy, 1952–1972.* Oxford: Clarendon Press, 1974.

Marx, Karl. *Capital: A Critique of Political Economy.* Vol. 1, *The Process of Capitalist Production.* Translated from the 3d German ed. by Samuel Moore and Edward Aveling. Edited by Frederick Engels. New York: Modern Library, 1906.

———. *Capital: A Critique of Political Economy.* Vol. 3. Translated by David Fernbach. London: Penguin, 1981.

Mayfield, James B. *Rural Politics in Nasser Egypt: A Quest for Legitimacy.* Austin: University of Texas Press, 1971.

McNeill, William H. *Plagues and Peoples.* Garden City, N.Y.: Anchor Press / Doubleday, 1976.

Meade, James, and Richard Strue. *National Income and Expenditure.* 2d ed. Cambridge: Bowes and Bowes, 1948.

Mehanna, Soheir, Nicholas S. Hopkins, and Bahgat Abdelmaksoud. *Farmers and Merchants: Background to Structural Adjustment in Egypt.* Cairo Papers in Social Science 17, Monograph 2. Cairo: American University in Cairo Press, 1994.

Mehta, Uday Singh. *Liberalism and Empire: A Study in Nineteenth-Century British Liberal Thought.* Chicago: University of Chicago Press, 1999.

Meskell, Lynn, ed. *Archaeology Under Fire: Nationalism, Politics and Heritage in the Eastern Mediterranean and the Middle East.* London: Routledge, 1998.

Mintz, Sidney W. *Sweetness and Power: The Place of Sugar in Modern History.* New York: Viking Penguin, 1985.

Mitchell, Timothy. "Everyday Metaphors of Power." *Theory and Society* 19, no. 5 (1990): 545–77.

———. *Colonising Egypt.* Berkeley: University of California Press, 1991.

———. "Worlds Apart: An Egyptian Village and the International Tourism Industry." *Middle East Report,* no. 196 (Sept.–Oct. 1995).

———. "Origins and Limits of the Modern Idea of the Economy." Advanced Study Center, University of Michigan, *Working Papers Series,* no. 12, Nov. 1995.

———. *Al-dimuqratiyya wa-'l-dawla fi al-ʿalam al-ʿarabi.* Damascus: Dar ʿIybal, 1996.

———. "Fixing the Economy." *Cultural Studies* 12, no. 1 (1998): 82–101.

———. "Society, Economy, and the State Effect." In *State/Culture: State-Formation after the Cultural Turn.* Edited by George Steinmetz, 76–97. Ithaca, N.Y.: Cornell University Press, 1999.

———. "The Stage of Modernity." In *Questions of Modernity.* Edited by Timothy Mitchell, 1–34. Minneapolis: University of Minnesota Press, 2000.

Mitchell, Timothy, ed. *Questions of Modernity.* Minneapolis: University of Minnesota Press, 2000.

Mohieldin, Mahmoud. "Causes, Measures and Impact of State Intervention in the Financial Sector: The Egyptian Example." *Working Papers of the Economic Research Forum for the Arab Countries, Iran and Turkey,* no. 9507. Cairo, 1995.

Moussa, M. Z., and T. T. Jones. "Efficiency and Farm Size in Egypt: A Unit Output Price Profit Function Approach." *Applied Economics* 23, no. A1 (1991): 21–29.

Mubarak, ʿAli. *Al-khitat al-tawfiqiyya li-misr al-qahira wa-muduniha wa-biladiha al-qadima wa-'l-shahira.* Cairo: al-Matbaʿa al-Kubra al-Amiriyya, 1886–88.

Nahas, Joseph F. *Situation économique et sociale du fellah égyptien.* Paris: Arthur Rousseau, 1901.

Newberry, David M. "Futures Markets, Hedging, and Speculation." In *The New Palgrave Dictionary of Money and Finance.* Edited by David M. Newberry, Murray Milgate, and John Eatwell. Vol. 2. New York: Stockton Press, 1992.

Nockrashy, A. S., Osman Galal, and Jay Davenport. *More and Better Food: An Egyptian Demonstration Project.* Washington, D.C.: National Research Council, 1987.

Owen, Roger. *Cotton and the Egyptian Economy, 1820–1914: A Study in Trade and Development.* Oxford: Oxford University Press, 1969.

———. "The Development of Agricultural Production in Nineteenth-Century Egypt: Capitalism of What Type?" In *The Islamic Middle East 700–1900:*

Studies in Economic and Social History. Edited by A. L. Udovitch, 521–46. Princeton, N.J.: Darwin Press, 1981.
———. "The Population Census of 1917 and its Relationship to Egypt's Three Nineteenth-Century Statistical Regimes." *Journal of Historical Sociology* 9, no. 4 (1996): 457–72.
Palgrave, Robert. *Palgrave's Dictionary of Political Economy.* 2d ed. London: Macmillan, 1925–26.
Patriarca, Silvana. *Numbers and Nationhood.* Cambridge: Cambridge University Press, 1996.
Piore, Michael J., and Charles F. Sabel. *The Second Industrial Divide: Possibilities for Prosperity.* New York: Basic Books, 1984.
Polanyi, Karl. *The Great Transformation: The Political and Economic Origins of Our Time.* Boston: Beacon Press, 1944.
Population Council. "Egypt 1988: Results from the Demographic and Health Survey." *Studies in Family Planning* 21, no. 6 (1990): 351.
Postone, Moishe. *Time, Labor, and Social Domination.* Cambridge: Cambridge University Press, 1993.
Posusney, Marsha Pripstein. *Labor and the State in Egypt: Workers, Unions, and Economic Restructuring.* New York: Columbia University Press, 1997.
Pottage, Alain. "The Measure of Land." *The Modern Law Review* 57, no. 3 (1994): 361–84.
Powelson, John P., and Richard Stock. *The Peasant Betrayed: Agriculture and Land Reform in the Third World.* Published in association with the Lincoln Institute of Land Policy. Boston: Oelgeschlager, Gunn & Hain, 1987.
Prakash, Gyan. "Writing Post-Orientalist Histories of the Third World: Perspectives from Indian Historiography." *Comparative Studies in Society and History* 32, no. 2 (1990): 383–408.
———. "Can the 'Subaltern' Ride? A Reply to O'Hanlon and Washbrook." *Comparative Studies in Society and History* 34, no. 1 (1992): 168–84.
———. *Another Reason: Science and the Imagination of Modern India.* Princeton, N.J.: Princeton University Press, 1999.
Radice, Hugo. "The National Economy: A Keynesian Myth?" *Capital and Class,* no. 22 (Spring 1984): 111–40.
Radwan, Samir. *Agrarian Reform and Rural Poverty: Egypt, 1952–1975.* Geneva: International Labour Organization, 1977.
Radwan, Samir, and Eddy Lee. *Agrarian Change in Egypt: An Anatomy of Rural Poverty.* London: Croom Helm, 1986.
Ragan, John David. "A Fascination for the Exotic: Suzanne Volquin, Ismayl Urbain, Jehan D'Ivray, and the Saint-Simonians—French Travelers in Egypt on the Margins." Ph.D. diss., New York University, 2000.
Ramadan, ʿAbd al-ʿAzim. *ʿAbd al-Nasir wa-azmat maris.* Cairo: Ruz al-Yusuf, 1976.
———. *Siraʿ al-tabaqat fi misr (1837–1952).* Beirut: al-Muʾassasa al-ʿArabiyya li-ʾl-Dirasat wa-ʾl-Nashr, 1978.

———. *Tatawwur al-harakah al-wataniyya fi misr: min sanat 1937 ila sanat 1948.* Cairo: al-Hay'a al-Misriyya al-ʿAmma li-ʾl-Kitab, 1998.

Rashad, Muhammad. *Sirri jiddan: min milaffat al-lajna al-ʿulya ʾli-tasfiyat al-iqtaʿ.* Cairo: Dar al-Taʿawun, 1977.

Reid, Donald M. *Cairo University and the Making of a Modern Egypt.* Cambridge: Cambridge University Press, 1990.

Renan, Ernest. *Qu'est-ce qu'une nation? What is a nation?* English translation by Wanda Romer Taylor. Toronto: Tapir Press, 1996.

Ricardo, David. "An Essay on the Influence of a Low Price of Corn on the Profits of Stock." [1815]. In *The Works and Correspondence of David Ricardo.* Edited by Piero Sraffa. Vol. 4, *Pamphlets and Papers, 1815–1823.* Published for the Royal Economic Society, 9–41. Cambridge: Cambridge University Press, 1951.

———. *On the Principles of Political Economy and Taxation.* London: John Murray, 1817.

Richards, Alan. *Egypt's Agricultural Development 1800–1980: Technical and Social Change.* Boulder, Colo.: Westview Press, 1982.

Richards, Alan, and Philip L. Martin, eds. *Migration, Mechanization and Agricultural Labor Markets in Egypt.* Boulder, Colo.: Westview Press, 1983.

Richards, Alan, and John Waterbury. *A Political Economy of the Middle East.* Boulder, Colo.: Westview Press, 1990.

Rieker, Martina. "The Saʿid and the City: Subaltern Spaces in the Making of Modern Egyptian History." Ph.D. diss., Temple University, 1997.

Rifaʿa Rafiʿ Al-tahtawi. *Al-aʿmal al-kamila.* Edited by Muhammad al-ʿImara. Vol. 1. *Al-tamaddun wa-ʾl-hadara wa-ʾl-ʿumran.* Beirut: Al-Mu'assasa al-ʿArabiyya li-l-Dirasat wa-l-Nashr, 1973–78.

Rizq, Yunan Labib. *Al-Wafd wa-ʾl-kitab al-aswad.* Cairo: Mu'assasat al-Dirasat al-Siyasiyya wa-ʾl-Istratijiyya, 1978.

Ruf, Thierry. *Histoire contemporaine de l'agriculture egyptienne: Essai de synthèse.* Bondy, France: Editions de l'Orstom, 1988.

Saad, Reem. "Agriculture and Politics in Contemporary Egypt: The 1997 Tenancy Crisis." In *Discourses in Contemporary Egypt: Political and Social Issues.* Edited by Enid Hill, 22–35. Cairo Papers in Social Science 22, monograph 4. Cairo: American University in Cairo Press, 1999.

———. "State, Landlord, Parliament and Peasant: The Story of the 1992 Tenancy Law in Egypt." In *Agriculture in Egypt from Pharaonic to Modern Times.* Edited by Alan Bowman and Eugene Rogin, 387–404. Proceedings of the British Academy, no. 96. Oxford: Oxford University Press, 1999.

Saad Mikhail, Reem. "Peasant Perceptions of Recent Egyptian History." D.Phil. thesis, University of Oxford, 1994.

Sachs, Wolfgang, ed. *The Development Dictionary: A Guide to Knowledge and Power.* London: Zed Press, 1992.

Sadowski, Yahya. *Political Vegetables? Businessman and Bureaucrat in the Development of Egyptian Agriculture.* Washington, D.C.: Brookings Institution, 1991.

Said, Edward. *Orientalism*. New York: Pantheon, 1978.

Sa'id, Rif'at al-. *Al-sihafa al-yasariyya fi misr, 1925–1948*. Cairo: Maktabat Madbuli, 1977.

St. John, J. A. *Egypt and Nubia, Their Scenery and Their People*. London: Chapman and Hall, 1845.

Sami, Amin. *Taqwim al-nil wa-asma' man tawallaw amr misr wa-muddat hukmihim 'alayha wa-mulahazat ta'rikhiyya 'an ahwal al-khilafa al-'amma wa-shu'un misr al-khassa*. Vol. 3., in 3 parts. *1264–1289 (1848–1872)*. Cairo: Matba'at Dar al-Kutub, 1936.

Sami, Salib. *Dhikriyyat Salib Basha Sami, 1891–1952*. Edited by Sami Abu al-Nur. Cairo: Maktabat Madbuli, 1999.

Saunders, Frances Stonor. *The Cultural Cold War: The CIA and the World of Arts and Letters*. New York: New Press, 1999. Originally published as *Who Paid the Piper: The CIA and the Cultural Cold War*. London: Granta Books, 1999.

Sayyad, Nezar al-. "From Vernacularism to Globalism: The Temporal Reality of Traditional Settlements." *Traditional Dwellings and Settlements Review* 7, no. 1 (1995): 13–24.

Schultz, Theodore. *Transforming Traditional Agriculture*. New Haven, Conn.: Yale University Press, 1964.

Schulze, Reinhard. *Die Rebellion der ägyptischen Fallahin 1919*. Berlin: Baalbek Verlag, 1981.

Scott, James C. *Weapons of the Weak: Everyday Forms of Peasant Resistance*. New Haven, Conn.: Yale University Press, 1985.

Seddon, David. "Commentary on Agrarian Relations in the Middle East: A New Paradigm for Analysis?" *Current Sociology* 34, no. 2 (1986): 151–72.

Shaw, Stanford J. *The Financial and Administrative Organization and Development of Ottoman Egypt, 1517–1798*. Princeton, N.J.: Princeton University Press, 1962.

Simmel, Georg. *Philosophie des geldes*. Leipzig: Duncker & Humbolt, 1900. English translation, *The Philosophy of Money*. London: Routledge and Kegan Paul, 1978.

———. "Die Grossstadt und das Geistesleben." In *Die Grossstadt*, Vorträge und Aufsätz zur Städteausstellung. Edited by K. Bücher et al. Gehe-Stiftung zu Dresden, Winter 1902–3, *Jahrbuch der Gehe-Stiftung zu Dresden*, vol. 9. Dresden: von Zahn & Jaensch, 1903.

———. "The Metropolis and Mental Life." Translated by Edward A. Shils. In *Second-Year Course in the Study of Contemporary Society (Social Science II): Syllabus and Selected Readings*. Edited by Harry D. Gideonse, Herbert Goldhamer, Earl S. Johnson, Maynard C. Krueger, and Louis Wirth. 5th edition, 221–38. Chicago: University of Chicago Press, 1936.

———. "The Metropolis and Mental Life." Translated by Hans Gerth with C. Wright Mills. In *The Sociology of Georg Simmel*. Translated by Kurt H. Wolff, 409–24. New York: Free Press, 1950.

Smith, Charles D. *Islam and the Search for Social Order in Modern Egypt: A Biography of Muhammad Husayn Haykal.* Albany: State University of New York Press, 1983.

———. "Imagined Identities, Imagined Nationalisms: Print Culture and Egyptian Nationalism in the Light of Recent Scholarship." *International Journal of Middle East Studies* 29, no. 4 (1997): 607–22.

Spivak, Gayatri Chakravorty. "Can the Subaltern Speak?" In *Marxism and the Interpretation of Culture.* Edited by C. Nelson and L. Grossberg, 271–313. Basingstoke: Macmillan Education, 1988. Reprinted in *Colonial Discourse and Post-Colonial Theory.* Edited by Patrick Williams and Laura Chrisman, 66–111. New York: Columbia University Press, 1994.

Springborg, Robert. *Mubarak's Egypt: Fragmentation of the Political Order.* Boulder, Colo.: Westview Press, 1989.

———. "Rolling Back Egypt's Agrarian Reform." *Middle East Report,* no. 166 (Sept.–Oct. 1990): 29.

———. "State-Society Relations in Egypt: The Debate over Owner-Tenant Relations." *Middle East Journal* 45, no. 2 (1991): 231–49.

Stark, David. "Recombinant Property in East European Capitalism." In *The Laws of the Markets.* Edited by Michel Callon. *Sociological Review* monograph series, 116–46. Oxford: Blackwell, 1998.

Stauth, Georg. *Die Fellachen im Nildelta: Zur Struktur des Konflikts zwischen subsistenz- und warenproduktion in Ländlichen Ägypten.* Wiesbaden: Franz Steiner, 1983.

———. "Capitalist Farming and Small Peasant Households in Egypt." *Review* 7, no. 2 (1983): 285–314. Reprinted in *The Rural Middle East: Peasant Lives and Modes of Production.* Edited by Kathy Glavanis and Pandeli Glavanis, 122–41. London: Zed Press, 1989.

Steele James. *An Architecture for the People: The Complete Works of Hassan Fathy.* London: Thames and Hudson, 1997.

Stewart, Frances, Henk Thomas, and Tom de Wilde, eds. *The Other Policy: The Influence of Policies on Technology Choice and Small Enterprise Development.* London: Intermediate Technology Publications, 1990.

Streeten, Paul. "A Cool Look at Outward-Looking Strategies for Development." *World Economy* 5, no. 2 (1982): 166–67.

Sufian, Sandra. "Healing the Land and the Nation: Malaria and the Zionist Project in Mandatory Palestine, 1920–1947." Ph.D. diss., New York University, 1999.

Taussig, Michael T. "Culture of Terror—Space of Death: Roger Casement's Putumayo Report and the Explanation of Torture." *Comparative Studies in Society and History* 26, no. 3 (1984): 467–97.

Taylor, Elizabeth. "Egyptian Migration and Peasant Wives," *MERIP Reports,* no. 124 (1984): 3–10.

Thomas, Nicholas. *Entangled Objects: Exchange, Material Culture, and Colonialism in the Pacific.* Cambridge, Mass.: Harvard University Press, 1991.

Tignor, Robert L. *Modernization and British Colonial Rule in Egypt, 1882–1914*. Princeton, N.J.: Princeton University Press, 1966.

———. "Nationalism, Economic Planning, and Development Projects in Interwar Egypt." *International Journal of African Historical Studies* 10, no. 2 (1977): 185–208.

———. *The State, Private Enterprise and Economic Change in Egypt, 1918–1952*. Princeton, N.J.: Princeton University Press, 1984.

———. *Egyptian Textiles and British Capital, 1930–1956*. Cairo: American University in Cairo Press, 1989.

Toth, James. *Rural Labor Movements in Egypt and Their Impact on the State, 1961–1992*. Gainesville: University Press of Florida, 1999.

Tribe, Keith. *Land, Labour, and Economic Discourse*. London: Routledge & Kegan Paul, 1978.

United States Agency for International Development. *Annual Budget Submission, FY 1990: Egypt*. Washington, D.C.: USAID, 1988.

———. *Congressional Presentation, FY 1990. Main Volume*, and *Annex II: Asia and the Near East*. Washington, D.C.: USAID, 1989.

United States Agency for International Development, Office of Agricultural Credit and Economics, Cairo. *Agricultural Data Base*. Cairo: USAID, 1989.

United States Agency for International Development, Public Affairs Office, Cairo. *Status Report: United States Economic Assistance to Egypt*. Cairo: USAID, 1989.

United States Congress, Senate Committee on Foreign Relations. *The BCCI Affair: A Report to the Committee on Foreign Relations, United States Senate, by Senator John Kerry and Senator Hank Brown*. Washington, D.C.: United States Government Printing Office, 1992.

United States Congress, Senate Committee on Foreign Relations, Subcommittee on Multinational Corporations. *Hearings on International Grain Companies*. 94th Congress, June 1976.

United States Department of Agriculture. *Egypt: Major Constraints to Increasing Agricultural Productivity*. Foreign Economic Report no. 120. Washington, D.C.: Department of Agriculture, 1976.

United States Department of Commerce, International Trade Administration. *Foreign Economic Trends and their Implication for the U.S.* Washington, D.C.: Department of Commerce, 1989.

Urbain, Ismayl [Georges Voisin, pseud.]. *L'Algérie pour les Algériens*. Paris: Michel Lévy Frères, 1861.

Urry, John. *The Tourist Gaze: Leisure and Travel in Contemporary Societies*. London: Sage, 1990.

Van der Spek, Kees. "Dead Mountain vs. Living Community: The Theban Necropolis as Cultural Landscape." Paper presented at the UNESCO Third International Forum, "University and Heritage," Deakin University, Melbourne and Geelong, Australia, October 4–9, 1998.

Vaucher, Georges. "La Livre égyptienne, de sa creation par Mohamed Aly a ses recentes modifications." *L'Egypte Contemporaine* 41, no. 256 (Jan. 1950): 115–46.

Villiers Stuart, Henry. *Egypt after the War, Being the Narrative of a Tour of Inspection.* London: John Murray, 1883.

Vitalis, Robert. *When Capitalists Collide: Business Conflict and the End of Empire in Egypt.* Berkeley: University of California Press, 1995.

Volait, Mercedes. *L'Architecture moderne en Egypte et la Revue Al-ʿImara, 1939–59.* Dossiers du CEDEJ 1987, no. 4. Cairo: Centre d'Etudes et de Documentation Economique, Juridique et Sociale, 1988.

Wald, Alan M. *The New York Intellectuals: The Rise and Decline of the Anti-Stalinist Left from the 1930s to the 1980s.* Chapel Hill: University of North Carolina Press, 1987.

Walras, Leon. *Eléments d'économie politique pure, ou, Théorie de la richesse sociale.* 1 vol. in 2. Lausanne: L. Corbaz, 1874–77.

Walz, Terence. *Trade Between Egypt and Bilad as-Sudan, 1700–1820.* Cairo: Institut Français d'Archéologie Orientale du Caire, 1978.

Warriner, Doreen. *Land and Poverty in the Middle East.* Westport, Conn.: Hyperion Press, 1948.

———. *Land Reform and Development in the Middle East: A Study of Egypt, Syria, and Iraq.* 2d ed. London: Oxford University Press, 1962.

Waterbury, John. *The Egypt of Nasser and Sadat: The Political Economy of Two Regimes.* Princeton, N.J.: Princeton University Press, 1983.

———. *Hydropolitics of the Nile Valley.* Syracuse, N.Y.: Syracuse University Press, 1979.

Weber, Max. *The Theory of Economic and Social Organization.* Edited by Talcott Parsons. Translated by A. M. Henderson and Talcott Parsons. New York: Oxford University Press, 1947.

———. *Wirtschaft und Gesellschaft: Grundriss der Verstehenden Soziologie.* 2 vols. in 1. Tübingen: Mohr 1972.

Wessel, James, with Mort Hantman. *Trading the Future: Farm Exports and the Concentration of Economic Power in Our Food System.* San Francisco: Institute for Food and Development Policy, 1983.

Wilbour, Charles Edwin. *Travels in Egypt (December 1880 to May 1891): Letters of Charles Edwin Wilbour.* Edited by Jean Capart. New York: Brooklyn Museum, 1936.

Willcocks, Sir William. *Irrigation of Mesopotamia.* London: E. & F. N. Spon, 1917.

Willcocks, Sir William, and J. I. Craig. *Egyptian Irrigation.* 3d ed., 2 vols. London: E. & F. N. Spon, 1913.

World Bank. *Trends in Developing Economies 1989.* Washington, D.C.: World Bank, 1989.

———. *Egypt: Alleviating Poverty.* Washington, D.C.: World Bank, 1991.

———. *Global Economic Prospects and the Developing Countries: 2000.* Washington, D.C.: World Bank, 1999.

World Commission on Dams. *Dams and Development: A New Framework for Decision Making.* November 2000. Available at www.damsreport.org.

World Commission on Environment and Development. *Our Common Future.* Oxford: Oxford University Press, 1987.

World Wildlife Fund Canada and World Wildlife Fund U.S. *Resolving the DDT Dilemma: Protecting Biodiversity and Human Health.* Toronto and Washington, D.C.: WWF Canada and WWF U.S., 1998.

Zaytoun, Mohaya A. "Income Distribution in Egyptian Agriculture and Its Main Determinants." In *The Political Economy of Income Distribution in Egypt.* Edited by Gouda Abdel-Khalek and Robert Tignor, 268–306. New York: Holmes and Meier, 1982.

Zelizer, Viviana A. *The Social Meaning of Money: Pin Money, Paychecks, Poor Relief and Other Currencies.* Princeton, N.J.: Princeton University Press, 1997.

NEWSPAPERS AND PERIODICALS

al-Ahram
al-Ahram al-iqtisadi
al-Ahram Hebdo
al-Ahram Weekly
al-Akhbar
Akhbar al-yawm
Business Monthly (Cairo)
Business Today Egypt
Cairo Times
al-Dustur
Economist
Egyptian Gazette
Financial Times
Guardian Weekly (London)
Middle East Times (Egypt edition)
Le Monde Diplomatique
New York Times
Observer (London)
Ruz al-Yusuf
al-Shaʿb
al-Wafd
Wall Street Journal

SERIALS AND ARCHIVES

Food and Agriculture Organization of the United Nations. *The State of Food and Agriculture.*

Food and Agriculture Organization of the United Nations. *Yearbook.*

Gouvernement d'Egypte, Département de la Statistique Générale. *L'Annuaire Statistique* (1910–).

Government of Egypt, Central Agency for Public Mobilization and Statistics. *Statistical Yearbook.*

Great Britain, Parliament. *Hansard.* Available at http://www.parliament.the-stationery-office.co.uk.

United States Congress, House of Representatives, Committee on Foreign Affairs, Subcommittee on Europe and the Middle East. *Foreign Assistance Legislation.*

United States Department of Agriculture. *Agriculture Fact Book.*

United States National Archives. Record Group 59, Department of State, Central Files, Egypt. Microform. University Publications of America, 1985.

United States Securities and Exchange Commission. Archives. Available at http://www.sec.gov/archives.

World Bank. *World Development Report.* Available at http://www.worldbank.org.

World Tourism Organization. *World Tourism Highlights.* Available at http://www.world-tourism.org.

Index

Compositor: Impressions Book and Journal Services, Inc.
Text: 10/13 Aldus
Display: Aldus
Printer and binder: Malloy Lithographing, Inc.